Post-Communist Welfare Pathways

Also by Alfio Cerami

SOCIAL POLICY IN CENTRAL AND EASTERN EUROPE: The Emergence of a New European Welfare Regime

Also by Pieter Vanhuysse

DIVIDE AND PACIFY: Strategic Social Policies and Political Protests in Post-Communist Democracies

Post-Communist Welfare Pathways

Theorizing Social Policy Transformations in Central and Eastern Europe

Edited by

Alfio Cerami
Sciences Po, France

and

Pieter Vanhuysse
University of Haifa, Israel, and European Centre for Social Welfare Policy and Research, Vienna, Austria

First published 2009 by
PALGRAVE MACMILLAN

Palgrave Macmillan in the UK is an imprint of Macmillan Publishers Limited,
registered in England, company number 785998, of Houndmills, Basingstoke,
Hampshire RG21 6XS.

Palgrave Macmillan in the US is a division of St Martin's Press LLC,
175 Fifth Avenue, New York, NY 10010.

Palgrave Macmillan is the global academic imprint of the above companies
and has companies and representatives throughout the world.

Palgrave® and Macmillan® are registered trademarks in the United States,
the United Kingdom, Europe and other countries.

ISBN: 978–0–230–23026–2

This book is printed on paper suitable for recycling and made from fully
managed and sustained forest sources. Logging, pulping and manufacturing
processes are expected to conform to the environmental regulations of the
country of origin.

A catalogue record for this book is available from the British Library.

A catalog record for this book is available from the Library of Congress.

10 9 8 7 6 5 4 3 2 1
18 17 16 15 14 13 12 11 10 09

Printed and bound in Great Britain by
CPI Antony Rowe, Chippenham and Eastbourne

Contents

Figures and Tables

Figures

Tables

Acknowledgements

In writing this book we have accumulated many debts. We thank, first of all, all contributors for having joined this project with their chapters and ideas. In addition, we would like to thank Vivien Schmidt for useful discussions on the role of ideas and discourses in institutional change, Anton Hemerijck, Frédérique Hoffmann, Karl Hinrichs, Bruno Palier, Ricardo Rodrigues and Jonathan Zeitlin for previous valuable discussions on welfare state change and inspiration. We also thank Mikko Kautto, and the organizers of the ESPAnet September 2008 Conference in Helsinki for having allowed a special session aimed at 'Learning from the Eastern Experience' in which several participants have provided helpful feedback on an early version of this manuscript. Alfio Cerami also wishes to thank Renaud Dehousse at the Centre for European Studies of Sciences Po for constant support during these years. Pieter Vanhuysse wishes to thank the European Centre for Social Welfare Policy and Research in Vienna and its Director, Bernd Marin, for having provided an excellent intellectual environment during the editing of this book.

Contributors

Jolanta Aidukaite (PhD in Sociology from Stockholm University) is a senior researcher fellow at the Institute for Social Research, Lithuania. Prior to taking up a position at the Institute, Jolanta Aidukaite was lecturing and conducting research on social policy development issues in the three Baltic States at the Södertörn University, Sweden. Her main research and teaching interests are comparative social policy, globalization, inequalities and poverty, and urban segregation. She is particularly interested in social policy development issues in Central and Eastern Europe. Her latest publication 'Old Welfare State Theories and New Welfare Regimes in Eastern Europe: Challenges and Implications' is forthcoming in the journal *Communist and Post-Communist Studies*. Jolanta's latest edited book *Poverty, Urbanity and Social Policy: Central and Eastern Europe Compared* was published by Nova Sciences Publishers (New York) in May 2009.

Alfio Cerami is a research associate at the Centre for European Studies of Sciences Po, Paris. He received his PhD degree in social science from the University of Erfurt (Germany). He has been a visiting lecturer at the University of Erfurt (Germany), at Sciences Po, Paris, and at the Centre for German and European Studies of the State University of St Petersburg (Russia). His research interests include comparative social policy, political economy, development economics, human and socioeconomic security. His most recent publications include 'Welfare State Developments in the Russian Federation: Oil-Led Social Policy and the "Russian Miracle"' (*Social Policy & Administration*, 2009, 43, 2: 105–20), 'New Social Risks in CEE. The Need for a New Empowering Politics of the Welfare State' (*Czech Sociological Review*, 2008, 44, 6), *Promoting Human Security: Ethical, Normative and Educational Frameworks in Western Europe* (together with P. Burgess et al., 2007, Paris: UNESCO) and *Social Policy in Central and Eastern Europe. The Emergence of a New European Welfare Regime* (Berlin: LIT Verlag, 2006).

Veerle De Maesschalck is a research assistant at the Herman Deleeck Centre for Social Policy of the University of Antwerp. Her main research interests focus on welfare state dynamics and social security issues. Recent publications include 'Social Redistribution in Federalised Belgium' (with B. Cantillon et al., *West European Politics*, 29:5, 2006) and *Réflexions sur le Fédéralisme Social* (co-editor with B. Cantillon, Acco, 2008).

Stephan Haggard is the Lawrence and Sallye Krause Professor at the Graduate School of International Relations and Pacific Studies (IR/PS) at the

University of California, San Diego (UCSD). He is the author of *Pathways from the Periphery: the Political Economy of Growth in the Newly Industrializing Countries* (1990) and *The Political Economy of the Asian Financial Crisis* (2000) and co-author of *The Political Economy of Democratic Transitions* (with Robert Kaufman, 1995), *Famine in North Korea: Markets, Aid and Reform* (with Marcus Noland, 2007) and *Development, Democracy and Welfare States: Latin America, East Asia and Eastern Europe* (with Robert Kaufman, 2008).

Tomasz Inglot is Professor of Political Science and Douglas R. Moore Faculty Research Lecturer at Minnesota State University, USA. He received his PhD degree in Political Science from the University of Wisconsin-Madison. He is the author of *Welfare States in East Central Europe, 1919–2004* (Cambridge University Press, 2008). His articles on comparative social policy and politics have appeared in *Communist and Post-Communist Studies, Perspectives on Political Science,* and *Polityka Społeczna* (Warsaw). He also co-edited a collective volume, *Fighting Poverty and Reforming Social Security: What Can Post-Soviet States Learn from New Democracies in Central Europe?,* published by the Woodrow Wilson Center for International Scholars in Washington DC in 2005. He is the recipient of numerous national and international fellowships and grants from IREX (International Research and Exchanges Board), Fulbright, and the American Council of Learned Societies (ACLS), among others. He is currently working on a new collaborative study of family policies in Central and Eastern Europe.

Robert R. Kaufman received a PhD from Harvard University, and is a professor of Political Science at Rutgers University. He has been a visiting professor at Yale, Princeton and University of Pennsylvania, a fellow at the Institute of Advanced Studies, Princeton and a fellow at Collegium Budapest. He has written extensively on democratization, the politics of economic reform and the politics of social policy reform. His most recent book is *Development, Democracy, and Welfare States: Latin America, East Asia, and Eastern Europe* (Princeton University Press, 2008), co-authored with Stephan Haggard. *The Political-Economy of Democratic Transitions* (1995), also co-authored with Haggard, won the 1995 Leubbert Prize for the best book in comparative politics, awarded by the Comparative Politics Section of the APSA. He is co-editor with Joan Nelson of *Crucial Needs, Weak Incentives: Globalization, Democratization, and Social Sector Reform in Latin America* (2004), which focuses on health and education policies in Argentina, Brazil, Colombia, Mexico, Peru and Venezuela.

Kristine Kern is assistant professor at Wageningen University (Netherlands) and has been visiting professor at Södertörn University (Sweden) and the University of Minnesota (USA) and a senior research associate at the Social Science Research Center Berlin (Germany). Her main research interests focus on the governance of multi-level systems, EU studies and environmental policy. Her publications include *Cities, Europeanization and Multi-level Governance* (2009), *Journal of Common Market Studies* (with Harriet Bulkeley), *Governing a Common Sea: Environmental Policies in the Baltic Sea Region* (2008), *London: Earthscan* (co-edited with Marko Joas and Detlef Jahn), *Zivilgesellschaft und Sozialkapital* (2004) (co-edited with Ansgar Klein, Brigitte Geißel and Maria Berger, Wiesbaden: VS Verlag) and *Die Diffusion von Politikinnovationen* (2000), Opladen: Leske +Budrich.

Claus Offe was until his retirement in 2005 Professor of Political Science at Humboldt University, Berlin, where he held a chair of Political Sociology and Social Policy. He earned his PhD (Dr rer. pol.) at the University of Frankfurt (1968) and his Habilitation at the University of Constance. Since 2006 he has taught at the Hertie School of Governance, a private professional school of public policy, where he holds a chair of Political Sociology. Previous positions include professorships at the Universities of Bielefeld and Bremen. He has held research fellowships and visiting professorships in the US, Canada, Australia, Hungary, Poland, Austria, Italy and the Netherlands. He was awarded an honorary degree by the Australian National University in 2007. His fields of research include democratic theory, transition studies, EU integration, and welfare state and labour market studies.

Mitchell A. Orenstein is S. Richard Hirsch Associate Professor of European Studies at Johns Hopkins University, Paul H. Nitze School of Advanced International Studies in Washington, DC. Orenstein's work focuses on the international political economy of policy reform, exploring the ways that democratic polities seek to adapt and adjust to pressures and politics of globalization. He is the author of *Out of the Red: Building Capitalism and Democracy in Postcommunist Europe* and *Privatizing Pensions: The Transnational Campaign for Social Security Reform*. His articles on the international politics of economic reform and democratization have appeared in *Comparative Political Studies, Comparative Politics, East European Politics and Societies, Europe-Asia Studies, Global Social Policy*, and *Journal of Democracy*. Orenstein is currently writing a book on the prospects for economic development policy after the financial crisis.

Miroslava Rákoczyová, PhD, is a researcher at the Research Institute for Labour and Social Affairs Prague, Research Centre in Brno. She is a specialist in labour market policy, poverty, social exclusion and the policy of social inclusion. Her latest publications include 'Local strategies of integration of immigrants in the Czech Republic' (with R. Trbola, 2008) and 'Labour migration and its regulation in the frame of Czech labour market policy' (with H. Porizkova, 2008). She is currently the coordinator of a research project funded by the Ministry of Education, Youth and Sports of the

Czech Republic, entitled 'Migrating People in the Czech Republic – Their integration in the labour market and social integration'.

Cristina Rat is a lecturer at the Sociology Department of the 'Babeş-Bolyai' University and a research fellow at the Research Centre on Interethnic Relation (CCRIT) Cluj-Napoca. She has been recently awarded with a doctoral degree in Sociology and her current work focuses on social inequalities, welfare reform and social policies targeting the poor and vulnerable categories in Central and Eastern Europe. Recent publications: 'Quasi-Marketization and Security in Health Care Systems: A Case Study of the North-Western Region of Romania' (2008) in *Studia Sociologia* (with Livia Popescu), 'The Effectiveness of Welfare State Transfers in Reducing Poverty in Romania and Hungary during the first Decade of Post-Socialist Transition' (2006) in *Studia Sociologia*, 'Romanian Roma, State Transfers, and Poverty' (2005) in *International Journal of Sociology*.

Tomáš Sirovátka is Professor of Social Policy at the Faculty of Social Studies, Masaryk University in Brno. He is also a head of the Brno branch of the Research Institute of Labour and Social Affairs. He has carried a number of national as well as international research projects on social policy and employment policy, has published numerous books in the Czech Republic and contributed to several comparative books on social and employment policies. He also has published regularly in peer-reviewed international journals such as *Journal of Comparative Policy Analysis, European Journal of Social Security, International Review of Sociology, International Journal of Sociology and Social Policy* and *Social Policy and Administration*.

Simona Stanescu is a PhD student in Sociology, Bucharest University and researcher at Quality of Life Research Institute, Romanian Academy. Her main areas of interest include comparative social policy, post-communist transformations, enlargement of the EU and the European social agenda. Selected publications of Stanescu include *The Encyclopaedia of Social Development* (co-editor with C. Zamfir, Polirom Romania, 2007), 'Social Policy Reform in Post-Communist Romania Facing the EU Changes' (*CEU Political Science Journal*, volume I, Budapest, Hungary, 2006), *Romanian Accession to EU: the impact on Romanian welfare state* (editor, Romanian Academy, 2004) and 'Romanian Minimum Income Provision as Mechanism of Promoting Social Inclusion' (with Simona Ilie, *NISPA*, volume V, Slovakia, 2004).

Dorottya Szikra has been an associate professor at Eötvös University in Budapest Faculty of Social Sciences since 2003. She has also worked for the Hungarian Ministry of Welfare from 2002 to 2004 as an independent adviser. She was invited to the Central European University, Budapest, Department of Gender Studies as a visiting professor in 2005/2006. Her main research interest includes the history of social policy and social work, history of and current development of family policies. Her recent publications include 'Tradition Matters: Child Care and Primary School Education in Modern Hungary' in Karen Hageman et al. (eds) *Child Care and Primary Education in Post-War Europe* (New York and Oxford, Berghahn Books, 2009), and (together with Dorota Szelewa) 'Welfare et socialisme: de certains concepts relatifs au genre' [Welfare under state socialism. An attempt to apply mainstream and gendered concepts], *Cahiers du Genre*, no. 48, 2009.

Hildegard Theobald is Professor of Organizational Gerontology at Centre for Research on Ageing and Society, Vechta University, Germany. Her research interests include international comparative welfare state research (care policies), professionalization, work organizations and social and gender inequality. Among her most recent publications: 'Care-Politiken, Care-Arbeitsmarkt und Ungleichheit: Schweden, Deutschland und Italien im Vergleich' (*Berliner Journal für Soziologie*, 2008, 18(2), 257–81, *Governing Home Care: A Cross-National Comparison* (Cheltenham: Edward Elgar, 2007) (together with V. Burau and R. H. Blank) and 'Care Resources and Social Exclusion: A European Comparison' (in G. Backes et al. (eds), *Gender, Health and Ageing. European Perspectives on Life Course, Health Issues and Social Challenges*, Wiesbaden: VS-Verlag, 2006, 241–66).

Béla Tomka is Associate Professor of Modern Social and Economic History at the Department of History, University of Szeged. He studied history in Szeged and Budapest, received his PhD (1996) and dr habil. degree (2004) in History at Debrecen University. He was Guest Professor and Research Fellow in Münster, Portland, Minneapolis, Amsterdam, Edinburgh and Berlin. He is the author of ten books including *Welfare in East and West: Hungarian Social Security in an International Comparison, 1918–1990* (Berlin: Akademie Verlag, 2004), editor of several other volumes and co-editor of *AETAS*, a quarterly journal of history. He also co-founded the International Social History Association in 2005. His current research interest is comparative history of twentieth-century East Central Europe, with an emphasis on social welfare, population, family and living standards.

Natascha Van Mechelen is senior researcher at the Herman Deleeck Centre for Social Policy in Antwerp. Her main research is the evolution of minimum income protection in a cross-country perspective. Her PhD research focuses on the institutional factors (such as the degree of segmentation and decentralization of social protection arrangements) explaining the cross-national variation in social assistance benefit levels.

Pieter Vanhuysse received his PhD from the London School of Economics. A former fellow of the Collegium Budapest Institute for Advanced Study, he is a lecturer at the University of Haifa and a research affiliate at the European

Centre for Social Welfare Policy and Research in Vienna. His work centres on the comparative political sociology and political economy of social policies and welfare regimes, education and human capital, and pathways of democratic transition and policy reform. It has appeared in over 20 journals, including *Journal of Social Policy, Public Choice, Journal of Public Policy, Journal of European Public Policy, Politics, Political Studies, Europe–Asia Studies, East European Quarterly, International Journal of Social Welfare* and *International Journal of Sociology and Social Policy.* Dr Vanhuysse's book *Divide and Pacify: Strategic Social Policies and Political Protests in Post-Communist Democracies* (CEU Press) was nominated for the American Sociological Association's Award for Distinguished Contribution to Scholarship, Section on Political Sociology, for 2006.

1
Introduction: Social Policy Pathways, Twenty Years after the Fall of the Berlin Wall*

Alfio Cerami and Pieter Vanhuysse

The year 2009 marks the fifth anniversary of the accession of eight formerly communist states in Central and Eastern Europe to the European Union,[1] and the twentieth anniversary of the fall of the Berlin Wall. This latter event ushered in a new post-Cold War era and a new wave of democratization and free markets in the heart of the European continent. Twenty years on from that eventful autumn day on 9 November 1989, the institutions and procedures of liberal democracy and the predominant role for free markets in economic life are well established as the only game in town in most though not all of the post-communist region, and they are solidly established in every one of the new EU member countries. But many challenges remain even in this latter group of eight (plus two, since 2007[2]), not least in the domain of welfare states. The long-term social consequences of transition still have to be ascertained, and already population ageing looms large as the next big threat in the decades ahead. Economic crises have repeatedly materialized in all countries of the region since 1989, most recently and severely in October 2008 in Bulgaria, Hungary, Latvia, Lithuania, Estonia and Romania. As Claus Offe notes in this volume, compared to the EU-15[3] member states, after 1989 even post-communist reform leaders, on average, were nevertheless confronted with generally higher levels of unemployment, poverty, social exclusion and income inequality and with lower levels of economic wellbeing and social justice.[4] These social ills are now likely to increase still further, widely across post-communist Europe. In addition, the export-led economic model embraced by Central and Eastern European (CEE) countries based on liberalized trade and capital markets and a high dependence on foreign direct investments has now turned into a possible impediment (Barysch, 2009). Whether the impact and extent of the global financial crisis are still unknown for Western European countries, their potential negative consequences for the less developed CEE countries are more obvious precisely because of their larger social ills and their particular economic models.

Against this background, there is no better time than now to explore what post-communist welfare states do, and how they have evolved over time and adapted to changing circumstances. The contributors to this book concentrate their attention on the main institutional, economic, political and social changes that have occurred in Central and Eastern Europe before, during and after communism, trying to assess the causal factors and institutional mechanisms that have been instrumental in shaping alternative welfare state pathways in the region. Specifically, they discuss the transformations and adaptations that have taken place in nine countries spanning three distinct post-communist sub-regions: the Czech Republic, Hungary, Poland and Slovakia (the Visegrad region), Estonia, Latvia and Lithuania (the Baltic area), and Bulgaria and Romania (South-Eastern Europe's new EU members). This choice of cases reflects institutional diversity within and between sub-regions. While all nine countries share a similar communist history with Bismarckian welfare institutions established in the pre-Second World-War period and readapted to communist and post-communist needs, there are significant country-specific and sub-regional peculiarities, including the respective legacies of the pre-war Austro-Hungarian (the Czech Republic, Hungary, Slovakia), Turk-Ottoman (Bulgaria, Romania), Prussian (Poland) and Soviet (Estonia, Latvia, Lithuania) empires. The three sub-regions display peculiar developmental problems. The strong economic ties established with Western Europe have greatly influenced the initial positive economic performance of the four Visegrad countries, while the slow rural–urban modernization of South-Eastern European economies may have hindered a fast catching-up process.[5] Far from being settled from the start, however, the question on the relative degrees of unity and diversity is one of the main topics tackled throughout this volume. Indeed, individual chapters entertain a lively debate on this issue, as they differ in the relative emphasis placed on homogeneity and heterogeneity within Central and Eastern Europe.

Tomasz Inglot's chapter, on the one hand, highlights intra-regional institutional differences and their historical origins predating the communist period. Inglot's review of the Czech, Polish, Hungarian and Slovak cases compares the distinct pathways that have evolved in these welfare states, with respect to their ideational foundation, their institutional consolidation, their maturation in terms of coverage and spending, their expansion and retrenchment cycles, and their major post-communist reforms. Inglot's case studies serve to bolster his theoretical claim that scholarship on contemporary Central and Eastern European welfare states until now has focused too narrowly on post-1989 developments, without fully understanding the influence of the pre-war and interwar period. Welfare states in this region, Inglot argues, ought to be conceived as deeply historically rooted, multi-layered and evolving entities that have accumulated successive layers of ideas, bureaucracy and social insurance schemes. In this account, Central Europe's history of instability, authoritarianism and meddling by foreign powers has led its nation states to develop 'emergency' welfare states – meant to be temporary, but which have become permanent over time. One of the main causal mechanisms in this account is institutional layering. Over the past century, moments of crisis and regime change have mainly added new layers onto already existing structures (see also Inglot, 2008; Thelen, 2004; Streeck and Thelen, 2005a; Cerami, this volume). As a result, says Inglot, path-departing welfare state changes in this region today tend to occur mainly at the margins, as new adaptations, rather than radical reforms.

The chapters by Haggard and Kaufman and Szikra and Tomka, on the other hand, tend towards the view that intra-regional commonalities were far greater than the differences, not least because of the transformative and homogenizing impact of the communist regime itself. The causal mechanisms involved in this process, these authors argue, are inherent to the economic, political and organizational logic of communist state ideology itself. Communism's very commitment to full employment, to the provision of cheap basic consumer goods and housing, and to the absence of private markets necessitated 'premature welfare states' (Kornai, 1992, 1996) or 'great redistributive systems' (Szelenyi, 2009a, 2009b) involving the state's full-scale involvement in social welfare and health on a wide if not universal basis (see also Cook, 1993; Offe, 1993, this volume). After the post-war communist takeovers, welfare benefits that were extended initially to urban workers naturally widened in coverage as the relative share of industrial employment grew over time, as a result of fast industrialization and the far-reaching collectivization of agriculture (with the partial exception of Poland). Other contributions provide a more variegated picture of institutional transformation in the region. For instance, the arguments by Cerami on mechanisms of institutional change, Vanhuysse on power politics and the policy causes of welfare status separation and ethno-linguistic segregation, Cerami and Stanescu on welfare transformations in South-Eastern Europe, and Szikra and Tomka on gender, highlight several complementary mechanisms that have taken place simultaneously, with elements of path-departure not necessarily materializing at the margins but rather within the core of the welfare architecture.

Mechanisms of path-dependency and path-departure in neo-institutional analysis

Neo-institutional scholarship has traditionally emphasized lock-in processes, self-reinforcing mechanisms, vested interests and influence of veto points as fundamental factors of institutional transformation.[6] Change in existing institutional settings is seen here as the product of a cumulative sequential transformation in which timing and sequencing are determinant. The possibility of abrupt institutional change, while not denied a priori, is viewed predominantly as caused by 'critical junctures' and/or the need to surmount unprecedented challenges which would otherwise put existing institutions under strain. The 'exhaustion' or 'cessation' of the main welfare functions makes abrupt transformative change more attractive than the status quo. But institutional change is not always the exclusive product of either a sequence of small incremental institutional adjustments or an unprecedented and unexpected environmentally generated catastrophe. There is often room for path-departing, path-breaking or path-creating transformations to operate. This volume addresses these issues, highlighting similarities as well as diversities in the variegated and multidimensional process of the CEE welfare state pathways since 1989.

Influential historical-institutional accounts[7] have tended to shy away from analysing path-departing, path-breaking or path-creating elements of institutional change. All too often, perhaps, the focus of analysis has concentrated on those elements that lead to status quo, gradual adaptive change and, more recently, path-stabilization. Recently, however, Ebbinghaus (2005) and Hall and Thelen (2009) have usefully analysed path-stabilization in terms of marginal adaptations to environmental changes without changing core principles: *plus ça change, plus c'est la même chose*. Stability is ensured through the institutionalization, reinforcement and consolidation of existing institutional practices, whereas lock-in processes, self-reinforcing mechanisms, vested interests and veto points can be both drivers of incremental institutional transformation and important path-stabilizing elements in an ongoing process of institutional consolidation (Ebbinghaus, 2005, p. 17). For example, when analysing Western pension reforms, Ebbinghaus (2005, 2006) distinguishes between unplanned 'trodden trails' that emerge through the subsequent repeated use by others of a path spontaneously chosen by one individual, and 'road junctures' that constitute a branching point at which one of the available pathways must be chosen. While the first model stresses the spontaneous emergence and subsequent long-term entrenchment of institutions, the second looks at the interdependent sequence of events that structure the alternatives for future change. Yet, in both models, institutional inertia remains the leading explanatory variable. Very little attention is paid, for example, to the diffusion of innovative ideas or the change of power coalitions that could create or enforce alternative pathways. Ebbinghaus (2005, p. 17) further distinguishes path-*departure* – the gradual adaptation through partial renewal of institutional arrangements and limited redirection of core principles – from path-*breaking* (or path-cessation) – the intervention that ends the self-reinforcement of an established institution and may give way to a new one. Finally, the creation of a new path can also occur through new forms of 'recombinant transformation' that result in the formation of unique institutional hybrids (Stark, 1996; Campbell, 2004; Crouch, 2005; Cerami, 2006, 2009a).

As regards post-communist welfare pathways, the authors of this volume share the view that the emerging model or models of post-communist welfare are likely to lead to peculiar institutional hybrids not responding closely to Esping-Andersen's (1990) three-worlds typology or other typologies that have followed in its wake. Like Ekiert and Hanson (2003), and Cook (2007a), this volume re-affirms that both history and politics matter. However, it also demonstrates that this has not precluded elements of innovation and path-departure. This volume portrays a distinctly dynamic picture, in which several drivers of institutional innovation have contributed to the establishment of multidimensional pathways of welfare transformation in Central and Eastern Europe. Socioeconomic factors, political competition, public beliefs and popular and interest group preferences, ideational diffusion and gendered political decisions and battles have all been influential in the process of welfare state innovation. As highlighted by Haggard and Kaufman (this volume), economic and developmental variables have provided incentives not only for path-stabilization but also for path-departure, path-cessation and path-creation. This volume explores the various institutional practices, veto points, lock-in processes and self-reinforcing mechanisms, as well as the role of supranational actors, ideational diffusion, and distributive conflict and elite strategies, that have alternatively driven and constrained the possibility for welfare state change and have influenced not only the stabilization of previously 'well-trodden paths' but have also opened windows for path-departure, path-cessation and path-creation, continuously creating new 'road junctures', 'blind alleys' and 'emergency exits'.

Drivers of institutional innovation in post-communist welfare states

New welfare institutions in post-communist Europe have been influenced not just by public beliefs and interest group preferences. Economic and institutional ideas as diffused and promoted by the most influential international organizations, such as the IMF, the World Bank and the European Union, and by other epistemic communities and advocacy coalitions, have also been key, as highlighted by Orenstein, Theobald and Kern, and Sirovátka and Rákoczyová (this volume). New privatization-based ideas and discourses created new synergies among the different elites (Stark and Bruszt, 1998), and they altered the existing 'power politics' by introducing new strategic policy instruments, in the form of three-pillar pension schemes, public–private mixes of health care, decentralization and privatization in the management of the social security, and basic safety nets in social assistance policies. In conclusion the new power politics of Central and Eastern European welfare state restructuring largely depended on existing historical institutional settings and socioeconomic cleavages where the battles of different national elites took place, but it was also mediated and influenced by international institutions such as the IMF, the World Bank and the European Union, and by other epistemic communities and advocacy coalitions. Sirovátka and Rákoczyová highlight the strong potential for institutional learning regarding the European agenda of social inclusion, which has changed the discourse and process of policy-making in the Czech Republic. While not a new topic in comparative welfare state research (e.g. Hall, 1993; Heclo, 1994), the relation between welfare restructuring and social learning has until recently only rarely been applied to the CEE case. Like Lendvai (2005), Vachudova (2008) and Hemerijck (2010), the chapters by Cerami and Stanescu, Inglot, Orenstein, Theobald and Kern, and Offe make some headway in this regard.

Consistent with a recent theoretical renaissance in Western scholarship, a number of contributions to this volume indicate that ideas and discourses, not least those promoted by influential international institutions, have been key to institutional innovation in CEE.[8] New economic paradigms historically emerge not only because important institutions have suddenly become dysfunctional but also because a new consensus among specific epistemic communities or advocacy coalitions is found.[9] In Central and Eastern Europe, several attempts to reform the central planned economy through the introduction of new forms of state-socialism took place, as was the case in Hungary during the Kádár era or in the Czech Republic during the Prague Spring. After 1989, new social policy ideas, often promoted by the World Bank, IMF, OECD and the EU, have involved privatization in pensions (Orenstein, this volume), health care (Cerami, 2006), elderly care (Theobald and Kern, this volume), decentralization (Van Mechelen and De Maesschalck, this volume) and social inclusion policies (Sirovátka and Rákoczyová, this volume). Similarly, battles for a more gender-equal society resulting from the transition to post-industrial and knowledge-based economies and the emergence of new social risks have had important repercussions for the institutional make-up of both Western and Eastern European welfare states.[10] Szikra and Tomka's chapter provides interesting insights in this regard, highlighting the different forms of 'maternalism' and 'familism' that characterize CEE countries, while sketching the historical pathways of transformation with their associated patterns of political mediation and contestation. During the Cold War, for example, different forms of 'implicit familism' became the leading feature of the communist system of social protection. Most social benefits were tied to employment status, but a dense network of childcare facilities was established to promote female labour market participation levels. At the same time, the provision of parental leave for mothers only meant that the regime wanted to stress the traditional gender roles in the family, against the initial Marxist idea of freeing women from domestic work. In the early years of post-communist transition, by contrast, an explicit maternalist discourse prevailed, aiming to withdraw mothers from the labour market into household functions. A more diverse discourse evolved during the EU accession process, supported by EU priorities for gender mainstreaming, which aimed at the increase of female employment, even though it was substantially higher than in many Western countries.

Permanent emergencies, causal configurations and welfare regime convergence

Which causal configurations and developmental strategies can be expected to be dominant in accounting for welfare state pathways? In their sweeping new historical-institutional theory, Stephan Haggard and Robert Kaufman (2008, this volume) highlight the regionally specific combinations of three distinct causal factors as crucial for explaining welfare regime pathways in the middle-income countries of Latin America, East Asia and Eastern Europe (excluding the Baltic area). These factors are 'critical realignments' in social policy formation, economic-industrial national development strategies, and regime type (democracy vs. autocracy). The notion of critical realignments is, of course, next-of-kin to the political coalitions studied in histories of Western welfare states (Esping-Andersen, 1990; Iversen, 2005; van Kersbergen and Manow, 2009). It is defined here as significant changes in the power equilibrium between political elites and key welfare state actors, especially unions, peasants and popular political parties. These latter groups were newly excluded/repressed or included/co-opted during these realignments; processes which subsequently determined their political and organizational capacity.[11] A second element in the Haggard and Kaufman account regards the specific macro-economic developmental strategy adopted in each region. In Latin America, uneven developments between the urban working class and the peasantry combined with an Import Substituting Industrialization development strategy without wide human capital investment. This led to social policies that were deep but narrow, mainly targeted at the urban working class. In East Asia, decolonization strategies combined with export-oriented growth strategies to encourage investments in education predominantly, at the expense of more standard social policies. In communist Eastern Europe, lastly, state-led industrialization and export strategies aimed at the Soviet Union led to 'universal' social policies and large perceived welfare entitlements that strongly narrowed the scope for post-communist welfare retrenchment.

How have these causal configurations been at play in post-communist welfare pathways? King (2002, 2007) distinguishes between two principal developmental models that have been pursued in the entire post-communist region: a backward patrimonial type in the post-Soviet CIS[12] that has relied heavily on raw materials exports, and a more economically progressive liberal type in CEE[13] relying on massive capital imports and manufactured exports. The capital-imports/manufactures-exports combination of course goes some way towards explaining the economic and budgetary troubles that have affected nearly the entire region so strongly since autumn 2008. *Within* post-communist Central and Eastern Europe, however, a crucial further distinction is the one made by Bohle and Greskovits (2006, 2007) between a 'straightforward neo-liberal' and an 'embedded neo-liberal' or social-liberal model of economic development.[14] The Baltic states have preferred the first model, combining flexible, deregulated labour market institutions with low taxation levels and low-value-added export strategies based on resource-intensive and/or unskilled (cheap) labour-based industrial production. This strategy has co-evolved with high growth rates, leading it to become known over the course of the 1990s as the 'Baltic Tiger' model. It has been functionally compatible with the increasingly liberal direction of welfare pathways in the Baltics, as described in the chapters by Jolanta Aidukaite and Pieter Vanhuysse, on which more below.

In contrast, the four Visegrad countries have adopted an embedded neo-liberal strategy, as a compromise between liberalization and social protection, one that is somewhat reminiscent of post-war continental Western European 'embedded liberalism' (Ruggie, 1983), but which places a much higher emphasis on social protection as a way to accommodate and facilitate the dominant macro-economic developmental goals of neo-liberal competitiveness (Bohle and Greskovits, 2007). The neo-liberal macro-economic dimension of the Visegrad model has been centred mainly around foreign direct investment and more complex exports (mainly of automobiles), based on production strategies that combined complex capital, technology and more advanced industry-specific human skills (on FDI, see Drahokoupil, 2008). The subordinated embedded side of the Visegrad model has consisted in its reliance upon a generous but ad-hoc and politically targeted welfare state architecture, as described in this book by Tomasz Inglot, Stephan Haggard and Robert Kaufman, and Pieter Vanhuysse. Compared to earlier analyses of social policy in Central and Eastern Europe,[15] these contributions jointly make theoretical progress by setting out more clearly the different sets of causal mechanisms and power configurations that have driven welfare pathways since 1989. In the process, they entertain a lively scholarly debate about the relative weight of communist legacies in post-communist transition, and how these legacies differed within the region.

Adding a power dimension: distributive conflict and strategic social policies

A further issue of crucial importance regards the relative weight of institutional mechanisms versus (elite) actor strategies in shaping post-communist welfare pathways. Pieter Vanhuysse's discussion of the cases of Hungary, Poland, Estonia and Latvia revisits 'generous' or 'emergency' welfare state interpretations as put forward in this volume also by Inglot, Haggard and Kaufman, and Szikra and Tomka. In particular, Vanhuysse concurs with the view that new democratic governments, especially in Central and Eastern Europe, have attached an uncommonly high priority by international comparison to setting up early safety nets aimed at compensating at-risk workers. But his chapter complements these accounts by adding an analysis of power-as-distributive-conflict and elite strategy. This once again brings to the forefront Haggard and Kaufman's concept of 'critical realignments'. Vanhuysse highlights how power-holders have chosen which social risks or status groups to accommodate in transition, and which social cleavages to play down or accentuate.

In the case of Hungary and Poland, policymakers have gone beyond providing generous 'emergency' safety nets by significantly *reshaping* the distributions of transition winners and losers, and welfare state contributors and dependants. Policies such as extensive early and disability retirement were used to separate seemingly similar at-risk workers into different interest groups with clashing material interests and weakening social network ties. The key causal mechanisms involved in Vanhuysse's account are sociological and material. They include decreasing weak ties among marginalized labour market outsiders as well as distributive conflict over ever-scarcer welfare state resources among once-similar actors, and individualistic coping strategies such as informal work, which replaced the pursuit of public goods through collective action. As time went by, there were likely to be further feedback mechanisms contributing to the progressive pacification of the polity.[16] Beyond safety net provision, Vanhuysse argues, social policies have modified the patterns of distributive conflict in the polity, by reducing the political salience of class cleavages and increasing that of the pensioner constituency relative to other groups of claimants of state resources. This helps to account for why even after the partial privatization of pensions systems, discussed by Mitchell Orenstein in this volume, and despite demographically still relatively young populations, these countries have witnessed public pension spending well above the OECD average (see also Vanhuysse, 2001). Moreover, the relative economic welfare of pensioners improved markedly after 1989–1990, both when compared to other at-risk groups and when compared to their own situation in late socialism.

The cases of Bulgaria and Romania, which entered the European Union in January 2007, provide further insights into the role of power politics. As Cerami and Stanescu show, these South-Eastern European countries have undergone important transformations since the early years following the Ottoman occupation. In the battles for social and economic modernization that have often pitted urban elites against rural elites, welfare institutions have helped to pacify largely underdeveloped and highly divided agricultural societies, thereby allowing a faster modernization process and facilitating fragile compromises between rural and urban elites with different modernization priorities. The Baltic welfare states, lastly, have been balancing between 'old' legacies of universalism and 'new' neo-liberal ideas in a larger context in which a weak civil society and a relatively mild influence of the EU social model have led to a top-down, elite-driven policy regime. Like Aidukaite (this volume), Vanhuysse (this volume) notes that non-citizens in Latvia and Estonia do not enjoy eligibility and voting rights in national elections. But he notes that even though non-citizens in both countries may have been nominally entitled to all social rights, they have, in actual practice, been marginalized, and pacified, along ethnic lines. Vanhuysse highlights the way in which the new titular elites have reshaped the distribution of transition winners and losers after Baltic independence in ways that made existing levels of ethno-linguistic heterogeneity politically more salient, at the expense of class and other social cleavages. These power strategies helped to break up the Russian speakers' capacity to coalesce with socioeconomically similar transition losers for class-based economic protests, which left them further marginalized *as* an ethnic minority. This shows how recent studies indicating the negative effects of ethno-linguistic heterogeneity on social solidarity (Alesina and La Ferrara, 2005; Putnam, 2007) could be complemented with more explicitly strategic analyses enquiring when (and how) such ethnic cleavages are made politically salient.

A closer emphasis on the power politics of social policy can also inform the larger debates about path-dependence and path-departure discussed above. The six cases discussed above constitute clear instances of path-departure, beyond mere incremental change or institutional layering. The dramatic reversal of the political clout of Russian speakers vis-à-vis titulars after independence in Latvia and Estonia was precisely *that* – a reversal, and a far-reaching instance of critical realignment. And the *de novo* creation of hundreds of thousands of working-aged Bulgarian, Hungarian, Polish and Romanian pensioners, while a well-known template from late socialism, accelerated so much in speed and scale after 1989 that it significantly perturbed the work-welfare composition of society. At a crucial juncture, supply-side policies reshaped the prevailing logics of distributive politics in these polities, *after which* mechanisms of institutional path-dependence could once again gather force.

Outline of the book

This book is divided into three main parts. Part I focuses on historical trajectories (Dorottya Szikra and Béla Tomka), mechanisms of institutional change (Alfio Cerami) and power politics (Pieter Vanhuysse) in CEE welfare pathways.

Dorottya Szikra and Béla Tomka (Chapter 2) discuss the main welfare state transformations that have taken place in East Central Europe since the first establishment of social insurance institutions at the end of the nineteenth century. Compared to previous studies on the topic, which have often neglected the gender dimension of social security reforms, Szikra and Tomka emphasize the different understanding of 'familism' and 'maternalism' in the historical development of CEE welfare states, and they denote current social protection regimes as hybrid systems that have gone through highly complex pathways of institutional transformation.

Alfio Cerami (Chapter 3) discusses the main mechanisms of institutional change transforming CEE welfare states. Cerami investigates the micro–macro linkages involved in any process of institutional transformation, highlighting also the relational and organizational character of institutional change. He discusses a wide array of complementary mechanisms that have influenced CEE welfare state institutions across three interconnected domains – ideas, institutions and interests. In order to make sense of the various patterns of institutional change, Cerami identifies an aggregating mechanism of recombinant transformation, or bricolage, as having played a key role in the overall process of welfare state restructuring.

Pieter Vanhuysse (Chapter 4) argues that post-communist rulers in Hungary, Poland, Latvia and Estonia have used their state power to design policies aimed at the preservation of social order via *protest* avoidance, as a necessary political alternative to *blame* avoidance (see Weaver, 1986) in a context of high social costs of fast reforms. At the critical juncture of post-communist transition, elites have proactively *reshaped* the distributions of economic winners and losers of transition in all four cases. In the two Visegrad cases, they have created Great Abnormal Pensioner Booms (Vanhuysse, 2004) by sending hundreds of thousands of working-age citizens into early and disability retirement, increasing all pensioners' policy clout in the process. In the two Baltic cases, political elites have designed public policies to silence and subdue their formerly powerful Russian-speaking minorities, in an effort to break their political voice in terms of electoral clout, collective action capacity and access to scarce state resources.

Part II is dedicated to country studies on the Czech Republic, Hungary, Poland and Slovakia (Tomasz Inglot), Estonia, Latvia and Lithuania (Jolanta Aidukaite), and Bulgaria and Romania (Cerami and Stanescu).

Tomasz Inglot (Chapter 5) compares the Visegrad systems of cash transfers and discusses national developmental pathways according to five dimensions: welfare discourse, the type of institutional consolidation, the timing of the maturation of the welfare state, sequencing of expansion and retrenchment, and prioritizing and timing of major social policy reforms. Emphasizing the relevance of historical and discursive institutionalism (see Schmidt, 2008) in these four countries, Inglot argues that although path-dependence prevails, rare path-departing openings can also occur, especially under conditions of national political reconstruction, as illustrated by the case of Slovakia.

Jolanta Aidukaite (Chapter 6) reviews Baltic social policy developments and concludes that historical legacies have had a greater impact on social policy change than right–left power resources or Europeanization. Important moments of path-departures such as the partial privatization of pension insurance, have nevertheless substantially altered the previous social insurance structures.

Alfio Cerami and Simona Stanescu (Chapter 7) review elements of path-dependence, path-departure and institutional innovation in the main welfare states' transformations in Bulgaria and Romania since the first establishment of social insurance institutions in the early twentieth century. In order to explain the main factors and causes of institutional change, they propose a modified version of the 'misfit' model whereby a misfit between new environmental requirements and existing institutional structures is a key driver for institutional change, together with mediating factors such as ideas, interests and institutions, and enabling factors such as socioeconomic variables, political conflicts and cleavages, and ideational diffusion.

Part III contains sectoral analyses of specific social policy areas: pensions and international organizations (Mitchell Orenstein), elderly care (Hildegard Theobald and Kristine Kern), minimum income schemes (Cristina Rat), the devolution of social security arrangements (Natascha van Mechelen and Veerle De Maesschalck) and the impact of the EU social inclusion strategy (Tomas Sirovátka and Miroslava Rákoczyová).

Mitchell Orenstein (Chapter 8) advances a transnational perspective on welfare state development and change, arguing that transnational actors have had a major impact on pension privatization in Central and Eastern Europe and the former Soviet Union. Extensive interviews and documentary evidence demonstrate the direct involvement of transnational actors in putting reform on the agenda, funding reform teams and ensuring implementation through post-reform technical assistance. According to Orenstein, advocacy coalitions and policy diffusion of ideas are crucial additional influences on institutional change, fostering path-departure and institutional innovation.

Hildegard Theobald and Kristine Kern (Chapter 9) highlight the profound changes that elderly care systems have faced in many Continental, Southern and Central and Eastern European countries, with a special emphasis on bilateral transfer processes between countries. They show intense processes of cross-country policy learning and ideational and policy transfer in different parts of Europe.

Cristina Rat (Chapter 10) investigates minimum income-guaranteed schemes in Bulgaria, the Czech Republic, Hungary, Poland, Romania and Slovakia. She draws attention to the social divisions which make certain categories of citizens particularly vulnerable to the inadequacies of social inclusion policies. Within the larger set of social inclusion policies, minimum income-guarantee schemes are last-resort benefits, which ought to secure subsistence while maintaining incentives to work. However, in the strongly polarized CEE member states, with poverty thresholds well below the EU-15 average, Rat argues that 'securing subsistence' means helping households far below the poverty threshold to obtain a minimal income, rather than the prevention and tackling of the different forms of poverty.

Natascha van Mechelen and Veerle De Maesschalck (Chapter 11) focus on decentralization reforms in CEE countries. They argue that despite sound theoretical arguments in favour of decentralization, the dominant assumption in this region remains that redistributive policies ought to be performed at the central level. Van Mechelen and De Maesschalck's analysis shows that although extreme forms of decentralization are generally associated with inadequate minimum income provision, more restricted versions of decentralization do not necessarily result in low benefit levels. Social assistance benefit packages are invariably below the poverty line in countries where municipalities decide autonomously on most of the package. But they are usually above the poverty line where central governments set the basic social assistance rates and housing benefits while sharing funding liabilities with the local government level. The authors conclude that the current trend towards more local involvement in minimum income provision in CEE countries should not necessarily lead to inadequate benefits, provided that there is strong central steering.

Tomáš Sirovátka and Miroslava Rákoczyová (Chapter 12) explore how Czech governments have implemented the new EU agenda of social inclusion, and how key actors at the national, regional and local levels perceive the problem of social exclusion, formulate strategies and implement policies. They conclude that while the agenda of social inclusion may bring positive future effects in terms of institutional learning and policy innovation, the low legitimacy of the social inclusion agenda, implementation deficits and contradictions between the national and local (regional) levels still represent significant barriers to policy change.

The last two contributions to this volume draw many threads together and offer a particularly broad-sweep analysis. Stephan Haggard and Robert Kaufman's essay (Chapter 13) compares the main developmental strategies put in place in the middle-income countries of East Asia and Latin America with those of the countries studied in this volume. In line with their previous work, Haggard and Kaufman emphasize the role of historical legacies and the importance of political mediation in the overall process of welfare state transformation. They also argue that a fruitful agenda for future research on CEE welfare pathways ought to include the construction of clear metrics to capture path-dependent and path-departing changes and the continued collection of qualitative and quantitative data that will permit more focused comparisons.

Finally, Claus Offe's epilogue reflects upon two sets of factors at the very beginning and the very end point of welfare state transformation: values, ideas, attitudes and expectations regarding social policy on the one hand, and the actual achievements and outcomes of social policies on the other. Regarding the first, Offe points to the legacy of pervasive popular expectations, discussed in a number of chapters in this volume, of a particularly comprehensive 'paternalist care' welfare state. With characteristic lucidity, Offe goes on to suggest that, far from vanishing simultaneously with the corresponding communist-type welfare policies, these paternalist state expectations may actually have survived or gained in strength in the post-communist context of reform hardship and nostalgia for the past among many sub-sectors of society. Regarding outcomes, Offe highlights the fact that the post-communist countries studied in this book, even the frontrunners among them, have actually been relatively poor performers in a wider international context, whether viewed in terms of the social justice of public policies such as poverty prevention, education, labour market performance, social expenditure on health and cohesion, income distribution, intergenerational justice and anti-discrimination policies (Merkel and Giebler, 2009), or in terms of the subjective satisfaction with conditions in post-transition and post-accession, particularly among older and poorer citizens (EBRD, 2007). Added to the current context of post-EU-accession *reform fatigue* and the unexpected global economic crisis of 2008–2009, which will undoubtedly reduce the macro-fiscal financial leeway, this particularly unsavoury constellation of conditions might well lead to new political dynamics for party competitition, democratic stability and social spending in the region. After this new critical juncture of CEE welfare pathways, which coincides with the twentieth anniversary of the fall of the Wall, path-departures, institutional ruptures, permanent emergencies and zero-sum distributive conflict are likely to figure prominently.

Part I
Theoretical Background

2
Social Policy in East Central Europe: Major Trends in the Twentieth Century

Dorottya Szikra and Béla Tomka

Introduction

East Central European countries and post-Soviet states have a common communist legacy, because of which they are looked at as countries with markedly different political and welfare cultures compared to 'Western' capitalist democracies.[1] The difference in the historical legacy has caused many authors to group these countries into one category of 'post-Soviet' or 'post-communist' states. The systematic analysis of the commonalities and differences of their welfare history has only started recently (Inglot, 2003, 2008; Tomka, 2003, 2005; Cerami, 2006), but these studies have mainly neglected the history of family policies in the region. Recent development of family policies and gender have attracted considerable attention (Pascall and Kwak, 2005, Fodor et al., 2002; Szelewa and Polakowski, 2008) but the historical roots of current family policies is a new field to be explored.

In this introductory chapter we argue that the similarities and differences that can be observed today lie partly in the historical legacies of these countries, dating back at least to the turn of the twentieth century. Peculiarities of pre- and post-war development and diverging political and economic arrangements under the transition period led to markedly different welfare outcomes in these new capitalist democracies. Still, we can observe some common features, both historically and today, and these make the label 'post-communist welfare' relevant. Besides arguing that social policies in the region are more mixed and volatile than in 'Western' capitalist democracies we point out the gendered nature of such policies. We argue that due to historical legacies and gendered political considerations, different forms of 'familialism' developed in the region, especially in the second half of the communist period, and despite the radical political and economic changes these patterns can still be grasped very well. Our argument will be underpinned with examples from the development of social insurance systems and family policies in East Central Europe, thus the Czech Republic, Slovakia, Hungary and Poland.

We share the concern of both Eastern and Western scholars about the difficulties of analysing the welfare systems of East Central European countries with the help of already existing frameworks (Saxonberg, 2000; Tomka, 2003; Inglot, 2008). Some would even argue that communist countries are placed 'outside the scope of Esping-Andersen's typology as well as its feminist variants' (Michel, 2006, p. 146). Although there has been much criticism against the framework of power-resources analysts, some of their analytical dimensions could well be utilized in East Central European welfare research (Tomka, 2003; Inglot, 2008). New-institutionalism and the theory of path-dependency have also been relevant to much of the scholarship, although with certain modifications. From the standpoint of historical institutionalism Tomasz Inglot comes to the conclusion that although there are important differences between social policy decision-making processes and outcomes within East Central Europe, the common and distinguishing pattern is their 'emergency' decision-making manner that is strongly linked to economic and political crisis throughout history (Inglot, 2008, and this volume). Although we think that historical institutionalism and the theory of path-dependency are crucial, we also suggest that 'welfare culture' as a concept can provide us with useful tools to interpret the different levels of resistance to the repeated neo-liberal challenges in the post-communist world (Müller, 1999; Pfau-Effinger, 2005).

Gendered research focusing on the development of family policies shines a light on social policies affecting gendered relations, and influencing the welfare chances of women and children (Saxonberg, 2000; Fodor et al., 2002; Heinen, 2002; Pascall and Lewis, 2004; Fodor, 2006). These studies could utilize concepts of 'maternalism' and 'familialism', developed by North-American scholars (Haney and Pollard, 2003). Maternalism describes how women played a central role in the process of welfare state formation, and how women as mothers became subjects of social policy (Koven and Michel, 1993). Familialism builds on the evidence that throughout history 'states attempted to mobilize families and deploy familial images for a variety of political ends' (Haney and Pollard, 2003, pp. 1–14). In their recent attempt Szelewa and Polakowski describe East Central European family policies relying on the framework developed by Leitner (2003), and describe different forms of familialisms in East Central European countries (Szelewa and Polakowki, 2008). Our chapter goes beyond their analysis by highlighting the different and changing forms of familialisms under communism.

Early histories of social policy in East Central Europe

Although there has been extensive research from the 1960s on the early years of the welfare states, East Central European countries were mainly

Table 2.1 Introduction of compulsory social insurance schemes in East Central Europe

	Injuries	Sickness	Old age	Unemployment
Czech Republic	1887	1888	1924	1918
Slovakia	1907	1891	1924	1918
Hungary	1907	1891	1928	1991
Poland	1924	1920	1927	1924

Source: Darvas (2000) with modifications.

left out of the analysis. The main reason for this was the difficulty to gain information on Eastern development. Communist countries have had their own Marxist–Leninist welfare historiography, but research in the region was fairly unsystematic and produced studies that were often heavily ideological. This is why there has been a need for former state socialist countries to write or rewrite their welfare histories after the fall of communism.

Authors dealing with the early years of social policy in East Central Europe stress their Bismarckian traditions (Szikra, 2000, 2004; Tomka, 2004; Cerami, 2006; Inglot, 2008). Indeed, the first compulsory social insurance schemes were introduced immediately following German and Austrian legislation in these countries. Austrian legislation applied directly to today's Czech Republic. Hungary (including what was later called Slovakia), being part of the Austro-Hungarian monarchy, closely followed this legislation. Poland's territory was divided between Germany, the Austro-Hungarian monarchy and Russia before its formation in 1919; thus the legislation of these countries were applied here before the First World War. Poland itself introduced compulsory social insurance legislation after its formation, in the 1920s. In Table 2.1, above, the years of the first social insurance legislations of East Central European countries are listed.

The table shows that the timing and sequence of social insurance legislation in East Central European countries was in line with Western European welfare history. The ambition of these countries to keep pace with social and economic development in Germany and Austria was a good reason to provide social insurance for workers at an early stage. This can be illustrated by the words of the Minister of Industrial Affairs in Hungary in 1891, referring to the economic environment of the country:

> I kept in mind that Hungarian employers and workers should not be put in a less favourable position than their counterparts in the other countries and kingdoms of the council of the empire with which we form a united duty zone. It is also evident that the way in which sickness benefits are arranged in the German Empire affects us. Our industrial

conditions have a certain natural connection with these countries. (Indoklás, 1890, p. 168)

The constant incentives to adjust legislations within the Austro-Hungarian monarchy might be viewed at as early examples of a 'harmonization process' within Europe. In addition to cultural and economic reasons, workers' demonstrations around the turn of the century made the leading elite believe that social insurance would pacify the working class. Peter Flora and Jens Alber are right when they argue that monarchies with limited suffrage, like Austria-Hungary, were more likely to introduce social insurance legislation at an early stage of development to secure the legitimacy of their ruling class. In the constitutional monarchies 'social welfare [is] an authoritarian defence against (full) political citizenship and [is] a consequence of competition for loyalty' (Flora and Alber, 1981, p. 46). This truly holds for the East Central European countries.

Early social insurance legislation clearly positions welfare regimes of East Central European countries in the typologies created by Richard Titmuss (1958) and Gøsta Esping-Andersen (1990). The emerging welfare systems before and immediately after the First World War were closest to what is often called 'conservative', 'etatist' or 'Bismarckian' welfare regimes. The most important characteristic here is the early introduction of workers' insurance schemes financed from contributions, with minimal or no state subsidy. Another important feature is the creation of separate schemes for civil servants, industrial workers and agricultural workers. Civil servants enjoyed favourable conditions in all of these countries and agricultural workers were mainly offered voluntary insurance with very poor conditions (Szikra, 2009). This is why a very low proportion of agricultural workers became covered by social insurance schemes before the Second World War. This, in itself, was not rare in Western Europe either. However, with the exception of Czechoslovakia, the agricultural sector dominated the economy in East Central European countries throughout the interwar period (Mitchell, 1980, pp. 162–8). Low coverage of the agricultural population, weak local administration and the relatively high number of small industries all contributed to the fact that the overall coverage of social insurance schemes remained lower than in most Western countries.

Austria-Hungary fell apart in 1918–1920 and several new successor states were created in the region. Social policy legislation constituted a significant element of the state formation process in all of these countries. In the newly created Czechoslovakia, sickness, disability and pension insurance for all employees except part-time workers was enacted in 1924 (Czech Social Security Administration, 2004). The first socialist government in Poland introduced compulsory social insurance, which soon became one of the most developed systems in East Central Europe (Inglot, 2008). Hungary lost two-thirds of the territories of the previous Hungarian kingdom. Here, legislation created a centralized body of social insurance, extended sickness

Table 2.2 Introduction of paid maternity leave and family allowance in East Central European countries

	Maternity leave	Family allowance
Czech Republic	1888	1945
Slovakia	1884	1945
Hungary	1884	1938 (1912 for civil servants)
Poland	1933	1948

Sources: Ferge (1991); Darvas (2000); Szikra and Szelewa (2008).

and injuries insurance, as well as introducing a fairly generous old-age and disability pension system in 1928. Here, the fear from the 'disappearance of the nation' led to the emergence of maternalist policy measures in the 1930s and 1940s (Koven and Michel, 1993). Family allowance for factory workers was introduced as early as 1938, and an extensive, means- and behaviour-tested loan was provided for poor agricultural families with many children (Szikra, 2008). The 1930s saw the rapid development of kindergartens and afternoon services for children of factory workers. These measures paved the way to what later became an 'optional familialistic' or 'public maternalist' development in Hungary (Leitner, 2003; Fodor, 2007; Szikra and Szelewa, 2009).

In Poland at this time, with its traditional commitment to Catholicism, family life was treated as 'sacred' and a private matter. This is the main reason why family policies played a marginal role in the newly formed state (Szikra and Szelewa, 2009). 'Implicit familialism', where the state does not create explicit family policies and puts the burden on families (Leitner, 2003), remained a long-lasting feature of the Polish state. At the same time, the rhetoric about the 'mother Pole' was very much present between the two World Wars, creating a paradox situation when the 'saviors of the nation' (Davis, 1997) were actually left alone with their caring tasks. In Czechoslovakia legislation of the Austro-Hungarian monarchy regarding childcare facilities and payments remained in place for a long time and the government refrained from extensive maternalist policies and concentrated more on the insurance of industrial workers than on their families (Haskova, 2007). Table 2.2 shows the dates of the introduction of paid maternity leave and family allowance in East Central Europe.

Major features of communist welfare regimes in East Central Europe

The concept of welfare state is usually applied for parliamentary democracies and market economies but not for communist countries. However, in communist societies the collective responsibility for the welfare of citizens also existed, and the relevant institutions were set up. The state was not the only agent taking responsibility for the well-being of citizens, but it had an exceptional significance in the welfare mix. Based on these considerations East Central European communist countries can plausibly be considered as welfare states as well (Haney, 2000, pp. 101–22). However, if we take the Marshallian perspective on the development of rights, according to which social rights are built upon civil and political rights, and these together form the basis of the welfare state, we can say that East Central European communist countries cannot be regarded welfare states (Marshall, 1950). For sure, with the banning of civil and political rights, these countries followed a different path to welfare, and if we take a broader view and consider 'well-fare' in the sense of 'well-being' we can say that the periods of massive political suppression in these countries do not call for the label 'welfare state', let alone 'welfare society'.

But if we put these theoretical considerations aside, we can also observe that in communist East Central Europe a specific structure of social rights emerged. The role of welfare arrangements and the width and depth of social rights, however, substantially changed over time within the communist era. The lack of civil and political rights and the system of privileges coupled with mass poverty contributed to the 1956 uprising in Poland and the revolution in Hungary in the same year. The same reasons can be grasped in the 1968 events in Czechoslovakia. After the revolts, the East Central European communist regimes changed their welfare policies. An unspoken contract between the state and the citizens was created: social rights and welfare were provided *in return* for the lack of political and civil rights. Social spending rose and new institutions were created. Thus both in respect of social security arrangements and family policies, two periods can be distinguished within communism: The first period lasted from the early years of communism until the mid- or, in other countries, late 1960s, and the second period from the late 1960s until the fall of communism. A more universal set of welfare policies can be observed in the second period, and this is the time of the development of generous family policies as well. To this we return later.

The major difference compared to Western Europe is that the foundation of social welfare was a compulsory employed status of the working-age population, even if it implied low levels of income. Other specific institutions of communist welfare included price subsidies for specific goods and services, and the system of social benefits offered by companies, both with altering significance over time. First we deal with these institutions, then we turn to the features and development of social security systems and family policies in the region.

The centrality of the right and obligation to work was guaranteed by the constitution in most cases. Working-age people out of employment, especially males, were persecuted and often imprisoned. To accomplish *full employment* the centralized allocation of the working force was established. Social policy also became a means to drive people into the state-run industries as most of the transfer payments were tied to employment in the public sector. Economic incentives and regulations encouraged companies to employ even those people for whom they were not able to provide appropriate work, thus creating hidden unemployment. The position of employees was relatively favourable in the situation of shortage economy and labour law made it difficult to fire employees. At the same time, all of this had its price since it harmed efficient employment: the shift of the working force from less effective sectors to more successful ones ran into difficulties. This regime of employment could only be maintained in the long run while companies were protected from the consequences of low productivity by the centrally planned economy.

In the East Central European communist countries the system of *price subsidies* for basic consumer goods and services was a major tool of welfare policy. The explicit goal of these measures was not only the increase of purchasing power but also the support of inefficient firms and branches. At the same time they had a moderate impact on social inequality, primarily because better-off segments of the society had much better access to them than the less privileged ones. In certain areas, such as health care or consumption of basic foods, they resulted in large-scale waste of resources (Andorka and Tóth, 1992, p. 442). Price subsidies in East Central European never grew so much out of proportion as in the GDR in the 1980s, where the funds allocated for subsidies surpassed social security expenditures (Therborn, 1995, p. 95).

In the East Central European communist regimes the system of *fringe benefits* became much more diversified and extensive than in market economies. Factories often established – depending on their size – kindergartens, sport and cultural facilities, health-care institutions and holiday resorts. Companies even distributed a fair share of goods in short supply, most importantly flats, but they often also provided such necessities as basic foodstuffs for their employees. At the same time fringe benefits mainly benefited the higher ranks of industrial workers and they rarely reached unskilled labourers of state-run factories.

The changes in the *functions of social security* were contradictory in communist East Central Europe. Alternative welfare systems, such as social assistance, sporadically existed on the local level but their role was marginal compared to capitalist democracies. This made the significance of social security programmes greater compared to capitalist democracies. Another special feature was that the earlier existing autonomy of social insurance administration was eliminated. The system was driven by direct political aims and became integrated into the complex system of the above-described fringe benefits and price subsidies.

Legislation in the aftermath of the Second World War, partly initiated by non-communist political forces, promoted the extension of social rights in East Central Europe. *Coverage* of the social security schemes continued to increase at a significant pace in the region after the communist takeover. At the same time, a policy of particularities and privileges rather than that of universalism emerged under early communism. The differentiation of social security eligibility remained long in place in all of the East Central European countries: industrial workers, members of the armed forces, the party and state bureaucracy were privileged (de Deken, 1994, p. 137). Parallel to this process was the politically motivated elimination of social rights obtained in the previous regime and the discrimination of certain social groups, most of all farmers (Minkoff and Turgeon, 1977, pp. 178–80). However, the crudest forms of class-based discrimination were abandoned by the early 1960s, not least due to the subsequent uprises and revolutions in Poland and Hungary in 1956. The growing significance of the solidarity principle of the 1960s and 1970s in the area of qualifying conditions resulted in the rapid increase of the coverage, and can be regarded as a move toward universality. Solidarity had its limits: there was a heavily work-related element in the system. Cash benefits (pensions, sick leave, etc.) were not merely closely linked to employment but also determined by the level of income. This characteristic of social security arrangements became even more pronounced over time.

Alongside similarities there were significant differences between the East Central European countries in terms of coverage. It was primarily the Polish, being different from the other countries due to the high number of private farmers, who were not eligible for pension insurance until the late 1970s. However, by the 1980s universalism gained ground in all three countries, and the differences within the region were simultaneously decreasing. In Hungary as well as in Czechoslovakia, the middle of 1970s was the turning point, when universalism became the underlying principle of social security. In Poland this development took place somewhat later, at the end of the 1970s (Okrasa, 1987, p. 14).

While social security coverage ratios in East Central Europe increased considerably in the post-war decades and soon became comparable to these of Austria or Germany, the absolute and even the relative *level of benefits* does not turn out so favourably in a Western European comparison. A striking feature of the communist welfare regimes just establishing themselves in Hungary and Poland was the relatively moderate level of *social security expenditures* both compared to welfare efforts in the interwar period and in a European context: In terms of social security expenditures relative to the GDP, Poland and Hungary diverged from Western Europe until the end of the 1970s. Moreover, in 1980 Hungary was still more behind the West than in 1930 (Hivatal, 1982, p. 387; Tomka, 2004, pp. 41–8). In contrast, Czechoslovakia had a high social security/GDP ratio in the first two post-war decades. By 1980 differences mostly disappeared between the three countries (Castles, 1986, p. 217). Growth in the relative level of social security expenditures in the 1980s was due to the economic recession reflected in the stagnation of the GDP, and also the efforts of the regimes to buy the support of the population in a period when their legitimacy was eroding quickly.

The expansion of social security programmes took place in East Central Europe with priorities different from those in Western Europe, with its prime considerations related to the efficiency of production and the mobilization of the workforce. In the first two decades, the most important characteristic of *structure of expenditures* was the low ratio of pension-related expenditures and the relatively high ratio of health-care spending compared to Western Europe. Between the 1960s and 1980s the relative decrease in health expenditures and the increase in family benefits represented especially strong divergences from Western European trends. As a significant difference, it is also important to mention the complete lack of unemployment expenditures in East Central Europe (Andorka and Tóth, 1992, p. 413).

In most Western European countries the state had an increasing role in the *administration* of social security in the decades following the Second World War. However, the complete nationalization of social security could be observed in East Central Europe. In Hungary, from 1951 until the mid-1980s the operation of social security was in the hands of trade unions, themselves an organic part of the power structure of the party-state. In Czechoslovakia and Poland social security was controlled by the state administration directly. In addition, there was no democratic control of any kind over social security schemes (Deacon, 1983, p. 155; Tomka, 2004, pp. 90–5). Elected self-governments did not exist and the lack of democratic control over the state administration made even indirect control impossible, thus turning the organizational aspect of social security into the area where differences from Western Europe were of the greatest degree.

Family policies under communism served primarily pronatalist aims but at the same time were relatively successful in diminishing poverty among families with children (Darvas, 2000). Early communist family policies were restrictive in all countries, with low state subsidy for childcare institutions and restrictive legislation on abortion. Recent research shows how the communist state pushed the responsibility of building kindergartens onto local communities and factories, thus actually withdrawing itself from public provision, which was contrary to the state's self-image as carer for 'our greatest treasure, the child' (Bicskei, 2007). After the uprisings and revolutions in the region in 1956 and 1968 welfare policies and also family policies changed substantially and became part of the social compromise between the state and the citizens.

A very good example for this turn is the system of extended parental leave, introduced from the late 1960s in all East Central European countries.

This leave is called 'parental leave' in the English-speaking literature to distinguish it from the former systems of short maternity leave, although they were only paid to mothers at the outset of the schemes. Former 'short' maternity leave systems still remained in place after the introduction of the new extended schemes. In Czechoslovakia and in Hungary it was a paid leave and was provided for all working mothers for 2.5 and later 3 years. Long parental leave was unpaid in Poland until 1981, when it became paid. At the same time, contrary to the other two countries, parental leave was income-tested from the very beginning in Poland (Szikra and Szelewa, 2009). Income testing made Poland diverge from the other two countries as this was a rather uncommon means to define eligibility under communism.

Long parental leave schemes were also significant in the sense that they represented a slight change from the earlier policies of driving women into the labour market. Providing the leave only for mothers clearly shows that the regime wanted to stress the traditional roles of men and women within the family and broke with the initial Marxist idea of freeing women from domestic work. On the other hand, the fact that long maternity leave was an option and not an obligation created considerable freedom for women in this region, especially in those countries where childcare facilities became accessible. This can be called 'optional familialism', which developed in Hungary in its clearest form. Czechoslovakia also succeeded in providing kindergarten places for almost all families until the mid-1980s, but Poland still left caring tasks with family members to a great extent. In Poland the state did not provide financial support for mothers (long paid maternity leave) either. Using Leitner's classification we can say that Polish family policies represented the ideal-type of 'implicit familialism' already under communism, which means that here the state 'neither offers de-familialisation nor actively supports the caring function of the family through any kind of familialistic policy [and where] (...) the family will be the primary caretaker since there are no alternatives at hand' (Leitner, 2003, p. 359). This can be illustrated by the fact that, for instance, 85.7 per cent of 3 to 6-year-old Hungarian children attended kindergarten in 1989, compared to only 48.7 per cent of children in Poland (Szikra and Szelewa, 2008). The attendance in nursery schools was 12–13 per cent in Hungary and Czechoslovakia (not as high as state propaganda would have suggested), but in Poland it was just around 4 per cent in the same year (Darvas, 2000). A common feature in all the countries was that there was no possibility to stay at home or work part-time after children reached the age of 3. This means that women had to take on the double burden of full-time paid work in the state sector and unpaid care work at home.

It can be plausibly argued that the *communist, social democratic, conservative* and *familialist* features and traditions were simultaneously present in East Central European social security and family policy schemes even if with changing significance over time. By the 1980s increasing numbers of benefits were granted universally, and from the late 1970s benefits of health care belonged to this category, similar to the British or Swedish systems. Furthermore, as with social democratic regimes, social security management was centralized and the state played a central role in administration. At the same time, other important social security services, e.g. pensions or sick pay, were closely tied to the contributions paid, regarding both their qualifying conditions and their levels, which was similar to the Western European welfare type often called conservative or corporatist (Sik and Svetlik, 1990, p. 276). Family policies in Czechoslovakia and Hungary bore the features of 'optional familialism' by the late 1960s (Leitner, 2003) with long maternity leave and growing access to childcare facilities. From another perspective it can be argued that in these countries family policies in this period served contradicting aims: They were promoting the employment of women and their caring tasks at the very same time (Szikra and Szelewa, 2009). The relative levels of maternity leave and family allowance were generous even as compared with Western countries (Kamerman and Kahn, 1978) which, together with full employment, prevented female and child poverty. An exception is Poland where the features of 'implicit familialism' were crystallized by the fall of the regime.

It is of interest to see what bearing this complex *legacy* had on East Central Europe during the course of the political, social and economic transformation of the 1990s. From this aspect the considerable scale of welfare efforts (including price subsidies and other welfare spending) can be regarded as a dividend of the legacy. Most of the differences compared to capitalist democracies can be derived from the political system, thus its democratization could eliminate major divergences. The fact, however, that welfare spending was connected to the communist economic system (price subsidies, fringe benefits in factories, the indirect and hidden costs of full employment) was a burden when transforming communist social policy, because the fall of the regime jeopardized their survival. Consequently, the fate of welfare arrangements after the regime change depended heavily on the success of transforming resources associated with the old system into a welfare system compatible with market economy.

Recent changes in East Central European welfare

At the beginning of the social, political and economic transformation process in East Central Europe, there were diverse *expectations* by observers regarding the possible futures of the region's welfare systems. In the early 1990s, Bob Deacon, one of the experts most familiar with social policy in the region, predicted the emergence of welfare regimes more or less consistent with the ones in Gøsta Esping-Andersen's typology: 'liberal-capitalist' welfare system in Hungary; 'post-communist conservative corporatism' in Poland; and 'social democratic' regime in Czechoslovakia (Deacon, 1993,

p. 196). Most experts, including Esping-Andersen, however, projected the dominance of liberal regimes in East Central Europe in the near future (Ferge, 1992, p. 220; Esping-Andersen, 1996a, pp. 1–31). The latter expectations were based on two factors. On the one hand, there was the consideration that international agencies (such as the IMF and the World Bank) preferring liberal welfare policies might have a large impact on the transformation process, especially in countries with large foreign debts. In contrast, other international agencies, first of all the ILO and the EU, that might have been expected to support an anti-retrenchment policy of welfare states, were fairly passive. The passivity of the EU in that respect can be considered remarkable since it had effective political and economic means to influence government policies in the region (Deacon and Hulse, 1997, p. 60). On the other hand, there was a line of political reasoning among experts; namely, that the 'most articulate and politically best-organized social forces' give preference to the liberal model (Ferge, 1992, p. 219). In the following, we describe the realization of these scenarios.

The *transition to market economy* deeply challenged the East Central European welfare systems in the early 1990s. Not only did the former practices of guaranteed employment and subsidized prices on basic necessities diminish, but the basis of a new social security structure compatible with market economy was also shaken. First of all, the social costs of the transition increased demand for welfare services, while the number of contributors to social insurance budgets significantly decreased as a result of mass unemployment, growing informal economy and the easy availability of early retirement and disability pension. Despite the economic recession – and the dominant liberal scenarios – the first years of economic transition did not witness a significant decrease in social expenditures. In Poland and Hungary the spending even increased in relative terms, since governments introduced costly programmes, such as unemployment benefits and new social assistance schemes, in order to meet the social needs created by the rise in poverty. The entitlements for the already existing major social security benefits remained largely unchanged for several years, although coupled with the erosion of real values (Ferge and Tausz, 2002, pp. 178–95; Inglot, 2008, pp. 256, 279).

All in all, the welfare system retained its *mixed character* in East Central Europe, albeit with a different composition. The communist features disappeared quickly and the mix of social democratic and conservative principles has prevailed. These patterns were deeply rooted not only in institutions but also in public attitudes. According to polls, the majority of the electorate has favoured a combination of universalistic social welfare arrangements (especially in health care) and work-related benefits (cash benefits) (Ferge, 2001a, p. 151).

Despite the considerable path-dependency in welfare institutions and public attitudes supporting the full-scale welfare state, liberal reforms have

challenged the welfare status quo. These tendencies have led to a considerable degree of *volatility* of the systems. In Hungary, for instance, as a part of
an austerity package a significant curtailment of social benefits was carried
out by the new socialist-liberal coalition in the middle of the 1990s.[2] In the
first two years of the socialist-liberal coalition (in 1995 and 1996) the loss in
social expenditures totalled to 5 per cent of the GDP – a fall from 29.5 to 24.3
per cent. The major means of the retrenchment of welfare was a conscious
policy of non-indexation of the benefits, at a time when the inflation was
galloping well over 20 per cent annually again, but some entitlements were
also cut back (Lelkes, 2000, p. 94). The new pension system, introduced in
1997, was modelled after Latin-American (Chilean and Argentinean) prece-
dents favoured by international agencies, such as the IMF and the World
Bank. In 1995–1997 the universality of family allowance, initiated quite
recently, in 1990, was also abolished. (Förster and Tóth, 1999, p. 26; Gábos,
2000, pp. 107–12). However, the new, conservative government after 1998
cancelled several aspects of the liberal measures. It reintroduced universal
family allowance and revised the pension law to ensure more revenues for
the public pension fund. This step could only partly counterbalance the
introduction of private insurance schemes; however, all in all, the pension
system has retained its predominantly public nature, with an almost universal coverage.

After 2002, the new socialist-liberal coalition stressed the need for a liberal
transformation of the welfare sector but they only embarked on the implementation of minor liberal reforms. Although they moderately increased
the social security contributions going to private insurance, they kept the
universality of family allowance and maternity benefits and even significantly increased the real value of universal benefits. In 2006 the re-elected
socialist-liberal coalition embarked on a neo-liberal transformation of the
social security system. One of their greatest attempts, the abolition of free
health care as a citizen's right was finally annulled by a referendum in 2008
which showed the popular dissatisfaction with neo-liberal politics. At the
same time, a slight social-democratic turn in the family policy system was
initiated in 2006 with the increased role of universal family allowances.

The case of Hungary can be regarded as typical of the region's rapidly
changing and volatile welfare development. At the same time the transition
of the individual countries showed some *unique features* in terms of social
policy. In Poland, the economic shock therapy went in tandem with the
slow transformation of the welfare system, but the pension reform received
relatively extensive support from the political elite – unlike in Hungary
(Inglot, 2003, p. 243). In the Czech Republic, the prevailing liberal economic phraseology went alongside a surprisingly solid subsidizing of social
security in the first half of the 1990s. Here, the most profound reforms
were carried out in the area of health care, where a system of competing
public health insurance funds was established, while benefits based on the

principle of citizenship and universalism remained intact (Deacon, 2000, p. 151). What made Slovakia unique was the even slower pace of changes throughout the 1990s taking momentum in recent years (Hurcíková and Pekník, 2002, pp. 249–76).

In the early transformation period an explicit *maternalist* discourse was prevailing in all the four countries with the aim of withdrawing mothers from the labour market (Fodor et al., 2002). Later, a more diverse discourse evolved supported by the accession process to the EU which stressed gender mainstreaming and aimed at the increase of female employment. The tradition of 'implicit familialism' in Poland, where the state refrains from direct intervention into the families' welfare has been continuing since the fall of communism (Szelewa and Polakowski, 2008). Here, most of the payments are restricted to the poorest families. Also, crèches are almost non-existent in Poland and only about half of the 3 to 6-year-old children are in kindergarten. The overall reliance on private familial care in Poland is called 'private maternalism' by other authors (Glass and Fodor, 2007). In contrast, in Hungary all children over 5 years of age attend kindergarten by law. At the same time only 10 per cent of children are in crèches, where long waiting lists demonstrate high demand. The complex system of long maternity leave, inherited from communism, and the relatively high level and availability of childcare institutions, has led to the name 'optional familialism' (Szelewa and Polakowski, 2008), the roots of which can be found in the late 1960s, as we pointed out above. At the same time, the discrimination of Roma and poor children in childcare institutions is striking, which leads to the situation where women with a good labour market position can benefit significantly more from the family policy system than women with bad employment records and prospects. This latter group includes Roma women disproportionately. Families in small villages in economically remote areas are also put in a disadvantaged position.

In the Czech Republic, although family allowance is bound by income tests, only the wealthiest families are excluded. Parental leave is provided for four years, and, just like in all the East Central European countries, can be used by fathers as well. At the same time, the 'combination of a long leave period with low benefit rates constitutes an explicit re-familization policy, which promotes separate gender roles for men and women, since few men will be willing to utilize their right to parental leave under these conditions' (Saxonberg and Sirovátka, 2006, p. 189). This 'explicit familialism' is most prevalent in the Czech Republic and Slovakia (Szelewa and Polakowski, 2008). This means that these two countries moved away from an 'optional' familialist system that was initiated under communism towards an explicit form of familialism in the 1990s. Here the state explicitly wants parents and not institutions to care for children and provides financial support for this. The common 'familialist' features of all East Central European countries means that, albeit in different ways and to a different extent, they are putting most of the responsibility of care work on women. Policies to encourage the equal share of caring tasks between men and women cannot be observed in either of the countries.

Outside political agencies and observers were, depending on their ideals, either disillusioned (IMF, World Bank) or satisfied (EU) by the realization that the fast, liberal transformation of the welfare systems, according to the US-model, has not been carried out in the region. For example, an EU publication declared that 'all health care financing reforms are in the mainstream of Western European tradition' (Consensus Programme, 1998). Important research findings also emphasize the lack of full-scale liberal transformation not only in the early period (Götting, 1998, pp. 261–84), but at the end of the 1990s and beyond as well (Deacon, 2000, p. 151).

Although the significance of private pensions has been growing in the region, there remained solidaristic elements in the multipillar pension system: a modest vertical redistribution among contributors still takes place. This latter characteristic of the public pension system has even been strengthened during the transformation years since indexation was often applied to pensions in a non-linear way, favouring lower pensions. Pension reforms in Poland and Hungary project a growing significance of private pension schemes for young employees who are obliged to enter the new, mixed system. Other major schemes of social security remained more or less universal, the most important of which are the cash and in-kind benefits of health insurance. Still, widespread corruption in the health-care system hinders the effective realization of social rights. The role of means-tested poor relief and other social assistance, often regarded as an indicator of the liberal regime, has remained subordinate. As an example, in Hungary the share of social assistance within social expenditures was well below the ratio of liberal regimes in Esping-Andersen's study – in the late 1990s it was only 3.3 per cent as opposed to 18 per cent in the USA and 16 per cent in Canada (Lelkes, 2000, pp. 101–2). In this respect, neither of the East Central European welfare systems would qualify as a liberal regime. However moderate the liberal tendencies were, they further strengthened the mixed character of the welfare systems.

Since popular attitudes have favoured an extensive welfare state in the East Central European countries, even moderate *liberal reforms* and tendencies call for some explanation. They can partly be elucidated by the pressures of international agencies with a liberal agenda (IMF, World Bank) and real or perceived pressures coming from the global economy (Horstmann and Schmähl, 2002, pp. 63–81). However, these can only be partial explanations. From the mid-1990s onwards especially, the activity and influence of these international institutions have considerably declined. Because of low labour costs the region has benefited from the growing internationalization of the economy so far, as a result of which globalization cannot be considered as a major explanatory variable either.

The deficiencies of social capital might serve as a partial interpretation for the lack of resistance against neo-liberal efforts in the region. Communist politics was built upon previous undemocratic regimes impregnated with feudal relationships (Ferge, 2008). Suppression of civil and political rights continued under communism and successfully prevented the evolution of civil society and traditional communities (Uslaner, 2003, pp. 81–94). This massive social decapitalization has lasting effects: the level of social capital is expressed in trust and group membership far lower in the former communist countries than in the West (Gabriel, 2002, p. 58). This may contribute to low levels of social solidarity and to difficulties of people in cooperating effectively within or among groups. The resulting organizational weakness and decreasing influence of welfare recipients vis-à-vis other groups interested in the retrenchment of the welfare state – coupled with the mixed features of welfare institutions – is a vital factor in explaining why external and internal pressures for the residualization of the welfare state can persistently challenge the welfare status quo since 1990 causing considerable unsteadiness of the welfare arrangements (Offe, 1993, pp. 649–85). At the same time, the resistance against the influence of the World Bank and internal forces of neo-liberal welfare retrenchment took place to a different degree in the East Central European countries and thus led to a divergent scope of privatization in specific fields of social policy (Müller, 1999). To grasp the complexity of cultural factors in welfare state development in East Central Europe would need further research, which might connect to the promising new direction of research on Western Europe (Pfau-Effinger, 2005, pp. 3–20).

Opinions in the literature are quite varied about the *future of the welfare systems* of East Central Europe, ranging from the ones predicting a liberal transformation (Ferge, 2001a, p. 151) and the ones reluctant take sides (Deacon, 2000, p. 152) to those highlighting the slow speed of change (Consensus Programme, 1998). According to the findings of several opinion polls, 'the majority of Central and Eastern European citizens are indeed very much in favour of the fully-fledged "European Model"' (Ferge, 2001a, p. 151), which suggests that the liberalization of welfare systems would clash with the will of voters. The more so, because democratic institutions now operate more transparently and reliably and reflect the preferences of voters to a greater degree than in the first stage of transition, and the political environment in East Central European countries has became highly competitive. The EU accession of the countries in the region also encourages the adoption and sustenance of the institutions of conservative and social democratic welfare systems dominant in the EU (Tomka, 2006, pp. 135–59). At the same time, due to the organizational weakness of social groups interested in the preservation of extensive welfare systems (Offe, 1993, pp. 649–85), those advocating the residualization of welfare systems stand the chance of realizing their programmes when repeatedly challenging the status quo.

Summary

The origins of the welfare development of East Central Europe can be found in their early Bismarckian legislation, part of which was enacted within the Austro-Hungarian monarchy. After the First World War, the state formation processes clearly elevated social legislation in the region. Social insurance schemes attracted increasing support. However, they solely focused on industrial workers. With the exception of Czechoslovakia, the dominantly agrarian character of these countries and the lack of insurance for agricultural workers, along with the often weak implementation of existing schemes, resulted in a relatively moderate coverage of the population by social insurance programmes. At the same time, strong and centralized social insurance institutions were created by the 1940s constituting the bases of further institutional development throughout the communist period. Significant maternalist family policies developed in Hungary from the 1930s but not in the other two countries.

The special characteristics of communist welfare policies included the lack of democratic control over social insurance, the elimination of civil society, (forced) full employment and the high employment rate of women within this, and, finally, centrally set prices and wages, and thus price subsidies for most basic goods. Very importantly, the Bismarckian tradition of linking social rights to full-time employment was in line with communist political and economic aims. Thus communist welfare 'rights' were strongly linked to employment. Alongside this, social assistance became almost non-existent. Growing legitimacy deficits of the regimes led to more inclusive welfare policies and by the end of the 1970s there was a definite move towards universalism. Poland was an exception to this, where certain social rights became linked both to employment and to income tests. A common feature of communist welfare was familialism: despite propaganda most of the care work was to be done by the families and, within that, women. In the second half of the 1960s, family policies became more extensive and, due to the gendered political considerations of political elites, long parental leave schemes were introduced alongside the increase in access to kindergartens and crèches. Here again, the Polish state remained the most reluctant to provide universal coverage for childcare services, and placed most of this burden on mothers. In the other two countries, limited but still existing options were provided for mothers with small children that enabled them to choose between employment and care work in the first three years of their children's lives.

The merging traditions of pre-war development and state-socialism have made East Central European welfare systems more diverse and mixed than their Western counterparts. This makes it difficult to place them into the categories of 'conservative-corporatist', 'liberal' and 'social democratic'. The constantly changing nature of the East Central European welfare regimes led some authors to describe the systems as 'faceless' (Lelkes, 2000), 'mixed' (Szikra, 2005) or 'institutionally volatile' (Tomka, 2005). At the same time welfare policies of East Central European countries were important in cushioning the effects of the transformation crises. The neo-liberal transformation of the welfare system did not take place anywhere in the region, although welfare policies diverged in several respects. Poland took a more radical way, while the Czech Republic applied a gradualist approach without an attempt at shock-therapy in welfare. In Hungary, no specific character of the welfare reforms can be grasped as succeeding governments have tried to undo with their predecessors' social policies. Slovakia seems to have become successful economically by the mid-2000s, although this is partly at the expense of social cohesion, with cuts in welfare rights and the introduction of privatization in major areas of welfare. Family policies in the region did not break with the tradition of familialism: they explicitly (Czech Republic and Slovakia) or implicitly (Poland) support the care work of families and, within that, women. The state still provides long parental leave to fulfil this aim in the Czech Republic, Slovakia and Hungary. In Hungary a wider option of facilities and payments is available for better-off families (optional familialism) but poor and Roma children are often excluded from quality childcare institutions. The state refrains from wider support in Poland, where the Catholic Church remained a major influence in family policies. Nowhere in these countries have successful programmes supporting the care work of fathers and the employment of mothers developed.

The social and political legacies of the communist regimes fostered the emergence of volatile welfare policies. On the one hand, we can see the high popular acceptance of the states' welfare activities and in traditional gender roles. On the other hand, we can find that the low levels of social capital and capabilities among worse-off welfare recipients and feminist organizations are especially weak. The weakness of such stakeholders leads to a situation where universal welfare institutions that could potentially foster class, gender and ethnic equalities are constantly challenged.

3
Mechanisms of Institutional Change in Central and Eastern European Welfare State Restructuring*

Alfio Cerami

Introduction

The study of Central and Eastern European (CEE) social policy has now reached the attention of the international academic community, but despite an increasing number of publications on the topic, the mechanisms of institutional change occurring in these welfare states in transition have, so far, remained partly unexplored and this in spite of the clear importance that such an investigation might have for future reform proposals.[1] How can better social policy reforms be implemented in the region if the paths and mechanisms of institutional change are not fully understood? In order to achieve this objective, this chapter investigates the mechanisms of institutional change in CEE welfare state restructuring adopting a mechanism-based explanation approach. Here, the focus is given not on relationships between variables, but on actors and the intended and unintended outcomes of their actions. Following Peter Hedström (2008), the explanatory power of a mechanism-based approach lies, in fact, in the explanation of an event, giving account of why it happened, not only by citing earlier events, but also providing (or suggesting) causal mechanisms (see also Hedström and Swedberg, 1998; Elster, 1998). For Jon Elster (1998), a mechanism explains by opening 'the black box' and showing the 'cogs and wheels' of the internal machinery. It also provides a continuous chain of causal intentional links between the *explanans* and the *explanandum*. As correctly emphasized by Hedström (2008), identifying the details of the mechanisms not only produces explanations that are more precise and intelligible, since it permits identification of structural similarities between processes that at first glance could seem completely dissimilar, but it also avoids an unnecessary proliferation of concepts. Moreover, the investigation of the mechanisms involved in an outcome can also allow the identification of a genuine causal relationship and not simply a correlation between variables. This ultimately allows the detection of models that otherwise would remain unknown.

Contrary to common assumptions and academic desires for single explanatory models, this chapter will highlight the impossibility of identifying one single mechanism of institutional change influencing CEE social policy. Rather, and this is the main argument, several mechanisms of institutional change took place simultaneously during the stages of institutional design and institutional transformation. This should, however, not surprise the reader. Institutional actors do not act separately from one another, and neither do mechanisms of institutional change. In the new-institutionalist tradition (see Hall, 1997), it will be argued that these mechanisms of institutional change, complementary to each other, have influenced the transformation in three different, but interconnected, domains. In the domain of ideas, these mechanisms have taken the form of ideational, communicative and coordinative mechanisms; in the domain of institutions they have taken the form of transformative adaptive mechanisms; and, finally, in the domain of interests they have taken the form of increasing returns mechanisms. These mechanisms have contributed to altering not only the pre-existing welfare institutions, but also the contemporary institutional relations and organizational features of the welfare state, ultimately affecting the politics, polity and policy spheres. The relational character of institutional change will, as a consequence, be highlighted and with it the key characteristics of recombinant transformation (or bricolage) as aggregating mechanism of institutional change in the overall process of welfare state restructuring. Finally, as shown by the case of international policy diffusion of ideas, causal chains of social and institutional mechanisms, such as *self-fulfilling prophecies*, can not only speed the implementation of specific policy preferences, but can also help to highlight so far unexplored pathways of institutional change, thus opening new avenues for future research on transition economies.

The chapter is structured as follows: section 1 provides a brief description of the mechanisms of institutional change attempting to highlight their main characteristics, while section 2 provides some examples of the way in which they influence the transformation in the domains of ideas, interests and institutions. Finally, section 3 provides some empirical evidence specifically tailored to the CEE case, while discussing the key characteristics of recombinant transformation.

New-institutionalism(s) and mechanisms of institutional change[2]

The investigation of the mechanisms of institutional change in CEE social policy must, inevitably, be situated in the current new-institutionalist analysis. Since the first days of its inception in the 1980s, this strand of social enquiry has been the object of a lively academic debate which has resulted in a substantial expansion in its explanatory power, but also in violent internal diatribes and, to some extent, not always justified theoretical misunderstandings. Exponents of rational-choice institutionalism (Hardin, 1982; Elster and Hylland, 1986; Shepsle, 1986; Fiorina, 1995; Bates et al., 1998; Weingast, 1998) have given primary attention to the fixed rationalist preferences of actors and institutions, proponents of historical institutionalism (Hall, 1986; North, 1990; Steinmo et al., 1992; Skocpol, 1995; Hall and Taylor, 1996; Thelen, 1999; Pierson, 2000) to the self-reinforcing mechanisms and historical paths, while the advocates of sociological institutionalism (March and Olsen, 1989; DiMaggio and Powell, 1991; Brinton and Nee, 1998) to the formal and informal rules that govern human behaviour. More recently, supporters of actor-centred institutionalism (Scharpf, 1997; Schludi, 2005) have emphasized the crucial importance of strategic interactions in the process of institutional change, while, in the newest, and probably less reductionist version, discursive-institutionalism (Schmidt, 2000, 2006, 2008; see also Campbell and Pedersen, 2001; Hay, 2001, 2006), the ideational and communicative side of institutional change has also been called into question. Despite significant differences in the power attributed to each single variable (whether rationalities, historical legacies, norms, tactical exchanges or discourses), all these new-institutionalism(s) have shared a common emphasis on ideas, interests and institutions as interrelated entities, as well as, and this will be the key point in this section, implicitly calling attention to the relational and organizational character of institutional change.

Ideas, interests and institutions are as interlinked as their relations with the actors involved in the process of institutional change. Institutions delimit the arena where the battles for change take place, interests crystallize the individuals' and institutional dominant concerns, while ideas provide the substantive reasons for immediate action (or inaction). Ideas, interests and institutions are, thus, mutually permeated (Hall, 1986; Lepsius, 1990; Palier and Surel, 2005). Policy action aimed at institutional change can only occur if situated in a clear institutional context (it would be impossible in an institutional limbo of procedures), if meeting specific vested interests and if corresponding to previously agreed set of ideas (or *paradigms* to use Kuhn's definition) (Kuhn, 1970). The process of institutional change becomes, in this context, a highly relational and organizational process, since it involves a continuous recombination of existing relationships (expressed also in terms of the *ways of doing things*) between the actors and the environment in which they are embedded.

Surprisingly, however, the relational and organizational character of institutional change has, to date, largely been neglected, especially when applied to comparative welfare state research. Here, the behaviour of actors (for example, individuals or other social and institutional units) has primarily been analysed in terms of their motives and objectives, neglecting the 'relational' factors that may exist between individuals, institutions, interests (and the substantive leading ideas) and the ways in which they are 'organized' together. Talking about mechanisms of institutional change in welfare state research becomes, in this context, a matter of talking about 'organizational relations' among actors (for example, veto players, policymakers, citizens or trade union members), among institutions (for example, ministries of finance, of labour and social affairs, and so on), among interests (for example, trade unions' specific concerns), among ideas (for example, neoliberal vs. social democracy), as well as among institutions, interests, ideas and actors themselves. From this perspective, mechanisms of institutional change can be understood as a sub-class of *social mechanisms* (Mayntz, 2003; Ettrich, personal communication), in the sense that they involve relations among spheres of social life. They are institutions-, interests- and ideas-permeated, as mentioned above, but also, and not less importantly, relations-permeated in the sense that they are embedded in a set of previously organized institutional relationships.

Mechanisms of institutional change must also be described according to the ways in which and how, mid-stages, a determined result is achieved from a set of alternative possible options (Mayntz, 2003). A mechanism can only then be identified when the process, linked to a special result and set-up condition, is shown. According to MacAdam et al. (2001) and Tilly (2001), a mechanism must include the set-up conditions, intermediate activities and termination conditions. On the basis of these considerations, these authors identify a threefold typology of 'environmental', 'cognitive' and 'relational' mechanisms. Environmental mechanisms influence the change in the 'conditions affecting life' and cognitive mechanisms involve psychological mechanisms that cause specific behavioural patterns, while relational mechanisms, to quote Tilly, change the 'connections among people, groups, and interpersonal networks' (Mayntz, 2003, p. 9).

Similarly, Hedström and Swedberg (1998) differentiate between 'situational' (macro–micro), 'individual action' (micro–micro) and 'transformational' (micro–macro) mechanisms on the basis of their levels of influence. According to the authors, 'instead of analyzing relationships between phenomena exclusively on the macro-level, one should always try to establish how macro level events or conditions affect the individual (macro–micro), how the individual assimilates the impact of these macro-level events (micro–micro) and how a number of individuals, through their actions and interactions, generate macro-level outcomes (macro–macro)' (Hedström and Swedberg, 1998, pp. 21–3). On the basis of Coleman's (1986) so-called micro–macro graph, Åberg and Hedström (2005) and Hedström (2008) further discuss this concept, illustrating how the gap between a model and reality can be narrowed creating a closer link between quantitative research and agent-based modelling. Social scientists usually explain social or macro-level outcomes with references to other social or macro-level phenomena. But simply providing a link between macro-level outcomes (for example, a specific social outcome) and social and macro-level phenomena (for example, the actions of others or other relevant environmental conditions), statistically or otherwise, would lead to a rather incomplete explanation, since the mechanisms that tell us about how and why they are related cannot be found at this aggregate level (Hedström, 2008, p. 331). Instead, Åberg and Hedström (2005) and Hedström (2008) propose to analyse how individuals' properties and orientations to action are influenced by the social environments in which they are embedded (mechanism 1), how these properties and orientations to action influence how they act (mechanism 2), and how these actions bring about the social outcomes we seek to explain (mechanism 3). Explaining the entire causal chain of mechanisms 1–2–3 instead of simply linking macro-level variables is the main logic of the mechanism-based explanation approach adopted in this chapter (see also Hedström, 2008, Figure 13.2, p. 331).

Identifying the causal chain (causal reconstruction) and the mechanisms according to which a phenomenon originates becomes crucial also for understanding the path and direction of institutional change (Mayntz, 2002, 2003). Mechanisms of institutional change, as repetitive processes that link particular set-up conditions with specific causal results (see Goodin, 1996; Elster, 1998), are seen, in this way, as steering procedures and processes that materialize through institutionalization, de-institutionalization and re-institutionalization processes. In other words, they construct, deconstruct and reconstruct previous ideas, interests and institutions in new forms, while changing the relations and the organizational structures among the constituting elements. Mechanisms of institutional change, as a consequence, not only play an important institutionalization function in providing a stable, recurring, repetitive, patterned behaviour of institutional change (see Goodin, 1996), but they also play a regulating as well as a stabilization function, in that they regulate and institutionalize social and institutional praxis.

In the course of this chapter, mechanisms of institutional change will be defined, in general terms, as 'recurrent processes generating a specific kind of outcome or event' (Mayntz, 2003, p. 1) and, more specifically, as steering procedures and processes, whose main characteristic is repetitive action aiming at pursuing a specific institutional change through an alteration of the main organizational relations. This alteration materializes through a causal chain in ongoing processes of construction, deconstruction and reconstruction of ideas, interests and institutions. As will be shown, taking as a case study the transformation of CEE social policy, several mechanisms of institutional change have materialized in the region affecting the politics (the welfare logic of a nation), the polity (through establishment of determined welfare institutions) and the policy sphere of the welfare state (including the alteration of specific policy features of the welfare arrangement, such as, for example, the retirement age).

Mechanisms of institutional change: some examples

In this section, a literature review of the main mechanisms of institutional change is carried out, since an exploration of previous works is crucial for understanding the ways in which institutions evolve, relate to each other and adapt to changing circumstances. Concepts such as discursive institutional change (see Schmidt, 2006, 2008), recalibration (Ferrera et al., 2000; Hemerijck, 2007, 2010) and incremental transformative change (Streeck and Thelen, 2005) are discussed here and then applied to the CEE case. These are all forms of adaptive transformative institutional change, which can have path-dependent (North, 1990; Pierson, 1996, 2001), path-departing (Ebbinghaus, 2005) and path-creating (Garud and Karnøe, 2001; Lessenich, 2003) characteristics.

Ideational, communicative and coordinative mechanisms

The role that ideas and discourses play in social policy change has now become the object of increasing scholarly attention (see, for instance, Schmidt, 2006, 2008; Béland, 2005, 2007; Cerami, 2008a). The reasons for such interest are easy to imagine. Ideas and discourses represent the background and foreground of political action, which then turns into specific programmes and policies. However, despite increasing attention, very few studies have put ideas and discourses in a specific institutional context. The most recent work of Vivien A. Schmidt is a noteworthy exception to this trend. In her article 'Discursive Institutionalism: The Explanatory Power of Ideas and Discourses', Schmidt (2008) moves the debate on new-institutionalism a step forward highlighting how ideas, as the substantive content of discourse, may be sub-divided into three levels – policies, programmes and philosophies – and two types – cognitive and normative. To clarify, policies, programmes and philosophies refer, respectively, to the policy solutions, to the specific agendas that underpin the policy solutions and to the paradigms that reflect the underlying assumptions and organizing principles. Policies, programmes and philosophies also contain two types of ideas. Cognitive ideas provide the recipes, guidelines and maps, while normative ideas refer to the values and norms attached. Discourse, by contrast, as the interactive process of conveying ideas, materializes in two forms: the coordinative discourse, among policy actors, and the communicative discourse, between political actors and the public. In the policy sphere, for example, the coordinative discourse consists of the individuals and actors at the centre of the policy construction who seek to coordinate agreement (for example, policymakers, civil servants, and so on), while in the political sphere, the communicative discourse consists of the individuals and groups at the centre of political communication who seek to communicate decisions to the public (for example, party leaders, government spokespeople, and so on). According to the author, the institutions in discursive-institutionalism are not external rule-following structures, but simultaneously structures and constructs internal to agents. Interests are then subjective ideas neither 'objective' nor 'material', while norms tend to be dynamic, inter-subjective constructs rather than static structures.

Even though Schmidt does not use this exact definition, ideational, communicative and coordinative mechanisms of institutional change are, in short, the key elements according to which each transformation in institutional relations occurs. In particular, ideational mechanisms of institutional change could be defined as those representing the interactive and creative processes and procedures caused by the exhaustion or obsolescence of old policy ideas (for example, Keynesianism or Thatcherism). These take form primarily through an image creation and a figurative representation of possible better alternatives. Communicative mechanisms of institutional change can, in this context, be described as the communicative processes and procedures caused by the necessity to communicate the new images and figurative representations to the actors involved (both institutional actors and the public) in the policy-making process. These mechanisms primarily take the form of announcement activities aimed at producing a change in policy orientation. Finally, coordinative mechanisms of institutional change represent the coordinative processes and procedures caused by the need of establishing new linkages (organizational relations) among the actors and institutions involved. These mechanisms aimed at achieving a specific set of goals take the form of synchronization activities among actors and institutions.

Transformative adaptive mechanisms of institutional change

A recent, but increasingly influential classification of mechanisms of institutional change taking place primarily in the sphere of institutions is the one provided by Wolfgang Streeck and Kathleen Thelen (2005) who emphasize the importance of incremental transformative change as main mechanism of institutional transformation. The authors offer a five-fold typology of types of institutional change (*displacement, layering, drift, conversion* and *exhaustion*) each one associated with a particular mechanism (*defection, differential growth, deliberate neglect, redirection* or *reinterpretation, depletion*). Displacement, which involves a slow rise in salience of subordinate to dominant institutions, takes place through a mechanism of defection when institutional incoherence opens space for deviant behaviour. This implies a cultivation of a new logic of action through the rediscovery and activation of dormant or latent institutional resources. Layering, on the other hand, materializes when new elements are attached to existing institutions gradually changing their status and nature. The main mechanism here is differential growth in which there is a faster growth of new institutions created on the edges of old ones (new fringe eats into old core). The third type of institutional change, drift, primarily concerns a neglect of institutional maintenance in spite of external change, resulting in slippage in institutional practice on the ground. The main mechanism here is deliberate neglect in which change in institutional outcomes are effected by strategically neglecting adaptations to changing circumstances. Conversion, the fourth type, entails a redeployment of old institutions to new purposes, which become attached to old structures. The main mechanism here is redirection or reinterpretation aiming at reducing the gap between rules and enactment, due, for example, to limits of institutional design, to ambiguity of institutional rules, or to changed contextual conditions. Finally, exhaustion is the more dramatic of these types of institutional change, since it takes place through a gradual breakdown of institutions over time. The main mechanism here is depletion, in which the normal working of an institution undermines its external preconditions representing serious limits to growth through 'decreasing returns' (see Streeck and Thelen, 2005, Table 1.1, p. 31). Streeck and Thelen's classification emphasizes, in short, the role of incremental change with transformative results in institutional relations. The authors see the welfare state as an evolutionary system, which mutates on the basis of changing circumstances, transforming and adapting its structure incrementally according the new environmental requirements.

Also for Ferrera et al. (2000), Pierson (2001) and Hemerijck (2007, 2010), the welfare state can be better described as an evolutionary system that undergoes a process of constant adaptation. The authors, however, propose the concept of recalibration[3] to describe the institutional learning processes that Western European welfare states are facing. Recalibration involves, in this context, an adaptive transformation that can take place in four crucial areas: functional, distributive, normative and institutional. Functional recalibration concerns a redefinition of the main functions that the modern European welfare states are called to cope with. At the beginning of the twenty-first century, these primarily involve coping with emerging 'new' social risks, caused by the de-industrialization and tertiarization of employment, women's entry in the labour market, increasing instability of the family structure, as well as by processes linked to the privatization of the welfare state (Esping-Andersen, 1999; Esping-Andersen et al., 2002; Taylor-Gooby, 2004; Armingeon and Bonoli, 2006; Cerami, 2008b). These 'new' social risks also involve 'new' categories of people, such as atypical workers, people with low education attainments or in long-term care. Distributive

recalibration, by contrast, involves a reallocation of social protection benefits across new and different policy clienteles. This results from an emerging
labour market segmentation between 'insiders' and 'outsiders' with a subsequent rise in inequality of income and life chances. Normative recalibration concerns, in this context, the norms and values promoted by a specific
welfare regime (see Esping-Andersen, 1990). Scandinavian welfare systems
still tend to promote universal values as the core of their normative foundations, while Continental and Anglo-Saxon welfare regimes continue to have
as their normative basis, respectively, the maintenance of the professional
status of workers (conservative welfare states) or a strict association between
market performance and citizens' coverage (neo-liberal welfare states).
Finally, institutional recalibration concerns a reform in the institutional
design. This involves, in more practical terms, a redefinition of the responsibilities attributed to the different levels of decision-making, the structure of social and economic policy governance, as well as the separate and
joint responsibilities of individuals, states, markets and families (Hemerijck,
2007, pp. 15–18). For the concept of recalibration, the key means for achieving the necessary institutional realignment is policy learning, even though
policy diffusion or policy transfer dynamics can also play a crucial role. In
short, welfare institutions evolve and adapt to the new environment, but
change in institutional relations tend to be the result of a learning process in which past mistakes are investigated, metabolized and, if possible,
adequately addressed.

Increasing returns as mechanisms of institutional change

Positive feedback and increasing returns are probably the more often discussed topics in comparative welfare state research. In very few words, the
main argument put forward by new-institutionalist social policy scholars
(Pierson, 1996, 2000, 2001; Bonoli and Palier, 2001, 2007; Hinrichs, 2001)
is that social policy programmes tend to generate their own set of interests,
which then spill over as political support from programme 'winners' for continuation (Weaver, 1986, 2008; Pierson, 2000). Positive feedbacks dynamics
(such as those linked to already acquired benefits, for example, occupational
pensions) thus tend to produce increasing returns for status quo maintenance influencing the preferences of actors and institutions involved in the
reform process. Increasing returns become, in this context, mechanisms
of institutional change that automatically constrain the policy options for
change (for example, precluding the road to alternative paths of reforms due
to sunk costs and transaction costs). When transformation takes place, this
usually takes the form of path-dependent incremental adjustments to the
status quo (see Streeck and Thelen, 2005).

The validity of the positive feedback argument has, however, also attracted
its critiques. In fact, not only path-dependent institutional change is possible, but also possibilities for path-departure exist (see Ebbinghaus, 2005;

see also Bonoli and Palier, 2007). In this case, decreasing returns caused by negative feedbacks can open windows of opportunities for substantial regime change. Programmes not only generate their own set of interests and winning constituencies, but may also generate growing and unsustainable demands on budgetary resources (negative feedback) forcing for regime transition. In addition, programmes can also generate oppositional coalition from programme losers or new demands from programme winners that cannot be satisfied within existing policy regime (Weaver, 2008). Decreasing returns become here crucial mechanisms of institutional change that automatically open policy windows for the search of alternative policy regimes or for the development of new policy paradigms. When this occurs, transformation can deviate from a previously established path (path-departure) (Ebbinghaus, 2005), or, potentially, even including several elements of innovation that might ultimately lead to the creation of a completely different and new path (path-creation) (for a definition of path-creation, see Garud and Karnøe, 2001; Lessenich, 2003).

Mechanisms of institutional change in CEE social policy

This third section provides some empirical evidence tailored to the CEE case. Here, the mechanisms of institutional change taking place in the sphere of ideas, institutions and interests are discussed. Two main stages of institutional change are identified. The first stage of institutional design (see Elster et al., 1998) involves the blueprint of the new welfare state that has been created in ideational terms and communicated to the actors involved and to the public, and the second stage of institutional transformation concerns the new welfare arrangement that has been implemented and adapted in order to meet the new emerging needs.

Ideational, communicative and coordinative mechanisms in CEE social policy

During the first stage of institutional design, in the immediate aftermath of the collapse of communism, new political ideas (policies, programmes and philosophies) no longer based on communist values were immediately discussed and agreed upon at cabinet meetings and at international round-table talks, while new political discourses (coordinative and communicative) were then developed and communicated to policymakers and the citizens. The newly agreed policies, programmes and philosophies covered a wide range of issues, and implied a substantial redefinition of the main welfare state functions, institutional settings and associated relations so far in place. In more practical terms, at the level of ideas, the new policies introduced involved a shift from universal to individual-based benefits, and from an equalization to a differentiation of their access and structure. New social policy programmes focused, by contrast, on a shift of agenda from benefits granted on the basis of the collective work-status in the central planned economy to benefits provided on the basis of the individual work perform-ance in a market economic environment. This evidently implied a drastic change of the underlying social policy philosophies that could no longer be centred on public responsibility; rather they now had to be based on pri-vate responsibility. In terms of cognitive ideas, detachment from market per-formance and unjustified equalization of benefits were now addressed as the real enemies to fight in the new welfare organization. Unconditional market orientation and individual merit were, especially during the first period of reforms, real objectives to pursue at any cost, even if these costs would have meant a temporary rise in income and social inequality. As the Czech Prime Minister Václav Klaus repeatedly stated, a 'market democracy without adjec-tives' (where 'social' was the adjective he was referring to) was what Eastern European citizens needed. This was not a rare policy vision in the region (see Haggard and Kaufman, 2008, ch. 8; also Aidukaite, this volume). In terms of normative ideas, new buzzwords such as activation, market achievements and independency from the welfare state were introduced as the new nor-mative foundations of the post-communist welfare state, appearing regularly in official documents and on ministry websites. These new leading ideas, very different from the ones present during communism, did not remain in an ideational limbo, but materialized in substantially new discourses (new since they involved the new democratic games occurring in a participatory democracy). Coordinative discourses involved the coordination of actions and beliefs of party members, ministries, policymakers, local authorities and not-for-profit organizations, while communicative discourses involved all cadres of the decision- and policy-making process called to communicate to the general public, in the most possible persuasive manner, the new circum-stances and the requirements of a market democracy.

This ideational and discursive redefinition of the state–society relations took place in national as well as in transnational arenas. During the years sub-sequent to the fall of the Berlin Wall an increasing number of intra- and inter-governmental meetings and round-table talks started not only in the capitals of the major CEE and Western European countries, where bilateral agreements, partnerships and cooperation between states was actively sought, but also in the offices of the most influential international organizations (Orenstein et al., 2008). These intra- and inter-governmental meetings had practical short-term objectives concerning, for example, the negotiations of loans in the case of the World Bank and IMF, of new social security standards, as in the case of the ILO, and the accession in the next wave of Enlargement as in the case of the European Union (Deacon, 2007), as well as more ambitious mid-term and long-term objectives through the diffusion and consolidation of new ideas, programmes and philosophies based on new market-oriented principles.

Policy diffusion of ideas achieved in this way a double, and to some extent, pervert objective. On the one hand it helped to alter the ideational basis of the existing welfare architecture along the new market-oriented policy priorities as set by the Washington and Brussels Consensus, while on the other it produced an important coordinative impact on the actions of national governments, now pushed to follow internationally established (and commonly shared) standards. Privatizing pensions (Orenstein, 2008a, also this volume), health (Cerami, 2006) or elderly care (Theobald and Kern, this volume), the new ideological priorities of a national and transnational campaign for social security reforms, became, at the same time, the source and the aim of future welfare state restructuring. To use Robert K. Merton's (1968) definition, a causal chain of *self-fulfilling prophecy* mechanisms[4] made the initial beliefs about the uncontested superiority of private provisions not only a reality, well before sound empirical evidence was provided,[5] but also the favourite option of several countries and their introduction subjected to a run.

Transformative adaptive mechanisms of institutional change in CEE social policy

After a first stage of institutional design where the new welfare state, as an image, started to have clearly defined borders, a second stage of institutional transformation through the establishment of a fully operational market-based welfare system took place. During this second stage of institutional change, politicians and policymakers have been called to transform and adapt the welfare arrangement existent during communism in order to make it compatible with the specific institutional culture of the nation or, in other words, attempting to make it sustainable in the long-term, but also 'environmental friendly'. Several mechanisms of institutional change took place simultaneously, overlapping with and complementing each other.

Within this stage of institutional change, the key elements of Streeck and Thelen's (2005b) classification based on incremental transformative change can be identified. Displacement through a mechanism of defection has occurred in all countries involving the politics, polity and policy spheres. The institutional incoherence that resulted from central planning opened up space to the cultivation of a new market-oriented social policy logic in which dormant latent institutions and policies have been both rediscovered and reactivated. This reactivation concerned the re-enforcement of Bismarckian characteristics already present during communism. These regarded the modes of access to social protection based on work performance and contribution records, earnings-related benefits, social contributions as a main financing mechanism and involvement of social partners in the management of the social insurance funds[6] (see contributions of Aidukaite, Inglot, Szikra and Tomka in this volume). Layering through a mechanism of differential growth has, in contrast, principally occurred at the polity and policy level where new elements (layers) have been attached to existing institutions. According to Inglot (2008, pp. 25, 26, 32), the post-communist welfare state in East Central Europe consists of a historical core of the interwar welfare state (1919–39) with institutions and laws pertaining to work injury, pension, disability, sickness and maternity insurance, followed by a post-war expansion of the welfare state (1949–89) with newer institutions and policies (such as pay-as-you-go financing of social insurance, national health service and family programmes) attached to existing layers, associated, finally, with reinforced earnings-related and market-oriented principles as introduced after the fall of communism (1989 onwards). Drift, characterized by a mechanism of deliberate neglect, has also taken place in the region but in specific social policy sub-fields in which existing institutions and institutional practices once linked to the functioning of the central planned economy have slowly disappeared. The best example here is probably given by the governments' abdication to artificial subvention of the price of products and the volume of the workforce, which has then resulted in a reduction of workers' purchase power and social protection (see contributions of Cerami and Stanescu, and Rat in this volume). Conversion through mechanisms of redirection and reinterpretation has also taken place, even though primarily at the polity and policy levels. Old institutions and policies already in force during communism have been adapted to new purposes and changing circumstances. A noteworthy example can be seen in the reforms of family benefits. These benefits have been maintained at a generally high level if compared to Western standards (for example, three years of childcare in Hungary), but adapted to the new emerging needs caused by changing family and employment structures (Szikra and Tomka, this volume). Finally, exhaustion through a mechanism of depletion has also taken place. The best example here is given by the dismissal of the communist party's over-centralized control over the functioning of the welfare system. The 'normal' working of this institutional practice would have seriously undermined the correct functioning of the post-communist welfare state.

During this stage of institutional transformation, the welfare state was not only transformed, but also adapted to changing circumstances. All key features of Ferrera et al.'s (2000), Pierson's (2001) and Hemerijck's (2007, 2010) concepts of recalibration (functional, distributive, normative and institutional recalibration) can be identified. Functional recalibration has implied, for instance, a redefinition of the main functional relations between institutions and actors and, in particular, this has involved the transition from a welfare state that aimed at preserving the communist status quo to a welfare state that accompanied the transformation towards a market-based economy. To use a famous definition developed by Fritz Scharpf (1999) in the field of European studies, the main functional recalibration occurring in the post-communist welfare state was, especially during the first period of reforms, associated to the necessity of ensuring 'negative' market-making integration through the introduction of market-based welfare provisions. While, in a second phase, the recalibrations also ensured some form of 'positive' market-correcting integration through the introduction of a social safety net able to cushion the negative repercussions of the economic transition (see 'emergency welfare states', Inglot, this volume). The transition had, in fact, to be conducted in a way so as not to neutralize the main social pacifying functions of the welfare state. Privatization of the economy and of the welfare organization was, in this context, coupled with the maintenance of a certain degree of public responsibility (see Vanhuysse, 2006a), then replaced by the social prerogatives promoted in the light of the future waves of Enlargement.

Distributive recalibration was also necessary. This primarily involved the reallocation of benefits across new policy clienteles, which, in the first period of transition, had meant a reallocation of benefits from the 'communist industrial worker' to new and more diversified occupational categories resulting from the privatization of the economy, while, in a subsequent period, it implied tackling the new emergent problem of poverty and unemployment. In fact, distributive recalibration has not only touched classical categories of workers, but also all CEE citizens due to, for example, the restructuring of the economy and dismissal of several state-owned enterprises (Szalai, 2005a). As can be expected, adapting the redistributive priorities and efficiency of a system, in which all benefits were decided and granted at firm level, was, of course, an extremely difficult task for which unprecedented policy efforts were required. The collapse of most of the state-owned enterprises required governments to take several distributive responsibilities for which they were institutionally not ready. These included establishing an extensive system of protection against unemployment and social assistance benefits so far almost inexistent (Rat, this volume), recalibrating family policies to the new labour market requirements (Szikra and Tomka, this volume), not to mention providing new sources of protection and insurance for elderly and the sick (Theobald and Kern, this volume).

Normative recalibration, that is, the adaptation of the norms and values attached to a specific welfare regime, was also an unavoidable consequence in this stage of institutional change. The refusal of a pure American-style neo-liberal model as promoted by the most influential financial institutions (notably the World Bank, the IMF and the OECD), replaced by the introduction or rather the reintroduction (or reinforcement) of a Bismarck-type social insurance was the easiest way to link the new welfare logic, now based on individual and performance-based achievements, with the new allocative priorities of a market democracy. In more practical terms, this implied a shift from universal and flat-rate benefits to contributions and earnings-related ones. Fortunately, however, this shift was not conducted from scratch, since it found some already existing institutional material in the pre- and post- the Second World War system of social protection of these countries, ultimately smoothing the post-communist reform process (Inglot, 2003, 2008; Szikra, 2004; Tomka, 2004; Cerami, 2006, 2009a; Haggard and Kaufman, 2008).

Finally, institutional recalibration has implied, on the one hand, the transformation from an authoritarian system, based on central planning to pluralist social policy-making (now the main characteristic of post-communist welfare states) in which different institutions take care of different aspects of the policy-making process, but also the reconfigurations and readaptations of existing institutional practices and relations in order to bring them in line with the bureaucratic requirements of a competitive market democracy. During this stage, the decentralization of power and responsibilities to local authorities was finalized, involving not only the establishment of new local and regional communities, but also new administrative institutions, such as more independent ministries of health, labour and social affairs. Due to emerging problems posed by unconstrained decentralization of responsibilities (see Van Mechelen and De Maesschalck, this volume) some recentralization of power also became necessary and the excessive devolution of responsibilities has now been often reconsidered. The most notable examples of this process of recalibration are, perhaps, the setting of minimum requirements for pension and health insurance funds as well as the legal obligations for central and local governments to ensure an ever-larger section of potentially unprotected population (for example, the unemployed, sick, disabled, etc.).

Increasing returns as mechanisms of institutional change in CEE social policy

In Central and Eastern Europe, increasing returns mechanisms have primarily involved on the one hand the vested interests that already existed as a result of the communist heritage, and on the other the new patterns of interest formation and representation that emerged as a result of the privatization of the economy. It comes, in this context, as no surprise that the social policy reform process was primarily negotiated within existing elites and only afterwards communicated to the public. This was mainly because those who were in the position of acting as veto players used their power to reduce the workers' mobilization capacity through access to relatively generous welfare benefits (Vanhuysse, 2006a). As argued by the author, the unusual increase in welfare provisions and beneficiaries that occurred in countries with a low budget capacity can be explained by the future political benefits that a social stabilizing strategy would have brought for these democracies in transition (see also Cerami and Stanescu, this volume; Vanhuysse, this volume). Increasing returns, especially during the first period of transition, took the form of the continuation of privileges granted to particular professional categories (for example, miners, soldiers, police, and so on) as present in Bulgaria, Estonia, Latvia, Lithuania, Poland, Romania, Slovak Republic and Slovenia (Cerami, 2006), but also to the continuation of state protection through early retirement and generous unemployment benefits. As noted by Vanhuysse (2006a, p. 89), between 1989 and 1996 the number of old-age pensioners increased by 5 per cent in the Czech Republic, by 20 per cent in Hungary and by 46 per cent in Poland. These corresponded in plain numbers to 93,000 new Czech pensioners,

261,000 Hungarians and 1,049,000 Poles. Once these increasing returns (as mechanisms of institutional change) could be ensured to the population at large, and the subsequent political support from potential programme 'losers' ('early winners') ensured, the path towards privatization could further be followed. In Albert O. Hirschman's tradition (Hirschman, 1978), governments have, in brief, reduced the voices of threatened workers by increasing their exit options, while providing, at the same time, sufficient incentives for loyalty.

Positive feedbacks, however, have not only materialized in the region, but also negative feedbacks have occurred. In fact, social programmes in force during communism not only generated their own set of interests and winning constituencies, but also an ever-larger set of losers, not to mention growing and unsustainable demands on budgetary resources calling for regime transition. Oppositional coalition from programme losers, as well as new demands from programme winners that could not be satisfied within the existing policy regime (for example, new elites), also existed. In case of status quo maintenance, these growing decreasing returns soon became evident to the policy community and the population at large, ultimately facilitating a selective policy and regime change, albeit in a highly ambiguous manner. Differentiation in the access and structure of benefits became, for example, the key features in pension and health insurance, but state responsibility continued to be guaranteed for non-solvent funds and unprotected citizens (Cerami, 2006). Similar considerations apply to the tax and distributive responsibilities given to local authorities (clearly not in the position of ensuring regional socioeconomic homogeneity), but also to the privatization of large state-owned enterprises (clearly not in the position of bearing most of the restructuring costs) (see Stark and Bruszt, 1998). In summary, increasing and decreasing returns played a key role in the process of welfare state transformation by opening and closing windows of opportunities (Jon Elster's black box or 'cogs and wheels' of the machinery; see Elster, 1998) for path-dependent as well as path-departing transformations.

Recombinant transformation as aggregating mechanism of institutional change

How do we make sense of all of these, at first glance, different patterns of institutional change? Which is, at the end, the dominant mechanism of institutional change in Central and Eastern European welfare state restructuring? The main argument put forward in this chapter is, indeed, that several mechanisms of institutional change have taken place simultaneously, all of them ultimately affecting the policy, polity and politics sphere. At the highest level of abstraction (the level concerning the construction of a welfare state which is a social construction of an unidentifiable object), an aggregating mechanism of institutional change, recombinant transformation (or bricolage), can be identified. In *Social Policy in Central and Eastern Europe. The Emergence of a New European Welfare Regime* (Cerami, 2006), I have argued that the transformation of CEE welfare states is characterized by the creation of 'unique hybrids' (see also Szikra and Tomka; Inglot, this volume) encapsulating elements of various worlds of welfare: the re-enforcement of Bismarckian-oriented policies as heritage of the Austro-Hungarian empire, the maintenance of egalitarian and universal aspirations as fostered during the communist period, coupled with the introduction of market-friendly welfare provisions as main social policy logic of the post-communist environment (see also Żukowski, 2009). Similarly, but with a substantially minor emphasis on the impact of universal provisions, other authors (Szalai, 2005b; Gans-Morse and Orenstein, 2006; Fuchs and Offe, 2009; Aidukaite, this volume) have highlighted how a combination of Bismarckian and neo-liberal features are now the main characteristics of the contemporary CEE systems of social protection, thus placing these welfare states in transition somewhere in between Esping-Andersen's conservative and neo-liberal world. Before these considerations, however, other scholars had already emphasized the recombinant properties of institutional changes. For example, David Stark (1996) has described the transformation of CEE capitalism as a form of 'organizational hedging in which actors respond to uncertainty by diversifying assets, redefining and recombining resources' (Stark, 1996, p. 993). Colin Crouch has emphasized similar properties of institutional transformation in the reform of European capitalist governance (Crouch, 2005) and Western European welfare states, while Wolfram Lamping and Friedbert W. Rüb (2004) have applied this model to the specific case of German welfare state reforms. Regardless of whether one decides to accept or to refuse the existence of one or several models of welfare capitalisms in Europe, the variegated character of each institutional transformation can only with difficulty be denied. In fact, welfare state restructuring means, in reality, continuous processes of construction, deconstruction and reconstruction of existing ideas, interests and institutions and with their associated organizational relations. If a constructive transformation then has to take place, this necessarily implies, like the DNA of an individual, a recombinant character aiming at mixing elements in new meaningful chains. It can therefore be affirmed that path-dependent, path-departing and path-creating characteristics are not necessarily mutually exclusive, but central elements of any institutional transformation.

Conclusion

This chapter has discussed the various mechanisms of institutional change that have influenced the transformation of CEE welfare states. The main argument has been that several mechanisms of institutional change have taken place simultaneously, all of them ultimately affecting the policy, polity and politics sphere. The organizational relational character of institutional change has also been highlighted. In particular, it has been affirmed that a correct analysis of welfare state change must investigate not only changes in institutional structures, but also changes in the organizational relations. These take the form of interactions among actors (for example, veto players, policymakers, citizens or trade union members), among institutions (for example, ministries of finance, of labour and social affairs, and so on), among interests (for example, trade unions' specific concerns), among ideas (for example, neo-liberal vs. social democracy), as well as among institutions, interests, ideas and actors themselves (for example, emerging patterns of interest-mediation and negotiations among veto players in a specific institutional context). By adopting a mechanisms-based explanation approach this chapter has also emphasized the causal chains that have linked a particular starting condition to a specific institutional outcome. Here, it has been affirmed that several mechanisms of institutional change, complementary to each other, have influenced the transformation in three different but interconnected domains. In the domain of ideas, these mechanisms have taken the form of ideational, communicative and coordinative mechanisms, in the domain of institutions of transformative adaptive mechanisms and, finally, in the domain of interests of increasing returns mechanisms. In order to make sense of the various patterns of institutional change, an aggregating mechanism of recombinant transformation (or bricolage) has been identified as playing a key role in the overall process of welfare state restructuring. Transformation in these spheres has, in fact, displayed not only path-dependent, but also path-departing, as well as path-creating, characteristics. To conclude, the results of this investigation are not only useful for scholars of comparative social policy, but also may open new avenues for future research in other areas related to the social and economic transformation of transition economies. As shown by the case of international policy diffusion of ideas, causal chains of social and institutional mechanisms, such as *self-fulfilling prophecies*, can not only speed the implementation of specific policy preferences, but can also help to highlight so far unexplored pathways of institutional change.

4
Power, Order and the Politics of Social Policy in Central and Eastern Europe*

Pieter Vanhuysse

> There is nothing more difficult to execute, nor more dubious of success, nor more dangerous to administer than to introduce a new order of things; for he who introduces it has all those who profit from the old order as his enemies, and he has only lukewarm allies in all those who might profit from the new.
>
> (Niccolò Machiavelli, *The Prince*, Chapter VI)

'Empowering' the analysis of post-communist pathways: the cases of Hungary, Poland, Latvia and Estonia

If there is one topic on which political science ought to be able to stake out a distinct claim to fame against other social sciences, it is power. From Machiavelli in the Renaissance Florence of the Medici to Bismarck and Pope Leo XIII in late nineteenth-century Prussia and Rome, rulers and their counsellors have been studied by political scientists in how they have used their state power to establish and consolidate political order. In the post-war decades, early post-behavioural theories by Peter Bachrach and Morton Baratz (1962) and Steven Lukes (1974) represented seminal breakthroughs. They emphasized the hidden faces of power, suggesting how the asymmetric distribution of political and economic rights can structure relations of dominance in society above and beyond any observable decisions taken by ruling elites. Even in the absence of manifest conflict – what Lukes called the first face of power – powerholders often have the ability to stack the deck of cards of social life in ways such as to avoid the making of decisions (the second face of power), for instance through institutional design and agenda setting. Moreover, powerholders can shape the definitions of subordinate actors' identities and interests, thereby forcing them to pre-emptively adapt to newly stacked decks of cards (the third face).

Yet despite these ominous early beginnings, not all is well with the study of power in public policy analysis today. In strongly worded clarion calls for a major theoretical redirection, Moe (2006) has recently pointed out that rational choice-influenced analyses in particular may well *discuss* power frequently, but nevertheless tend to entertain a naive 'one-sided – and overly benign' view of what it entails. Moe therefore proposes a substantive analytical shift away from seeing politics predominantly in win–win and efficiency-enhancing terms and towards explicitly win–lose conceptions of power as distributive conflict.[1] This clarion call has been preceded by disparate earlier studies[2] and has been echoed more recently by Frances Fox Piven's (2008) ASA Presidential Address, by the reception of the expanded 2005 edition of Lukes' classic 1974 essay (Dowding, 2006; *Political Studies Review*, 2006), and by similar calls within historical institutionalism (Thelen, 2004; Hall and Thelen, 2009). The message is clear: centuries after the publication of one of its founding texts, *The Prince*, political science as a discipline still has a lot more puzzling to do about power.

To students of social policy, these debates may, at first sight, merely appear to be old wine in new bottles. The unequal (re)distribution of material resources is, after all, the bread and butter of many welfare programmes. Both power-resources and power-order interpretations of social policy have had influential proponents, on which more below. Yet, today, such interpretations are no longer paradigmatic. Especially since the seminal contributions of R. Kent Weaver (1986) and Paul Pierson (1994, 1996), the politics of social policy in the rapidly maturing advanced democracies of the post-1970s era is now predominantly analysed from the point of view of blame avoidance theory and retrenchment logics. The rationale is straightforward. Re-election-seeking government parties pursuing welfare cutbacks need to try and shift blame or obfuscate responsibility for these unpopular measures, especially in the face of well-documented psychological mechanisms of loss aversion, myopia and other preference inconsistencies. The electoral risks that accompany painful policy reforms, even when these are known to be generally efficiency-enhancing, are further compounded by a range of formidable political obstacles confronting reforming politicians.[3] Reform costs tend to be concentrated and/or to hurt well-organized stakeholders, while reform benefits are often dispersed and/or spread over less well-organized target populations. The perception of costs and benefits is often asymmetric, independently of their distribution. In addition, the political gains from reforms typically take time to become clearly apparent to their intended beneficiaries, or are not easily linked to complex reforms. Lastly, *ex ante* uncertainty about the identity of reform winners and losers may lead voters to reject reforms that they know to be socially efficient, resulting in status quo bias. It is therefore not surprising that current political theories of blame avoidance and economic reforms still follow Niccolò Machiavelli's classic argument. New policies may not win rulers as many supporters as they will cost them opponents. Once again, it appears, we end up at our starting point – *The Prince*.

Yet sometimes change just has to happen. When the status quo is simply untenable, the urgency of costly reforms hurting major sub-strands of the electorate is often such that governments are *neither* able to avoid reforms, *nor* able to entirely avoid blame for them. One example, arguably the single most salient instance of large-scale social change after the Second World War, are the transitions from communist one-party states and planned economies to liberal market democracies in East Central Europe. In this chapter I argue that post-communist rulers in this context have used their state power to design policies aimed at the consolidation of a particular vision of the new regime and at the preservation of social order via *protest* avoidance as a necessary political alternative to *blame* avoidance (Béland and Marier, 2006). As a result, ethnically less 'desired' or economically less 'market-conform' categories of citizens have been sidelined in terms of collective action capacity and policy influence at a time when the political arena of these nascent democracies was being reshaped. In the process, I make the case for infusing both path-dependence and path-departure theories of social policy with more explicitly power-sensitive accounts. Social policies, after all, are rarely purely technocratic or win–win processes of risk-protection or needs-alleviation; least of all at critical junctures such as the 1990s in post-communist Europe.

My four country cases comprise two core members of each of the two main sub-clusters that have emerged within a distinct European *post-communist* public policy model (Castles and Obinger, 2008; Bohle and Greskovits, 2007): Hungary and Poland for the Visegrad sub-cluster; and Estonia and Latvia for the Baltic sub-cluster. My treatment is influenced by historically informed studies of welfare state formation suggesting how, decades if not centuries ago, changing social and religious cleavages have been key in shaping the core political coalitions – or critical realignments – that have determined social policy at historically critical junctures (Esping-Andersen, 1990; van Kersbergen and Manow, 2009; Korpi, 2001, 2006). It also revisits path-dependency and 'generous' or 'emergency' welfare state interpretations of post-communist social policy put forward in this volume. In particular, I concur with Inglot (this volume) in viewing post-communist welfare states as having been designed as emergencies and temporary creations, yet having become de facto permanent structures highly resistant to reforms. But I side with Haggard and Kaufman (2008, this volume) in viewing the temporal point of post-communist transition as a theoretically and empirically critical juncture. The force of communist institutional and policy legacies was particularly strong up to that point, and the degree of intra-regional convergence in social spending levels, structures and growth rates more striking than that of intra-regional divergence.

This chapter seeks to add a more strategic dimension to these analyses by highlighting how, especially at such junctures, elites can to a significant degree *choose* which social risks or status groups to accommodate (and how), and which social cleavages to play down (or accentuate). Thus, I argue that Hungarian and Polish policymakers have not merely provided generous 'emergency' safety nets for exogenously given groups of at-risk citizens. They have proactively *reshaped* the distributions of economic winners and losers in transition, and of contributors and dependants in the welfare state. In so doing, they have modified the subsequent patterns of distributive conflict in the polity, for instance by reducing the political salience of class cleavages and increasing the policy clout of the pensioner constituency. My two Baltic cases in turn represent a study of the use of power along yet another dimension – ethnicity. Recent advances in political economy (Alesina and La Ferrara, 2005; Bridgman, 2008) and social capital theory (Hooghe, 2007; Putnam, 2007) have documented the manifold negative effects of ethno-linguistic heterogeneity in groups, cities and states, both on public policies and on socioeconomic variables such as productivity, growth, public goods provision and other forms of social solidarity. My interpretation of the two Baltic cases reverses the causal analysis somewhat. I point out that here too the power strategies of the new elites mattered crucially, in that they proactively remodelled the distribution of transition winners and losers along ethnic lines. In so doing, Estonian and Latvian power-holders have designed public policies and shaped social solidarity in ways that made existing levels of ethno-linguistic heterogeneity politically more salient, at the expense of class and other existing social cleavages.

Splitting up at-risk workers: Bismarckian social policies in two Visegrad democracies

Numerous observers have pointed to the near-inevitable yet often unexpectedly protracted social costs that accompanied transition reforms. Those post-communist governments who were strongly committed to fast transition progress were generally not able to prevent protracted reforms costs. As the present volume makes abundantly clear, the socialist inheritance of relatively secure jobs and social rights for all workers led voters to expect that the government would intervene extensively in the provision of job security and social safety nets also during transition. After 1989, the pro-welfare-state electoral constituency was certainly considerably stronger in Eastern than in Western European democracies (Alesina and Fuchs-Schündeln, 2007; Haggard and Kaufman, 2008; Corneo and Gruner, 2002). Post-communist governments consequently faced strong hurdles in retrenching welfare programmes and hardening social policy budget constraints.

Beyond anti-reform voting, active resistance against reforms among subsets of the workforce provided another likely political scenario. Workers in communist societies had become accustomed to very high levels of employment security by international standards. In transition, they enjoyed, by definition, higher levels of freedom and political resources to organize reform protests. And many had good reason to do so, given the fast-rising levels and longer duration spells of unemployment, and the ever more visible gaps between reform winners and losers. Widely across post-communist Europe, with the initial exception of the Czech lands, unemployment shot up very rapidly in the 1990s after many decades of near-zero official levels. This scenario appeared to spell trouble. As Piven and Cloward's (1977, 1993) classic studies indicate, in periods of rapid and large-scale social change, unemployment has been a particularly significant trigger for disruptions of social order.

The incidence and distribution of job losses and related social hardship appeared further conducive to 'Latin American' scenarios for large-scale disruption in the polity and ensuing reversals of reforms (Greskovits, 1998; Haggard and Kaufman, 1995; Roberts, 2008). Crucially, the threat of job losses was not equally distributed, but strongly stratified along geographical (urban–rural) as well as educational lines (Scarpetta and Wörgötter, 1995; Rashid et al., 2005).[4] In all four Visegrad countries, for instance, the variation in regional unemployment levels tended to be significantly larger than in Western economies (Boeri et al., 1998). Exposed workers were closely linked in terms of both socioeconomic and professional status and geographic location. Since active social networks occur naturally at workplaces, these form an ideal environment for grievance sharing, coordinating and mobilizing workers for reform protests. The greater the specificity of the attribution of blame for reform costs, the greater the probability of protest was likely to be (Javeline, 2003). It is in such contexts that powerholders committed to reforms may use public policies in an effort to ensure political order. Strategic social policies can then become a useful tool of pre-emptive protest avoidance. Korpi's (2001) rational-action account of Western welfare state development suggests that rulers have a number of policy tools at their disposal through strategies involving Lukes' (1974) second and third face of power. For instance, rulers can shape subordinate actors' definitions of their interests and identities in ways that increase the latter's mobilization costs in setting up collective action.

As explored extensively in my book *Divide and Pacify* (2006a), Hungarian and Polish governments in the early 1990s attempted to reduce the threat of large-scale reform protests by splitting up groups of well-networked and formally organized at-risk workers into different subgroups with conflicting material interests and fewer common social ties. In the first seven years of democracy alone, literally hundreds of thousands of workers were transferred out of the labour force and onto early pensions and disability pensions. These policies led to Great Abnormal Pensioner Booms. Whereas the number of 60-plussers remained stable in Hungary and grew by 10 per cent in Poland between 1989 and 1996, the number of old-age pensioners increased by respectively one-fifth and 46 per cent. In the same period of just seven years, the number of disability pensioners also increased by one-half in Hungary and by one-fifth in Poland (Vanhuysse, 2006a). Reform losers were hereby separated, de facto and administratively, into four different social status categories. In addition to regular old-age pensioners, citizens of labour market age were divided into regular jobholders, unemployed workers and 'abnormal' pensioners on early or disability pensions.

The hard power core of these 'emergency power policies' revolved around two essentially Bismarckian mechanisms (see also Fuchs and Offe, 2009). First, material benefits were selectively provided to particular target groups whose opposition to reforms would have been especially effective in disrupting economic reform progress. Second, these policies 'created' distributional conflict between groups that until that moment had shared similar objective interests, by dividing at-risk workers into three different social and administrative status categories. The end result was that a likely scenario of reform protests organized by encompassing interest coalitions was replaced by one of social quiescence, as a joint outcome of outright competition for state resources among these newly competing status groups, decreasing social ties among marginalized labour market outsiders, and individualistic coping strategies such as informal economy activities by working-age pensioners and unemployed people.

The strategic use of welfare state programmes thereby allowed coalition parties to dilute, or defuse, a potentially explosive social mix of soaring reforms costs hitting well-organized clusters of workers in a short (or at the same) moment in time. To be sure, especially in Hungary, early retirement had been a frequently used policy template also under late socialism (e.g. Inglot, this volume). The strategy of offloading workers at risk of job losses onto the public pension systems has long been a strategy for politically convenient labour force reduction in the advanced welfare states of continental Western and Southern Europe (Ebbinghaus, 2006). What was novel about the abnormal pensioner booms in post-communist Hungary and Poland was the sheer speed and scale of early exit post-1990. These policies have had significant further consequences for post-communist political economies, along classic path-dependency lines.

After the pensioner booms: path-dependency in the emergency welfare states

At the formative historical turning point of 1989–1990, the social policies described above helped to reduce the incidence of disruptive conflict, but at the cost of subsequently constraining the fiscal leeway available in social policy. However, if critical junctures are marked by the multiplicity of institutional choices and policy alternatives, they are necessarily followed by a subsequent contraction of this feasible set. In Katznelson's (2003, p. 293) words, junctures are characterized by 'a transition of initially very high uncertainty and possibility to less, from a wide array of policy options to fewer, and by institutional innovation that reduces uncertainty and inscribes content and limits to policy'. In the Hungarian and Polish cases, the Abnormal Pensioner Booms, once enacted, were inherently difficult to reverse. Consequently they led to soaring pension system dependency rates and necessitated partial pension privatization later, towards the latter part of the 1990s (Orenstein, this volume). However, at-risk workers no longer represented disruptive political dynamite that needed to be defused, *now*.

As *unemployed workers*, at-risk workers now represented a numerically marginalized group that could be squeezed *later*. Thus, immediately after 1989–1990, Hungary and Poland offered the second and third most generous unemployment replacement rates respectively (70 and 65 per cent in the first six months) within a sample of ten post-communist states. But by the late 1990s, Hungary had cut those rates marginally (to 55 per cent), while Poland had enacted the most drastic cuts of the entire sample (by 30 per cent) (Vodopivec et al., 2003, p. 20). Similarly, while these two countries offered by far the most generous maximum duration periods for payment of unemployment benefits in post-communist Europe in the early 1990s (24 months), they had severely cut these payment periods (by 12 and six months respectively) by the end of the decade (Vodopivec et al., 2003, p. 21). Other indicators of eligibility and generosity similarly show that after an initially generous starting point in early transition, unemployment benefits were significantly retrenched subsequently (Boeri and Terrell, 2002).

Conversely, as *early and disability pensioners*, at-risk workers now represented a medium-term time bomb undermining the welfare system's finances, *later*. Moreover, pensioners at once became significantly more numerous. Their increased electoral clout could now pre-emptively influence the policy platforms of politicians and it made it harder than before to retrench pensions. Towards the end of the 1990s and into the present decade, public expenditures for elderly generations were made increasingly at the expense of younger generations. For instance, in Hungary the systemic pension reforms from 1997 onwards shifted most reform costs onto younger workers and future taxpayers, while continuing to favour current pensioners (Müller, 1999). But public pension spending in Hungary and Poland, at 11.4 and 8.3 per cent of GDP respectively between 1999 and 2003, was well above the OECD average (7.5 per cent), even though these countries boasted demographically younger populations than most other OECD countries (own computations from OECD, 2007). Not surprisingly therefore, Verhoeven et al.'s (2009, pp. 113–14) analysis of three socioeconomic groups with few economic resources (those with no education living in rural areas) indicates that in Hungary and Poland the relative incomes of pensioners were higher in 2002 than they had been in 1991. More importantly, in both countries the relative incomes of pensioners were markedly higher than those of both unemployed people and workers with few economic resources in every single year between 1991 and 2002. In the case of Poland, the same observation – better relative incomes for pensioners than for workers and the unemployed – held true for most of the transition period also when analysing three other population samples: all persons living in urban areas, all persons with five years of education, and all persons with ten years of education (Verhoeven et al., 2009).

Only as late as December 2008 was a measure fiscal prudence restored in the case of Polish pension finances. Various early retirement schemes covering more than one million Poles were abolished by the Polish Sejm in spite of President Kaczynski's veto. Starting on 1 January 2009, nobody covered within the universal (basic/mandatory) system based on individual accounts (the vast majority of Poles born after 1948) will be able to start claiming pensions before they reach 60 (for women) or 65 (for men). However, many longstanding exceptional pension privileges such those for the uniformed services and for farmers will remain excluded.[5] In Hungary, by contrast, pensioner-favouring policies have continued unabated, at great public financial cost. Left of centre government parties have started paying pensioners a thirteenth month of pensions, thereby accelerating the already worrying rise in public deficits. Towards the start of the twenty-first century, a string of political and economic crises in Hungary have been accompanied by upsurges in protests and violence. These culminated in the events of autumn 2006. Ostensibly reacting to Prime Minister Gyurcsany's leaked admission of lying during the election campaign, groups of right-wing radicals occupied central parts of Budapest in violent protests during the commemorations of the 1956 Revolution. Long overdue reforms in health care and pensions, in the context of an economy particularly hard hit by economic crisis after October 2008, may instigate further unrests. The peaceful pathways of post-1989 welfare may thus have come to an end in today's new post-EU-accession era.

In sum, the logic of reform protests may have been replaced in part by one of intergenerational public policy conflict in these Visegrad states (on generational policy conflict, see Tepe and Vanhuysse, 2009). This process appears also to have been accompanied by a steady radicalization of these polities, as silenced reform losers have increasingly resorted to politically illiberal parties and protest forms (Vanhuysse, 2008b). Below I turn to a less frequently recognized instance of power politics and its hidden faces in post-communism, and one that appears to have been yet more blatantly illiberal – ethnic discrimination in the Baltic region.

Silencing linguistic minorities: ethnic stratification in two Baltic democracies

In the Baltic area, the scope for power politics in social policy might appear to have been much more limited – at first sight. After all, governments in this region have far outdone all other post-communist first-round EU accession members in 'shrinking the state'. This was accomplished by means of fast and far-reaching macro-economic and industrial liberalization programmes after 1991 (Bohle and Greskovits, 2006, 2007; Feldmann,

2007). This liberalization drive also extended to pensions and social policy more generally.[6] It is now generally agreed that on most of the commonly used indicators of programme coverage, eligibility conditions and benefit generosity, Baltic welfare regimes are significantly less generous and less encompassing than the other new EU member states. While it has become commonplace to refer to most post-communist welfare states as hybrid forms recombining various aspects of different regime types (Cerami, 2006; Inglot, Szikra and Tomka, this volume), Baltic welfare models can be more unreservedly qualified as 'neo-liberal' or, at the very least, 'basic'. Latvia's welfare state is particularly lean and mean. For instance, between 1999 and 2004, Minimum Income Guarantee Programmes Spending ranged from 0.02 to 0.05 per cent of GDP in Latvia and between 0.17 and 0.41 per cent in Estonia, compared to 0.19–0.44 per cent in Poland and 0.38–0.48 per cent in the Czech Republic. Similarly, average monthly social assistance benefits and family benefits amounted to 1.5 and 6 per cent of the minimum wage in 2004 respectively, as compared to 10 and 10 per cent in Hungary, and 14 and 6 per cent in Poland respectively (Ringold and Kasek, 2007, pp. 53, 33).

Underlying this general shrinking of the state, power strategies have ruled supreme along ethnic lines. My argument does not apply to Lithuania, which was the most ethnically homogenous of the three Baltic states to start with, and where the citizenship law of 1989 allowed all residents to apply for naturalization regardless of ethnicity (Aidukaite, this volume; Pettai and Kreuzer, 1998). It applies to Estonia and Latvia, where newly independent coalition parties have aggressively used their state power through deliberate strategies of *ethnic-linguistic* discrimination against their Russian-speaking minorities. To illustrate the argument, I reinterpret insights from a string of descriptive World Bank documents and work by other institutional and academic observers of this region (for example, Laitin, 2007; Bloom, 2007, 2008), most notably *Identity in Formation*, David Laitin's (1998) path-breaking political ethnography of identity (and linguistic) strategies and status changes among Baltic minorities.

As Laitin (1998) notes, the Russian-speaking minorities in the Baltic area constituted up to a third of the population, and they had already been struck by the 'double cataclysm' of the passage of the republican Language Laws in 1989 and the collapse of the Soviet Union in 1991. But subsequently, successive Estonian and Latvian governments, headed by strongly nationalistic political parties, have deliberately denied their Russian-speaking minorities basic political rights, let alone a key voice, at the most crucial early formative moment of these new nation states. As in the case of Hungarian and Polish pension policies, these Baltic transitions developed remarkably peacefully, despite strong prior expectations of ethnically based protests (Laitin, 2007). Here too, timing was of the essence, and path-dependence mechanisms mainly kicked in *after* initial elite strategies had changed the political game.

Baltic Russian speakers, post-independence: the wheel of fortune reversed

At the critical juncture of early post-1991 nation building, there was a strategic incentive for titular Baltic parties, to move first by delaying Russian speakers' political influence *in the short run*. Substantial fractions of the Russian minorities, most of whom who had arrived decades earlier, were initially denied automatic citizenship on the grounds that Soviet rule had been an illegal occupation (Pettai and Kreuzer, 1998; Bloom, 2008). These early discrimination measures, in this strong form, could be expected to be temporary, valid until international outcry towards the end of the 1990s and subsequent EU conditionality would force titular governments to liberalize their citizenships laws and to better safeguard the status of ethnic minorities.[7] But crucially, *before* this happened, these measures opened up a policy window that could set the Baltic nation states onto a distinct political and economic pathway, give a first-mover advantage to titular Baltic interest coalitions, quickly push up the economic value of the titular language at the expense of Russian, and disproportionately impose social and economic costs on ethnic Russians.

In Estonia, a citizenship law passed by the first post-Soviet Estonian government under Tiit Vähi required all non-citizens to either pass an examination in Estonian or, failing that, to first establish ten years of 'legal' residence. As a result, the great majority of Russian speakers were simply denied any voting rights in the 1992 elections. These elections brought to power the vehemently nationalist Fatherland (Isamaa) coalition, which moved quickly to stop state subsidies for Russian-language schools. In summer 1993 Isamaa passed a far-reaching 'Law on Aliens' requiring non-citizens to register and be eligible for temporary residence permits only, or else to face deportation (Laitin, 1998, pp. 94–5). In a move widely perceived as being intended to slow down naturalization of Soviet-era immigrants, the Estonian government passed a new citizenship law in January 1995 that added another civics examination to the naturalization procedure, and subsequently waited over three months before it even issued specific information about this exam (Laitin, 1998, p. 6). Russian speakers frequently reported recurrent and unexplained delays and even disappearing documents in their citizenship applications (Laitin, 1998, pp. 6–7, 354–5). As with the tacit encouragement of early retirement in Hungary and Poland, the informal practices of administrators and street-level bureaucrats furthered this process behind the scenes.

Similar strategies were employed in Latvia. An operating pre-independence coalition between Latvian titulars and Russian speakers was declared null and void by October 1991. It was replaced by proposed laws stipulating a 16-year period before Russian speakers (at least the vast majority which did not descend from interwar Latvian passport holders) could even apply for citizenship. While this law was never ratified, Latvian governments managed to delay the passing of a more moderate law, and thereby all naturalization procedures for Russians, until as late as 1994 (Dreifelds, 1996). In addition, a so-called 'window process' was implemented to limit eligible citizenship applications by age sets (Laitin, 1998, p. 95). Given that a 1991 Latvian Supreme Council ruling had refused non-citizens all rights to travel abroad, own land, hold state office and many other jobs, and vote, the initial refusal and subsequent delay of citizenship to Russian speakers sufficed to deny them of much political and economic power. Right up until 1994, non-citizens were refused the vote even in *local* elections (Laitin, 1998, p. 98). Note that although titular Latvians represented only 54 per cent of the Latvian population (and less than half of the 19–44 age group), they had constituted 79 per cent of all voters in the 1993 elections. Only 39 per cent of the ethnic Russians, who represented *one-third* of the population, had been able to vote in those same elections (Dreifelds, 1996, pp. 143, 150–1, 86). In this light, the Latvian titulars' silencing tactics towards Russian speakers amounted to a stunning power grab. However, it would be a mistake to interpret these policies as exclusively or blindly motivated by irrational ethnic/nationalistic sentiment. Rather, the ruling Baltic titulars strategically played the ethnic card in order to guarantee social order and to make fast progress with economic reforms in ways that disproportionately benefited their own ethnic group.

Order and power: silent non-exit through broken voice

Baltic titular groups may well have wanted to force Russian speakers into actual *'physical exit'* – and, conversely, to prevent additional entry from Russia into their own territory.[8] But this was likely to be an altogether limited strategy. Hirschman's (1970) exit mechanism is more likely to have operated mainly in the case of a different group at the other end of the opportunities market, by directing workers with marketable skills *west*ward. The streams of Baltic (as well as Polish, Moldavian and Bulgarian) workers that have moved to work in the old EU-15 member states have generally tended to be rich either in general human capital (e.g. doctors and engineers) or, more frequently, in scarce and high-quality industrial skills (Culic, 2008; Woolfson, 2007). At this high end of the opportunities market, exit set in motion a classic cream-skimming mechanism. Hirschman (1970, p. 47) famously remarked that precisely those actors who care most about the quality of any organizational product are normally the most effective agents of voice. Therefore they may also be – for that very reason – most likely to exit first in case of organizational decline (for a formalization, see Gehlbach, 2006). In the Baltic case, those with the best opportunities exited first, thereby diluting the human capital base of Baltic political economies, driving them further along their distinctly low-skill, low-quality, low-value-added export production pathway (Bohle and Greskovits, 2006).

At the low end of the opportunities market, I suggest that Baltic titular governments were well aware of the limited scope and the high international blame attached to an enforced *east*ward exit strategy regarding their Russian-speaking minority populations. The scope for enforcing exit among the economic losers of transition was admittedly higher in these cases than it was in the case of Hungarian or Polish transition losers. Nevertheless, the longstanding residence and homeownership of Russian speakers on Baltic territory, their (mutually) tenuous links with the new Russia as opposed to the old USSR, and the Baltic states' (until recently) better current levels and future prospects of economic prosperity all combined to strongly reduce the incentives for the vast majority of Russian speakers to exit eastwards.[9] Despite their rhetoric (which served other ends), Baltic governments therefore rationally reverted to an alternative main strategy – one of imposing what Brian Barry (1974) called '*silent non-exit*'. Playing the ethnic card and employing harsh nationalist rhetoric increased silent non-exit in two distinct ways.

First, ethnically motivated citizenship restrictions directly muted the Russians' option of '*peaceful voice*' by simply foreclosing the power of the polling booth for many. This in turn allowed the titular governments to safely target economic policies along ethnic lines. By reorienting trade away from Russia and towards the West, titular powerholders could build on their first-mover advantage and reap economic benefits. In contrast, the Russian-speaking minority, which was predominantly employed in those industries that had been built up during the Soviet empire, such as electronics and heavy industries, suffered heavy employment losses in the 1990s (Aasland, 1998; Bite and Zagorskis, 2003; Bohle and Greskovits, 2007). In addition, Russians' re-employment chances were hampered by a double obstacle – lack of language ability and the unlearning of outdated skills in favour of new, marketable ones.

The geographical and ethno-linguistic incidence of unemployment is a case in point – one that reveals striking similarities not just with Hungary and Poland in the 1990s, but also with Britain in the 1980s.[10] Estonian governments deliberately neglected the industrial base in the Russian-dominated east of the country after 1991. This led to an unemployment rate of up to 40 per cent in that part of Estonia as compared to near-zero in Tallin, the capital (Laitin, 1998, p. 358). In 2001, unemployment varied from a low of 7.7 per cent in Hiiumaa county (West Estonia) to much higher rates in the south-east and north-east of the country, with a maximum of 20.6 per cent in Jõgeva county (East Estonia). At 18 per cent, the unemployment rate among non-Estonians was 7 per cent higher that year than that of ethnic Estonians (Leppik and Kruuda, 2003, p. 82).

In Latvia, the share of jobseekers aged 15–64 was 13 per cent for people with Latvian language skills in the late 1990s, and 20.8 per cent for people without those skills (Bite and Zagorskis, 2003, pp. 93–5, 66). Yet this ethnic divide was no major electoral threat, as scores of Russian speakers had been, essentially, disenfranchised. As Bloom (2008, p. 1584) indicates, Russian speakers were disproportionately concentrated among Latvia's seven largest (and richest) cities, where they accounted on average for 62 per cent of the population (ranging from 48 per cent in Jelgava to 86 per cent in Daugavpils). Yet on average, an amazing 40 per cent of these cities' populations were non-citizens without basic voting rights. Even in regions with strong Russian minorities that did hold citizenship, such as Latgale, Russians were politically sidelined: not one single party representing minority voters has ever taken part in any of Latvia's 13 post-Soviet coalition governments (Bloom, 2008, p. 1577). Not surprisingly the significant lack of peaceful political voice (voting and government inclusion) translated into redistributive biases of public policies. For instance, Latvia's seven big 'Russian-speaking' cities received on average a mere 4 per cent of their local government revenue in the form of transfers from the national government in 1996, as compared to 44 per cent in the case of more 'indigenous' rural provinces such as Zemgale and Kurzeme (Bloom, 2008, p. 1580). Bloom's (2008, Table 1A) insightful study of Latvian fiscal appeasement furthermore shows that, even after controlling for socioeconomic needs such as unemployment levels, the share of non-citizens (for example, non-voters) at the district level was systematically negatively correlated with a wide range of fiscal transfers throughout the 1990s.

Beyond voting, a second mechanism by which Baltic titular governments imposed silent non-exit on their Russian-speaking minorities was by breaking their *'disruptive voice'* in terms of strikes and protests. Anti-Russian policies and rhetoric deliberately created permanent uncertainty and fear of deportation. However, in classic Bismarckian fashion, they also heightened the political salience of ethnic as opposed to class cleavages within the polity. Specifically, these strategies helped to further break up the Russian speakers' capacity to coalesce with *socioeconomically similar but ethnically different* transition losers (such as, for instance, poor farmers and displaced blue-collar workers of titular origin). As we have seen, once-similar Hungarian and Polish at-risk workers had been divided post-1989 into numerically smaller and politically competing groups of workers with jobs, unemployed workers and early retirees. Similarly, the inability of Baltic Russian-speaking (numerical) minorities to coalesce for economic (that is, *class*-based) protests left them further marginalized politically, *as* a mere ethnic minority. Thus the 1993 Estonian Law on Cultural Autonomy of National Minorities, which granted minority groups with more than 3,000 members special cultural and educational rights, was designed to further subdivide Russians from other ethnic minorities: 'One effect of this law – and one of its drafters told me in confidence that this was intentional – will be to divide the Russian-speaking minorities into separate political forces, thereby diminishing their overall impact in opposition to the Estonian culturalist program' (Laitin, 1998, p. 357). And tellingly, Laitin (1998, pp. 96–7) reports that:

in confidential interviews, officials of the Isamaa government confided to me that the anti-Russian government rhetoric played a crucial economic role.

With it, there was an electoral coalition of urban business (which wanted economic reform) and rural folk (farmers and pensioners) which was willing to accept the harsh realities of economic reform as long as the Russian population was being threatened. Without the chauvinism, I was told, a coalition of Russian and the rural elements would have defeated reform.

Political voice became ethnically stratified also along other dimensions. Beyond voting less, by 1999, Slavic inhabitants in Estonia and Latvia were significantly less likely than the titular ethnic inhabitants to engage in a wide range of political and civil activities, including membership or financial support of organizations or movements, political activities other than elections, the collection of signatures or the signing of petitions, as well as participation in strikes or political rallies (Aasland and Fløtten, 2001). To a significant degree therefore, the political voice of Russian speakers was broken by state policies that narrowed the social foundations for anti-reform collective action and even peaceful voice.

Lastly, the analysis also indicates mechanisms by which, even in these seemingly *universally* lean Baltic welfare states, the power politics of social policy may have crept in via the back door after 1991. Against a backdrop of generally high social hardship levels resulting from economic liberalization programmes that were radical even by post-communist Polish or UK-Thatcherite standards, the policies discussed above are likely to have translated into yet higher social costs for Russian speakers *specifically*. Unemployment was the single most important cause of poverty in the Baltic economies in the 1990s. For instance, in Latvia between 1996 and 2000, poverty ranged from 28 to 30 per cent among households with one unemployed member, and from 44 to 60 per cent among households with two unemployed members. Compared to average households, those in the unemployment-stricken Eastern region of Latgale, where a large Russian minority lived, had a 23 per cent higher likelihood of being poor in 1996, and a 75 per cent higher likelihood in 2000.[11] As unemployment disproportionately affected Russian speakers, Russians' poverty rates were likely to be much higher as well. By the turn of the century, the disadvantage of Slavic inhabitants vis-à-vis the titular ethnic group remained statistically significant along a number of indicators of social exclusion in both Estonia and Latvia. This ethnic stratification was evident, for instance, regarding (a) the share of unemployed, discouraged or not actively jobseeking workers, (b) those fearing job loss, (c) those lacking economic resources for participation in social life, (d) a synthetic additive index of social disadvantage (Aasland and Fløtten, 2001). Titma et al. (1998) similarly report a marked reversal of economic fortune for Russian speakers soon after Estonian independence: controlling for situational variables, income differentials quickly shifted from a slight advantage to a substantial disadvantage for Russian speakers vis-à-vis titular groups.

Take-up rates of social assistance services similarly reflected ethnic divisions. Ethnic Latvians were generally better informed about social assistance. They received social assistance benefits more often than other ethnic groups, even though application rates were similar for Latvians and Russians (Ringold and Kasek, 2007). In a strongly decentralized social assistance system such as the Latvian one, this was in part due to administrative and tax revenue capacities of different local governments. For instance, of those who had applied for social assistance, 73 per cent of Latvians, 59 per cent of Russians and only 50 per cent other ethnics were granted the requested benefits in full, whereas 11 per cent Latvians, 20 per cent of Russians and 30 per cent of others received nothing (Bite and Zagorskis, 2003, pp. 93–5).

The successful Baltic economic reforms in the 1990s dismantled the power of trade unions but also of the Russian minority, which might have become a strong opponent of reforms (Vanhuysse, 2007). In Bohle and Greskovits' (2007, p. 451) words, the Russians were 'as much silenced in interest group as in democratic politics. Political exclusion was coupled with and buttressed by social exclusion'. It may therefore be true that legally residing Russians in Estonia and Latvia are nominally entitled to all welfare rights such as social services, health care, family benefits and housing. But beyond *de jure* appearances and statements, the de facto access to (and exercise of) such rights can nevertheless be significantly restricted. This ethno-linguistic composition and targeting of social policies and social costs (such as poverty, labour market exclusion, pension rights, and mental and physical ill health) is a feature that has thus far been overlooked in country studies of Baltic welfare.[12] Yet it may turn out to have been another significant hidden face of power. In the same vein, whereas between 1990 and 2004 the Estonian state administration grew relatively little, in Latvia the number of state administrators more than quadrupled, putting the country in first place among a sample of nine post-communist cases in terms of the exploitation of state resources for patronage purposes (Hanley, 2008). All evidence reviewed in this chapter leads one to expect that these state employment patterns may have been heavily biased among ethnic lines in favour of Latvian titulars. Like the ethno-linguistic distribution of unemployment, the ethnic composition of new state employment and of social assistance by the state constitutes a promising avenue for future explorations in the power politics of post-communist societies.

Conclusions: order and disorder in post-communist politics

> When the degree of asymmetry in power increases, the terms of exchange of the weaker actor are likely to deteriorate, but at the same time her probability of successful resistance tends to decrease, thereby decreasing the probability of manifest conflict between these actors. (Korpi, 2001, p. 248)

As many students of social policy have noted, the strategic use of social policies to enhance political order and to stabilize contingent power regimes is as old as the welfare state itself – whether in democratic Western Europe (Korpi, 2001, 2006; Offe, 1984; Fuchs and Offe, 2009), or in communist Eastern Europe (Cook, 1993; Kornai, 1992, 1996). The very first social insurance laws in late nineteenth-century Europe were not proactive efforts by socialist movements, but conservative-reactionary attempts by state elites to stifle the threats raised by these emerging movements to the existing order (Korpi, 2006, pp. 175–6). In the 1880s, Bismarck introduced social insurance programmes that were prototypes of state-corporatist segmenting institutions, with separate programmes for various occupational categories. In continental Europe, the Catholic Church, aided by Pope Leo XIII's 1891 *Workers Encyclical*, supported such efforts (see also van Kersbergen and Manow, 2009). Essentially, these early social policy strategies segmented the labour force into internally homogenous occupational communities that differed between them in terms of socioeconomic resources and risks. Beyond preserving social order in the short run, these strategies changed power relations through an elaborate set of principles 'intended to engineer institutions which would foster social peace by molding preferences and identities and to counteract broad-based collective action by the dependent labor force in ways reflecting class cleavages' (Korpi, 2001, p. 251). Similarly, Levy (2005) argues that French governments after 1983 implemented a 'social anaesthesia' strategy by cushioning the social costs of industrial reforms through fiscally expansionary measures such as public employment, subsidized private employment, worker training and early retirement.

I have argued that post-communist governments in Hungary, Poland, Latvia and Estonia have successfully resorted to similar social anaesthesia strategies. Other instances of such strategies remain to be explored in further research. For example, the substantial Roma minority populations in countries like Slovakia, Hungary, Romania and Bulgaria appear not to have been subject to such blatantly orchestrated forms of ethnic discrimination. Yet their socioeconomic and civic fate and bureaucratic treatment in these countries, both in communism and after transition, have been similar in more than one respect to that of the Russian-speaking minorities in Estonia and Latvia post-1991 (Ringold et al., 2005; Ringold and Kasek, 2007). As these Roma populations constituted a hard *ethnic* core within the larger pool of economic transition losers, their continued marginalization in terms of democratic voice, collective mobilization and, possibly, social benefit take-up rates may have similarly served to defuse some social dynamite by reducing the likelihood of *class-based* anti-reform collective action.

Albert Hirschman (1970) emphasized long ago that the option of exit can atrophy the art of voice. But even in the absence of that option, powerholders have plenty of further ammunition at their disposal to try and silence the powerless. The two sets of post-communist policy packages discussed here have differed in their main target groups. But they had a power core in common. Russian-speaking minorities in Estonia and Latvia, just like at-risk workers in Hungary and Poland, have been sentenced to silent non-exit by state policies aimed at creating and/or exacerbating distributive conflict among 'objectively' similar economic reform losers. As had happened historically with welfare states in West Europe (Esping-Andersen, 1990; van Kersbergen and Manow, 2009) and in middle-income countries (Haggard and Kaufman, 2008), the particular interest coalitions that usurped power at this critical juncture of post-communist state-building could thereby structure the emerging shape and distributional logic of the new policy regimes. In both the Baltic and the Visegrad cases, power politics have helped to break up the social foundations for anti-reform collective action, and they have consolidated the particular democratic capitalist pathway chosen (respectively neo-liberalism and embedded liberalism).

The dramatic reversal of the political clout of Latvian and Estonian Russian speakers after independence and the large-scale creation of new (working-aged) Hungarian and Polish pensioners constitute clear instances of path-departure, beyond mere institutional layering. At a crucial juncture, the particular policies implemented in these two sets of countries – and not, for instance, in comparable cases such as Lithuania and the Czech Republic respectively – have reshaped the prevailing logics of distributive politics in these four polities. Lastly, in both sets of countries, these strategies have either embodied or contributed to a distinctly illiberal turn in political life. The 'liberal backsliding' observed across much of post-communist Europe over the past few years has been well documented. It has been evident in decreasing levels of support for liberal politics (as measured by class-based economic protests, electoral turnout levels, and support for liberal and non-extremist parties), coupled with rising levels of political anomie (as measured by high levels of dissatisfaction, disengagement and disillusion regarding the new political and economic order).[13] As argued above, the first stage of post-communist politics in the early and mid-1990s has led to broadly successful damage control strategies, by which government elites used emergency public policies to prevent large-scale reform protests and consolidate democratic and market consolidation. But in the second stage, towards the late 1990s and into the present decade, the very success of these earlier policies may have turned angry workers increasingly towards protests votes for illiberal populist parties (Vanhuysse, 2008b). A third, more contentious stage may have been ushered in by the worldwide economic crisis from late 2008 onwards; a crisis that has hit countries such as the erstwhile 'Baltic Tigers', Hungary, Bulgaria and Romania particularly hard, due to the national-developmental and macro-fiscal strategies they have adopted. For instance, following its IMF-led 10 billion-euro emergency package in October 2008, the Latvian government has announced real public sector wage cuts of 30–35 per cent, while its economy was forecast to shrink by 8–10 per cent in 2009 (Barysch, 2009). In this light the eruptions of riots and violent protests observed in January 2009 alone on the streets of cities such as Vilnius, Sofia, Bucharest and Riga (the worst since Latvian independence) may prove to have been a harbinger of more economic protests in the near future.[14]

Popular disillusionment with the liberal politics and policies of the early post-communist era has been especially pronounced among the economic losers of transition, and it is almost invariably stratified along educational and regional lines (Paczynska, 2005). In terms of peaceful voice, voting turnout rates have been artificially inflated in the Baltic cases due to the straightforward exclusion of scores of Russian speakers. Even so, here as elsewhere in Central and Eastern Europe, voting turnout has declined fast after the first post-communist 'founding' elections, to reach very low levels by international standards. Turnout rates slumped to 66 per cent on average in Hungary and to 69 per cent in Latvia over the second-to-fifth general elections, and to respectively 46, 61, 71, and 74 per cent in Poland, Estonia, the Czech Republic and Slovakia over the second-to-sixth elections.[15] As Arend Lijphart (1997, p. 2) famously argued, low voter turnout means unequal and socioeconomically biased turnout. The use of voting as an expression of political protest could therefore be expected to be diminished by the well-known tendency of economically weak actors to record low levels of actual involvement in politics (Anderson, 2001). In sum, decreasing voting turnout levels of the kind observed in post-communist democracies are likely to have disproportionately reduced the policy influence of socioeconomically disadvantaged groups in electoral as well as collective action terms. Flying high over post-communist Europe like the devil in *The Master and Margarita*, even the ghosts of Machiavelli and Bismarck might have learnt a thing or two.

Part II
Country Studies

5
Czech Republic, Hungary, Poland and Slovakia: Adaptation and Reform of the Post-Communist 'Emergency Welfare States'

Tomasz Inglot

Introduction

The investigation of post-communist social policies has centred on two general topics: a possible emergence of a new type of welfare state regime in the former Soviet bloc and the search for the major determinants of social policy development and reform in the region. Many scholars have recommended the designation of a separate regime type to distinguish between Western and Eastern systems of welfare protection (Müller et al., 1999; Aidukaite, 2004; Cerami, 2006). Moreover, arguably institutionalism and the power resources approach have become the most popular explanatory frameworks of 'transformational' post-communist social policy. Their adherents stress the determining influence of institutional constraints, veto points and international financial organizations (Müller, 1999; Orenstein and Haas, 2005; Orenstein, this volume) or political factors, for example, the impact of political parties, ideologies, interest groups and bureaucratic stakeholders, on social policy development (Hasselmann, 2006; Vanhuysse, 2006a, and this volume; Cook, 2007b).

This chapter concentrates on the four new democracies of East Central Europe – the Czech Republic, Poland, Hungary and Slovakia – to demonstrate the explanatory potential of a comparative analytical framework of *historical institutionalism* (Amenta, 2003; Pierson, 2004) in combination with *discourse institutionalism* (Schmidt, 2008; Cerami, this volume). On the fundamental level, all four countries share the Bismarckian foundations of the European welfare state. They currently spend on the average 10–15 per cent of GDP annually for their major social insurance programmes. Therefore, in a narrow sense, they represent 'conservative', contributory or Bismarckian (based on social insurance principles) regimes (Esping-Andersen, 1990).

Nonetheless, I argue that the post-communist welfare states have evolved into much more complex 'hybrid' structures and policies that defy standard classifications. They all consist of a combination of basic institutional 'layers' dating as far back as the early twentieth century (see also Szikra and Tomka, this volume). In a broad historical perspective, the Czech, Polish, Hungarian and Slovak welfare states share four stages of development: imperial origins (1880–1918), incomplete institutional consolidation during the interwar period of independent state-building (1919–1939), over four decades of adaptation, expansion and crisis (retrenchment) of the national welfare states during communist rule (1945–1989), and, finally, the recent 15-year period of a 'transformation shock', preceding their accession to the European Union (1989–2004).[1] Nonetheless, as I will explain below, we must also note that these countries differ quite significantly from one another in terms of the *timing* and *sequencing* of specific institutional and policy changes during each historical stage. The second dimension of this enquiry concerns the causal factors behind welfare state development in the post-communist region. It involves a long-standing debate, also highlighted in this volume, between the arguments in support of *path-dependence* (Inglot, 1995, 2003, 2008; Tomka, 2004) and those that stress *path-departing* changes and reforms undertaken by political agents or policy entrepreneurs (Vanhuysse, 2006a), often with heavy involvement of foreign actors (Müller, 1999; Orenstein, this volume).

A mounting body of empirical evidence has consistently favoured the path-dependence perspective as the most suitable to the understanding of the period of 1989–2004 and perhaps also beyond the EU accession. As I argue in this chapter, while path-departing changes do occur, they tend to appear at the margins of the major welfare state institutions and programmes,[2] as new 'layers' and adaptations, rather than core reforms that would alter the fundamentals of these century-old systems of social protection. Regrettably, many scholars have focused rather narrowly on the developments since the fall of the old regime (Kramer, 1997; Elster et al., 1998; Müller, 1999; Vanhuysse, 2006a; Cook, 2007a, 2007b), with only passing reference to either common or more distinct legacies of communism, not to mention the earlier periods. In so doing, however, we minimize the significance of the welfare state as a historically grounded, evolutionary phenomenon that has continued to function more or less without interruption for almost a hundred years. This 'multilayered', evolving entity incorporates an accumulated baggage of institutions, ideas and practices that continue to live on under different successive political and economic regimes. In the post-communist cases we should pay particular attention to the impact of the alteration of democratic and authoritarian (totalitarian) systems of rule, for example, a complex metahistorical and institution-forming process which made convergence with the Western or even the Eastern (Soviet Union) models of the welfare state extremely difficult, if not outright impossible.

A classic, contextualized historical enquiry into the path-dependent nature of state institutions and policies, including the welfare state, usually entails the identification of the so-called 'critical junctures' that determine future 'trajectories' of development in various countries (Pierson, 2004). Analyses of Central and Eastern Europe (CEE) most frequently single out the key regime changes and systemic crises as historical turning points, the most recent one occurring in 1989 (Elster et al., 1998; Müller, 1999; Cook, 2007a; Vanhuysse, this volume). I contend, however, that in CEE we are dealing with a much less clear, convoluted and uneven process without a single, clearly identifiable critical juncture. Instead, I argue that the *misdeveloped* national states with long history of instability, authoritarianism and foreign intervention tend to engender similarly misconstructed or 'unrealized' systems of welfare protection that I call *emergency welfare states*. By definition emergency welfare states are designed as temporary creations but in reality they have become de facto permanent structures, no less resistant to reform than the commonly recognized welfare regimes. Although inherently unstable, they all have experienced several successive, alternating periods of expansion and retrenchment (reform), a cyclical pattern that has prevented the establishment of a lasting equilibrium between two interlinked processes: the process of state- (and nation) building on one hand, and the more narrowly defined process of *welfare state-building* on the other. The key periods of regime change or major instances of regime crisis and reform added new layers of ideas (welfare doctrine), decision-making structures (bureaucracies) and programmes (social insurance schemes) on top of the existing ones. Just as it happened in case of labour market policies in Western Europe (Thelen, 2004), here also repeated cycles of renegotiation of traditional approaches and entrenched policy patterns allowed enough room only for limited or 'bounded' changes.

Serious opportunities for transformative reforms open up only when the equilibrium between the processes of state-building as a whole, and welfare-state building in particular, is seriously undermined by the following factors: a change in the political regime (including foreign intervention, occupation and most significantly the winning of national independence), a prolonged period of political instability and unrest, and/or a deep socioeconomic crisis. Usually the occurrence of only one of these contingencies would be insufficient to challenge the institutional or ideational status quo or to alter longstanding patterns of social policies in a major way. When two or three of these overlap, more noticeable path-departing reforms could occur. It is important to note, however, that regime change by itself may not be a sufficient pre-condition even to initiate meaningful transformations. Yet each of these three factors by itself creates powerful incentives for creative *adaptations* of the existing structures to the new political and socioeconomic conditions. In sum, my argument concerning the most important determinants of social policy development in East Central Europe points to the crucial impact of parallel historical sequences of key events and crises, as well as governmental responses they engender.

The seemingly ambitious reform agendas and external shocks applied to these political and social systems throughout history tend to obscure the fact of the surprising endurance of the basic institutional and policy patterns of the Czech, Polish, Hungarian and Slovak welfare states. All of them, we might argue, represent relatively well-consolidated and comprehensive but also permanently 'unfinished' or 'unrealized' European models of social safety nets that apparently function the most effectively, if not necessarily efficiently, during political and socioeconomic emergencies. In the remaining part of this chapter I will briefly compare and contrast distinct national pathways of the four welfare states with special attention to five features: (1) the origins, timing and the content of the main welfare discourse (or the ideational foundation of the welfare state); (2) the type of institutional consolidation; (3) the timing and historical significance of the 'maturation' of the welfare state (coverage completion and the peak levels of spending in relation to the GDP); (4) the sequencing of expansion and retrenchment; and (5) the prioritizing and timing of major post-communist reforms.

Czech Republic

Welfare discourse

In 1993 the Czech Republic inherited welfare laws and institutions of the Czechoslovak federation, many dating back to the mid-twentieth century and even earlier. Czechoslovakia stands out from the rest of East Central Europe because of the attempted 'revolutionary' transformation of social policy in the late 1940s. The National Insurance Act, adopted in April 1948 but prepared in advance of the February 1948 Stalinist *coup d'état*, created a modern, well-integrated system of social protection in the country, based on near universal coverage and social-democratic syndicalism that flourished in the Czech reformist circles during the Second World War and its immediate aftermath (De Deken, 1994). It combined Bismarckian and Beveridgean models in the context of a relatively advanced, industrialized region (Bohemia and Moravia) which survived the ravages of the war much better than its neighbours. More importantly, this synthesis took place before the full imposition of Stalinism, allowing Czech reformers and planners much more flexibility in shaping their own developmental path. In fact, throughout the 1940s Czechoslovakia was praised within the Soviet bloc as a leading model of a post-war 'socialist welfare state'.[3]

The National Insurance Act of 1948 still serves as the major pillar of the welfare state in the Czech Republic. Further adaptations to this law took place during 1950–56, under direct pressure from Moscow, and later as a result of domestic politics and internal ideological tensions with the Czechoslovak Communist Party, in the 1960s and 1970s. In 1968, for example, the liberal policy planners tried to strip the national welfare state of its Stalinist distortions but their work was interrupted by the Soviet invasion. Similar efforts were revived again in the late 1980s but it was only in the early 1990s, with the coming to power of the new generation of democratic reformers, that they gained real momentum (Tomeš, 2002). In essence, the Czech Republic inherited a welfare system in an early phase of a second attempted social-democratic 'renewal'.

The model of the national welfare state promoted since 1993 by the first Czech Prime Minister, Václav Klaus combined 'social-democratic' entitlements (pensions, family protection) and liberal incentives for the middle class (voluntary private pensions and tax breaks). As Sirovátka and Rákoczyová argue in this volume, the Czech government skilfully combined pro-market rhetoric with active welfare policies. More precisely, it actually attempted to 'reconstruct' certain previous welfare settlements, including the universalistic goals of the National Social Insurance Act of 1948, along with the better integration of social policy laws with the labour market and the changing economic system of the country, and also assure the maintenance of a widely popular and balanced mix of cash benefits and social services developed during the communist era. Democratic reconstruction of post-communist Czechoslovakia and then its successor, the Czech Republic, seems to have rested to a large degree on the widespread popularity of this welfare model and its implied past accomplishments, at least from 1969 until the stagnation of the late 1980s. In this context, for example, we might better understand the seemingly paradoxical resistance of the 'neo-liberal' Klaus government to the international pressures to abandon excessive state intervention in the labour market and his opposition to mandatory private pensions (Müller, 1999; Macha, 2002; Hasselmann, 2006).

Institutional consolidation

The apparent stability and prosperity of the Czech welfare state for most of the time since 1993 can be also explained by the institutional inheritance. The National Insurance Act of 1948 created a powerful welfare ministry which ran a highly disciplined administrative apparatus in an efficient and tight manner. In the post-war period the country also established a single, central social insurance agency to administer pensions and family benefits. Even though the Stalinist planners soon after replaced this agency with the Soviet-style trade union bureaucracy, the Czechoslovak welfare state administration still differed significantly from its communist neighbours in East Central Europe. The union officials in charge of social policy came from the ranks of left-wing social democrats with previous knowledge and experience in the area where labour had played an unusually large role since the 1920s (Korbel, 1977, p. 57). Considerable overlap in personnel and expertise between the state and the trade union bureaucracies made the preservation of the national Czechoslovak model much easier, even under the most hostile conditions of the command economy.

Curiously, democratic Czech governments, which have wholeheartedly embraced free market, have also resisted pressures to decentralize and open up the welfare system to greater participation from civil society groups. Details of social security budgets remain a tightly guarded secret, spurring widespread speculation about the true financial condition of the system (Potůček, 1999; Bautzová, 2006). Moreover, the prolonged resistance to the 'three tier' pension system, advocated by the World Bank and adopted in Poland and Hungary, could also be at least partially attributed to the fact that the closed decision-making process and the conservative nature of the inherited Czech institutions provide little opportunity for an open debate on fundamental systemic reforms.

Maturation of the welfare state

Early maturation of the Czechoslovak welfare state, in terms of coverage for major social insurance programmes and peak social expenditures, helped its successor, the Czech Republic, to maintain stability but also made it more resistant to change than the other countries in the region. With the possible exception of rural groups in the less developed parts of the country, the expansion of pension, sickness, maternity insurance and also a number of other family related benefits had been completed by the late 1940s. Therefore in 1993 the Czech Republic could boast almost 50 years of experience in managing a system of social benefits that could have performed no worse than a comparable *social-democratic* Western welfare state, if not for the foreign intervention and the well-known dysfunctions of the Soviet-style command economy. Moreover, in the mid-1960s Czechoslovakia already reached the social spending level (for cash transfers) estimated at about 12 per cent of the Net Material Product (NMP).[4] It coincided with the slow-down of the economy and resulted mainly from a fresh wave of retirements under very favourable conditions granted to public sector employees during the late 1950s. But the relatively skilful and effective handling of this crisis later served as a useful precedent for both the communist and post-communist social policy reformers as they struggled to keep welfare state finances in balance during the 1980s and the early 1990s (Tomeš, 2002). Much later, the speedy recovery from the crisis of 1997–98, when the Czech government temporarily cut social expenditures (Král, 2003; also see Table 5.1), confirmed the overall impression of the exceptional endurance and effectiveness of the Czech (and Czechoslovak) 'emergency' welfare state irrespective of the type of a political or economic regime.

Sequencing of expansion and retrenchment

Communist Czechoslovakia, like all its neighbours in the Soviet bloc, experienced periods of serious economic and political crises that forced reductions in welfare spending. When the Prague Spring began, however, the worst socioeconomic crisis had already passed and the government had managed to fix a serious pension crisis through a combination of fiscal austerity, benefit cuts and various work incentives for the first large wave of post-war retirees (Tomeš, 2002). Actually, the Czechoslovak welfare state experienced a major retrenchment only twice in its history, in the early Stalinist period, and again in the mid-1960s. These crises, however, were followed by rapid expansion of spending for cash benefits; in the second case also aided by temporary Soviet economic aid and increased productivity of the Czechoslovak economy under renewed political repression (Stevens, 1985, p. 189).

Two decades later the democratic rulers of Czechoslovakia inherited a stagnated economy and deteriorating quality of social benefits and services. Yet because at that time the welfare state was in considerably better shape than anywhere else in the region the new government was able to balance its budget without much social disruption, at least in the short term. The sharp downturn of 1991–92 affected mostly the poorer Slovakia which suffered the brunt of the initial pain of transition amid collapsing heavy industry and large unemployment (see Table 5.1). Freed of the burden of the Slovak crisis after the velvet divorce of January 1993, however, the Czechs soon got a fresh chance to implement necessary changes in the inherited welfare state with much less cost than previously anticipated.

Priorities and timing of the post-communist reforms

In the early days the Czech government apparently had one major social priority – an active labour market policy that focused on subsidized employment for workers, the protection of the basic standards of living and the preservation of nearly universal access to cash transfers and social services. Indeed, this approach worked relatively well into the mid-1990s in large measure thanks to the 'velvet divorce' with Slovakia (Kabaj, 1995; Tomeš, 2002). The standard of living, however, was well protected only for the first year, and already in early 1992 not only Slovaks but also some Czechs began to experience palpable deterioration of social insurance payments. As we can see in Table 5.1 and in later discussion below, the Czechoslovak policymakers, and later also the Czech government approached the anticipated social emergency quite differently than their counterparts in Poland and Hungary. They pursued a much more conservative policy of fiscal restraint, initially even favouring a mild retrenchment rather than escalation of spending.

Moreover, regardless of the growing fiscal burden until the late 2000s the Czechs never seriously pursued pension reform, except during a brief period of economic slowdown in 1997–98 (Král, 2003). Prime Minister Klaus continued to favour the traditional pension system[5] and the lack of budgetary transparency and the centralization of the decision-making process allowed the government to ignore the mounting fiscal deficit that in 2004 reached an unprecedented 12 per cent, the highest level among the new EU members (Deficit (Nadwyżka), 2004). The social policy budget avoided major cuts due

Table 5.1 GDP growth, unemployment rate and social security expenditure of GDP in the Czech Republic, Hungary, Poland and Slovakia, 1990–2002 (in %)

Year	1990	1991	1992	1993	1994	1995	1996	1997	1998	1999	2000	2001	2002
CZECH REPUBLIC													
GDP annual growth	-1.2	-11.5	-0.5	0.1	2.2	5.9	4.3	-0.8	-1	0.5	3.6	2.5	1.9
Unemployment rate	0.8	4.1	2.6	3.5	3.2	2.9	3.5	5.2	6.5	8.7	8.3	8	7.5
Social Security Exp. % GDP	n.d	n.d.	*10.2*	*9.7*	*9.9*	*10.1*	*10.3*	*11.1*	*10.8*	*11.1*	*11.5*	*11.3*	*11.6*
HUNGARY													
GDP annual growth	-3.5	-11.9	-3.1	-0.6	2.9	1.5	1.3	4.6	4.9	4.2	6	4.3	3.8
Unemployment rate	1.9	7.4	9.3	14.5	12.4	12.1	9.9	8.7	7.8	7	6.4	5.7	5.8
Social Security Exp. % GDP	*14.9*	*16.2*	*16.2*	*16.1*	*16*	*13.6*	*12.2*	*11.7*	*n.d*	*n.d*	*n.d*	*n.d*	*n.d.*
Pension & Sick pay exp. % GDP	*10.9*	*11.8*	*11.9*	*12*	*12.3*	*11.1*	*10.2*	*9.8*	*10.2*	*10.2*	*9.8*	*10*	*10.6*
POLAND													
GDP annual growth	11.6	-7	2.6	3.8	5.2	7	6	6.8	4.8	4.1	4	1	1.4
Unemployment rate	6.3	11.9	14.3	16.4	16	14.9	13.2	8.6	10.2	13.4	16.4	18.5	19.8
Social Security Exp. % GDP	*10.8*	*16.2*	*16.7*	*16.4*	*17*	*16.1*	*16*	*16.2*	*14.9*	*15*	*13.7*	*14.6*	*14.7*
SLOVAKIA													
GDP annual growth	-2.5	-14.6	-6.5	-3.7	4.9	6.5	5.8	5.6	4.2	1.5	2	3.2	4.1
Unemployment rate	n.d.	n.d.	10.4	14.4	14.6	13.1	12.8	12.5	15.6	19.2	17.9	18.7	17.9
Social Security Exp. % GDP	*n.d.*	*n.d.*	*n.d.*	*11*	*10.4*	*10.5*	*10.5*	*10.2*	*10.4*	*10.2*	*9.8*	*9.5*	*9.4*

Sources: Data included in this table were collected from various governmental agencies and independent organizations in the four countries. Social Security total includes all pensions, family benefits and sickness & maternity payments for all insured employees. For more detailed information see Inglot 2008. GDP and unemployment figures originated from *Transition Reports* (1991–2007), European Bank for Reconstruction and Development (ERBD).

largely to a fresh influx of foreign investment that helped restart the economy twice already, in 2000, and again following the EU accession in 2004–05. The social reform package of December 2007 proposed by the fragile centre-right coalition of Marek Topolanek came in response to yet another crisis cycle but again focused on rather minor savings in sickness insurance and family payments, to compensate for the growing pension burden.[6] As such it illustrates once again the general continuity in the traditional 'emergency welfare state' with its strong preference for conservative solutions and excessive confidence in the over-centralized micromanagement of national social policy that shuns public input (see also Sirovátka and Rakoczyová, this volume).

Hungary

Welfare discourse

The Hungarian welfare ideology in many ways represents the polar opposite of the Czech experience. Despite the early origins and development of Bismarckian insurance for workers and white-collar professionals in the 1880s–1920s (see Szikra and Tomka, this volume); subsequent political shifts from the extreme right to the radical left prevented an emergence of a clear and forward looking consensus on a national welfare ideology before the Second World War. In the 1950s the Stalinist rulers further damaged any prospects for improvement in this area by imposing especially severe policies of forced industrialization, social cutbacks and discrimination in traditional cash benefits (Tomka, 2004, pp. 78–9).

A temporary settlement on the national welfare doctrine was reached only in the mid-1970s. From now on the uniform social insurance laws covered almost all population, marking the peak achievement of the post-Stalinist order constructed by Janos Kádár after the failed national uprising of 1956. These laws, however, had neither the breadth, consistency nor the transformative character of the Czechoslovak National Insurance Act, but instead reflected a fragile truce between ambitious welfare reformers who envisioned a modernized and wide-ranging 'societal policy' in socialist Hungary, and the economic planners of the New Economic Mechanism (NEM) who preferred the existing, more limited social insurance system under tight fiscal controls (Ferge, 1979). This doctrinal 'hybrid' began to unravel in the mid-1980s under pressure from accelerated economic liberalization. In essence, the late timing, weak political support and internal inconsistency of the Hungarian welfare ideology combined to produce an especially challenging legacy for the new democratic era.

Institutional consolidation

A highly dysfunctional decision-making structure, including a decentralized, fragmented and largely disempowered social insurance bureaucracy, posed another significant challenge. During most of its modern history

Hungary lacked an influential welfare ministry, which in a conventional European (Bismarckian or Beveridgean) system serves as the main conduit and a forceful advocate for social policy. Instead, the welfare state agenda and policy coordination fell under direct supervision of the interior or finance ministries which viewed welfare as low priority for the nation. Meanwhile, trade union bureaucracies and later also local government administrators never acquired enough experience, resources or support at the top echelons of government (and the communist party) to be able to fully implement their ambitious plans of a modern system of social benefits. Meanwhile, the Hungarian welfare state remained heavily 'monetized', with new, more generous cash benefits directed toward the family (childcare assistance) administered by parallel structures outside of the traditional social insurance schemes (Haney, 2002). These schemes competed for limited resources with the traditional social insurance but lacked a stable, sympathetic intermediary at the top of the government (Góralska and Wiktorow, 1988).

In the early 1990s the conservative government of Prime Minister Joseph Antall attempted to strengthen the role of the welfare and labour ministries and helped reintroduce the long-defunct self-government of social insurance. These reforms, adopted in 1994 and supported by the ex-communist trade unions eager to regain political support within the newly created Pension and Health Insurance Boards, soon backfired, however. Paradoxically, the electoral victory of the 'left' (the ex-communist Socialist Party), opened the way for accelerated economic liberalization, pushing aside the incipient ideas of an expanded welfare state. In a nutshell, not only the lack of a permanent ideational consensus (Gedeon, 1995) but also the late development and weak consolidation of the institutional infrastructure created severe obstacles to the reform of the Hungarian 'emergency welfare state' during the 1990s.

Maturation of the welfare state

By the late 1970s and early 1980s Hungary achieved full social insurance coverage against all major risks (Tomka, 2004, Tables 10–12), marking the end of an unprecedented expansion of social spending during the communist era (*c.*12 per cent of GDP). A serious retrenchment effort followed in the early 1980s (Inglot, 2008, Table 3.6, p. 186). The late maturation and belated expansion of coverage, however, meant that the idea of a fully developed, generous and all-encompassing welfare state still remained an unfulfilled expectation for many Hungarians at the time of transition. Cash benefits, for example, had functioned for the most part as two independent spheres of the safety net, the traditional and moderately egalitarian system of 'earned' social insurance transfers such as pensions and sick pay, and the new 'modern' and rather generous income protection schemes for mothers and children (GYES and GYED). While the government occasionally moved resources and sometimes also benefit allocation between the two systems, outside of the narrow circle of social policy reformers no significant challenge arose to either the ideational or the institutional inertia or the policy status quo.

Sequencing of expansion and retrenchment

The early 1990s ushered in an unprecedented explosion of social spending that helped to cushion accelerated transition to democracy and the market (Inglot, 2003, 2008; Vanhuysse, 2006a). In fact it represented a second major period of the widely anticipated and sustained improvement in the scope and the level of social benefits. The previous one began in the initial Kádár period of 1957 and lasted for more than 20 years, until about 1979. This time, however, serious austerity measures began much sooner, in 1995. Yet, just like in the former instance, the actual changes toward the leaner and much less generous welfare state were much less dramatic than what the economic reformers hoped for. The fairly reliable but institutionally deficient and increasingly expensive system of cash transfers was extremely resistant to change. The previous cycle of sharp spending reductions in the final years of communist rule gave way to the steady expansion and growth of expenditures during 1988–1994 (Table 5.1; Inglot, 2008, Table 3.6, p. 186). The outgoing communists and the new democratic rulers both seized upon the pre-existing 'emergency' practices to protect their political interests, which in turn prevented any fundamental reform of the increasingly costly pension system.

Priorities and timing of the major post-communist reforms

In the early 1990s, despite a rapid increase in social security spending during the time of transition and a comparatively high burden of social expenditures, the reform priorities of the Hungarian government focused almost exclusively on the institutional transformation of the welfare state. Just as the emergence of new political parties and competition between them in 1988–89 symbolized the advent of democracy, the reintroduction of social insurance self-government was supposed to showcase the rebirth of a new, more accountable welfare state. Meanwhile, even though the government continued relatively high level of social insurance spending, the prolonged economic recession and increasing inflation (Table 5.1) hit the society particularly hard. These efforts turned out to be grossly inadequate to maintain the standard of living of many beneficiaries of social policy, especially the pensioners. They also exacerbated deep divisions within the ruling elite among the advocates of continued welfare spending, moderates and economic reformers who were especially alarmed by the escalating budget deficit. In contrast to the Czech Republic, where for many years pension reform was relegated to skilful fiscal manoeuvring, the existence of separate and more transparent pension accounting in Hungary made it more difficult to hide even the smallest signs of trouble. Nonetheless, despite increasing international pressures, the government found it impossible to control the pension budget until the late 1990s, and settled instead on smaller cuts in family benefits and education (Table 5.1; Inglot, 2003; Vanhuysse, 2006a).

Several years of political wrangling, resulting again in the political marginalization of both the pension fund and the welfare state, led in 1997–98 to a difficult political compromise on a new three-pillar pension system. We might argue, however, that in the larger perspective, the overall dynamic of the Hungarian welfare state development in the post-communist era has depended much less on the process and the outcomes of the pension reform than many observers have claimed. As Zsuza Ferge and Katalin Tausz (2002) rightly note, we can distinguish roughly two periods of social policy-making in the country: 1989–1994, and since 1995. The continuation of relatively high social spending in the first period was essential for social stability under an especially severe economic downturn (Vanhuysse, 2006a). Since then successive governments led by the ex-communists and the national-liberal politicians regularly attempted and failed to rein in social expenditures in many categories despite the fact that they managed to alter the pension laws and also reverse the institutional decentralization of the early 1990s. The first decade of post-communist social policy also produced little improvement in the social conditions and the quality of social provision in the country as a whole (Ferge and Tausz, 2002). Thus, by the late 2000s, with budget deficits still surpassing 6 per cent of GDP (Deficit (Nadwyżka), 2004) the traditional Hungarian *emergency welfare state* remained very much alive, with little new evidence of convergence with Western European models of social provision.

Poland

Welfare discourse

The Polish welfare doctrine originated in the Great Depression and the political turmoil of the 1930s. A series of laws adopted during 1933–35 consolidated the emerging ideology of a paternalistic welfare state, built on the imperial Bismarckian foundations by the followers of Marshall Józef Piłsudski, or the so-called 'Sanacja' regime. Deeply conservative and inegalitarian in character, this doctrine rested on enhanced government guarantees and political controls over the ailing system of social insurance benefits. Post-war Stalinist planners skilfully adopted this 'statist' welfare ideology to their needs and rebuilt the post-war welfare state in a similar, centralized fashion but with greatly reduced cash benefits. As elsewhere in the region, 'Sovietization' (including union-led decentralization) of social policy was tried in Poland, but it happened late, in 1954–55, and lasted only briefly. More significantly, however, in the subsequent decades the Polish communists tried to reinvent their own national welfare doctrine in a major way twice: first in the 1960s, through a partial return to a conservative

Bismarckian model, and again during the 1970s, in a much more ambitious attempt to develop a more modernized and universalistic 'socialist welfare state'.

Still, the basic tenets of the conservative model of social protection survived almost intact. The failed effort to upgrade social policy during the 1970s left an especially bitter legacy of unfulfilled social expectations as the country plunged into long economic and political crisis from which it began to seriously recover only in 1992. The Polish post-communist governments seem to have learned a crucial lesson from the past experience, since they all defended the long-established principle of state guarantees and controls that often substituted for the lack of generous and universal benefits. Instead, social privileges and bonuses for the already most favoured groups of state employees (miners, steelworkers, railroad workers, the security apparatus and so on), and now also for private farmers, continued to expand as part of a larger effort to guarantee of social stability and peace (Inglot, 1995, 2003, 2008; also Vanhuysse, 2006a and this volume).

Institutional consolidation

The early Polish welfare state has been remarkably successful in the establishment and consolidation of the decision-making structure and the administration of the basic social insurance programmes. The creation of a unified country out of diverse elements of three different imperial bureaucracies (German, Austro-Hungarian and Russian) gave the nation-builders necessary experience and confidence to confront future emergencies, including those in the sphere of social policy. Already at the outset of the Second World War Poland had a powerful and well-managed welfare ministry and one centralized Social Insurance Institution (Zakład Ubezpieczeń Społecznych – ZUS). The latter also run hospitals, clinics and rehabilitation centres. Its large assembly of trained professionals was essential for the post-war reconstruction of the welfare state in terms of both revenue generation and administration of expenditures (Jackowiak, 1991).

Throughout the whole post-war period the ZUS survived repeated attempts at institutional reform relatively intact. First, the Stalinists tried but failed to eliminate this institution in the mid-1950s. Their policies quickly backfired, as the government-controlled unions themselves asked for the re-establishment of ZUS as the stable guarantor of social payments to all key occupations. Second, during the 1970s, many of its duties such as sick pay and family payments were temporarily transferred to the state enterprises, resulting in escalating costs and declining quality of social provision. Finally, after the fall of communism, the ZUS again came under attack, this time as a 'relic' of the old, overly centralized Marxist-Leninist regime (Opinie Do Senackiego Projektu..., 1992), but in the end it also survived these and the other further restructuring attempts rather well. This vast government bureaucracy successfully resisted not only the most controversial reform proposals (the creation of parallel structures that would take over revenue collection and payment of key social benefits) but also moderate changes agreed upon by all major political parties (technological modernization, the upgrading of social services for the disabled and increased democratic controls by the parliament). The continued importance and political clout of the ZUS is best illustrated by the latest government proposal that gives it considerable power in the administration of the second, privatized pension pillar introduced in 1999.[7]

Maturation of the welfare state

The Polish welfare state reached its peak social insurance coverage only in the early 1980s. The timing of this development was especially precarious because it coincided with the worst economic downturn in post-war history, a severe political crisis of the regime, and also the highest level of social spending in relation to the national wealth (12 per cent of GDP). In this aspect, we can notice a striking resemblance to Hungary, where social expenditures rose above 10 per cent of GDP at approximately the same time. Nevertheless, the Polish situation turned out to be more severe, both in terms of the depth of the crisis and the type of government response. While the Hungarian crisis accumulated gradually throughout the decade and engendered a more cautious and incremental reaction from the communist rulers, the Polish debacle started and ended in rather an abrupt fashion. At first it appeared that the martial law regime of General Wojciech Jaruzelski would quickly restore stability to the economy and the welfare state under the cover of political repression, in a manner resembling Pinochet-style, market-oriented policies in Chile, or perhaps in a milder form reminiscent of the Kádár period in Hungary.[8] Instead, social expenditures remained at a high level through the mid-1980s, with all serious efforts to reform the welfare state effectively suspended until 1989.

The incoming Solidarity government of Prime Minister Tadeusz Mazowiecki inherited a fully mature and relatively well-developed welfare state that nonetheless required urgent reforms. The 'round-table' agreements that ultimately led to the restoration of democracy empowered the newly reconstituted independent trade unions (Solidarity and the government-backed official unions) to interfere with decision-making at the highest levels. To the regret of many reform-minded experts within a small but vibrant social policy community, the idea of 'democratic' consultations with the unions quickly morphed again into a traditional pattern of dispersed and particularistic bargaining over special occupational interests in defence of the entrenched social privileges.[9]

Sequencing of expansion and retrenchment

Among all four countries of East Central Europe, Poland appears to have been the most prone to a specific pattern of cyclical development where political and economic crises usually coincide with sudden increases in social spending. This was the case immediately after the Second World War, during the post-Stalinist recovery of the late 1950s, the early 1970s, and again during the Solidarity period of 1980–81. Conversely, as social peace ensued and the economy began to grow again, the government almost immediately tried to slow down or reduce welfare spending (see Table 5.1). This pattern of social policy development severely weakened the Polish welfare state, further enhancing its particular 'emergency' characteristics. While old programmes such as pensions grew rapidly and new schemes such as family benefits and childcare were later added, the key policy-making traditions and tendencies remained largely intact.

The Polish social insurance system, originally built to confront a serious crisis of national survival after the First World War, and once again during the Second World War, was repeatedly tested throughout the rest of the century. In the light of past developments, for example, the construction of the solid administrative infrastructure (ZUS) and also previous experiences in handling various crises, we can understand much better why it performed so well during the most difficult early years of the post-communist transformation, 1990–92. As many studies have shown during this time the elderly were relatively well protected (Inglot, 1995, 2003, 2008; Vanhuysse, 2006a), yet at a very heavy price as the total spending climbed to unprecedented levels of 16–17 per cent of the GDP and remained high for many years to come (Table 5.1). The slowing economy eventually forced mild retrenchments in the late 1990s and early 2000s, but, as had happened before on numerous occasions, the final results were disappointing. If we consider the fact that the farmers' insurance now remains mostly hidden from view in a separate government account and many pension entitlements (for the military, police and so on) are no longer financed directly by the ZUS budget, the total social security spending still remains at an extremely worrisome level of about 18 per cent of GDP.

Priorities and timing of post-communist reform

Contrary to what most observers have argued, the post-communist social policy reform in Poland, as opposed to the economic reform, was neither radical in its goals nor deeply transformative in its consequences. Just as in Hungary, it can be roughly divided into two major stages. The first stage lasted until 1995 and involved intensive efforts to protect the living standards of all major social groups during the shock therapy. Available data shows that this was a rather successful operation, especially with regard to cash transfers for the major occupational groups (Inglot, 1995, 2003, 2008). We must add, however, that the delivery of these social programmes relied almost exclusively on the inherited institutions of the welfare state (welfare ministry, ZUS) which traditionally performed well under crises. Meanwhile, outside of the establishment of a new network of basic public assistance and unemployment protection and the recalibration of pension payments in 1991, in the first few years there was little momentum toward major systemic reforms in social policy.

The second stage of welfare transformation, from the mid- to late 1990s, focused almost exclusively on the long-delayed old-age pension reform. The new 'pillar' of privately invested pensions created an additional 'layer' of support installed on top of the restructured government scheme. Undoubtedly, as in Hungary, the continuing heavy pension burden and the ensuing budget deficit made it difficult for any government to ignore both internal and external calls for reform (Orenstein, this volume). In the end, however, a domestic political compromise between the more conservative (ZUS, welfare ministry bureaucracies) and more reformist (the finance ministry and key policymakers in the government, including the new minister of labour) factions, appears to have been domestically generated rather than forged under foreign pressure (see also Haggard and Kaufman, this volume). As many Polish and international experts concede (Batty, 1997) the reform as a whole aimed first and foremost to shore up the existing system, for example, generating long-term savings for the government, and not to radically transform the welfare state and its doctrine of social support. During the 2000s, despite repeated calls for radical, neo-liberal reforms, the government (Ministry of Labour), the ZUS, and also the major union lobbies, have remained the main guarantors and the most significant opponents of further changes that could undermine traditional state paternalism and alter the 'emergency' (crisis-managing) character of the Polish welfare state in a meaningful way.[10]

Slovakia

Welfare discourse

In 1993, as a newly founded state, Slovakia faced a very different challenge than its East European neighbours when it tried to define a national welfare doctrine for the post-communist era. The country inherited a well-developed branch of the federal Czechoslovak welfare state that had been officially decentralized since 1968. But in reality, the Czechs actually shaped the country's social policy from the start from within the central ministry in Prague and they in fact were the real successors of the dissolved federation. The Slovaks, who suffered a much greater pain of transition from communist rule (Table 5.1), had to quickly find a new direction and a new identity for what now became their own national welfare state.

The search for a 'genuine' Slovak welfare doctrine also went through two distinct phases, the first lasting from 1993 to approximately 2000, and the second beginning in 2000. Initially, disappointed by the results of a mixture of social-democratic and liberal market policies of the early Czechoslovak era, the nationalist government of Prime Minister Vladimír Mečiar opted for the so-called 'third way' (Mečiar, 1993). This approach was based on a specific version of a social-democratic ideology of 'social solidarity' with a strong preference for corporatist governance (see Ministry of Labour..., 2001). It highlighted the role of the trade unions in the large industrial sector and among public employees; a politically influential group that made up the core of Mečiar's constituency and the mainstay of his party, the HZDS. In connection with this an attempt was made to translate the crucial core of the original Czechoslovak welfare doctrine, or more precisely its egalitarian, social democratic component, into a national Slovak welfare ideology which now emphasized both traditional social insurance (pensions) and the reorganized family benefits and public assistance (*statni socialni podpory*) for the poor (Potůček and Radičová, 1998).

In August 2000 the new, more openly pro-Western and pro-European government of Miroslav Dziurinda moved to radical redefine the national welfare ideology (Ministry of Labour..., 2001). Following in the footsteps of Poland and Hungary it proposed a pro-market vision of an accelerated and simultaneous privatization of the country's economy along with a radical retrenchment of its social safety net. In reality this new vision of the Slovak welfare state, complete with multipillar pensions and substantially reduced, means-tested benefits, closely resembled the Hungarian model of the mid-1990s. We can also argue that the severe institutional weaknesses (lack of domestic social policy expertise) and grave political mistakes of the Mečiar government (anti-democratic style, nationalist rhetoric, and conflicts with the pro-Western president) in the first decade of independence created a serious crisis of confidence in the ruling elite, preparing the ground for a possible path-departure in the future, although not necessarily the end of the post-Czechoslovak 'emergency' welfare state altogether.

Institutional consolidation

Throughout the 1990s Slovakia has remained severely disadvantaged in terms of policy leadership and necessary social policy expertise (see Radičová and Potůček, 1998). Early on the Bratislava branch of the federal Ministry of Labour was converted into the national Ministry of Labour, Social Affairs, and the Family (*Ministerstvo Práce, Sociálni Vecí a Rodiny*) while the republican branch of the Czechoslovak Social Security Agency in charge of pensions became the National Social Insurance Agency (*Všeobecná Narodná Poist'ovňa*). Soon after, however, the new Slovak welfare state began to break away from the Czechoslovak traditions. The National Social Insurance Agency was granted independent status under a tripartite board, chaired by the minister of social affairs. The financing of social insurance was now based on three separate funds – pensions, sickness and health. Furthermore, in 1995 the agency split into two entities, Social Insurance Agency (*Socialna Poist'ovna*), dealing with pensions and sickness insurance, and the Health Insurance Agency (*Zdravotna Poist'ovna*), in charge of health care, now closely resembling the Hungarian rather than the Czech model.

The formal institutional reorganization alone hardly constitutes a radical break with the past. Still, as some Slovak scholars argue (Butorá and Butorová, 1993; Potůček and Radičová, 1998; Jakoby, 2002) a combination of an accelerated nationalist push for a final separation from the Czechs and the lack of sufficient domestic bureaucratic capacity and expertise seems to have opened up the way for the adoption of new, foreign-inspired models.[11] We have to keep in mind, however, that in reality the Ministry of Labour in Bratislava remained firmly in charge of the new welfare state as a whole, mainly through the chairmanship of the supervisory board but also through many informal channels of fiscal policy, reminiscent of the old Czechoslovak system.[12]

Maturation of the welfare state

In the post-war period the Slovak population benefited rather substantially from the Czechoslovak National Insurance Act of 1948. During 1946–1950 the number of persons covered by pension insurance grew by almost 130 per cent, as compared to 46 per cent in the Czech lands, and about 61 per cent for Czechoslovakia as a whole. This was, of course, partly attributable to rapid Stalinist-era industrialization in Slovakia, but we must note that already in 1948 pension coverage increased there by as much as 87 per cent. Initially the communist rulers, eager to consolidate power in the aftermath of the February 1948 coup, also greatly expanded social pensions that bene- fited mostly the much poorer population in the eastern part of the country (Inglot, 2008, Tables 2.4 and 2.5, pp. 74–5).

In terms of the total social spending, however, the two parts of the coun- try did not reach 'maturity' at the same time. Overall, it took Slovakia about two decades to catch up to the Czech lands in the area of pensions. The overall level of spending climbed very rapidly only in the aftermath of the Soviet invasion of 1968. Previously, at the peak of the maturation of the Czechoslovak welfare system and during the economic crisis of 1963, the gap between the pension spending in the Czech lands and Slovakia was still considerable but it declined significantly by the later 1980s. In the final year of communist rule, 1989, the Slovak social safety net apparently came out almost even in terms of funding for both federal republics (Inglot, 2008, Tables 4.2 and 4.4, pp. 229, 240).

Sequencing of expansion and retrenchment

The Slovak welfare state experienced several significant periods of expan- sion that generally overlapped with the trends in the Czech lands and Czechoslovakia as a whole, but the two nations differed in the emphasis and the long-term impact of expansion and retrenchment. After initial rapid growth Slovakia was severely hurt by substantial cutbacks in pen- sion spending (especially social pensions) and sick pay during the harshest years of Stalinism, 1951–1953. However, social spending quickly rebounded, reaching a rather high, peak level of 12.3 per cent in 1963. In Slovakia, as opposed to the Czech lands, the emphasis has begun to shift also quite visibly to family policy. Following the deep economic downturn of the mid- to late 1960s, the Soviet invasion of August 1968, and the 'federalization' of Czechoslovakia, all social spending levels rebounded again, surpassing the 1963 top figure almost a decade later, in 1972 (Inglot, 2008, Table 4.4).

During this crucial period of crisis and Soviet-imposed 'stabilization' of Czechoslovakia, Slovak maternity benefits recovered by 1968 and expanded quite rapidly during the 1970s. It took a full decade, however, to recoup the total losses caused by the fiscal austerity of the 1960s. Slovak family policy spending peaked at above 4 per cent of the NMP in 1963 but reached this level again only 20 years later, during the time of the rise of the Solidarity movement in Poland in 1980–81. Pension and sickness spending also reached rather alarming levels, especially given the stagnant economy. We must note that by 1985, for example, Slovakia was spending more than 9 per cent of NMP for pensions, catching up quickly with the Czechs, who already had reached this point in the mid-1960s, only to suffer a long stagnation in payments in the following decades.

Finally, as we compare previous periods of crisis and retrenchment in the still united Czechoslovakia, it is hard to ignore parallel developments of the late 1960s and the early 1990s. In both cases the federal state made a concentrated effort to maintain a stable safety net in the traditionally poorer Slovakia. In the 1960s, however, the first severe welfare state retrenchment happened there much more quickly and was experienced more painfully than in the Czech lands. Still, Slovakia became relatively privileged later on, even gaining a slight edge in most categories, especially in the area of family policy under the Husak regime. However, in the last days of communist rule again Slovakia suffered the brunt of an attempted cutback in social spending. In 1990 under the new democratic government the trend continued, with the welfare effort dropping by almost a full percentage point, twice the rate of the Czech lands. A year later the federal government apparently made a genuine attempt to remedy this. Slovak expenditure for cash transfer rose in conjunction with a massive consumer subsidy conversion plan (Tomeš, 2002; see also Table 5.1), whereas the Czech spending continued to fall. In the long run, however, this situation was unsustainable, due mainly to a continued economic downturn that primarily hurt the Slovak lands. In many ways, we can argue that the roller coaster spending pattern helped justify the push for independence (Mečiar, 1993) but, as we have seen above, was unable to delay austerity for long once the Slovaks were now forced to confront the crisis on their own.

Prioritizing and timing of the post-communist reforms

The first Mečiar government focused primarily on institutional reforms judged necessary for the process of state and nation-building in the country. Meanwhile, until at least the mid-1990s, we could notice significant policy continuity, primarily in family-related benefits. As we recall, these benefits played a significant role during previous crises of communist rule. In the early 1990s the federal (Czechoslovak) government also attempted, with mixed success, to maintain a stable level of family-oriented payments in the Slovak lands. As the economy gradually struggled to recover, during 1993–1995 the newly independent Slovaks targeted pensions for limited reductions, while family and maternity allowances remained relatively generous and widely accessible. The situation began to reverse in 1995–1996, when the economy began to slow down again and Mečiar suffered his first temporary political defeat. Thus a combination of economic and political considerations, for example, the fear of industrial unrest among the key constituency of the HZDS-led coalition, seems to have contributed to the serious reassessment of national welfare priorities. In addition, the World Bank pressure for more means-tested and 'rationalized' family benefit structure appears to have played a role as well (Jakoby, 2002).

In the late 1990s Slovakia entered a second stage of policy reform with a strong emphasis on the maintenance of stable pension spending levels at about 7.5 per cent of GDP (Table 5.1) and gradual reduction of family payments (allowances for children, parental benefits and so on). The latter was accomplished mainly by shifting the responsibility to the local welfare agencies. For this reason the actual extent of the spending reductions for family policy may not be as great as evidenced by the figures provided by the Social Insurance Agency since their budget no longer funds many of the payments that are subject to strict means-testing. This general trend seems to have continued until the late 2000s, now under a left-centre coalition government.

Even though the fall of the Mečiar regime ushered in a new, pro-market era in Slovak social policy, it appears that regardless of a much more rapid effort in the area of institutional reform, change on the policy level remains uncertain, with noticeable influence of the past legacies still prevailing in many areas. For instance, while the new government placed a much greater emphasis on pension reform, for example, introducing the second privatized pillar in January 2003, apparently it gave in to social pressure with the return to a more universal, Czechoslovak-style system of family support. In 2002 it reintroduced the old-style payments along with slightly more strict work and income requirements. As the Slovak experts themselves acknowledge, this illustrates the central dilemma of the current government: how to best reconcile the more traditional 'motivational aspects of social policy' with the newer idea of ensuring the 'flexibility of the labor market' (Stanek et al., 2007). Recent announcements of the Slovak government about the possible 'renationalization' of the private pension funds raise serious doubts about the lasting effect of the neo-liberal policy course set in motion by the Dziurinda cabinet in the early 2000s (Palata, 2008). Instead it raises the prospect of an Argentinian-style 'cyclical' process of crisis decision-making that in this case may be somewhat lessened only by more decisive EU intervention. Therefore the judgement is still out whether or not the retrenchment of the early 2000s, in combination of the state-building efforts of the previous decade, will actually constitute a lasting, path-departing change that could decouple Slovakia once and for all from the legacy of the Czechoslovak 'emergency welfare state'.

Conclusion: The future of the post-communist 'emergency welfare states' in the Czech Republic, Hungary, Poland and Slovakia

Before 1989 several resilient and adaptable 'emergency' welfare states had already emerged in Central and Eastern Europe. In all cases, the pre-existing institutional infrastructure absorbed the initial shock of transition relatively well but in the longer term every country had to adjust its policy-making bodies, bureaucracies, and modus operandi to the rapidly changing political and socioeconomic environment, domestically, regionally (EU) and globally. Still, almost everywhere, with the possible exception of Slovakia in the early 2000s, we could observe clear continuity in terms of the welfare discourse, institutional consolidation, and also in maintaining a rather destabilizing pattern of alternating expansion and retrenchment of social expenditures.

The first two elements to a large extent augmented the negative effects of the third one. Generally, all four countries fared quite well in terms of upholding the accumulated social insurance rights and providing immediate assistance to the jobless under extremely difficult conditions of economic collapse and rising unemployment. Yet they did so in different ways. Czechoslovakia, and its direct successor, the Czech Republic, where the welfare state matured early and learned how to manage previous crises under tight centralized control during the communist period, turned out to be much more resilient, if not generous in absolute terms, than Hungary and Poland, both countries where greater political and economic liberalization preceded the ultimate collapse of the old regime. All of these countries have also differed substantially in terms of prioritizing and timing of attempted reform in different segments of the welfare state such as pensions and family policy. Nonetheless, despite their differences they all continued to function in an emergency mode throughout the 1990s and early 2000s, drawing sharp contrast from much more stable and predictable welfare regimes of Western Europe.

As Alfio Cerami rightly argues in his theoretical contribution to this volume, more attention to the parallel mechanisms of social policy development allows us to better understand the seeming paradox of simultaneous path-dependence and path-departure across different countries and their own social benefit schemes. Furthermore, I agree with Pieter Vanhuysse's claim that 'power politics' must be seriously considered as the crucial force shaping the nature of the post-communist welfare state but I place much more emphasis on the historical and institutional opportunities and constraints that influence the potential agents of change and their relationship with the public. In other words, the study of the four CEE countries illustrates the need for a multidimensional approach that connects the examination of the former communist bloc to the mainstream scholarship, but also, as Haggard and Kaufman note in this volume, recognizes the distinct processes that make these welfare states worthy of separate investigation as new, emerging democracies and economies burdened with the consequential legacies of communist rule.

This chapter has focused for the most part on the crucial period prior to EU accession but contemporary researchers are likely to wonder whether or not we are witnessing a second, no less crucial stage of transformation of these welfare states in the post-2004 era. Indeed, several new elements increasingly point in a new direction. On the one hand, the economic expansion of the private sector and also increased emigration following the EU accession (especially in case of Poland) has provided an important, if only temporary, cushion for many vulnerable groups. In short, these groups tend to be less organized and offer less resistance to social cutbacks since they no longer rely as much on traditional government-provided employment and social support.[13] On the other hand, the EU has unquestionably provided not only more long-term developmental support but also an important 'psychological-legal' comfort zone for each country. Citizens and pro-welfare politicians are now confident that the basic rules and norms of social protection will be in place, even if in many cases implementation of crucial improvements in everyday life continues to lag behind. In essence, the legal culture of the EU by itself creates a counter-trend to neo-liberalism. It also simultaneously emboldens powerful pressure groups and opens new opportunities for less influential individuals and civil society groups to seek broader social rights and protections.

It is true that the emergence of a new, large group of middle-class owners/ entrepreneurs who usually tend to resist welfare state burdens may turn out to have a negative effect on the quantity and quality of welfare provision in each country. As the Czech case has shown, however, this may not necessarily usher in radical market liberalism and fiscal restraint on the national scale. In many cases family business owners do not so much resist the heavy burden of welfare taxation but rather seek better terms for their incorporation into a relatively generous network of privileges already enjoyed by the hired employees in the national insurance systems such as, for example, sick pay provision, extended maternity leave and early retirement (Tymorek, 2008). Finally, the weakness of labour in the new private sector of the economy (Crowley and Ost, 2001; Ost, 2005) has not yet resulted in the emergence of influential business lobbies[14] that would be inclined to challenge the social policy consensus (based on the traditional state paternalism of the early twentieth century) in a meaningful way. If this happens we might be able to argue that the CEE countries will have reached a true milestone on the road to becoming more conventional European welfare regimes rather than continue to function in a typical way as better adapted but still well-entrenched, post-communist 'emergency welfare states'.

6
The Transformation of Welfare Systems in the Baltic States: Estonia, Latvia and Lithuania*

Jolanta Aidukaite

Introduction

This chapter aims to give a general overview of the main problems and reform challenges of social protection in Estonia, Latvia and Lithuania since the collapse of the Soviet regime. Baltic social policy offers an interesting case study, as the experience of Soviet authoritarian rule between 1940 and 1990–91 had an impact on their subsequent trajectories, while post-communist economic and social restructuring has coincided with population ageing and the increasing impact of globalization and Europeanization in recent years. The Baltic economies have experienced rapid economic expansion during the last years of the transition (2000–2007) and had the fastest growing GDPs in Europe (see Table 6.1).[1] Consequently, employment opportunities have increased in the Baltic region and unemployment has decreased considerably. However, despite comparatively good economic indicators and GDP growth, Baltic societies spend much less on social protection as compared to the EU-15 and the EU-27 average. The share of GDP spent on social protection in the three Baltic states (12–13 per cent) is among the lowest in the European Union (Keune, 2008, p. 13). Thus, it is not surprising that the income inequalities expressed as a 'Gini coefficient' are also the highest in these societies, ranging from 36 in Estonia and Lithuania to almost 38 in Latvia (Table 6.2). The absolute poverty rate is non-existent in the EU-15 countries and also in the Czech Republic, Slovenia and Hungary, but it is still present in the three Baltic states. With regard to the relative poverty rate, again the Baltic states are the leaders, with Lithuania (29 per cent) having the highest relative poverty in the EU at present. Furthermore, the Baltic states are among the new EU member states with the highest share of a shadow economy. The share of GDP in the shadow economy amounts to 39 per cent in Latvia, 38 per cent in Estonia and 30 per cent in Lithuania. Only Romania (51 per cent) has a bigger shadow economy than Estonia and Latvia. Lithuania, however, has

Table 6.1 Total expenditure on social protection (SP) (current prices, percentage of GDP), minimum wage (MW) and real GDP growth rate (GR) in the Baltic states (%)

	1998	1999	2000	2001	2002	2003	2004	2005	2006	2007	2008
Estonia (SP)	–	–	14.0	13.1	12.7	12.6	13.0	12.7	12.4	–	–
Latvia (SP)	–	17.2	15.3	14.3	13.9	13.8	12.9	12.4	12.2(p)	–	–
Lithuania (SP)	–	16.4	15.8	14.7	14.0	13.5	13.3	13.1	13.2(p)	–	–
EU-15 (SP)	–	26.9	26.8	27.0	27.3	27.7	27.6	27.7(p)	27.5(p)	–	–
Estonia (MW)	–	–	–	–	118.0	138.0	159.0	172.0	191.7	230.1	278.0
Latvia (MW)	–	74.7	84.4	89.3	107.0	116.0	121.0	116.0	129.2	172.0	229.4
Lithuania (MW)	–	91.7	106.3	120.0	120.0	125.0	125.0	145.0	159.3	173.8	231.7
Estonia (GR)	–	-0.1	9.6	7.7	7.8	7.1	7.5	9.2	10.4	6.3	-1.3(f)
Latvia (GR)	–	3.3	6.9	8.0	6.5	7.2	8.7	10.6	11.9	10.2	-0.8(f)
Lithuania (GR)	–	-1.5	4.2	6.7	6.9	10.2	7.4	7.8	7.8	8.9	3.8(f)
EU-15 (GR)	–	3.0	3.9	1.9	1.2	1.2	2.3	1.8	2.9	2.7	1.1(f)
EU-27 (GR)	–	3.0	3.9	2.0	1.2	1.3	2.5	2.0	3.1	2.9	1.4(f)

Note: (p) = Provisional value; (f) = Forecast.
Source: Eurostat (http://epp.eurostat.ec.europa.eu/).

Table 6.2   Basic economic and social indicators of the Baltic states

	GDP per capita, PPS, 2008	Relative median poverty gap, % in 2006	UN Gini Index (per capita)	Ratio of richest 20% to poorest 20% (2006)	Absolute poverty rate (%), $2.15/day, 2002/2003	Shadow economy, % of GDP, 2004/ 2005
Estonia	70.5[f]	22	35.8	5.5	5	38.2
Latvia	58.6[f]	25	37.7	7.9	3	39.4
Lithuania	62.3[f]	29	36.0	6.3	4	30.2
EU-15	110.9[f]	22	29.0	4.7	0	18.2
EU-27	100.0	22	30.0	4.8	3.4	24.6

Note: (f) = Forecast.
Source: Eurostat; UNDP, 2008; World Bank, 2005; Noelke, 2008; Schneider, 2007; own calculations.

a smaller shadow economy than Latvia, Estonia, Bulgaria and Romania (for more details see Aidukaite, 2009). One of the reasons, according to Chandler (2002), why the shadow economy in the three Baltic states is more pervasive than in the other EU member states is that people in the Baltics believe that the governments do not deserve financial support, since they provide poor-quality services. Indeed, it could be argued that the low quality of public social services and the relatively low level of social benefits contribute to this situation, and not only in the Baltics, but also in other post-communist societies. The 2002 opinion survey carried out in all three Baltic states indicated that overwhelming majorities (about 90 per cent) of the citizens in the three Baltic states believe that the government does not guarantee the social security of its citizens, and they have to rely more on the market or the family for support (Aidukaite, 2005). Furthermore, Estonia, Latvia and Lithuania are among the European nations whose citizens are most dissatisfied with their health-care systems and health (EFILWC, 2004).

A number of scholars (Bohle, 2007; Guogis and Koht, 2009; Lendvai, 2008) have attempted to group Estonia, Latvia and Lithuania into the neo-liberal welfare state regime, according to their low levels of social spending, high-income inequalities and low decommodification. Why do the Baltic states, despite impressive economic indicators, perform less well with regard to social indicators and social effort? The aim of explaining welfare state development in affluent capitalist democracies has spawned a plethora of welfare state theories and approaches. The emergence, variation and development of the welfare state have been explained by the degree of organized labour and the legacy of the politics, where strong left-wing party power ensures more comprehensive and universal social policies (for example, Esping-Andersen, 1990; Korpi, 1983; Korpi and Palme, 2003). Other important explanatory factors are demographic change, affluence and the economic performance (e.g. Wilensky, 2002), the importance of previous policy choices (path-dependency), and the strength of interest groups in the welfare state (for example, Pierson, 1994). Towards the end of the twentieth century, the impact of globalization (Deacon, 1997) and Europeanization (Kvist and Saari, 2007) has started to gain ground, in particular when Eastern European social policy is discussed. With few exceptions (for example, Aidukaite, 2004; Cerami, 2006), relatively few attempts have, however, been made to test or develop welfare state theories on postcommunist countries. Few studies have emphasized in one way or another the importance of adopting a multidimensional approach to studying social policy development in Central and Eastern Europe (CEE). In my previous study of the three Baltic states (Aidukaite, 2004), I have suggested studying social policy as if embedded in the societal, economic, political, cultural and historical aspects of a given society. As Granovetter's embeddedness approach (1992) implies, the behaviour and institutions to be analysed are so constrained by the ongoing social relations, that to construe them as independent is a serious misunderstanding. Cerami (2006) has suggested the neo-classical social policy approach to studying the CEE welfare states. This approach emphasizes not only historical legacies, culture, institutional structures, political organizations and social interaction, but also focuses on the strategic interactions of economic, political and social actors as well as the set of formal and informal rules which govern human behaviour. Yet, in this volume Cerami suggests viewing the welfare state change as the outcome of interactions among actors, institutions, interest groups and ideas and also within each of these domains. In addressing the initiatives above, this chapter takes a multidimensional approach to social policy development and reviews social policy change in the Baltic states, taking into account the major explanatory variables of welfare state research: previous policy choices (path-dependency), the legacy of the politics and organized labour, the impact of the economy, and the impact of globalization and Europeanization. These variables do not compete with each other but, on the contrary, form a causal complexity from which a specific outcome (welfare state change) is derived. Furthermore, these variables also imply that the ideas, actors, institutions and norms are behind them.

The Baltic type of welfare: previous policy choices and their impact on the present

The first social security programmes in the three Baltic states date back to as early as 1919 (Aidukaite, 2004; Kore, 2005; Rajevska, 2005). Social security during the interwar period (1919–1940) resembled the

Bismarckian system of social insurance. However, the number of insured people was low and only permanent state employees had the right to a state pension. The money that went into the pension fund was mainly obtained from employer and employee contributions. Farmers were totally excluded from the social insurance system (Macinskas, 1971). After the Second World War, Estonia, Latvia and Lithuania were incorporated into the Soviet Union and were subjected to the same social policy regulations as the whole empire. The social policy was organized through employment in the USSR. Everybody had to work and everybody was insured for all social risks. The social security system's coverage was universal, albeit with rather low benefit levels. Everybody was guaranteed security in all cases of loss of working capacity, old age, invalidity, illness and the loss of the family breadwinner. This extensive social policy (full employment, free education and health care) and social security, with its huge redistributive mechanism, promoted class equality among the various social groups (Aidukaite, 2004). Some studies (for example, Deacon, 1992), however, indicate that there was an upper class, namely the so-called 'nomenclature' that profited more from the benefits of the authoritarian welfare state than did other social groups. Other studies (Hartl and Večernik, 1992) have also underlined the negative aspects of the former Soviet system, such as no indexation of benefits, the poor quality of health care and other services and housing shortages. Nevertheless, according to Deacon (1992), there was job security for many in the former Communist countries, workers' wages represented a high percentage of the average wage, and cheap housing and free health care were available to everybody.

All the features of the Soviet system were present in the social protection systems of the independent states of Estonia, Latvia and Lithuania in 1991, and they were transformed gradually. Estonia was the swiftest, and Lithuania the slowest, in destroying the Soviet-era social security system. In general terms, the social security system of Estonia and Latvia can be described as a mixture of the elements taken from the basic security (where eligibility is based on contributions or citizenship, and flat-rate benefits are provided) and corporatist (with eligibility based on labour force participation, and earnings-related benefits) models. Weak elements of the targeted model (where eligibility is based on proven need, and the level of benefits is minimal) can be found too. Lithuania has seen a combination of corporatist and the basic security models, however, with much stronger elements of the targeted model in the social security system (Aidukaite, 2006). Nevertheless, in all three countries the current system has become less universal and comprehensive. Housing has become the private responsibility of the individual. Currently, citizens have a choice, either to use public health-care services, financed through the sickness fund (obligatory health-care insurance financed through the social insurance contributions and state subsidies) or to visit private health-care clinics or hospitals that have no agreements with the sickness funds, requiring full coverage for their services from the patients. Student fees have been introduced at the universities in the Baltic states, and private universities have appeared, offering alternative degrees and professions compared to those from the public higher education. The ideology has shifted from a full, state commitment to the safety of everybody in every situation to providing a safety net for its population, where people's primary responsibility is for their own welfare (Aidukaite, 2004).

Overall, the welfare systems of the three Baltic states can be referred to as a distinct post-communist welfare regime. This regime deviates from the other three delineated by Esping-Andersen (1990) and is already gaining acceptance within comparative welfare state research (see Aidukaite, 2004, 2009; Cerami, 2006; Deacon, 2000). Generally, the post-communist regime is characterized as having traits from both the liberal and conservative corporatist regimes as well as some distinct features of the post-communist societies. These features are as follows: a high take-up rate of social security, but relatively low benefit levels; the experience of the Soviet type of welfare state, which implies still deeply embedded signs of solidarity and universalism; and a low level of trust in the state institutions. The Baltic states, specifically, exhibit a number of particular features. Namely, insurance-based schemes play a major part in the social protection system and this is not surprising seeing as the former Soviet system was based on employment. However, the same programmes cover everyone. In many cases, universal benefits still overshadow means-tested ones. Nevertheless, the relatively low benefit levels do not create enough incentives for people to be honest and declare their income for taxation. Even if the state plays a vital role in protecting its citizens from social risks, the market and the family are still two of the most important agents for guaranteeing an adequate standard of living for the population. These three countries have well-developed and extensive social security systems which cover everyone in need in various social risks (Aidukaite, 2004, 2006). Nevertheless, the benefit levels are low. For instance, the replacement rate for the old-age pension is maintained at low levels and accounts for only 30–40 per cent of the gross average wage (Müller, 2002a). This is low by Western European standards. The situation is similar for other benefits such as unemployment, universal child allowances and other social benefits.[2] It also needs to be kept in mind that in the Baltic states the general level of wages is low compared to the 'old' EU countries. Thus, for example, as Regnard (2007) demonstrates, among the member states and the candidate countries statutory minimum wages, in January 2007, varied between €92 and €1,570 per month. In the three Baltic states, the monthly minimum amounted to €230 in Estonia, €174 in Lithuania and €172 in Latvia. Even when the minimum wages were measured in Purchasing Power Parities (PPPs), the ranking among EU and candidate countries remained almost unchanged. Out of the 21 European countries

measured, Estonia, Lithuania and Latvia came 16th, 18th and 19th respectively (Regnard, 2007, Figures 1 and 2).

   To sum up, when it comes to social policy structures and the coverage
of the population, the Baltic welfare state still shows more comprehensive
solutions to social problems than residual ones. Nevertheless, when it comes
to the social benefit levels, minimum salaries and the share of GDP spent on
social protection, the Baltic welfare state shows disadvantages compared to
the well-developed welfare states. The relatively lower levels of social benefits, even if they cover all those in need, do not contribute enough to ensure
an adequate standard of living for their population, and hinder the successful poverty solutions as well as the expansion of their welfare programmes.

Does politics matter? The legacy of the politics and organized labour

Communist successor parties have not been very successful after the collapse of the communist regimes in Estonia and Latvia, despite the resources
they inherited from the past and other purported advantages (see Table 6.3).
Orenstein (1998) claims that communist successor parties can only suc-
ceed if they lose their association with the past regime and form cross-class
alliances with pro-reform nomenclature business elites and workers, pensioners and other groups. The crucial factor here is the ability to forge links
between institutionalized trade unions and a new capitalist class of former
nomenclature entrepreneurs. In the Baltic case, only Lithuania, despite having quite weak trade unions, has managed to retain quite strong socialist
parties (Orenstein, 1998, p. 495). In Latvia and, in particular, in Estonia, the
negative attitude towards socialist parties, together with quite weak trade
unions, makes it difficult to see the emergence of a strong socialist party
in the near future (Paluckiene, 2000). Numerous studies (Esping-Andersen,
1990; Korpi and Palme, 2003) have demonstrated that countries that have
strong left-wing parties, powerful labour unions and a significant working-
class presence in the decision-making apparatus also have a more highly
developed welfare system than those with strong right-wing parties. If we
examine the elections in the three Baltic states, it is obvious that mainly
right-wing or centre-right parties have dominated all elections, except for
many of the elections in Lithuania. The Baltic states did not move towards
a comprehensive social-democratic model, but instead have chosen a more
liberal approach because of the predominant right-wing ideology in politics
(Guogis and Koht, 2009; Lauristin, 2003). However, political parties in this
region, unlike in the 'old' Western democracies, do not have a clear vision of
social policy in their programmes (Aidukaite, 2004; Guogis et al., 2000).

   In Estonia, the liberal right-wing coalition has been in power since 1992
(see Table 6.3). This must be one of the major reasons why Estonia chose a
more liberal approach to social policy. The ruling right-wing coalitions have

Table 6.3   Parties which dominated the parliamentary elections in the Baltic states

Party	Year	Ideology
Estonia		
National Coalition Party *Pro Patria*	1992	Right-wing
Coalition and Rural People's Party	1995	Centre-right
Estonian Centre Party (EK)	1999	Right-wing
Estonian Centre Party (EK)	2003	Right-wing
Res Publica (RP)		
Estonian Reform Party (R)	2007	Centre-right
Estonian Centre Party (EK)		
Latvia		
Latvian Way Union (LC)	1993	Right-wing
Master Democratic Party (DPS)	1995	Centre- Right-wing
Latvian Way Union (LC)		
People's Party (TP)	1998	Right wing
Latvian Way Union (LC)		
New Time (or, New Era) (JL)	2002	Right-wing
People's Party (TP)	2006	Right-right
Lithuania		
Homeland Union (TS)	1990	Right-wing
Lithuanian Democratic Labour Party (LDDP)	1992	Left-wing
Homeland Union (TS)	1996	Right-wing
Brazauskas Social Democratic Coalition (ABSK)	2000	Left-wing
Labour Party (DP)	2004	Centre-left
For a Working Lithuania:		
Lithuanian Social Democratic Party (LSDP)		
New Union (NS[SL])		
Homeland Union – Lithuanian	2008	Centre-right
Christian Democrats (TS-LKD)		
National Revival Party (TPP)		

Source: Kalnins, 2003; Parties and Elections in EU (www.parties-and-elections.de/); *The Economist*, 2007a, 2007b.

implemented a proportional tax system and there has been a considerable decline in the universal schemes in favour of the introduction of means-tested ones (Trumm, 2006). The efforts of the social-democratic wing in the governments led by Prime Minister Mart Laar in 1992–94 and 1999–2002 have succeeded in the implementation of some elements of a universal social security scheme concerning mandatory pension, health and unemployment insurance and universal family benefits. However, because the fiscal policy in these coalitions was in the hands of right-wing parties, these schemes were never backed with the appropriate financial tools (Lauristin, 2003, p. 9). Estonia does not really have leftist parties, nor are there extreme right-wing parties in the polity (*Estonica*, 2008, pp. 3–4). The Communist Party in Estonia was dissolved in 1992 and was never able to make a political comeback. The ideological differences between the parties are small and hard to ascertain. The only exceptions are the Reform Party and the Social Democratic Party, which have been represented in the parliament. The former has throughout its existence striven firmly for a liberal position in its policy documents. The latter declares in its constitution that the Nordic welfare model and the ideals of social democracy are its starting points.

In Latvia, right-wing or centre-right parties have dominated all national and local elections since 1991 (see Table 6.3). The left-wing parties, however, have managed to form a coalition, For Human Rights in United Latvia, which has been a ruling power in the municipality of Riga since March 2001. In their political manifesto, the Social Democrats support the enhancement of social policy and moderate economic reforms in order to avoid social tensions. However, they have never been in a position nationally to implement their manifesto (Kalnins, 2003). Most Latvians are still wary of any political grouping even remotely associated with Soviet-era communism (*The Economist*, 2007a).

Lithuania represents an interesting case, because the Social Democratic Party managed to win several elections (see Table 6.3). Since 1991 the voters have shifted between the Conservatives (right-wing party) and the Social Democratic Party founded by the former ex-Communist Party members. Despite its left-wing ideology, by the mid-2000s the Social Democratic Party had become a centrist party, and it has continued in power in coalitions with other parties. Nevertheless, power resource theory does not hold true for Lithuania. According to Guogis and Koht (2009), the provisions of social support are relatively low in Lithuania, and the Lithuanian Social Democrats who were in a ruling coalition with the Social Liberals, in 2001–2004 and together with other parties later (until 2006), did not substantially change matters. The minimum wages still remained low as well as various social benefits. Left-wing parties, and particularly, the Lithuanian Social Democratic Party, which was in power, did not aim to create a social democratic welfare state. Guogis and Koht argue that this can be explained by the recent experiences and memories connected to the Soviet period of Lithuanian history. A comprehensive study by Guogis et al. (2000) on political parties' attitudes towards social security in Lithuania revealed that most political parties were against the universal (social-democratic) model of social policy and were in favour of a marginal (liberal) model. It is interesting that no left-wing party had come out in favour of the universal model of social policy. It is even more surprising, as Guodis et al. claim, that no party stated their support for the supremacy of the corporatist model based on social insurance, which, according to them, actually exists in the country at present.

In general, the party system started to develop in the Baltic states, when they first regained their independence. The political legacy from 1990 onwards is characterized by the frequent formation of new political parties and their high volatility and fragmentation. For instance, according to Kalnins (2003), the Latvian party system is still not completely stable. The number of parties represented in parliament changes with every new election. The Lithuanian political landscape is also marked by the fragmentation of the party landscape, the impact of personal rivalries and corruption scandals, and the limited costs of instability in a context of broad policy consensus (*The Economist*, 2007b). Similar tendencies can also be observed in Estonia (*Estonica*, 2008). Generally, the Baltic countries have followed many of the trends seen in other post-communist countries in terms of their party fragmentation, electoral volatility and ideological divisions (Pettai and Kreuzer, 1999). Pettai and Kreuzer predict that in the future in Latvia and Estonia ethnic divisions will manifest themselves in the emerging party systems. There are around 22 per cent 'non-citizens' in Latvia and 13 per cent in Estonia (Wilson, 2002). The numbers, however, have been gradually declining each year. In the case of Latvia, non-citizens do not enjoy eligibility and voting rights in national or local elections. In Estonia, non-citizens do not enjoy voting rights in national elections and cannot stand as candidates in local elections or be members of political parties. However, non-citizens legally residing in Estonia can vote in local elections. Non-citizens in both countries are entitled to all social rights: social services, health care, family benefits and housing according to the criterion of residency. Nevertheless, obviously the socioeconomic conditions of non-Estonians and non-Latvians have declined considerably. Numerous studies (Aidukaite, 2005; Heidmets, 2008; Leinsalu et al., 2004) have pointed out the deteriorating social status, health and income of the Russian minorities in Estonia and Latvia. Furthermore, the Russian minorities are over-represented among the unemployed in these countries (Heidmets, 2008; Vanhuysse, this volume). Hence, while demographically the two countries continued to be multiethnic, electorally they are now much more homogeneous because of a quite large number of non-citizens among the Russian-speaking population. It is expected that the number of non-citizens will continue to decrease due to the process of naturalization and that might lead to the emergence of new parties representing the interests of the ethnic minorities (Pettai and Kreuzer, 1999; Vanhuysse, this volume).

It should be mentioned that politics has been little affected by ethnic differences in Lithuania. Lithuania is the most ethnically homogenous of the three Baltic states. In contrast to the corresponding legislation in Latvia and Estonia, the 1989 Lithuanian Citizenship Law allowed all residents to apply for naturalization, regardless of ethnicity (*The Economist*, 2007b). Overall, unlike in the West, the political parties in the Baltic countries do not have long traditions. In the West, the development process of parties took about half a century. For instance, the Social Democrats have made a significant impact on social policy development in Sweden, since they have been in power for more than 60 years (for more details see Olsson, 1990).

Other social actors have similarly been rather weak in the Baltic states. Civil society is weak in these countries and people have a low level of trust in the main state institutions (Paluckiene, 2000). Unions are weaker still, whether in terms of coverage, density or mobilization. More than anywhere in CEE, the labour movement in the Baltics forms a classic case of 'workers without power' (Vanhuysse, 2007). According to the latest statistics, only 11 per cent of the labour force belong to trade unions in Estonia, 12 per cent in Lithuania and around 16 per cent in Latvia, while in the Nordic countries it is 80–90 per cent. Collective agreements, in turn, cover 80–90 per cent of the workforce in Nordic countries, whereas in the Baltic countries the coverage is about 25 per cent (Kohl, 2008; Sippola, 2006, p. 16; Vanhuysse, 2007). Some public sector trade unions, such as those of the teachers and bus drivers, have been active at times, but this is counterbalanced by the fact that there are few trade unions in the private sector in the Baltic states (Aidukaite, 2004). In Latvia, trade union membership is today overwhelmingly concentrated in the public sector, with less than 10 per cent of employees in the private sector members of trade unions (Woolfson, 2008, p. 81). There no longer exists any strong party or organization which can represent the interests of wage earners in Lithuania, Latvia or Estonia (Aidukaite, 2004). Vanhuysse (this volume) explains that the weak power of the unions in the Baltics is due in part to the way in which broad coalitions of at-risk workers were prevented by governments through ethnic tactics dividing the titular economic losers from the Russian-speaking economic losers. However, this does not explain why trade unions are especially weak in Lithuania which is not divided by ethnic cleavages. Strong trade unions are an important key to expanding the social rights of citizens (see Esping-Andersen, 1990; Korpi, 1983). The distorted activity of the trade unions during the Soviet era, when they were more involved in property distribution than in defending the rights of the working people, has currently left a deep scar on the development of the trade unions. Furthermore, trade union membership has declined in many Eastern European countries and still is doing so. Even though a trend towards declining membership has also characterized Western Europe since the mid-1970s, it has not been to such an extent and it has not yet undermined the minimum standards at work, not least due to well-functioning structures of bilateral social dialogue and the accompanying legal regulations (Kohl, 2008, pp. 110–15). Nevertheless, according to Vanhuysse (2008a, p. 146), the inevitable early decline in trade union membership does not mean that post-communist unions could not be turned into assertive actors with reinvigorated political clout. Transition provided unseen new opportunities for upward mobility for political, economic and cultural elites. Ambitious unionists had similar chances to rebrand themselves by fighting combatively for workers. After all, it is precisely the 'opening up' of multiple aspects of politics and society which made the 1990s particularly conducive to actor agency. The labour unionization rate in many post-communist countries and especially in the three Baltic states has declined not only because of the legacy factor, but also due to such factors as the impact of foreign direct investment and international institutions, and structural economic changes such as privatization, the move towards smaller-sized enterprises, and the shift to a service economy have contributed to this situation (Vanhuysse, 2007, pp. 504–8). The three Baltic states being the most neo-liberal economies in Europe are especially reluctant to promote a social dialogue between employers and trade unions.

The impact of the economy, globalization and Europeanization

The dramatic decline in GDP, the financial crises, the high inflation during the first years of independence, the rapid GDP growth and the stabilization of financial sectors are still having an impact on the affordability of Baltic welfare states. In the face of current global financial crises, the governments in the three countries have been discussing the cutbacks and retrenchment opportunities in social policy. However, even in developed capitalist democracies, successful or unsuccessful economic performance cannot fully explain the differences between welfare state regimes. As noted, the rapid economic progress of the Baltic states over recent years has not necessarily brought a more universalistic approach to the expansion of social policies. Nevertheless, a gradual but minor increase in benefit levels and a minimum wage is observable in all three countries (see Table 6.1). At present, the transformation of social policy in Estonia, Latvia and Lithuania is determined not only by budgetary constraints, but also by population ageing, which was particularly dramatic in Estonia and Latvia during the first decade of the transition (Lauristin, 2003; Rajevska, 2005; Trumm, 2006). The reasons for the depopulation of Baltic societies include the declining birth rate and high mortality among young men due to stress-related accidents and diseases. The little emigration to the West to seek better-paid jobs or education has also affected this situation, however not necessarily significantly. The negative demographic development characterized by the shrinking and ageing population has deeply affected pension insurance and family policy developments in the Baltic states. Retired people currently make up around 16 per cent of the population in Estonia (see Bernotas and Guogis, 2006, p. 227) and this proportion is expected to increase further (Müller,

2002a). In these circumstances, governments in all three countries have raised the retirement age in order to maintain sufficient supplies of labour. By 2008–2016 Latvia and Estonia are due to have the same retirement age for the two sexes (62 for women and 63 for men), while in Lithuania the age will be 62.5 for men and 60 for women (Aidukaite, 2004, Appendix 1, p. 86). Furthermore, in response to the unfavourable demographic situation, Estonia, Latvia and Lithuania have opted for the privatization of the pension systems in order to ensure the financial sustainability of the pension insurance. The three-pillar pension reform implemented in the three countries was propagated by the World Bank (see Casey, 2004; Aidukaite, 2006). The first pillar is a compulsory, state-managed, non-funded scheme based on current contributions or taxes (pay-as-you-go) and started to operate in Lithuania in 1995, in Latvia in 1996 and in Estonia in 1999. The second pillar already started to operate in Latvia (a state-funded compulsory pension scheme) in 2001 and in Estonia (a compulsory privately managed and funded pension scheme) in 2002. In Lithuania, the second pillar is a voluntary privately managed funded pension scheme, implemented in 2004. The third pillar is a voluntary funded private pension scheme. It started to operate in Latvia and Estonia in 1998, and, in Lithuania, the third pillar was implemented as late as 2004 (for more details on pension reform in the Baltics see Aidukaite, 2006; Casey, 2004). With the implementation of the second and third pension insurance pillars, the high-income groups can protect their standard of living through private insurance. The implementation of the privatization of pension insurance meant an important shift in the social policy design of the Estonian, Latvian and Lithuanian welfare systems as well as significant implications for their future development.

Officially, the second and third pillars were developed to increase individual interest and responsibility in the pension system, as well as to avoid a drop in the pension replacement rate due to unfavourable demographic developments. However, the impact of global organizations, such as the International Monetary Fund (IMF) and the World Bank, has been crucial here. For instance, Casey (2004, p. 32) has pointed out that the Baltic countries were recipients of substantial World Bank loans. And although in no cases were these loans tied to pension reform, the countries' willingness to adopt appropriate pension reform made them 'suitable' candidates for assistance. Thus, the implementation of the World Bank's recommendations is quite apparent. The influence of Europeanization, however, was not so visible and definitely more limited.

In Lithuania, external donors, including the EU contractors and experts, do influence the form that social policy takes, particularly when it coincides with the dominant discourses propagated nationally (De la Porte and Deacon, 2002, 2004). Nevertheless, the EU's impact, mainly through the PHARE and Consensus programmes, seems to be rather weak in the absence of either strict requirements for the accession countries or a clear vision of how social policy should be reformed in the new member states. Moreover, according to Ferge (2001b), the Commission's proposals for the social reforms in the accession countries have many elements similar to what is usually termed the neo-liberal agenda that used to be represented by the supranational monetarist agencies. She claims that there is a not very hidden agenda in the EU reports that pays little attention to the essential features of the European model and hints at the necessity of changing the structure of social protection through privatization or marketization. For EU membership, Lithuania was only required to comply with the narrow legally binding acquis, which does not constitute the core of European social policy. The Lithuanians were required to participate in the European Employment Title, but its recommendations (as for EU member states) are not binding (De la Porte and Deacon, 2002, p. 91). In contrast with the EU's ambiguous role, the World Bank's influence was more marked. Its vision coincided very much with that of the other local players in Lithuania such as notably the liberal parties, the Free Market Institute, and the media.

The World Bank and the IMF were also highly influential in Estonia and Latvia (see, for example, Kore, 2005; Rajevska, 2005; Woolfson, 2008). For instance, the IMF arrived in Latvia in 1992 and imposed stringent economic requirements in order to achieve macroeconomic stability. The World Bank supported initiatives that promoted social reforms by providing loans and expert consultation. With the help of World Bank consultants, Latvia established means-tested social welfare schemes and a system of welfare provision that channelled state money to social service institutions on the basis of the number of clients these institutions served (Rajevska, 2005, p. 32). In Estonia, the World Bank supported a health-care insurance reform and in the mid-1990s it attempted to influence the principle of paying child benefits (Kore, 2005).

With regard to Estonia, several researchers (Lauristin, 2003; Leppik, 2005; Kore, 2005) have pointed out that the direct influence of EU social legislation on Estonian social policy has been rather limited. The desire to achieve EU membership was the main goal of the national policy and one of the most influential variables, in that it stimulated Estonia's desire to achieve astonishing results in various fields of economic and political life. However, regarding the field of social policy, indirect influences are most readily detectable. One of these is the ratification of the European Social Charter in 2000, through which Estonian policymakers accepted European social values in the field of social policy, such as higher expenditures in the social sphere, efforts to raise living standards, and more active labour market policy measures, health care and support to families (Lauristin, 2003).

Latvia, like its Baltic neighbours, obediently adopted each and every requirement imposed by the EU. The transposition of EU legislation in the social sphere actively took place between 2000 and 2002. Latvia ratified the European Social Charter in 2002 (Rajevska, 2005). Using the OMC,

Latvia, like the other Baltic states, signed a Joint Inclusion Memorandum in 2003 to fight poverty and social exclusion as well as preparing a National Activity Plan for Social Inclusion in 2004. Nevertheless, the influence of Europeanization can be mainly assessed, as stated by Palier and Guillén (2004, p. 204), through the concept of 'cognitive Europeanization', i.e. a way for policymakers to construct attitudes to and perceptions of social problems and to tackle them. Cognitive ideas provide the recipes, guidelines and maps that in the future may materialize into the desired outcome (Cerami, this volume). The Open Method of Coordination (OMC) obviously enriches domestic policy debates in the Baltic states by bringing new dimensions to it and providing a new framework for comparisons. Thus, in the long run, the indirect impact of the OMC might make considerable impact on the development of social rights. However, the OMC's impact remains quite marginal to date.

Overall, the general shift towards neo-liberal ideology and the free market economy made it easy to implement neo-liberal reforms in the Baltic states. Moreover, the current neo-liberal environment can even undermine the broad European policy goals such as social dialogue. According to Woolfson (2008), Latvia shows how the implementation of vocational education and training, regarded as crucial for creating a highly skilled workforce capable of adapting to an intensified competitive environment, can fail because of the inherited weakness in the character of social dialogue between employers and trade unions. The aggressively free market domestic preferences of the dominant political and business elites together with the weak trade unions make it difficult to implement policies enhancing social dialogue and lifelong learning in Latvia. Latvia has adopted some of the most neo-liberal policies in order to attract foreign investment. A global ranking of 155 nations on key business regulation reforms provided by the World Bank noted that Eastern Europe in general has achieved the highest rate of reform of any region in the world. Overall, Latvia is ranked 26th in the world in terms of 'ease-of-doing-business', with all three Baltic states commended for their 'remarkable achievement' in gaining a top-30 ranking in the decade and a half since the introduction of market reforms (World Bank, 2005, quoted by Woolfson, 2008, p. 80).

Conclusion

This chapter has reviewed social policy development in the three Baltic states using major explanatory variables of welfare state research: path-dependency, the legacy of the politics and organized labour, the impact of the economy, and the impact of globalization and Europeanization on social policy reforms. The discussion has revealed so far that the historical legacy (with its current impact not only on social policy structures, but also on the civil society and the social dialogue between employer and employee) has had a greater impact on social policy change than the impact of the current right-left political balance in the parliaments of the Baltic states or the impact of Europeanization. The path-departures, however, are also obviously observable in the Baltic states. The partial privatization of pension insurance has especially altered the previous social insurance structures, which in future may reveal even more increasing inequalities in the Baltic societies.

The current right–left political balance in the parliaments of the Baltic states, however, cannot accurately explain why the particular type of social policy model prevails in Estonia, Latvia and Lithuania. Rather, the explanations could be sought in the various reasons affecting social policy change. Namely, the previous policy structures, the impact of the economy, the legacy of the politics, the level of civil society and the impact of Europeanization and globalization form complex causal constellations in which social policy is preserved, designed and transformed.

This chapter has demonstrated that the Baltic welfare state is balancing between the 'old' ideas of universalism and solidarity and the 'new' ideas stemming from the free market economy and neo-liberal ideology. The weak civil society, political elites' obvious preferences for liberalism, the strong impact of globalization and the so far still moderate influences of Europeanization create the situation where social rights are determined mainly by the social policymakers and other political elite and therefore are easily retrenched without strong resistance from the grassroots level. The ethnic divisions in Estonia and Latvia, meaning higher social costs for Russian speakers (Vanhuysse, this volume), whose voices are not yet clearly heard in the political arena, keep Estonia and Latvia divided and therefore reduce the formation of organized labour to claim its social rights.

The future of social policy in the Baltic states depends on whether the ideas of the European social model become a valuable discourse for the elites of the Baltic states, which can counterbalance the benefits gained by the marketization, liberalization and reintegration with the global markets. So far the Baltic elites see more benefits from the neo-liberal transition than from the solidaristic and universal welfare state. Social policy should become a priority not only for those dependent on it, but also for those who take the decisions to reform it.

7
Welfare State Transformations in Bulgaria and Romania

Alfio Cerami and Simona Stanescu

Introduction

This chapter discusses the main welfare state transformations occurring in Bulgaria and Romania since the establishment of the first social insurance system at the beginning of the twentieth century. As shown by other investigations in this volume (see contributions of Aidukaite, Inglot, Szikra and Tomka), post-communist welfare state restructuring did not start from scratch, but was built on pre-existing institutional layers. However, due to their more complex political, economic and social situation, the Bulgarian and Romanian transition towards democracy has not only been more difficult than in other Central and Eastern European (CEE) countries, but welfare reforms have also proceeded at a lower speed.

'Emergency welfare states', to use Tomasz Inglot's definition (2008, also this volume), were not simply those implemented in the four Visegrad countries (Czech Republic, Hungary, Poland and Slovakia), or in the three Baltic states (Estonia, Latvia and Lithuania), but included, perhaps, even more importantly, the emerging systems of social protection in the two South-Eastern European states under investigation here. In addition, following Pieter Vanhuysse's remarks on the four Visegrad countries (Vanhuysse, 2006a) and on the Baltic states (Vanhuysse, this volume; see also Aidukaite, this volume), it will also be argued that the use of strategic social policies was crucial, especially during the first years of transition, in lowering the political mobilization capacity of citizens, while, at the same time, smothering the difficult political, economic and social transition.

In contrast to what is often affirmed by the classical new-institutionalist literature (see Pierson, 1996), in the course of this chapter, it will be shown that welfare reform trajectories followed not only previously established pathways of institutional change (welfare reform trajectories based on subsequent stages of incremental transformative change) (see Streeck and Thelen, 2005), but also included more frequent moments of path-departure and innovation, as the introduction of private provisions shows (Orenstein, this volume). In order to explain how changes in environmental conditions have subsequently influenced welfare state transformations, a revised version of the 'misfit' model (March and Olsen, 1989; Risse et al., 2001; Börzel and Risse, 2003) is proposed. Here, not only is the misfit between new environmental requirements and domestic structures discussed, but also the influence of other mediating and enabling factors is included. These include the mediating role of existing ideas, interests and institutions as important *filters* of institutional change, as well as the enabling function of specific socioeconomic conditions that a country is facing, of its socio-economic and political conflicts and cleavages, and of international policy diffusion of ideas, which represent important *policy windows*[1] able to speed up, or hinder, reforms.[2]

The chapter is structured as follows: section 1 discusses the heritage of Bismarck and Stalin in the formation of the current systems of social protection. Section 2 proceeds with an investigation of post-communist welfare reforms by highlighting the role of emergency and strategic social policies in the establishment of the first semi-consolidated systems of social protection, and drawing attention to the role of policy diffusion of ideas as important, path-departing, elements of institutional innovation. In the concluding section, a revised version of the 'misfit' model is introduced with the aim of highlighting the key elements that have influenced the complex series of transformations in the Bulgarian and Romanian systems of social protection.

The heritage of Bismarck

Bulgaria and Romania share a similar history of social protection, which dates back to the communist and pre-communist period. The first legislation concerning old-age was established in Romania in 1912 and in Bulgaria in 1924 following the social insurance principle. Also health and sickness insurance followed the Bismarckian understanding of social solidarity dating back in the case of Romania to 1912 and in the case of Bulgaria to 1918 (ISSA, 2006). Interestingly, at first glance, the presence of a social insurance system in primarily agricultural societies could seem to contradict the most basic assumptions of the power resource model (Korpi and Palme, 2003) in which social insurance systems would be the favourite option in primarily industrialized economies, while universal and tax-financed social policies would be the preferred choice of agricultural societies (Baldwin, 1990). In the first case, such as in the Germany of Bismarck, social insurance-based welfare institutions would pacify the possible destabilizing social democratic aspirations of industrial workers, while, in the second case, such as in the Scandinavian countries, a universal and tax-financed system would more closely meet the needs of farmers, increasing their privileges, while at the same time ensuring the system-stabilizing necessities of a society where most of the people would still be too poor to pay for their own contributory benefits (Baldwin, 1990).

However, in the case of Bulgaria and Romania, the choice of introducing Bismarckian institutions in primarily rural societies was far from being a hazardous political decision, especially if the history and the social conflicts present in these countries are considered. For a long part of their history, Bulgaria and Romania remained under the influence of the Turkish Ottoman Empire. During this period, lasting several centuries (from the fourteenth century to the nineteenth century in both Bulgaria and Romania), agricultural and crafts products were not only produced and consumed locally, but passed through the main cities, exported into the vast territory of the Empire. These territories ranged from Istanbul to Egypt and Iraq. This system of distribution of products and welfare permitted a substantial economic growth for the counties under the Empire, but it also resulted in a peculiar rural–urban cleavage, where the main social conflicts arising in Bulgaria and Romania were not the ones between the working class and the bourgeoisie (the working class in both countries remained underdeveloped until the end of the Second World War), but rather the ones that were emerging between the peasants, with little political and economic power, and the most powerful and richest political and economic elites concentrated in the main urban areas (Hristov, 2008). Some observers described the social conflicts between peasants and urban elites in terms of 'modernization conflicts' (Hristov, 2008).[3] These forced state policies to confront a double resistance. On the one hand, redistributive policies aiming at catching up rural to urban areas would have required heavy taxation, and, therefore, faced the resistance of the peasants with already low budget capacity. The chronic absence of funds available to ensure local development subsequently relegated the less developed rural areas into a steady poverty trap (Hristov, 2008), while on the other, redistributive policies particularly targeted to disadvantaged rural areas also met the resistance of the urban elites who more clearly favoured interventions for urbanization and subsequent waves of industrialization. These, however, occurred in countries where a strong agricultural background could have only been transformed into a modern industrial society thanks mainly to heavy public transfers. The tensions arising between these two main social forces resulted in several violent demonstrations followed by policy blockages that hindered successful reforms.

In terms of welfare state formation, the systems of social protection implemented during the first years of the twentieth century clearly reflected these existing political and socioeconomic tensions, being characterized by an ambiguous mechanism of redistribution. Welfare institutions were based on the Bismarck insurance principle, thus meeting the requests of the most powerful urban political and economic elites, but these institutions did not correspond to the real needs and the socioeconomic structure of primarily agricultural populations, which continued to suffer from low level local development, associated to a lack urban and industrial modernization.

The heritage of Stalin

After the end of the Second World War, these systems of social protection were established primarily to meet the requirements of the urban political and economic elites, but owing to the absence of a real industrial working class (the only professional category who would have benefited from a social insurance principle), were slowly associated with and expanded by a system of social protection that more closely resembled Stalin's understanding of social modernization, in which universal and egalitarian principles had to be strictly linked to industrial development. The introduction of universalism in the new welfare arrangement helped, in this way, to meet two contrasting needs. On the one hand, it continued to meet the requests and the aspirations for urban development and industrial modernization already set by the political and economic elites of the main cities, while, on the other, it also aimed at targeting and pacifying the rural populations more directly, ensuring, at the same time, a system-legitimation and a social modernization function for the newly introduced communist regime.

During a first period of communist social policy reorganization, where reforms proceeded at a slower speed, towards the end of the 1960s, pension, health care and sickness insurance were finally also provided on an universal basis, being accessible, albeit at a lower quality, to rural populations. Benefits continued to be granted according to the occupational status of citizens, but since the entire population was employed in the central planned economy and wage differences were practically non-existent, the Bismarck system of social insurance still in place succeeded in achieving universal aspirations. This also concerned the management of welfare benefits and of social security funds, which, in theory decentralized to state-owned enterprises, depended in reality on the discretionary decisions of local bureaucrats and party officials who through the central planned economic system succeeded to redistribute the wealth to the most disadvantaged rural areas (Cerami, 2006, 2009a).

To what extent was this social and economic system successful in ensuring the often desired social and industrial modernization among the different CEE countries? Despite the fact that the Soviet satellite states shared similar institutional features due to the presence of similar and strictly linked systems of central planning, communist societies did not show similar economic performances, either in terms of internal production or in terms of social development. The four industrialized Visegrad countries and the three Baltic states performed not only economically better than the two South-Eastern European countries under investigation here, but were also less poor societies. The reasons for these differences are easy to imagine.

These can be explained by the less developed industrial organization, as well as by the persistence of regional disparities and more obsolete agricultural structures.

However, despite the existence of structural socioeconomic differences, the transformations of the welfare systems in the different European regions under communist control followed, in several instances, similar pathways of development characterized by similar welfare trajectories. This was primarily due to the presence of similar welfare institutions (e.g. the common Bismarck and Stalin heritage) and by similar exogenous constraints (e.g. the oil crisis of the 1970s). Constant and increasing demands for expanding the coverage and level of benefits in order to continue to ensure the legitimizing capacity of the communist regime were not only present in the four Visegrad countries and in the three Baltic states, often characterized by attempts of revolts, but were also existent, perhaps even more importantly, in Bulgaria and Romania, where the more difficult socioeconomic situation made requests for increasing redistribution particularly urgent. These growing requests clearly put the productive capacity of the central planned economy, already grown to its limits, under severe pressure. As argued for the case of the four Visegrad countries (Cerami, 2009a), the only possibilities available for communist policymakers were, at this point, either to renounce to the system-legitimizing requirements (see Offe, 2006) of the communist regime (this was clearly not a viable political option), or, and this was the choice of all governments in the region, to continue to ensure distribution through an increase in external debt. At the end of 1980s, Central and Eastern European governments were, as a consequence, not only highly indebted to international financial institutions (Cerami, 2009a, 2009b), but their system-stabilizing capacity through the use of strategic social policies had also come to an end.

In more practical terms, what did these common socio-political dilemmas that all communist regimes were facing really imply in the specific cases of Bulgarian and Romanian social policy transformations? On the one hand, the presence of similar Bismarckian and communist welfare institutions existing in both countries made them similarly resilient as other CEE countries to external pressures. The presence of similar welfare logics (Bismarck professional orientation associated to communist egalitarianism) resulted, in fact, in the existence of similar lock-in processes (Pierson, 1996) that tended, if not completely to block, at least to hinder path-departure from the status quo (for Bulgarian and Romanian as well as for other CEE policymakers it was clearly unthinkable to move away from the Soviet economic system). On the other hand, however, despite the existence of similar lock-in processes, the commonalities that the two South-Eastern European countries shared in terms of less modernized industrial and agriculture structures made their adaptation both to the communist and to the new 'global' environment not only more difficult, but asked simultaneously for differential and more urgent reforms. During the entire history of communism (and even beyond), Bulgaria and Romania suffered, in this way, from a double disease. They experienced the negative economic consequences deriving from a monolithic Soviet economic structure that provided uniform policy responses in the global arena, and also suffered from internal structural deficiencies that made their population not only poorer, but also more vulnerable to exogenous pressures.

It comes as no surprise then that the political and economic transition took a much more tortuous and, in some instances, violent road in Bulgaria and Romania than in other CEE countries. While in November 1989 opposition forces in Bulgaria succeeded in overthrowing the communist government of Todor Zhivkov relatively quickly, replacing him with the less exposed party member Andrei Lukanov and avoiding in this way potentially politically disruptive demonstrations, in communist Romania political transition took a different road in which a widespread use of police violence and intimidation of citizens became the key characteristics of a desperate strategy that aimed to block the democratic aspirations of the opposition groups and the civil society. The violent demonstrations, concluded on 25 December 1989 with the death sentence of Nicolae Ceausescu, represent not only the most emblematic image of the fall of communism, but perhaps the most dramatic images of the different socioeconomic performances and socio-political cleavages in Eastern Europe (Cerami, 2006, pp. 23–6).

What this political, economic and social chaos meant in more practical terms for the populations of Bulgaria and Romania can also be easily imagined. From 1989 to 1995, GDP per capita, already the lowest among CEE countries, decreased from US$1,859 to US$1,564 per year in Bulgaria and from US$2,013 to US$1,742 in Romania (the CEE average ranged between US$3,000 and US$5,000). In 2006, it increased only up to US$2,249 in Bulgaria and to US$2,249 in Romania against a CEE average that ranges from US$5,000 to US$12,000 (Unicef, 2008). The annual inflation rate also constantly rose, reaching a peak of 300 per cent in 1991 in Bulgaria and 250 per cent in 1993 in Romania (CEE average ranged from 2 per cent to 6 per cent). In 2006, it stabilized at 4 per cent in Bulgaria and 9 per cent in Romania (Unicef, 2006). Unemployment, so far a non-existent (or better-hidden) problem during communism, jumped year after year, reaching 11 per cent of total active population in 1995 in Bulgaria and 9 per cent in Romania. In 2006, it was equal to 10 per cent in Bulgaria and to 5 per cent in Romania (Unicef, 2008).

Post-communist social policy

As in other CEE countries, even in Bulgaria and Romania the first answers of policymakers to cushion the negative impacts of transition corresponded to the introduction of a first system of social safety nets made up of basic unemployment insurance and social assistance provisions. In the early 1990s, these emergency welfare programmes were also associated with an extensive use of early retirement policies, which, as argued by Vanhuysse (2006a), had two primary objectives: first, they 'pacified' the potentially most disruptive political professional categories (such employees of state-owned enterprises, miners, etc.), who, due to the dismantling of the central planned economy, were more at risk of poverty, and second, they also 'divided' these professional groups granting them a secure access to benefits and with it lowering their mobilization capacity. In addition to this two-fold *divide and pacify* strategy (Vanhuysse, 2006a), early exit options, to paraphrase Albert O. Hirschman (1978), also followed a *legitimize strategy* for the process of transformation providing the first tangible economic benefits to all those segments of the population who would otherwise have been the powerless losers of the democratic transformation.

As a result of the government decisions to expand early retirement privileges to several occupational categories, the number of persons in the late 1990s benefiting from early pensions reached 630,000 workers in Bulgaria (Consensus Phare, 1999a, p. 55), while it grew exponentially year over year in Romania, from 316,800 in 1989 reaching over 3 million in 1995 (Consensus Phare, 1999b, p. 52). Early pensioners were, during the difficult transition in Bulgaria and Romania towards democracy, a far from negligible social group, corresponding in the second half of the 1990s to approximately 9 per cent of the total population in Bulgaria and to 13 per cent of the total population in Romania (authors' calculations based on Consensus Phare, 1999a, p. 55; Consensus Phare, 1999b, p. 52). Interestingly, this strategic use of social policies did not stop immediately after the first and most difficult decade of economic and social transition, but continued during the entire process of transformation, replaced, this time, by an increase in disability benefits, whose number of beneficiaries has abnormally grown from 233,017 in 1995 to 487,144 in 2006 in Bulgaria (Tsolova et al., 2006, p. 13) and from 657,000 in 1995 to 842,900 in 2006 in Romania (Stanculescu and Zaman, 2006, p. 22; see also Haggard and Kaufman, 2008, ch. 8).

The introduction of these 'emergency welfare states' (see Inglot, this volume) ensured, in this way, not only a smooth transition towards capitalism, but also empowered and legitimized these fragile democracies. Whether these 'emergency welfare states' based on dividing, pacifying and legitimizing strategies were fully successful to smoothen the negative impact of transition is still the subject of academic debate. As shown by Cristina Rat (in this volume), the social safety net put in place by national authorities was, unfortunately, far from sufficient to bring people out of poverty, especially in those countries such as Bulgaria and Romania that were not only characterized by more fragile socioeconomic structures, but also characterized by a lack of capital for restructuring their economies due to attracting fewer foreign investments (Drahokoupil, 2008).

In terms of welfare state restructuring, after almost a decade of delayed reforms and discontinuous economic growth (Sotiropoulos et al., 2003), Bulgaria and Romania have fully introduced a three-pillar system of old-age protection (1999/2007 in Bulgaria and 2000 in Romania respectively), a system of heath insurance based on differentiation and privatization of provisions (1998/2004 and 1998/2006), a scheme, albeit still underdeveloped, of protection against unemployment (1991/1999/2007 and 1991/2000) coupled with an even less extensive system of family policies (1999/2002/2007 and 2000) and of social assistance provisions based on guaranteed minimum incomes (2005 and 2001).

The reasons for the late implementation of social protection reforms in these countries, and so remaining as 'frozen landscapes'[4] for longer periods when compared to the reforms that occurred in other CEE countries (for a recent review, see Haggard and Kaufman, 2008), can be explained by their more difficult socioeconomic situation, which made an effective modernization of the countries more difficult, and also, following Stein Rokkan (see Flora et al., 1999), by the strong political and social cleavages that existed between rural and urban areas. As can be expected, these cleavages resulted in continuous policy blockages since every reform proposal of the social protection system was also dissatisfying to large sections of the population (both rural and urban). Political parties in both countries were thus confronted, once again in their history, by the dilemma of simultaneously ensuring convergence of rural areas to urban standards, while at the same time promoting further modernization of urban areas so as to ensure a faster alignment towards the standards present in other CEE and Western countries. In times of deep economic crisis, these attempts of simultaneous catching-up and further modernization could only have been made possible through a heavy increase in taxation that, obviously, no one was willing or able to afford.

It comes then as no surprise that the Bulgarian and Romanian welfare states not only remained 'immovable objects' (Pierson, 1998) for longer periods of time, but also that the political battles among the different parties present in the parliaments only rarely resulted in successful policy action. As Haggard and Kaufman (2008, p. 331) have correctly emphasized, existing institutional structures and the instability of governments coupled with more complex economic conditions have all contributed towards influencing the post-communist social policy reform processes. In Bulgaria and Romania, for example, several centre-left and centre-right coalitions have alternated during the first 20 years of the post-communist transition. In Bulgaria, three left coalitions took office between 1989 and 1994, five right coalitions in 1990, 1991, 1997, 2001 and 2009, and one left–right grand coalition in 2005. Similarly in Romania, several centre-left and centre-right coalitions took office in a highly volatile political environment characterized by a deep economic recession and often followed by violent mass demonstrations. After the death of Ceausescu in December 1989, the power passed to left-oriented governments until 1996, to a centre-right coalition up to 2000, to a centre-left coalition until 2003, to a centre-right government from the subsequent elections of 2004 and, in 2008, to a contested centre-left coalition of the two parties that had stayed in strong opposition for several years – the centre Democratic Liberal Party and the left Social Democratic Party (see Table 7.1). Interestingly, the socioeconomic tensions present in

Table 7.1   Parliamentary elections in Bulgaria and Romania (1989–2009)

Bulgaria

1989	Left	Bulgarian Socialist Party
1990	Centre-right	Coalition led by Union of Democratic Forces
1991	Centre-right	Coalition led by Union of Democratic Forces
1994	Centre-left	Coalition led by Bulgarian Socialist Party
1997	Centre-right	Coalition led by Union of Democratic Forces and People's Union
2001	Centre-right (personalist)	Coalition led by National Movement of Simeon II
2005	Right–left grand coalition	Grand coalition led by National Movement of Simeon II, Bulgarian Socialist Party and others
2009	Centre-right	Coalition led by Citizens for European Development of Bulgaria

Romania

1990	Left	National Salvation Front
1992	Left	Coalition led by Social Democratic Party of Romania
1996	Centre-right	Coalition led by Democratic Convention of Romania
2000	Centre-left	Coalition led by Social Democratic Pole of Romania
2004	Centre-right	Coalition led by National Liberal Party, Democratic Party and Democratic Alliance of Hungarians in Romania
2008	Centre-left	Coalition led by Democratic Liberal Party and Social Democratic Party

Source: Cerami (2006), pp. 23–6; Parties and Elections in Europe (www.parties-and-elections.de/).

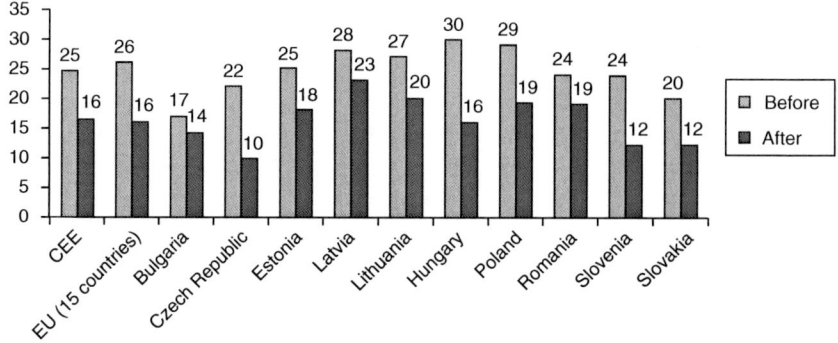

Figure 7.1 At risk of poverty before and after social transfers (2006)
Source: Eurostat. populations and social conditions. http://epp.eurostat.ec.europa.eu/

the countries often also spilled over into political tensions within existing leading coalitions, often leading to alternation of prime ministers.

With regard to the impact of the Bulgarian and Romanian welfare states in poverty reduction, this political impasse has resulted in less developed and less performing systems of social protection than those present in other CEE countries. As shown by Figure 7.1, in 2006 poverty rates after social transfers corresponded to 14 per cent in Bulgaria and to 19 per cent in Romania (CEE and EU-15 average: 16 per cent), with a reduction of poverty rates substantially lower than in other CEE and Western countries (only –3 per cent in the case of Bulgaria and –5 per cent in the case of Romania). As argued, the reasons for this negative performance can be found, on the one hand, in the more complex socioeconomic structure of these countries, that has hindered through subsequent developmental lock-in processes a successful modernization, while, on the other, also in mistakes in the implementation of welfare programmes with an excessive emphasis given to the privatization of provisions, which was unlikely to provide sufficient coverage and protection in less performing and less modernized market economies.

International policy diffusion of ideas

Were welfare state transformations in Bulgaria and Romania simply the result of incremental path-dependent institutional change, or did elements of innovation also play a role in the process of welfare state restructuring? As argued by various authors in this volume (see, for instance, Aidukaite, Cerami, Inglot, Szikra and Tomka), path-dependency was certainly one of the main characteristics of post-communist welfare state reforms. This transformation often took the form of subsequent adjustments and recombinations of existing institutional layers in which several features already present in the pre-communist and communist system of social protection were merged together in new and, to some extent, unique hybrid systems. Incremental path-dependent change, to use Streeck and Thelen's (2005) definition, was, however, not the only feature that characterized the post-communist institutional transformation. The diffusion of ideas, an important path-breaking character of international policy, should also be emphasized. Here, the most emblematic example can probably be given by the transnational actors' involvement in pension privatizations. As argued by Orenstein (in this volume), transnational policy actors helped to shape new pension reform agendas in a variety of different ways, becoming vessels of ideational influence on politics worldwide through the creation and diffusion of new policy ideas, norms, metrics, values and technical expertise (for detailed information, see also Orenstein, 2008a). In more practical terms, these policy ideas, norms, metrics and values took the concrete forms of well-known publications, such as *Averting the Old-Age Crisis* (World Bank, 1994), that highlighted the merits of private provisions (often underestimating the possible shortcomings), and also pre-reform technical assistance, which, empowered by the conditionality clausal attached to the granting of loans, represented advanced forms of social learning based on *increasing returns* mechanisms. The case of pre-reform technical assistance is a good example of this. In fact, from the period 1994–2004 both countries received constant advice from the World Bank on how to privatize pensions reforms. This pension reform strategy was not carried alone but often conducted in cooperation with USAID and the IMF. As for the World Bank, USAID pension reforms materialized in technical assistance programmes, in help for drafting laws and regulations, and in public relations campaigns (Orenstein, 2008a, p. 52). Notable here is the case of José Piñeira, the leading Chilean pension reformer, who was invited to give a talk via satellite to various World Bank offices in the region (Orenstein, 2008a, p. 85). The influence of transnational organizations in the post-communist reform process has not only been limited to pension privatization but it has also involved a number of spheres of influence including the restructuring of the health care (Cerami, 2006) and social assistance policies (World Bank, 2007), the banking sector (Epstein, 2008) and minority rights (Jacoby, 2008), to name but a few.

However, it is not only Washington-based transnational organizations that have influenced the post-communist reform process; the Brussels-based European Union has also played an important role in the process of systemic transformation. Even though the social dimension of the European Union has often been addressed as a missing element in the accession process (Lendvai, 2004; Sissenich, 2005), and more generally in the overall process of European Integration favouring 'market integration' and only secondarily 'social integration' (see Scharpf, 1999), recent studies with a more specific focus on policy diffusion of ideas (Guillén and Palier, 2004) have highlighted how, despite difficulties in observing a direct top-down impact of the EU in the social dimension, a significant indirect impact has been achieved in cognitive terms. Here, the EU succeeded to promote, despite some ambiguities, new social policy ideas, interests and institutions that lowered the potential impact of market-orthodoxy as promulgated by the most influential Washington-based organizations (Cerami, 2008a). In fact, if European Integration is not understood in simplistic terms as a top-down process of policy transfer at EU level followed by policy downloading at national level, but rather as a complex process of top-down and bottom-up influences characterized by multi-level governance (Hooghe and Marks, 2001) in which different actors at different levels of the European decision-making (EU, national, regional and local) all contribute to steer national and EU policy outcomes (Schmidt, 2006; Graziano and Vink, 2007), then we see that the impact of the European Union in the social dimension has, in reality, been far from insignificant. This has materialized not only in terms of new social policy, ideas, interests and institutions introduced as a result of policy diffusion, but also in terms of more complex, even though more difficult to measure, leverage effects (Vachudova, 2008).

For Vachudova (2008), two different types of leverage effects acted at the EU and national levels, amplifying the impact of the European Union in Eastern European policy change. According to the author, passive leverage consists of 'the traction that the EU has on domestic politics of credible candidate states merely by virtue of its existence and its usual conduct' (Vachudova, 2008, p. 25). This effect has been linked to the political and economic benefits of membership, such as the expectations of becoming politically stronger and more influential countries in the global environment, or associated to the prospects of attracting more foreign direct investments, of benefiting from more integration in the European markets, and of being the object of increasing transfers of know-how. Active leverage depends, in this context, on the fact that these substantial benefits created further incentives for states to satisfy the enormous entry requirements, thus, enacting political and policy adaptations. As Vachudova has argued, the accession processes, centred on a strategy of gate-keeping of different stages (screening, opening negotiations after satisfying the Copenhagen Criteria, closing particular chapters in the negotiations, etc.), all represented important forces that pushed for compliance to EU expectations (see Falkner et al., 2005; Falkner and Treib, 2007). In addition, other important forces helped to translate these leverage effects into domestic political and policy change. Here, one could argue *conditionality* (Schimmelfennig and Sedelmeier, 2005) as a key driver of institutional change (please note, however, that the most recent research seem to display contrasting results, see JEPP, 2008), but also, and perhaps even more importantly, constructivist mechanisms of social learning (Epstein, 2006) and internalization of EU rules adopted for instrumental reasons (Grabbe, 2006).

Misfit hypothesis revisited

One of the increasingly most discussed explanatory models employed to understand the main causes and factors of institutional change is centred on the 'goodness of fit' or 'misfit' hypothesis developed by March and Olsen (1989) in organizational sociology and applied by Risse et al. (2001) and Börzel and Risse (2003), more recently, to European studies. According to its basic version, the compatibility of domestic structures vis-à-vis external pressures for change is the key to determining institutional transformation. One of the misfit's core assumptions is, in fact, that the less compatible existing institutional structures are with the new environmental requirements, then the greater the pressure on domestic structures to adapt (Beichelt, 2008, p. 23). In this model, policy blockages are not excluded a priori, but pressures deriving from changes in environmental conditions (environmental misfit) automatically result in pressures for domestic change (institutional misfit) through the simple mediation of intermediary institutions and actors (opportunity structures). In subsequent, slightly modified versions of this model, other intervening variables are also addressed as being able to affect change in the politics, polity and policy spheres. These include, for example, the number of veto points, social learning processes and presence of formal and informal institutions (Börzel and Risse, 2003; Featherstone and Radaelli, 2003; Beichelt, 2008). Despite the fact that several other elements, such as those concerning the effectiveness of domestic governance, the existence of strong political pressures for compliance, or the presence of unfavourable economic conditions (e.g. unemployment) (for a review, see Toshkov, 2007), could also be included in this analysis, the basic assumptions of the 'misfit' model cannot so easily be abandoned. In the majority of cases, in fact, some form of unbalance between external environment and structural conditions is a necessary precondition in order to start reflections on the necessity and feasibility of change, making it more attractive than the status quo.

In the case of Bulgaria and Romania, a revised version of the 'misfit' model is not only useful to improve our understanding of the most recent social policy reforms in one specific area (e.g. pensions schemes), but, more importantly, in improving our understanding of the process of welfare state restructuring as a whole, highlighting the different pathways of change. As elucidated in previous sections, processes of environmental transformation due to the fall of the Berlin Wall resulted in an increasing environmental and institutional misfit between what the new environmental conditions of a market economy required and what already-existing domestic structures established during the communist and pre-communist period were able to provide. This environmental and institutional misfit produced rising pressures for action that made institutional change not only more attractive than the status quo, but also a desirable political option if the survival of these countries' institutions wanted to be achieved.

Even though, at first glance, this standard version of the 'misfit' model could already seem sufficient to explain the basic reasons why processes of institutional change had to be initiated, it is still too simplistic to assume that a misfit between new environmental requirements and structural inadequacies would have automatically resulted in successful policy and institutional change. As highlighted during the three main phases of welfare state change, the Bismarckian, Stalinist and post-communist periods (see also contributions of Aidukaite, Cerami, Inglot, Orenstein, Sirovátka and Rákoczyová, Szikra and Tomka, Vanhuysse in this volume), other *mediating* and *enabling* factors have played a vital role in the process of welfare state restructuring. These important mediating factors have included, for instance, a recalibration (Hemerijck, 2007, 2010; Cerami, this volume) of the leading ideas, interests and institutions that constituted the basis of the already established system of social protection. The dominant social policy ideas, interests and institutions inherited during the antecedent phases of institutional transformation played, in fact, the important function of *filters*, influencing, very often in a path-dependent way, the way in which policy and institutional change was conducted in subsequent waves of welfare state restructuring.

However, pressures for change stemming from the new environmental requirements, and filtered by the already existing ideas, interests and institutions, would not have been sufficient to result in successful institutional change, if, for example, after an early period of status quo, the increasingly dramatic socioeconomic situation of these countries, coupled with long-lasting socioeconomic and political conflicts and cleavages, would not have made reforms in these systems of social protection particularly urgent. These could, only to some extent, have been smothered by the use of strategic social policies. In addition to this, the presence of international policy diffusion of ideas, such as those concerning the privatization of the welfare state, made institutional change not only more attractive than the status quo, but also enabled, in the beginning of 2000s, the implementation of social policy reforms that have remained blocked for too long, representing important policy windows for new pathways of institutional transformation (see Figure 7.2).

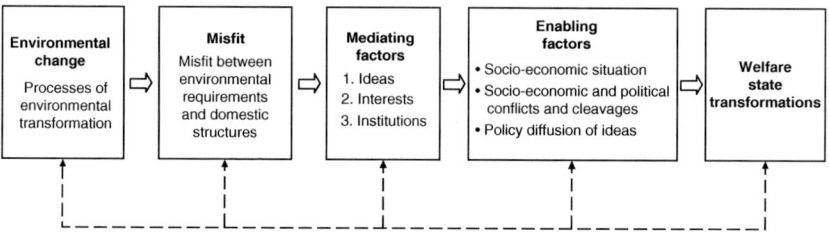

Figure 7.2 Welfare state transformations

Conclusion

This chapter has investigated the main welfare state transformations that have occurred in Bulgaria and Romania since the establishment of the first social insurance principle in the early years of the twentieth century. The main argument is that path-dependency has been a key characteristic in the process of welfare state restructuring, but moments of path-departure and innovation have also been present. In order to explain the main factors and causes of institutional change, this chapter has proposed a modified version of the 'misfit' model. Here, not only has a misfit between new environmental requirements and existing institutional structures been addressed as key for determining institutional change, but other *mediating* and *enabling* factors have also been identified as crucial. These mediating factors have included, for example, already existing ideas, interests and institutions established during the communist and pre-communist period, while enabling factors have involved the socioeconomic situation of a country, and, following Stein Rokkan, the long-lasting socioeconomic and political conflicts and cleavages as well as, more recently, international policy diffusion of ideas. These have represented, in the case of the mediating factors, important *filters* of institutional change, and in the case of the enabling factors important *policy windows* that have facilitated or hindered path-departure. Even though we do not aspire to provide an all-embracing explanatory model capable of including all possible variables that may influence institutional change in the region, we believe that an investigation of the reasons and causes responsible for institutional transformation associated with an exploration of the main mediating and enabling elements can represent a fruitful theoretical instrument for improving our understanding of welfare state transformations in Central and Eastern Europe and beyond.

Part III
Sectoral Analysis and Challenges

8
Transnational Actors in Central and East European Pension Reforms

Mitchell A. Orenstein

Introduction

The literature on welfare states in developed democracies has been dominated by a national political economy perspective in which key decisions about welfare state development and change are determined by national politics, economic forces, and demography (Cameron, 1978; Garrett, 1998; Katzenstein, 1985; Pierson, 1994). One school of thought views welfare state programmes as national responses to economic pressures caused by openness to international trade (Cameron, 1978; Katzenstein, 1985) while another emphasizes path-dependencies caused by political interest groups defending the benefits they derive from specific government programmes (Pierson, 1994). Much of this national politics literature has sought to refute the proposition that globalization has greatly impacted developed welfare states in Western Europe (Garrett, 1998; Iversen, 2005; Swank, 2002). Yet the highly visible campaign by the World Bank, United States Agency for International Development (USAID) and other organizations to promote pension privatization by replacing social-security-type systems with those based on private, individual pension savings accounts has prompted a growing enquiry into the role of transnational actors in developing country welfare states (Brooks, 2004; Cerami, 2006; Chłon-Dominczak and Móra, 2003; Cook, 2007a; Deacon, 1997; Madrid, 2003; Müller, 2003; Nelson, 2004; Orenstein, 2008a; Weyland, 2004).

This chapter demonstrates that transnational actors have played an important role in setting the pension reform agenda in Central and Eastern Europe (CEE) and the former Soviet Union (FSU). Transnational actors have influenced countries in multiple ways, by inspiring and recruiting reformers to pursue pension privatization, forming coalitions with domestic supporters to win battles in favour of reform, helping to convince domestic opponents to support reform, and otherwise devising strategies to neutralize opposition to reform. I build on a network or coalition approach to transnational politics in making this case (Jacoby, 2004; Keck and Sikkink,

1998; Sabatier, 1999). While drawing the various social science institutionalisms, this literature has placed a greater emphasis on the ideational dimension of transnational influence. Schmidt (2008) for instance speaks of a 'discursive' institutionalism that integrates a causal power of ideas in institutional development and change. While domestic factors remain important, studying the role of transnational actors is necessary, if not sufficient, to explain the rapid spread of pension reform in the former communist countries of Europe and Eurasia.

Standard political economy analyses fail to account for three key aspects of the reform process in Central and Eastern European pension reforms: (1) the content of reform, which conforms closely to the approach advocated by the World Bank in its 1994 publication *Averting the Old-Age Crisis* (World Bank, 1994); (2) the timing of reform, which in all cases came after the World Bank undertook a major effort to promote the pension privatization in CEE; and (3) case study evidence that shows the deep involvement of transnational actors in domestic reform processes. Transnational actor influence, through a variety of ideational and resource-based mechanisms, helps to account for the rapid spread of pension privatization in Central and Eastern Europe.

National political economy approaches

While scholars of the political economy of pension reform have begun to emphasize the role of transnational actors, domestic political and economic factors retain their pre-eminent place in the literature on pension system development and change. Myles and Pierson (2001), for instance, employ an institutional path-dependency approach based on Pierson's earlier (1994) work, arguing that countries with smaller income-related pension systems are more likely to implement individual, private pension savings accounts. Whereas countries with smaller pension systems have the fiscal room and domestic demand to add individual, private pension accounts, countries with large state pension systems have less need and ability to do so.

While Myles and Pierson's findings hold for the small number of West European countries included in their study, prior pension system size shows little correlation with pension privatization decisions in Central and Eastern Europe and the former Soviet Union. Instead, some of the largest and smallest pension systems in the region have adopted pension privatization. One pioneer of the new pension reform trend is Poland, whose pension system is an outlier in terms of overall size (see Table 8.1). In the mid-1990s, Poland spent 16 per cent of GDP on income-related state pensions. At the same time, reform also occurred in countries (or jurisdictions) with relatively small pension systems, such as Kosovo, consistent with the predictions of the Myles and Pierson argument. There is some evidence that countries with smaller pre-existing pension systems were more likely to adopt 'substitutive' rather than 'mixed' reforms (Kazakhstan and Kosovo),

Table 8.1 Public pension spending as percentage of GDP in
Central and Eastern Europe and the former Soviet Union

Country	Pension spending/ GDP	Year
Poland	14.4%	1995
Slovenia	13.6%	1996
Croatia	11.6%	1997
Latvia	10.2%	1995
Hungary	9.7%	1996
Slovakia	9.1%	1994
Czech Republic	9.0%	1996
Macedonia	8.7%	1998
Ukraine	8.6%	1996
Belarus	7.7%	1997
Moldova	7.5%	1996
Bulgaria	7.3%	1996
Estonia	7.0%	1995
Kyrgyz Republic	6.4%	1997
Lithuania	6.2%	1996
Russia	5.7%	1996
Uzbekistan	5.3%	1995
Albania	5.1%	1995
Romania	5.1%	1996
Kazakhstan	5.0%	1997
Armenia	3.1%	1996
Tajikistan	3.0%	1996
Azerbaijan	2.5%	1996
Turkmenistan	2.3%	1996
Georgia	1.7%	1996

Note: Countries in bold have implemented pension privatization.
Source: Palacios and Pallares-Miralles (2000).

indicating an important path-dependency. However, the Myles and Pierson
thesis cannot explain which countries adopted pension privatization in CEE
and FSU and why. The trend has been far more pervasive than their explanation would suggest.

   Within the political economy of pension reform literature in developing
countries globally, a number of domestic economic and political explanations

for the adoption of pension privatization have been advanced. Most explanations centre on political or economic conditions that may make reform more likely, such as economic or pension system crisis (Müller, 2003), high external debt (Müller, 2003), political fragmentation (Brooks, 2005), or low public support for the existing pension system (Hasselmann, 2006). While such factors may be important in explaining the propensity to reform in CEE and FSU countries, they cannot explain its content. Pension privatization marks a major path-departure from established norms of pension provision in Europe. Crisis alone, high debt, or other background conditions may create a likelihood of reform, but they do not dictate a particular path. Müller argues that high external debt makes countries more vulnerable to advice from international financial institutions (Müller, 2003). This argument neatly combines national political economy factors that explain a propensity to reform with transnational factors that determine their shape.

A further explanation is proposed by Weyland, who argues that the timing and regional diffusion patterns of pension privatization can be explained by studying the cognitive heuristics of domestic decision-makers (Weyland, 2005). Policymakers, Weyland argues, are not rational learners, who carefully study all the reform options before them and carefully consider the compatibility of various models with domestic political and economic decisions before making a choice. Instead, Weyland argues that they use cognitive heuristics such as 'anchoring' and 'availability' that predispose them only to consider a narrow range of seemingly available options and ones that seem to work well in neighbouring countries. The use of these cognitive heuristics explains why reforms seem to spread more rapidly within regions like Latin America and Central and Eastern Europe than between regions and why similar reforms are adopted in country after country in a relatively short period of time. While Weyland's exploration of the psychology of domestic reformers is a welcome contribution, the emphasis on domestic decision-makers learning from neighbouring countries cannot fully explain reforms undertaken in CEE and FSU. While Latin America had the Chilean example and reformers in other countries may have copied from there, CEE had no Chile. The World Bank, as we will see, was deeply involved in the reform process in Hungary and Poland, the first countries to adopt pension privatization in the CEE region. The deep involvement of transnational actors in putting pension privatization on the agenda and financing the development of reform legislation in CEE and FSU suggests that the involvement of these actors went beyond feeding 'available' models to policymakers eager for reform short cuts. They were creating their own markets for the reform ideas that they wished to disseminate by deploying a wide variety of resources to make pension privatization easier for domestic actors to support and implement.

As this brief review suggests, explanations based on national political and economic factors can only partially account for the wave of pension privatization in CEE and FSU states starting in 1998. Domestic political and economic conditions such as the economic crisis of the post-socialist welfare state, lack of confidence in communist era institutions, and political system fragmentation clearly created a propensity for reform in post-communist countries. None of these conditions, however, necessitated pension privatization. They did create fertile ground for transnational actors to promote a wide variety of radical liberal policy solutions. Under these circumstances, the influence of transnational actors was largely ideational – developing and promoting reform solutions that decision-makers in crisis could use.

Transnational actor influence

Content and timing of reforms

Pension reforms in the late 1990s and 2000s in Central and Eastern Europe were developed under the heavy influence of a policy campaign led by the World Bank starting in the early 1990s. The idea of pension privatization – defined as the replacement of social security type systems with ones based on private, individual pension savings accounts – arose in US universities in the late 1970s and was first implemented in Chile in the early 1980s (Edwards, 1998; Kurtz, 1999). However, these reforms were not widely known or seriously discussed in CEE and FSU policy circles until after the 1994 World Bank report. The only known exception is Poland, where two social policymakers circulated a short paper suggesting a switch to a mandatory, funded system in 1991. At the time, the proposal was shelved, in part because the World Bank representative in Poland, Nick Barr, a prominent opponent of pension privatization, refused to support it (interview with Nick Barr, 2007).

During the early 1990s, most Central European governments enacted emergency reforms (Offe, 1993) that ran counter to the logic of pension privatization. Whereas pension privatization is enacted to reduce the strain of pension expenditures on government budgets, most Central European governments dramatically expanded pension spending in the early 1990s. Their main objective at the time was to stem the effects of a serious economic crisis, rather than to cut pension spending. In some countries, such as Poland, the expansion of pension spending was dramatic, increasing to more than 16 per cent of gross domestic product due to using early retirement as a way to reduce unemployment (Cain and Surdej, 1999; Inglot, 2008). As a proportion of GDP, Poland continues to have one of the most generous public pension programmes in Europe.

When pension privatization emerged on the policy agenda in CEE and FSU, it did so with a vengeance. Between 1998 and 2004, 14 former communist countries from Hungary to Uzbekistan adopted these reforms (see Table 8.2). The Central and East European reforms did not generally follow the Chilean 'substitutive' model of reform, whereby the prior social security type system is

Table 8.2 Types of pension privatizations

Substitutive	Mixed	Parallel
Chile 1981	Sweden 1994	UK 1986
Bolivia 1997	Hungary 1998	Peru 1993
Mexico 1997	Poland 1999	Argentina 1994
El Salvador 1998	Costa Rica 2001	Colombia 1994
Kazakhstan 1998	Latvia 2001	Uruguay 1996
Dom. Rep. 2001	Bulgaria 2002	Estonia 2001
Nicaragua 2001	Croatia 2002	Lithuania 2002
Kosovo 2001	Macedonia 2002	
	Russia 2002	
	Slovakia 2003	
	Romania 2004	
	Uzbekistan 2004	

Sources: Madrid (2003), Müller (2003), Fultz (2004), Palacios (2003), Holzmann and Hinz (2005), Becker et al. (2005); and web resources from World Bank, IDB and USAID.

completely replaced (or substituted) by a pension system based on private, individual pension savings accounts. Instead, these reforms mostly followed the 'mixed' model advocated by the World Bank in its 1994 report, which called for scaling down public social security systems and replacing them in part with mandatory pension savings accounts. 'Parallel' reforms enable both the social security and individual account systems to operate side by side, with participants having the choice of which system to join (Müller, 2000).

Note that reforms sometimes characterized as 'mixed' in the literature are coded here as 'parallel', particularly Argentina and Estonia. One could include in this chart countries that have converted optional, funded, occupational pension systems to mandatory ones, including the Netherlands, Switzerland, Denmark and Iceland. However, this process differs from the partial or full replacement of social security pension systems, so these countries are left out of the narrow definition of the pension privatizations applied here, though they are part of the broader new pension reform trend.

The 'mixed' model of pension privatization was popularized with the 1994 publication of *Averting the Old-Age Crisis*, a World Bank report which defined a new approach to reforms. The report was the result of a research project initiated by World Bank Chief Economist Larry Summers in the early 1990s, and the final report represented a major advance in pension reform thinking. The Bank later backed up this expert authority with substantial resources devoted to pension reform technical assistance and lending.

While the exact extent of these resources is unclear, since pension reform assistance has often come in the context of other loans, a recent World Bank study estimates that that between 1984 and 2004 the World Bank made 93 loans with a pension component to 25 countries in its Europe/Central Asia region for a total of $1.6 billion (Holzmann and Hinz, 2005).

The report also precipitated a measurable policy shift in World Bank pension policy. Before its publication, the World Bank did not consistently advocate the pension privatization and individual pension accounts in its policy advice. Instead, the World Bank prior to 1994 offered a multiplicity of advice given by individual consultants and reform teams (Deacon, 1997; Nelson, 2004). In a systematic search conducted by the author of publicly available World Bank online documents on pensions, it is clear that several World Bank publications as late as 1993 warned against pension privatization, arguing that it would not solve fundamental problems facing systems in Central and Eastern Europe (cf. Barr, 2005). Between 1994 and 2004, however, no project documents by the World Bank diverged from the ultimate objective of pension privatization, indicating that a policy shift within the Bank took place in conjunction with the publication of *Averting the Old-Age Crisis*.

Averting the Old-Age Crisis also reshaped pension reform debates in countries worldwide by turning attention to the newly defined problem of demographic ageing. Generating a new problem definition around demographic ageing provided a key justification for radical reforms. The report found that a tripling of the global elderly population (over age 60) between 1990 and 2030 from 500 million to 1.4 billion would put growing pressure on existing pension arrangements in developed and developing countries alike (World Bank, 1994). A global pension crisis was thus in the making. The report synthesized a neo-liberal critique of existing welfare state arrangements and argued that existing, social-security-type pension systems would be unable to cope with emerging demographic pressures. With demographic ageing, the number of people receiving pension increases and the number of workers declines, causing budget deficits to occur. As a result, social security systems would face long-term fiscal crises. Furthermore, the report highlighted administrative and political challenges to the stability of social security systems. It argued that in developing countries in particular, pay-as-you-go systems are vulnerable to moral hazard on the part of politicians, while state administrations for social security often experience severe administrative difficulties, including providing negative returns (World Bank, 1994). Overall, the report argued that social security systems provide low returns on investment and leave many people uncovered, while benefiting already privileged sectors of the labour force, particularly in developing countries.

Averting the Old-Age Crisis translated this critique into a comprehensive alternative to public social-security-type pension systems that would rationalize the delivery of income-related benefits while also enhancing the redistributive aspects of pension systems. To achieve these multiple goals, the report advocated a mixed, or what it calls a 'multipillar' or three-pillar, approach to pension reform that neatly divides redistributive and income-related benefits into separate 'pillars'. It called for: (1) A first pillar of state-provided, redistributive benefits, such as a flat, minimum pension, pension guarantee, or reduced social security system; (2) A second pillar of mandatory pension savings in private individual accounts; (3) A third pillar of voluntary, funded individual or occupational pension plans.

The pension privatization model advocated by the report went significantly beyond the Chilean model that preceded it. First, it did not advocate a complete replacement of the former pay-as-you-go pension system, as had been done in Chile. Instead, it offered a broad policy template that could be mixed and matched in a variety of formats to suit individual country conditions. Importantly, it opened the way for so-called 'mixed' reforms that reduced the public pay-as-you-go system and replaced it only in part. By making advice more flexible than doctrinaire advocacy of the Chilean approach of complete replacement of the existing social security system, the report created a transnational policy approach more appealing to a broader array of countries without giving up individual, privately managed, funded accounts.

It also argued that one of the primary benefits of pension privatization was facilitating capital market development and investment in developing countries. It argued that countries could attain a major benefit for development through the creation of large pools of domestic pension capital that could be used to finance private sector development, stimulate economic growth and insulate developing countries from capital market flight (Müller, 2003).

Other organizations followed the World Bank's lead in advocating pension privatization worldwide. In 1994, the Inter-American Development Bank (IDB) also began to call for three-pillar reforms in Latin America, echoing the approach in *Averting the Old-Age Crisis*. It argued for increasing the linkage between contributions and benefits and increasing reliance on funded, privately managed pensions (de Oliveira, 1994). USAID also worked closely with the World Bank to advocate and implement pension privatization in Central and Eastern Europe and the former Soviet Union (Snelbecker, 2005), though it has differentiated itself by emphasizing the financial sector development aspects of pension reform in the countries where it has worked (interview with Charles Becker, USAID consultant in Central Asia, May 2005). The Organization for Economic Cooperation and Development (OECD) released an extensive publications series and organized conferences to promote new pension reform ideas in OECD and developing countries. These organizations have coordinated their work through a variety of formal and informal mechanisms. For instance, USAID conducts a thorough evaluation of the work already taking place in support of the pension privatization before designing a complementary work strategy for a country (interview with Denise Lamaute, Senior Pension Reform Adviser, USAID).

This transnational advocacy coalition was not without opponents. Pension privatization was opposed by another coalition composed primarily of the International Social Security Association (ISSA) and the International Labour Organization (ILO), organizations deeply involved in the spread of the early social security model pension systems. These coalitions occasionally debated with one another directly (Beattie and McGillivray, 1995; Fultz, 2004; James, 1996; Queisser, 2000) and also competed in the field. However, ILO had far less funding than the World Bank and was not successful in blocking its norms creation and diffusion mission (interview with Elaine Fultz, ILO Central and East Europe Team, May 2005). As the World Bank-led coalition moved from success to success, the ILO/ISSA-led coalition looked increasingly like it was fighting a rearguard action. In 2000, the ILO issued a book (Gillion et al., 2000) accepting pension privatization as one possible option for reform, though not without faults. Increasingly, ILO provided support on pensions to countries where the World Bank did not advocate pension privatization, particularly in poorer developing countries in Africa, Asia and Europe.

Transnational actors played a tremendous role in pushing Central and East European countries towards the mixed model of pension privatization. The adoption of reforms that so clearly mirrored the World Bank's advice on pension privatization provides once strong piece of evidence of the crucial role that transnational actors played in pension reform decisions in the post-communist European countries. A second piece of evidence is timing. No CEE or FSU country (with the exception of Poland) considered pension privatization prior to 1994. Nearly all CEE and FSU countries considered these reforms after 1994, when the World Bank began its campaign in earnest. Prior to 1994, all CEE and FSU countries introduced emergency measures that rapidly changed their pension systems, mainly with a view to bringing fiscal balance to systems under severe stress by raising contribution rates and cutting benefits in an ad hoc fashion. Pension privatization was never an explicit or implicit part of these changes. Pension privatization was put on the agenda in CEE and FSU countries by a transnational campaign coalition that began its activity in the region in 1994 by spreading and popularizing pension privatization ideas.

Direct involvement in reforms

In addition to the content and timing of reform, the impact of transnational actors needs to be considered because of their extensive involvement in placing the pension privatization on the agenda in CEE and FSU, working with governments on reform design, and supporting the implementation of reforms in cooperation with national governments. While the West European literature has revolved around the influence of globalization, in

Central and Eastern Europe the direct influence of transnational actors on the reform process is undeniable. Table 8.3 shows that all CEE and FSU countries implementing these reforms have enjoyed a range of assistance from transnational actors. While the extent and type varies from country to country, transnational actors have been an omnipresent force in the creation of new pension reform systems.

One of the primary ways that transnational actors have been important in facilitating reform in CEE and FSU is the dissemination of reform ideas and technical information about the pension privatization. Prior to the 1994 publication of *Averting the Old-Age Crisis*, few in CEE or FSU had heard of pension privatization. The World Bank-led effort to spread information about these reforms globally was an important factor in the decisions of many policymakers to support these reforms. For instance, central bank head Grigori Marchenko of Kazakhstan reports that it was his attendance at a World Bank-sponsored conference on pension privatization that convinced him to scrap the reform programme he was working on for Kazakhstan and instead push for the adoption of the pension privatization (interview, July 1998). Chilean economists such as Labour and Social Affairs Minister José Piñera often worked together with the World Bank and USAID to inspire CEE and FSU policymakers about pension privatization and their benefits (interview, 2006). The World Bank and USAID also organized numerous conferences where policymakers were trained in the ideas and techniques of these reforms. In countries considering pension privatization, the World Bank and USAID often paid for journalists and legislators to visit Chile and Argentina to learn more about new pension reform models (Brooks, 2004; Holzmann and Hinz, 2005).

A second lever of transnational actor influence has been the funding of reform teams dedicated to pension privatization. Transnational actors have normally formed coalitions with at least one major domestic partner in each country, usually a Minister of Labour or Minister of Finance (Chłon-Dominczak and Móra, 2003; Müller, 2003). They also have joined with these domestic partners to convince other, more sceptical members of the government and parliament to support pension privatization (interview with Palacios). This process of convincing actors to form or change their preferences on pension reform has multiple aspects including expert debate, public relations campaigns focused on policymakers and the general public, and politically targeted concessions in the design of the pension reform programme. The activities of transnational organizations in these campaigns are to win new supporters and counter the arguments of opponents of reform. In several cases discussed below, transnational actors have worked closely with their domestic partners to craft these debates, public relations campaigns and concessions in order to pass reform legislation. While this process has many stages, generous funding and technical assistance to government reform teams has been a primary means of transnational actor influence. Funding of such reform teams gives pension privatization a special priority within the government agenda. It ensures that this reform will be

Table 8.3 Transnational actor interventions in campaign for pension privatizations

Country	Prior conference attendance	Reform team funded	Pre-reform technical assistance	Implementation assistance	Date of reform	Reform type
Bulgaria	WB	USAID/WB	USAID/WB	USAID/WB	2002	Mixed
Croatia	WB	WB	WB	USAID/WB	2002	Mixed
Estonia	WB/USAID	WB	WB		2001	Parallel
Hungary		WB	WB	WB/USAID/Treas	1998	Mixed
Kazakhstan	WB/USAID	N/A	USAID	WB/USAID	1998	Substitutive
Kosovo		USAID	USAID	USAID	2001	Substitutive
Latvia	WB/USAID	WB	USAID	USAID	2001	Mixed
Macedonia	WB	USAID/WB	USAID/WB	USAID	2002	Mixed
Poland	USAID	WB/USAID	WB/USAID	WB/USAID	1999	Mixed
Russia	WB/USAID	WB	WB		2002	Mixed
Slovakia	USAID	WB	USAID/WB		2003	Mixed
Romania	WB	USAID/WB	USAID/WB		Ongoing	Mixed
Ukraine	WB	USAID	USAID		Ongoing	Mixed
Lithuania	WB/USAID		WB/USAID	USAID	2002	Parallel
Kyrgyzstan		WB	WB		1997	NDC
Uzbekistan	WB				2004	Mixed

Note: WB = World Bank; USAID = US Agency for International Development; Treas = US Treasury Department.

funded, despite other competing priorities. It provides the very best technical assistance in the development of programmes, drafting of reform legislation, and public relations efforts. It therefore enables reformers to use enormous resources unavailable to other parties in the debate to win new supporters and neutralize opponents, countering their arguments in expert and public debate and casting reforms in the most favourable possible light.

A third lever of influence is the provision of post-reform technical assistance and loans. While it may seem unlikely that post-reform assistance influences the reform process, since it takes place after legislation is passed (Holzmann and Hinz, 2005), the fact that governments can rely on extensive assistance during implementation lowers the risk for policymakers in backing the reform. Loans and other assistance may also prevent pension privatization from crowding out other government priorities, thus allowing alliances to form that may have been impossible without assistance. It may also enable side-payments to groups who would otherwise oppose reform.

Together, the timing of reforms in Central and Eastern Europe, the content of reform that reflects the 'mixed' model advocated in that report and evidence of the direct involvement of the World Bank and allied organizations in putting pension privatization on the agenda in multiple countries suggests that these organizations had a major impact on pension reforms reform in CEE and FSU.

Case studies

The following case studies provide examples of the nature of transnational actors' influence on the adoption of pension privatization in CEE and FSU. They show that this influence has included: (1) inspiring reformers by providing them with new information about the benefits of pension privatization; (2) forming coalitions with reformers to win domestic political battles in favour of reform; (3) helping to convince political actors that did not initially support reform; (4) helping to craft compromises with interest groups to insure their support of reform; (5) helping to neutralize opponents of reform. This evidence of deep involvement of transnational actors in domestic reform debates provides a clear mechanism for the influence of transnational actors on seemingly domestic processes of reform. It suggests that reforms have been substantially co-determined by coalitions of domestic and transnational actors. These case studies have been selected to represent a wide range of early (Hungary, Poland, Kazakhstan) and later (Croatia, Romania) reformers across the post-communist region, including East-Central Europe (Hungary, Poland), South-Eastern Europe (Croatia, Romania), and the former Soviet Union (Kazakhstan). Together, they represent more than one-third of total cases.

Hungary

In Hungary, transnational actors were so deeply involved in the pension reform efforts that their involvement must be viewed as necessary, if not sufficient determinants of reform. Reform would not have played out the same way without their involvement, if it had moved ahead at all, and the World Bank helped to put pension reform on the political agenda in Hungary by funding and assisting a working group within the Ministry of Finance to assemble a detailed proposal for new pension reforms in Hungary including mandatory, individual pension savings accounts. It also briefed or financed the briefing and training of numerous government officials in pension reform ideas and techniques. While these efforts had the strong support of Finance Minister Lajos Bokros, it would have been difficult for Hungarians to develop plans for the type of reforms proposed without extensive technical assistance, given that few lawyers or economists in the country had any knowledge or experience of funded pension systems in the late 1990s. Hungary did have a system of voluntary mutual benefit societies, but the reforms proposed by the Ministry of Finance in 1997 did not follow this prior model, but instead mirrored reform models adopted in Chile and Argentina. The Ministry of Finance working group on pension reform drew heavily on international experts to design the reform programme.

At the same time that the Ministry of Finance was working on new pension reform proposals with extensive World Bank assistance, other government agencies were working on reform proposals that reflected greater continuity with the existing pension system in Hungary. The Ministry of Finance's plan had to win support within the cabinet, government coalition and the Prime Minister's office before moving forward. This process depended on winning internal governmental debates that depended on mobilizing public legitimacy, expertise, and public relations. The World Bank worked closely with the Ministry of Finance to back up its proposals with detailed analyses designed to prevail in these internal debates. The World Bank provided modelling software that enabled the Ministry of Finance to independently test opposing proposals and to find them lacking. It helped to convince experts from other government departments of the benefits of its new pension reform proposals and played a major role in these internal debates within the Hungarian government. The World Bank additionally appointed two of its own pension reform experts to work full-time with the inter-ministerial working group in Hungary, assisting with all aspects of reform design, political strategy and public relations.

Transnational actors were also deeply involved pre- and post-reform in providing technical assistance to the Hungarian government agencies charged with implementing the reform and regulating private pension funds. USAID conducted extensive technical assistance projects during the first three years of reform implementation in Hungary from 1998 to 2001, strengthening the regulatory agency for the new private funds and providing a range of other technical support (interview with Denise Lamaute, Senior Pension Reform Adviser, USAID, 5 July 2005).

Pension privatization would not have been implemented in Hungary without extensive involvement and support from transnational actors. While the World Bank and USAID found willing partners in Finance Minister Lajos

Bokros, it is unlikely that Bokros' Finance Ministry had the technical capacity, resources or political power to have designed the reform programme in the same way without the assistance of these organizations. Nor did the Finance Ministry necessarily have the ability to take on the entrenched institutional interests represented by the Ministry of Welfare without World Bank technical assistance. The World Bank provided the ideas behind Hungary's pension reform, the resources that enabled its domestic partners to pursue their work and to win the technical and political battles to achieve their reform objectives. Subsequently Hungary, a leading reform country in Central and Eastern Europe, became a powerful model for other countries in the region and exported its pension reform experts to other countries in the region, often via the World Bank and USAID.

Kazakhstan

Transnational actors also played an important role in putting pension privatization on the agenda in Kazakhstan. Kazakhstan's reform was spurred by leading reformer Grigori Marchenko's attendance at a World Bank sponsored conference on pension reforms, where he heard a speech by Chilean reformer José Piñera (Ellerman, 2001) and returned to Kazakhstan convinced of the benefits of a funded system. USAID provided immediate technical assistance to help in this project, including paying for travel of officials to Chile and other countries to study global pension system models. USAID also provided reform design services and technical assistance of various types. The World Bank ultimately agreed to support the Kazakh reforms and loaned Kazakhstan $300 million to finance transition costs although the Bank was unhappy with several design features and attempted to use loan conditionalities to change them. USAID provided post-reform technical assistance for the first six years of implementation, working on drafting regulations and laws, improving administrative and regulatory systems, and creating better investment opportunities for pension funds.

Conducted in an authoritarian regime, the reform process in Kazakhstan did not require extensive negotiation with actors outside the government. Nonetheless, USAID funded a campaign of public consultation that enabled opponents to voice their mostly ineffectual opposition to the proposed reforms. USAID and the World Bank played a very limited role in helping to convince domestic actors in Kazakhstan to support reform, but a much greater role in ensuring the smooth implementation of reform in an environment that presented many technical and administrative challenges. Ultimately, USAID spent eight years assisting reform implementation in Kazakhstan, helping to establish a central database to record pension contributions, set up a regulatory agency to oversee private pension funds, and draft and revise laws and regulations. Reform in Kazakhstan was thus deeply influenced by the ideas developed and promoted by transnational actors and by the resources that made reform technically feasible in a country with a low level of infrastructure development. Pension privatization would not have made it to Kazakhstan without the effects of the transnational ideational campaign led by the World Bank.

Poland

Poland is a country where transnational policy actors played a large role in putting pension privatization on the domestic policy agenda. In 1991, two leading social policy officials had proposed a privatization of the Polish pension system, but it went nowhere and was quickly dropped from consideration by the government. After the publication of *Averting the Old-Age Crisis* in 1994, the World Bank began advocating pension privatization in Poland and was deeply involved in reform planning. While such reforms were opposed by many within the government and Ministry of Labour and Social Affairs, they were promoted by the left-wing Finance Minister Grzegorz Kołodko. The Ministry of Finance and later the Office for the Plenipotentiary for Pension Reform received substantial assistance from the World Bank and USAID to prepare reform legislation, convince legislators from various parties of the benefits of pension privatization, develop modelling software, and to prepare governmental institutions for reform implementation. The World Bank even seconded one of its leading pension reform officials, a Polish citizen, Michał Rutkowski, to head this Polish government office. The World Bank and USAID were also critical in reform implementation, as Poland experienced severe administrative difficulties in its social security administration, ZUS. Without World Bank support, it is unclear that the Polish government would have been able to move forward with an ambitious reform effort in the face of multiple sources of domestic opposition and delay. USAID even funded a major public relations campaign that helped to win public support for the pension reform effort. USAID and the World Bank continued to provide technical assistance for several years after the initial implementation of reform. These substantial resources cannot be underestimated in terms of their ability to mobilize governmental support and to subdue political opposition. Poland's reform efforts were controversial in part because the International Labour Organization produced a reform claiming that Polish private pension funds produced negative real rates of return and also because of severe difficulties in making its computerized accounts systems function appropriately. However, these negative impacts were minimized by the continued transnational aid effort, including World Bank and USAID funding for a domestic campaign to inform policymakers and thought leaders to learn about pension privatization, funding for many years of policy development, and loans and technical assistance to facilitate smooth implementation of the programme. Domestic path-dependencies and interest groups were swept away in the campaign for pension privatization in Poland and a major path-departure ensued, transforming Poland into an important model for other countries in the region.

Croatia

Transnational actors also played a strong role in influencing the Croatian government to adopt new pension reforms in 1999. Croatia's previous pension system provided one of the most generous benefits in Europe at a 90 per cent average replacement rate, compared to previous earnings (Müller, 2003, p. 94), while previous reform efforts in the 1990s had not included individual pension savings accounts (Müller, 2003, p. 96). The World Bank, together with a small NGO, the EastWest Institute, organized the governmental conference in 1995 that helped to put pension privatization on the political agenda in Croatia and to spread information in the policy community about their nature and benefits. The World Bank and USAID funded an interministerial working group for pension reform and provided a wide range of technical assistance. Along with other transnational actors, the World Bank and USAID were also deeply involved in convincing Croatian reformers to enact pension privatization and provided extensive technical assistance to make the reforms a reality. The World Bank also granted a leave of absence to a Croatian employee and former deputy minister of finance of Croatia, Zoran Anušić, to lead the pension reform effort (Müller, 2003, p. 97). The closeness of the World Bank and the Croatian government is evidenced by Zoran Anušić's work for both organizations. After leading reform efforts in Croatia, he was hired back by the World Bank to advise reform efforts in Macedonia and other Central and East European countries. Croatia's pension reform passed the legislature in 1999, but with the death of President Franjo Tuđjman, the new government first reviewed and then ultimately enacted the reform in 2002. The transnational coalition for pension privatization helped to put reform on the agenda in Croatia, and provided the local leadership for the reform effort domestically, as well as loans and grants for reform development and implementation. The ideational influence was arguably most significant, though backed up with substantial resources that enabled a path-departure in Croatian pensions, one of the largest as a percentage of GDP in the CEE region.

Romania

Romania shows the influence of transnational policy actors in planning reform while engaging in long-term struggles with various governments not committed to reform. Romania has legislated, but not yet implemented, its new pension reform system based on individual accounts. Cashu (2005) shows that despite a deep crisis in Romania's pension system in the 1990s and World Bank technical advice to address it, the World Bank initially did not promote pension privatization in Romania, nor did pension privatization figure on the agenda of the governing Party of Social Democracy from 1990 to 1996. The Ministry of Labour and Social Protection's first proposal designed to address the fiscal imbalances of the pension system did not contain provisions for mandatory pension savings, but rather targeted retirement age, eligibility criteria and benefit formula rather than systemic restructuring. It further supported the development of private, voluntary pension schemes. While the proposal reached the parliamentary stage of the process in the summer of 1996, it received no priority because of the imminent general elections in the fall and the Party of Social Democracy was defeated at the polls by a four-party centre-right coalition led by Emil Constantinescu. The new government withdrew the draft pension law from the parliament but later reintroduced it without significant changes, and began to discuss the creation of a mandatory savings scheme in 1997 championed by Minister of Labour Alexandru Athanasiu. At that point, the World Bank granted a loan to the Romanian government to finance reform-related projects. A group representing the drafting team, political parties and social partners travelled to Chile to study the Chilean model at first hand. Also with World Bank support, the Ministry of Labour held an international conference in Bucharest in 1999 featuring the architect of the Chilean reform, José Piñera.

The new pension reform proposal reached parliament, but failed to make any headway beyond the specialized committees. As general elections in November 2000 drew closer, chances of its passage dimmed as the centre-right coalition began to disintegrate. Prime Minister Mugur Isărescu then introduced the new pension system through an emergency ordinance, a constitutional provision allowing the executive to approve draft laws pending their formal adoption by the legislature within one year. Parliament then approved pension privatization in early 2000 and USAID launched a project to provide technical assistance. However, after new elections, the new government abrogated the Isărescu decree and invoked the need for a conventional parliamentary procedure proportionate to the social importance of this law, thus dragging its feet on reform during 2000–04. Laws on voluntary and mandatory private pension funds were finally passed in June and October 2004 respectively, only a month before general elections. Not only were the laws similar to the one passed in 2000, but implementation was left to the next government. At the time of this writing, the World Bank and USAID are involved in setting up administrative and regulatory aspects of the new pension system, though it is yet to be implemented. The Romanian case demonstrates that even in the face of strong government resistance, the World Bank and USAID have not given up their effort to pass legislation enabling pension privatization. While Romania has yet to implement this reform, showing the continued importance of domestic actors in determining reform outcomes, the transnational campaign for pension privatization will likely continue over the long term until it finds a government willing to implement reform.

Conclusion

A World Bank-led transnational advocacy campaign for pension privatization has had a powerful impact on the course of welfare state development after communism in CEE and FSU. While domestic political and economic factors have also been important in explaining the propensity of CEE and FSU countries to conduct reform and determine the shape reform has taken, transnational actors are essential in understanding the timing of reform and its content. In particular, this chapter has shown that no CEE or FSU country seriously considered pension privatization prior to 1994, the year of the World Bank publication *Averting the Old-Age Crisis*, which created a template for pension privatization worldwide, despite the existence of severe pension systems crises starting in 1989. Almost every country in the region, however, began to consider such reforms after the publication of this report and the transnational advocacy coalition that it unleashed in the mid-1990s. The World Bank and other organizations that cooperated with it, including USAID, played a tremendous role in putting pension privatization on the agenda in CEE and FSU. They did this by organizing training and briefing sessions to inform policymakers about new developments in pension system design and funding small reform teams that helped to craft new pension reform proposals with the assistance of numerous international consultants. In many cases, transnational actors helped their domestic partners to win political battles by providing staff that worked closely with reformers to help them prevail while also providing post-reform implementation assistance. With the support of transnational actors, domestic reformers have proven able to convince sceptics within the government and parliament of the benefits of reform. Transnational actors often spent several years providing technical assistance to address through the complex issues of computer systems design and operation and regulation of private funds which help to insure reform success and tip the balance in favour of reform in other countries that may look to their neighbours for stories of success or failure. Without the strong advocacy of these new pension reforms by the World Bank and USAID, it is unlikely that so many countries would have adopted these reforms in such a short period of time.

Implications

These findings raise important questions for scholars of welfare state development and change, path-dependency and the 'Europeanization' of Central and Eastern Europe. While welfare state studies have been dominated by a national perspective that argues that welfare state decisions remain strongly rooted in national, not international, political, economic and demographic trends, this chapter shows that transnational actors have had a powerful role in setting welfare state policies in Central and Eastern Europe. This raises questions about how to integrate the role of transnational actors into welfare state theory. This chapter has suggested that transnational actors may have the authority, particularly in middle-income developing countries, to overcome domestic institutional path-dependencies because of greater resources and ideational or expert authority.

Second, these findings suggest that the size of pension systems does not determine the propensity to reform in Central and East European welfare states. While Myles and Pierson (2001) suggest that countries with smaller state pension systems are more likely to adopt pension privatization, in Central and Eastern Europe, some of the countries with the most highly developed systems were the first to adopt such reforms. Other countries at all levels of pension system development followed.

Third, despite the long and growing literature on the 'Europeanization' of Central and Eastern Europe (cf. Schimmelfennig and Sedelmeier, 2005; Vachudova, 2005), it has been the World Bank, not the EU, that has had the most pervasive influence over pension reform in the region. The transnational actors involved in pension reform have been based largely in the US and advocated reforms substantially different from EU models. While there is some evidence to suggest that the European Commission did not oppose the implementation of pension privatization in Central and Eastern Europe (Orenstein, 2008b), it was certainly not a major actor in these reform processes (Pochet, 2003). This suggests that the transnational dimension of transition in Central and Eastern Europe goes far beyond the influence of the European Union alone and involves the integration into a broader set of international organizations. In any given policy area, a variety of transnational actors have been involved in policy; research into their activities and cooperation will reveal which actors have been most important. A presumption that the EU has been the central influence does not appear to be warranted.

This chapter has shown that welfare state developments in Central and Eastern Europe do not fully conform to the national perspective on welfare state development and change. Welfare state development in this region and other middle-income regions of the world are significantly affected by the agendas and actions of a variety of transnational actors. The World Bank and USAID have been the primary movers in Central and East European pension reform. They have found domestic partners and pursued a radical reform agenda that constitutes a major path-departure for welfare states in the region. This dramatic example of welfare state path-departure should cause analysts of developing and developed welfare states to better integrate the study of transnational actor influence into prevailing models of welfare state.

9
Elder Care Systems: Policy Transfer and Europeanization

*Hildegard Theobald and Kristine Kern**

Introduction

Since the 1990s, demographic and social changes in a situation of welfare state constraints have challenged prevalent elder care approaches in many Western countries and resulted not only in the restructuring of existing elder care systems but also in the creation of new systems. In Central and Eastern European (CEE) countries the fundamental shift of most welfare systems since the 1990s led to the advent of home-based elder care, which is a rather new phenomenon in this part of Europe.

A comparison of various policy approaches reveals common traits of the reforms in most countries, such as the introduction of market principles in care provision. In contrast, the establishment of separate funding systems started in some Continental European countries and, after being transferred to other countries in Continental Europe (and even to Japan), policy transfer can now be traced to countries in Southern and Central Europe. National care policies have been generated by the complex interplay of actors, ideas and institutions and, despite a trend of path-dependency, prevalent welfare systems change to meet the challenges of 'new' social risks. New welfare state policies are adapted to the existing basic principles and the country-specific goals and are embedded in the interplay of national and transnational actors, ideas and institutions. Our findings confirm the adaptation of prevalent national elder care policies to new social situations and the interplay of national and transnational actors.

In this chapter we analyse the factors that determine the change of elder care systems, including internal factors, such as the emergence of new actor constellations, and external factors, such as foreign models or EU politics. The changing design of national care systems will be explained by the complex interaction of factors originating within and beyond nation-states. Due to the distinctive features of the policy area of elder care, local-state relations and the interplay of the different levels need also to be taken into account.

148

Theoretically, the chapter draws, first, on approaches created by international comparative welfare state research, in particular in the area of social and elder care, to specify the significant dimensions of the policy field and preconditions for change. Second, we address research on policy diffusion and policy transfer concentrating on well-established research areas such as pension policy. The question of how individual countries learn, not only from their own experiences with elder care but also from the experiences of their peers, has not been analysed systematically. Third, the chapter is based on research concerned with the new modes of European governance. As in other fields of social policy, in the area of health and long-term care the Open Method of Coordination (OMC) has been introduced by the EU to support the institutionalization of best-practice transfer between member states.

Empirically, the chapter compares changes in care provision, funding and social rights in CEE countries (in particular in Estonia) with the development in Continental Europe (in particular in Germany and Austria) and Southern Europe (in particular in Italy and Spain). Thus, the analysis includes CEE countries, in which a lack of care provision and funding existed at the beginning of the 1990s. Moreover, elder care policy changes have taken place in the CEE countries within the framework of a general shift in welfare policies.

The analysis of the countries selected for our comparative study enables us to examine the influence of internal and external factors and their complex interaction at the national level systematically. Therefore, the next section starts with some theoretical explanations for the change of elder care systems. This includes (i) factors at national level, (ii) (bilateral) policy diffusion and policy transfer, and (iii) internationalization and Europeanization. Based on this conceptual framework, we empirically analyse the influence of these three factors on selected elder care systems.

Welfare state change: theoretical considerations

National level

Despite the influence of transnational processes, in elder care policy, national and subnational initiatives remain central to policy change. The development of elder care policy is characterized by its embeddedness in social and family relations and the combination of different societal sectors but also by the complex interplay of policies at central, regional and local level.

Based on cultural values, the family has traditionally been viewed as being responsible for the provision and funding of elder care. Only gradually has elder care responsibility – in terms of cultural values, funding and provision – become defined as a public concern governed in addition by the state and the market (Anttonen et al., 2003). In her approach Pfau-Effinger (2004) emphasizes cultural values and ideas, which are related to the state–market–family mix governing elder care in different countries. She points to three particularly significant concepts and ideas, which differ considerably between countries:

- the welfare mix (combination of different societal sectors);
- the state–market relationship;
- the dominant concepts of justice and redistribution.

Different theoretical-conceptual concepts have been established for the analysis of welfare state change. The concepts 'critical junctures' and 'formative moments' have been created to explain more radical welfare policy change not in line with existing policies (see Pierson, 2004; for elder care see Brodin, 2005; for CEE countries see Inglot, this volume). When a critical juncture is reached, structural conditions change and existing institutions are destabilized. Critical junctures are formative moments, which enable agents to form new institutions and to choose between different options without being restricted by existing institutions. During formative moments ideas held by the actors involved in the political struggle become decisive. They function as a lens for the interpretation of the changing environment, but when they become embedded in new institutional settings, they give meaning to political actions within the established framework.

In contrast, Thelen (2004) argues that most policy change takes an incremental form. In this line of research welfare states are defined as evolutionary systems constantly adapting to new situations, which can take place in four areas: functional recalibration, that is, a new definition of the main functions; distributive recalibration, that is, reallocati on of benefits between beneficiaries; normative recalibration, that is, change of norms and values; and institutional recalibration, that is, change of levels and sectors of policy-making (Ferrera et al., 2000; Hemerijck, 2007). Cerami emphasizes a continuous process 'of construction, deconstruction and reconstruction of existing ideas, interests and institutions' (Cerami, this volume). Characteristic for transformative processes are their recombinant character, that is, combining pre-existing and new elements.

Welfare state changes are viewed as the result of the interplay of ideas, actors and interests embedded in institutional frameworks. Ideas impact policy change in different ways (see Béland, 2009). As economic and social assumptions ideas can (de)legitimize existing welfare and political institutions, they can be used as political weapons. Ideas become influential only when they interact with powerful political actors and institutional forces. Institutional forces offer opportunities or create major constraints that affect both the strategies of the actors and the diffusion of their ideas. Decentralization and institutional fragmentation can have a major influence on policy-making.

Political institutions in the field of elder care policies stretch simultan-eously across local, regional and central levels and the interplay of these levels become crucial for policy development. In his approach to explain care policies within countries, Alber (1995) suggests that the key factor is their vertical (de)centralization. Traditionally, elder care policies were developed and implemented at local level, but country-specific central–local relations have now become decisive (Anttonen et al., 2003). Furthermore, vertical (de)centralization is important for policy development and implementation in a multi-level system (see Rauch, 2005; Burau et al., 2007). Despite the significance of debates and actors at national and subnational level, exter-nal influences – particularly the transfer of ideas and approaches between countries and the initiatives of international and transnational actors – increasingly impact on policy development and elder care policy design.

(Bilateral) policy diffusion and policy transfer

Policy diffusion and policy transfer is by no means a new phenomenon in the area of social policy. Research on the early development of pensions pol-icy shows that Germany's system, which can be characterized by a high level of continuity, served as a model and spread to the neighbouring countries in continental Europe. The Bismarckian system had a strong influence on Luxembourg, Belgium, France and Austria-Hungary. Moreover, research reveals that Germany and Austria-Hungary learned lessons from each other (Glootz, 2003, pp. 51f., 253) and that developments in Germany and Austria-Hungary had a direct impact on the social policy of today's Czech Republic, Slovakia, Hungary and Poland (Cerami, 2008a; Szikra and Tomka, this volume).

The transfer of ideas, institutions and policies plays a particularly import-ant role when policy change is taking place due to strong pressure for reform or due to the creation of new institutional arrangements, such as elder care systems in CEE countries. Such a situation opens up new opportunities for policy entrepreneurs and may, eventually, lead to policy changes. The social policy reforms of the 1990s in post-socialist countries were influenced by ideas developed by other countries as well as by international organizations. Diffusion processes became most visible in the context of pension privat-ization. This process began in 1981 with the privatization of the Chilean pensions system. Although this radical model shows rather unique features, similar approaches emerged in the 1990s not only in South America (for example in Peru, Argentina, Columbia, Bolivia) but also in almost all new EU member states in Central and Eastern Europe (Orenstein, 2008a).

The general discussion on this phenomenon concentrates on several strongly related concepts such as policy diffusion, policy transfer, lesson-drawing and policy convergence (Kern, 2000; Rose, 2005; Bulmer et al., 2007, Holzinger et al., 2008). While diffusion studies are more concerned with the timing and the sequence of adoptions than with what is done

(Rose, 2005, p. 23), the convergence literature focuses primarily on policy effects, and both lesson-drawing and policy transfer are more interested in the policy process (Bulmer et al., 2007, p. 14).

Rogers (2003, pp. 5, 11) defines diffusion as 'the process by which an innovation is communicated through certain channels over time among the members of a social system'. Based on this classical definition, best-practice transfer depends, first, on the existence of a policy innovation that is recognized as best practice, second, on a pioneer with the capacities to develop and label best practice and, third, on a group of potential adopters with adequate absorptive capacities and the willingness to adopt. However, best-practice transfer is far from being a smooth flow of ideas and policies from the best-practice source to the recipient. Instead learning from best practice is shaped by national institutions and may include contentious policy debates. Richard Rose (2005, p. 81) describes various ways of drawing a lesson which range from copying and adaptation to hybridization and synthesis and, finally, to pure inspiration and selective imitation. For the CEE countries Jacoby (2004, p. 6) argues that copying occurred in some cases but that it was rather rare and that CEE elites often tried to make significant local adaptations to foreign templates.

The regional spread of policy innovations in concentric circles that is originating from the centres of innovation can be explained by the fact that the knowledge necessary for the adoption of a policy is far more accessible to neighbours. Neighbourhood effects were first confirmed through studies on the diffusion of policy innovations among the United States. It can therefore be assumed that pioneering countries, such as Germany in the case of the establishment of the first pensions system and Chile in the case of pension privatization (Weyland, 2005), became centres of regional diffusion clusters because neighbouring countries tend to imitate and emulate the forerunners. Apart from geographical proximity, cultural proximity (in a particular language) can become a crucial factor for the adoption of a policy innovation from abroad.

Pioneers need considerable capacities to develop, test and label best practice. This requires different forms of networking with experts and policy entrepreneurs in other countries, ranging from participation at international conferences to establishing transnational expert networks. Such formalized networks shape the communication relations among pioneers and potential adopters and determine the transfer process. Two types of best-practice transfer can be distinguished here. It appears to be crucial whether direct bilateral relations dominate, for example between two neighbouring countries, or communication is channelled through multilateral networks. Transfer mechanisms and learning patterns may change with the increasing institutionalization of best-practice transfer through transnational networks, which have characterized European social policy from its outset (Kaelble, 2005). With their objective of spreading ideas, knowledge and best practice, transnational networks change communication patterns, influence the selection of best practice and create new arenas for transnational policy learning and lesson-drawing.

Europeanization and internationalization

Thus, social policy is not only influenced by policy transfers between countries but also by international organizations and the European Union, which may develop and promote their own policy models. The spectrum of international and European policies ranges from legally binding regulations to simple benchmarking and recommendations (Citi and Rhodes, 2006, p. 469). International organizations, in particular the International Labour Organization (ILO), played an important role in the worldwide spread of policy approaches following both World Wars. Competition emerged in the 1990s between two advocacy coalitions led by the World Bank and the ILO (Orenstein, 2008b, p. 69; Brooks, 2005). In contrast to the situation in Latin America, pension privatization in CEE countries was driven primarily by the World Bank's influential report *Averting the Old-Age Crisis* from 1994 (Orenstein, this volume). Although the World Bank was less influential in other areas of social policy, conflict and cooperation among international organizations (World Bank, OECD, ILO, WHO, and so on) and the formation of (opposing) transnational advocacy coalitions appear to have been a crucial factor for social policy reforms in CEE (cf. Cerami, 2006).

The influential role of international organizations for the development of social policy in CEE countries may be explained by the fact that EU social policy has been dominated by 'soft' forms of control because the EU refrained from the creation of a uniform social protection system and the imposition of social policies 'from above'. Harmonization has therefore been limited to just a few areas. Europeanization through legally binding regulations is clearly not as advanced in social policy as it is in other policy areas. Thus, EU conditionality played a rather limited role for social policy reforms in CEE accession countries (cf. Orenstein, 2008a; Sissenich, 2007). However, capacity building and policy reforms were supported by twinning projects and were subsidized through EU funding programmes such as PHARE (Cerami, 2006, p. 67).

In the absence of legally binding regulations, organizations such as the OECD and the EU have started using the concept of benchmarking. This approach has become an important management tool since the 1950s (Arrowsmith et al., 2004, p. 312). Benchmarking systems create institutional settings that make differences more transparent and allow comparisons between the countries. Rankings are based on a strategy of naming and shaming, thus creating a coercive dynamic through the disclosure of information and peer pressure that appears to promote compliance. The definition and use of process and performance indicators facilitate systematic learning from best practice and help to find measures to improve performance. Performance measurement can be seen as a step towards the systematic benchmarking of national policies. While best-practice transfer focuses primarily on the league leader, benchmarking offers a choice between different programmes with a high standard of performance (Rose, 2005, pp. 39, 54).

The idea of benchmarking has influenced the development of new forms of European governance. In the EU, 'benchmarking seems to be every-where' (Arrowsmith et al., 2004, p. 311). Starting with the EMU's Maastricht membership criteria and the Stability and Growth Pact, the practice of benchmarking has been transferred to other policy areas in which the EU's competences are rather limited. Since the late 1990s, a new form of regu-lation, the Open Method of Coordination (OMC), has been applied in the area of employment policy and subsequently extended to other policy areas such as pension reform policy and health-care policy.

The introduction of the OMC implies that the transfer of certain pol-icy elements and the sporadic adoption of foreign policy innovations have been replaced by an institutionalized form of transnationalization which is based on the systematic comparison of the performance of all EU member states. The OMC typically involves a decentralized but systematically coor-dinated benchmarking process that goes far beyond voluntary actions. As a result, pressure on the individual countries has intensified and tools have been created which ensure functionally equivalent services in all member states. Various combinations of benchmarking with voluntary or legally binding regulations and a structured coordination process can be found in the EU (Citi and Rhodes, 2006, p. 469). Although the OMC has created new forums for mutual learning, its strong reliance on peer pressure (Borrás and Jacobsson, 2004, p. 194) and the absence of sanctions and enforcement mechanisms can be seen as its major weakness (Heidenreich and Bischoff, 2008; Arrowsmith et al., 2004).

Elder care changes in a cross-country comparison

The conceptual approaches discussed above demonstrate, first and foremost, the importance of national factors for the development of elder care systems. At the national level the interplay of state, market and family as well as the local–central relations are crucial for policy development. Second, it can be assumed that elder care systems are influenced by foreign models, which are frequently transferred between countries, in particular between countries that show a high degree of geographical and cultural proximity. Finally, inter-national organizations and the European Union can also be expected to influ-ence national care systems. In the following empirical section, all three factors and their interaction in the selected countries are analysed comparatively.

National level

In the following, the newly established elder care policies and developments at national level are discussed based on a process-tracing approach, which focuses on the interplay of ideas, actors and institutions. Since the 1990s, in Continental and later on in Southern Europe demographic and social changes coupled with a lack of public elder care support triggered an intense societal debate. Care-dependency was not accepted as a social risk, which resulted in a significant 'underinsurance', for example high private costs for the elderly and their families, high levels of dependency on social assistance and a high care burden for the families (see Pacolet et al., 2000; OECD, 2006). Besides, a lack of adequate funding and home-based care provision was also stated in the CEE countries, in which the health and social care systems had been heavily oriented towards institutionalized care during the communist era.

The changes are analysed in the three clusters of countries – Continental Europe, Southern Europe and CEE countries. Within the Continental European countries societal debate centred around the question of the establishment of a new collectively funded social security system in a situation of welfare state constraint and the suitable modes of funding (Eisen and Mager, 1999; Pacolet et al., 2000; OECD, 2006). Debates have also highlighted care provision and asked how a high-quality and efficient care provision can be ensured. In line with general criticism on the welfare state care delivery by private providers together with the promotion of care within the family framework were viewed as a means to expand and improve care provision.

The debates related to funding ultimately resulted in the introduction of universal social rights and separate funding systems – either tax- or social insurance-funded or a combination of both – in various Continental European countries such as Austria (1993), Germany (1995/96), Luxemburg (1999), Flanders (Belgium) (2002), France (2002) and even Japan (2000). With the exception of Flanders separate funding systems have been introduced at central level. In contrast to the increasing public responsibility related to funding, the opening-up of a publicly financed care provision for private providers strengthened market elements. In addition, the family should be supported on the basis of a cash benefit and/or formal care provision. The restructuring has profoundly changed the state–market–family nexus with regard to funding and care provision (see Burau et al., 2007).

These changes and policy processes will be analysed in a greater detail using the example of Germany as a forerunner country. Owing to the federalist and corporatist orientation of Germany's political institutions, the ensuing process of policy development involved politicians from all governmental levels, representatives of the health care insurances and civic society actors, for example unions, employer organizations, organizations of pensioners and provider associations (Meyer, 1996).

The increasing costs at local levels for residential care provided the main incentive for the establishment of Long-term Care Insurance (LTCI) in 1995/96 (Campell and Morgan, 2005). On the basis of a mandatory social insurance – in line with the German social insurance tradition – funds were allocated to the sector and the state–market–family mix changed profoundly (see Meyer, 1996):

- The new law introduced a universal social right concerning care dependency instead of the existing residual social right based on the Federal Law on Social Assistance. In contrast to the German health-care tradition, only basic funding was granted. At the beginning of the LTCI debate most of the political and civic society actors argued for a more comprehensive funding level comparable to the health-care sector; in the end, however, the more economically oriented actors within the political parties prevailed.
- In line with the predominant discussion on the role of the market and already existing private care provision, the opening-up of a care market on equal terms for private providers was promoted as a precondition to increase efficiency, contain costs and strengthen user choice.
- The introduction of cash benefits as symbolic payment for family carers corresponds to traditional ideas on the role of families in elder care, while simultaneously signalling a departure from the health-care tradition. In particular, pensioners' or handicapped organizations demanded – unsuccessfully – a cash benefit on the payment level of service provision.
- The responsibility for the organization of care provision shifted to a new actor constellation that included politicians at regional and local levels, representatives of the care insurance funds and the provider organizations.

In contrast in Southern Europe, the family's responsibility for care provision was still emphasized during the 1990s related to a considerable lack of funding and care service provision (Bettio and Plantenga, 2004). It is only recently that a tax-based National Fund for Dependency has been introduced in Italy. Furthermore, a tax-funded scheme for long-term care provision has been established in Spain to expand and promote care provision (Simonazzi, 2008). In Italy the complex central–local interplay combined with a situation of welfare state constraints has impeded the introduction of new funding systems (for the development in Spain see section on policy transfer). In Italy the establishment of care services has been considered a local responsibility and has led to uneven and very restricted care provision. The limited public funds available for care provision and the significant local and regional differences fostered political initiatives to establish a sound funding system at central level. Centre-left governments in the 1990s favoured the introduction of a new national policy but reform was delayed until 2008 by the principle of cost-neutrality (Ranci, 2007; Lamura, 2007).

Since the mid-1990s, CEE countries have started initiatives to develop new elder care policies oriented towards home-based care. Owing to their legacy of institutionalized health and elder care services during the communist era, home-based care services in CEE countries were heavily underdeveloped until the early 1990s (Nospickel, 2005; Cerami, 2006). Public support related to elder care now comprises a range of different benefits that includes benefits for family carers, as well as different types of home-based services. Characteristic of elder care support is its coverage by different legal frameworks with different eligibility criteria and sources of tax and social insurance based funding (European Commission, 2007a, 2007b). In general, benefits covered by the welfare system – social care – are mainly residual, that is means-tested and family-oriented. The emphasis on the role of the family related to social elder care corresponds to the strong emphasis on family care prevalent in CEE countries, while in health care more universalistic attitudes prevail (Alber and Köhler, 2004; Ferge, 2001b).

Restricted and regionally uneven home-based care delivery and the residual orientation of social care services impede the access to service provision in most countries. In her analysis of the development of social care services in CEE countries Nospickel (2005) found that care services – limited and with low-quality standards – were already introduced at local level but regulated at central level during the 1980s. Following the fall of communism, the main goals were the decentralization of responsibility to the local level, the expansion and diversification of care delivery and the opening up of care provision to private providers. Recently, the problems of adequate funding for care provision have resulted in efforts to introduce separate funding systems in the Czech Republic and Slovenia, which resemble Continental European approaches (see section on transfer processes).

The analysis of the development in Estonia offers a more detailed insight into the process of change. As in many countries social care support has been developed within the social welfare system and home nursing-care within the health-care system. Social care benefits are provided at the municipal level within the framework of the 'Social Welfare Act' (1995). The law introduced a cash benefit for the support of disabled people in need of assistance and provided the basis for the establishment of care services oriented towards a community care model (Jesse et al., 2004). In case of old age, the obligation of the family to take care of family members is stipulated by Estonian law, and the state is only responsible if the family is not available or cannot afford care provision (Burau et al., 2007). The family responsibility and the devolution of care provision to the local level correspond to a tradition already established in Estonia during the period of independence. In the communist era, social services were regulated by the central government, but self-help movements have already organized support for disabled people since the mid-1980s (Kivisaar and Scots, 2006). During the reform social care provision was opened up to private providers, although public providers still dominate (Burau et al., 2007). Thus, social care policies combine ideas related to the Scandinavian model with liberal ideas of private care provision and ideas prevalent during the period of independence, for example the emphasis on family-based elder care.

Home-nursing services in Estonia have been established since 2003 within the framework of the health-care system related to the goal of de-hospitalization, but they are still widely underdeveloped (Jesse et al., 2004; Burau et al., 2007). Characteristic for the development of health-care policy in Estonia is the idea of combining public responsibility and universalism in terms of funding from the communist era with the reintroduction of a Bismarckian-oriented social insurance from the period of independence and the market-oriented provision of services (Jesse et al., 2004; Cerami, 2006, 2009a).

Over the years the roles of key interest groups in the reform process of health care have changed (see Jesse et al., 2004). During the first phase of the reforms the Estonian Medical Association was very influential; for example, even before independence this association began work on a concept for compulsory health-care insurance. New political actors emerged during the reform process, such as the 'Estonian Patient Representative Union' (EPRU) or representatives of the health insurance funds, and they are now regularly involved in reform processes.

(Bilateral) policy diffusion and policy transfer

Transnational factors have influenced policy changes at national levels. Policy transfer can be general in nature, that is involving a wide range of countries with distinct elder care approaches, or it can be limited to clusters of countries with certain policy approaches. The opening-up of care provision to private providers can be found in different countries with very different approaches. Transfer processes related to the establishment of separate funding systems exist in Continental European countries and even in Japan and, in addition, have recently been transferred to some Southern European and CEE countries.

The establishment of the Long-term Care Insurance (LTCI) in Germany and the care allowance in Austria had crucial effects on policy developments in other countries. The risk of care-dependency was formally covered for the first time in Austria in 1993. By defining different levels of care needs the tax-based Austrian system aims to guarantee universal access to cash benefits, which are directly provided for the care users to purchase professional services or to support care within the family (Mager and Manegold, 1999). These developments in Austria had repercussions on the debate in Germany as Austrian experts served as advisers in Germany. Since the late 1990s, the German model has inspired and influenced the development of separate funding systems in Luxemburg, Japan, Flanders and France (Köstler, 1999; Pacolet et al., 2000; Matsumoto, 2003; Lebihan and Martin, 2008). Characteristic of the transfer process is the adaptation of the funding system to the conditions of the individual country. Transfer is seen here as a policy process, based on the interplay of transnational and national actors embedded in certain political institutions.

Most impressive in this respect is the example of Japan. Like other Western countries, the traditional Japanese elder care model emphasized family care supplemented by tax-funded local care provision mainly targeting the lower socioeconomic classes (Burau et al., 2007; Izuhara, 2003). Emerging problems caused by demographic changes, increasing costs for the health-care system, the failure of two governmental programmes, combined with extensive lobbying from outside, provided the preconditions for change (Ikegami et al., 2003). In fact, Japanese history shows that the country has frequently adopted European ideas, including social security models (Tanaka, 2004). The introduction of a social insurance system was supported by a comprehensive analysis of the German approach and the invitation of German experts to Japan (Matsumoto, 2003). Within the country the transnational influences were taken up by new political actors – the Women's Association, the Citizens Committee and the Welfare Majors – that were in favour of the idea of a social insurance as a means to establish more public responsibility. In the process the conventional social-welfare policy community was destabilized, thereby allowing non-established political players to enter the arena (Eto, 2001).

More recently, countries and regions in Southern Europe have introduced separate funding systems as a means to secure a sound financial basis. In Spain a tax-funded system was introduced, based on the 'Law on the Promotion of Personal Autonomy and Care for People in a Situation of Care-dependency'. Like the Austrian model it is a tax-funded system, although the choice between service provision and a cash payment for family carers, the regulation of service provision at regional level and the opening-up of a care market make it closer to the German model (European Commission, 2007b). In Italy, the difficulties of establishing adequate funds for elder care provision at the national level resulted in the introduction of a new policy scheme at the regional level. Based on the reports of German and Austrian social policy experts, the Italian province South Tyrol, a region that borders Austria, introduced a care allowance system in 2007 which resembles the Austrian one.[1]

During the reform process in the CEE countries, transnational influences played an important role and led to a combination of different policy models. In two CEE countries new funding systems related to social care have recently been or are going to be established. In the Czech Republic a tax-based allowance oriented towards the Austrian system has been introduced (European Commission, 2007a). In Slovenia, plans have been developed to introduce a new compulsory LTCI system (European Commission, 2007b). The transfer of policies from Germany and Austria to Flanders, Luxemburg, South Tyrol, the Czech Republic and Slovenia reveals that neighbourhood effects are important for the diffusion of policy innovation.

German and Scandinavian influences played a significant role in the health-care and social-care reform in Estonia. During the country's process of establishing social health-care insurance, experts from both countries promoted the introduction of their own models. The Social Welfare Act was inspired by Scandinavian welfare traditions and even includes copies of paragraphs from several Scandinavian countries (Trumm, 2006). Furthermore, a Swedish consultancy became involved in policy efforts to shorten hospital stays in order to establish a less institutionalized system of health-care provision. Ultimately, the laws stipulating mandatory health-care insurance in Estonia can be interpreted as a compromise between the more expensive German health insurance model and the more affordable Scandinavian model (Jesse et al., 2004; Cerami, 2006).

Europeanization and internationalization

Although decisions on social policy are primarily made at national level, EU politics has had various impacts on the development of social policies in its member states. This concerns direct effects on social policy, emanating from social policy campaigns or, more recently, from the Open Method of Coordination (OMC) and – in particular for CEE countries – from programmes, funds and reports related to accession. In addition, during the welfare shift in the CEE countries, international organizations (World Bank, IMF, OECD, WHO) influenced the welfare state development significantly.

The creation of a European Ageing Policy already began at the end of the 1980s because demographic and social changes in EU member states became evident and the effects of European integration on the elderly, for example in terms of freedom of movement, also became apparent. An initial approach was provided by the European Social Charter of 1989, which called for, inter alia, economic security for the elderly and adequate benefits in case of illness for all EU citizens. The first action programme for the elderly (1991 to 1993) provided a key impulse for the emergence of a stronger Europe-oriented ageing policy (BMFSFJ, 1994). The main objectives were concretized within this process and became a part of the implementation of the European Social Charter.

The EU's Ageing Policy initially targeted the voluntary adoption of best practice, while the harmonization of national policies was completely rejected (BMFSFJ, 1994; Schulte, 2001). The introduction of the OMC in different social policy areas at the European Council summit in Lisbon in 2000 marked the adoption of a more coordinated transfer of ideas and regulations. The OMC on 'Health and Long-term Care' launched in 2004 and combined with the OMC Social Inclusion and Pension in 2007 defines three objectives for health and long-term care: (1) the accessibility of care services; (2) the provision of high-quality care; and (3) the financial sustainability of the policies. Due to the complexity of the health sector and national differences, no system of benchmarking has been applied, but the exchange of information on best practice – with the participation of all relevant actors at regional, central and EU levels – were defined as suitable measures for the application of the OMC. At EU level the OMC was stressed as a means to improve efficiency in European health-care provision. Social policy and financial goals are not regarded as conflicting goals, but as mutually reinforcing each other (Hervey, 2008).

In her analysis of national reports and reviews Hervey (2008) starts from the assumption that the OMC on Health and Long-term Care can be seen as a promoter of neo-liberal ideas, which rest upon keywords such as privatization, liberalization, provider competition and consumer choice. Instead of confirming this assumption, her findings show that a variety of reform approaches in the area of health care are discussed in the reports. Tjadens (2007) criticized that the developments at regional and local levels are neglected, civil society participation is inadequate and family carers are seen primarily as a source for cost savings.

In contrast to research results that show that the EU has only a marginal impact on the social policy of its member states, Cerami's (2008a) findings suggest that the EU, and particularly the OMC, is significant for the development of social policy in the new member states. It appears that ideas which prevail within certain policy areas at the European level gradually trickle down and can later be found in policy descriptions at national level, while the obligation to deliver national reports may lead to the development of new actor constellations at national level (for difficulties related to implementation see Sirovátka and Rákoczyová, this volume). The PHARE programme, launched by the EU between 1994 and 2004 and intended to support modernization of social security systems, had far-reaching consequences for the development of social policy.

Different EU programmes promote the establishment of social services in CEE countries (Nospickel, 2005). Of the projects financed by the PHARE and the PHARE-TWINNING programme, 30 per cent supported the establishment of adequate administrative structures. In addition, the ACCESS programme, which was financed by the PHARE programme, supported the development of civil society organizations. A survey among 120 state and non-state actors in the social service sectors in Hungary, Poland, Slovakia and the Czech Republic revealed that 50 per cent of the actors had received financial support within the framework of an EU programme (compare Sirovátka and Rákoczyová, this volume).

In addition, reports on 'Progress towards Accession' included a chapter on social policy, which revealed best practice in this policy area. As political actors relied on (positive) reports to avoid negative repercussions on their accession process and secure access to different EU funds, these reports gained importance. This even applies to Estonian health policy, and in particular to the choice of policy priorities. Legislative initiatives were restricted because priority was given to the harmonization of national and EU legislation (Jesse et al., 2004; Trumm, 2006).

International organizations impact significantly on the general development of welfare policies in CEE countries. The World Bank, IMF and OECD tended to favour privatization, liberalization and a more residual welfare state. In contrast, the WHO involved within health care reform did not promote a specific model but called for a more egalitarian health-care system (Cerami, 2006). In the case of Estonia, Jesse et al. (2004) cite the WHO Regional Office for Europe as an example of an organization that decisively influenced the reform. In addition, the authors state that the World Bank's Estonia Health Project (1995–1999) was key to the reform process.

Elder care policy changes – national, transnational and international influences

Demographic and social changes that have increased the care needs during a period of welfare state constraints are the reason why many European countries have experienced considerable changes of their elder care policies. Institutional and policy changes resulted in a redefinition of the level and mode of public responsibility, the preferred forms of care provision, and the introduction of new modes of funding. Thus, elder care reforms have significantly altered the nexus between the state, the market and the family in this policy area.

The changes are the result of the complex interplay between actors, ideas and institutions at the national level, but they were also influenced by ideas and actors originating from spheres beyond the national realm. Two distinctive modes can be found: bilateral transfer between countries and transfer promoted by the European Union and international organizations. Although policy designs and policy developments depend on the dominant care models, increasing care needs in a situation of economic constraints may result in the introduction of new policies, which take the experiences of other countries and the recommendations of international transfer agencies into account, thus departing in various important dimensions from previously dominant models. While the importance of models developed in other countries and by international organizations is well researched in long-established areas such as pension policy, the significance of external factors has not been analysed systematically for elder care systems.

The countries examined in this study were selected in a way which allows for a comparative analysis of differing elder care systems, and in particular for the examination of the complex interplay of internal and external factors in the context of prevalent ideas, actors and institutions at national level. In addition, the countries selected are characterized by limited funding and care provision at the beginning of the 1990s, which required profound policy changes, even leading to the establishment of new social rights and separate funding systems. New policy designs proved to be not simply copied but adapted to the country-specific elder care approaches.

With regard to a system of care provision in step with neo-liberal ideas, efforts to open up a care market to establish a more cost-efficient and user-friendly care service delivery can be detected in the countries compared in our study. In addition, care provision within the family framework was supported based on family values related to elder care. An increasing number of countries have responded to the lack of public funding with the establishment of separate funding systems and the introduction of more comprehensive social rights. Beginning with Continental European countries and Japan, the recent introduction of separate funding systems has been extended to Southern Europe and to CEE countries. A strong neighbourhood effect is revealed within these transfer processes, for example in South Tyrol, the Czech Republic and Slovenia along the Austrian border. In general, such separate funding systems are the result of intense transfer processes between the pioneering and the adopting countries, which requires adapting the model to the national (or regional) conditions. Institutional and policy changes appear to be a complex mixture of both path-dependency and the departure from existing systems.

Following the fall of communism and a more general welfare shift, CEE countries even combined new welfare policy approaches with administrative structures inherited from the communist era. In Estonia, for example, the establishment of a home-based elder care system is an example of the development of a hybrid system in two respects. First, different approaches established under two different regimes – before and during the Soviet period – were combined. And, second, other countries (such as Sweden and Germany) and international organizations (such as the WHO) influenced the development of a hybrid elder care system.

Despite social policy being defined as a national responsibility of the member states, the EU has undertaken various efforts to influence the development of social policy, generally by soft forms of control such as information campaigns or by facilitating policy transfer between countries. With the introduction of the OMC on Health and Long-term Care in 2004, the EU launched a new strategy, which entails the promotion of reforms and the institutionalization of exchange processes. Research on the CEE countries suggests that the OMC and also other EU programmes and funds influence the basic ideas within the area of health care. Such funding facilitates the emergence of new actor constellations, supports the establishment of administrative structures, and thus contributes directly to social policy development. During the accession phase the political influence of the EU grew – even in the area of social policy – owing to the compulsory provision of accession reports and the necessity to adapt to EU regulations and harmonize certain policies.

Although the EU has undoubtedly gained in importance with regard to social policy in its member states, essential decisions are still made at nation-state level and determined by actor constellations within the member states. Nonetheless, national policy changes are strongly affected by external factors, including foreign models, transnational expert networks, international organizations and the European Union.

10
The Impact of Minimum Income Guarantee Schemes in Central and Eastern Europe*

Cristina Rat

Introduction

The minimum income guarantee (MIG) constitutes as a policy response to the new social risks of poverty and social exclusion, providing a last resort benefit that ought to secure subsistence while maintaining incentives to work.[1] The emphasis on social inclusion through measures of labour force activation resonates with the general turn towards using social policies in order to manage labour rather than correct market failures (Carmel, 2005; Offe, 1982; Standing, 2003), and to develop MIG schemes aimed at enabling individuals to integrate on the labour market (Gough, 2001; Kazepov, 2005; Pena-Casas, 2005; Sainsbury and Morissens, 2002; Standing, 2003).

In the comparative research on potential typologies of CEE welfare states (Deacon and Szalai, 1992; Lendvai, 2008; Manning, 2004; Sotiropoulos et al., 2003) and path-dependence versus path-departure towards neo-liberal policies (Cerami, 2006; Ferge and Juhász, 2004; Haggard and Kaufman, 2008; Inglot, 2008; Kovács, 2002; Popescu, 2004a), the development of social safety nets received less attention than the insurance-based components of state social protection, with some notable exceptions (Braithwaite et al., 2000; Kramer, 1997; Standing, 1996; Szalai, 2005b; Szelényi, 2002). Existing studies commonly assert that, during the first decade of post-socialist transition, social protection served mainly to smooth the negative corollaries of economic liberalization, although high social expenditures in Hungary, the Czech Republic and Poland were detrimental to economic development in the second phase of the transition (Kramer, 1997). In Bulgaria and Romania social spending was much lower, partly because of the devaluation in real terms of insurance-based benefits, most notably of pensions, partly because of the delays in implementing adequate income-support benefits for the needy. In the case of these two 'late reformers', welfare reforms were delayed and economic subsidies maintained longer (Popescu, 2004a). Kramer (1997) and later Cerami (2006) highlight the 'dual role' of welfare provisions: to foster public support for the ongoing economic reforms and to consolidate democratic institutions. Cerami (2006) considers that the current social minimum contains several elements of policy innovation, but also socialist legacies, which penetrated the development of MIG schemes.

Moving beyond the leitmotiv of studies on CEE welfare states, which locate the roots of modest outcomes in poor financing and weak administrative capacities, this chapter tries to unfold why social safety nets remained precarious and ineffective overall. It comparatively analyses the impact of social assistance benefits in Bulgaria, the Czech Republic, Hungary, Poland, Romania and Slovakia, looking at country-specific data on welfare legislation and implementation in order to map out policy pathways of 'unfavourable inclusion' (Sen, 2000) that endanger the quest to tackle the 'new social risks' of poverty and social exclusion (Armingeon, 2004; Bonoli, 2007; Cerami, 2008b; Taylor-Gooby, 2004).

The first section examines the development of MIG schemes, seeing them as cases of 'policy transfer' (O'Connor, 2007) implemented, to paraphrase Eyal et al. (1998), 'not on the, but with the ruins' of the socialist welfare state (Eyal et al., 1998). Based on indicators of welfare input, output and outcome, the second section evaluates the effectiveness of social safety nets, and portrays clusters of 'poverty regimes' (Leibfried, 1992) among CEE countries. The third and fourth sections investigate neo-liberal articulations in eligibility conditions and means-testing (proving 'deservingness') and work incentives and behaviour constraints (proving 'discipline'). The last section draws attention to social divisions that make certain categories of the up-to-work population particularly vulnerable to the inadequacies of social inclusion policies, providing a detailed analysis of the situation of the Roma minority.

The development of minimum income guarantee schemes

In the second decade of post-socialist transition, MIG schemes replaced the previous means-tested local assistance benefits throughout the CEE countries, with the notable exception of Hungary. These transformations were intrinsically linked to embracing the European definition of poverty in terms of 'the risks of poverty and social exclusion' (Atkinson et al., 2002; Council of Europe, 2001; Kazepov and Sabatinelli, 2005; Marlier et al., 2007; Pena-Casas, 2005) and replacing general subsidizing policies with selective social protection targeting the most deprived categories of the population. Poverty is no longer defined as the socialist legacy of general scarcity and impoverishment (particularly harsh in Bulgaria and Romania) or as a corollary of the post-socialist transition, which turned large segments of the working class into 'losers' of the economic reforms (Ferge et al., 2002; Szelényi, 2002). It becomes a 'new social risk' (Bonoli, 2007; Ferrera et al.,

2000; Pierson, 2006; Taylor-Gooby, 2004) faced by those who lack educational qualifications and marketable skills in the emergent knowledge-based economy (Armingeon, 2004; Cerami, 2008b).

Social safety nets were not introduced in an institutional vacuum: even if they required the setting of new agencies, these borrowed in the initial phase regulations, offices and staff from already existing institutions. At the same time, local assistance benefits legislated during the late 1990s defined new public competences and a new category of clientele, whose existence was vehemently denied during state-socialism: the needy. Deservingness criteria drew new social divisions, which were nevertheless framed in the old containers of the honest and hardworking labourers *versus* the parasitic up-to-work others. Braithwaithe et al. (2000), who offer one of the first extensive analyses of the impact of social policies on economic deprivation in post-socialist countries using survey data from 1993, conclude that none of these countries offered substantial assistance for the poor at the time. They describe the social security system as 'dispersed' in Russia and Hungary (small benefits for a relatively large number of households), 'concentrated' in Poland and Estonia (considerable benefits, but delivered only to a few households), and 'irrelevant' in Bulgaria (only a few of the needy households received benefits, but their level was too low to make a difference) (Braithwaite et al., 2000).

Before the introduction of MIG schemes, social assistance benefits were administered and financed at the local level. This institutional design led to cost containment and low coverage, given that the territorial-administrative units with high rates of long-term unemployment and poverty had small revenues and modest redistributive capacities. The MIG programmes brought on financing from national budgets, although the administration of benefits remained at the local level. The new scheme was shaped by initial legislations on social assistance (such as means-testing procedures and the conditionality of benefits) and local-level practices (for example, the tolerance of social workers for delays in submitting the required documents and discretion in benefit award).

Consequently, MIG schemes hardly constitute a straightforward case of 'policy transfer' (O'Connor, 2007), although the influence of the EU as a transnational policy actor is apparent in the adoption of the 'risk of poverty and social exclusion' framework and the formulation of national strategies (Ferge and Juhász, 2004; Pena-Casas, 2005). The most explicit recommendations to adopt common criteria for sufficient resources and social assistance was set forth by the Council Recommendation 92/441/EEC from June 1992, which asserted that the protection of minimum resources should be rights-based, without time limitation, universal (not categorical), conditioned by availability to work and accompanied by activation measures and complementary services and benefits (health care, housing, education and vocational qualification) (Pena-Casas, 2005). European states have shown considerable variation in the implementation of these recommendations, and the landscape of welfare remained patterned by 'poverty regimes' (Leibfried, 1992). A tendency of convergence with regard to the role of means-tested benefits to either complement or replace employment-related benefits might be nevertheless identified (Sainsbury and Morissens, 2001, p. 26).

Looking at the poverty-reduction effectiveness of MIG schemes for vulnerable categories (unemployed, lone-mothers, and the elderly) Sainsbury and Morissens (2001) conclude that Hungary, the Czech Republic and Poland (the only post-socialist countries included in EU-SILC and thus in their analysis) cluster along other EU countries into various 'poverty regimes' (Sainsbury and Morissens, 2002, p. 28). Analysing the structure of social assistance benefits and their replacement rates, Kazepov and Sabatinelli (2005) reach slightly different conclusions: CEE countries can be grouped into a 'transition model' characterized by ambiguous patterns and policy discourses, where social assistance benefits have secondary importance. In these countries, social safety nets fail to address the vulnerability of specific populations (such as the Roma or families with children), and maintain a fragmented and categorical nature of benefits (Kazepov and Sabatinelli, 2005, p. 61).

In a simplified account, the early reformers from CEE countries (Hungary, the Czech Republic and Poland) do not differ considerably from other EU member states in terms of outcomes of social assistance benefits (as indicated by the poverty reduction effectiveness analysed by Sainsbury and Morrisens, 2002), but their policy outputs are rather unclear and weakly articulated (Kazepov and Sabatinelli, 2005).

Applying the criteria[2] set by Eardly et al. (1996) in their influential clustering of social assistance schemes in OECD countries,[3] all CEE countries that introduced MIG apparently reveal the features of 'integrated social assistance'. Bulgaria, the Czech Republic, Poland, Romania and Slovakia embrace a residual but rights-based approach, with strict targeting and means-testing, granting benefits to households rather than individuals or nuclear families within the household. Although the legacy of full employment and heavy state subsidies resemble the Keynesian economies of Nordic countries with 'citizenship-based residual assistance', CEE countries diverge from this model as they lack the tradition of linking benefits to counselling services within 'traditional casework' (Eardly et al., 1996). Hungary clusters into the 'dualist social assistance' model, characterized by the prevalence of categorical assistance and a general basic safety net. Szalai (2008) considers that the post-socialist Hungarian welfare state is 'bifurcated': it offers adequate protection only for the gainfully employed contributors, discounting the needs of the poorest segments of the population, who are supposed to receive income-support benefits through locally administered and funded welfare programmes (Szalai, 2008).

Are MIG schemes effective? Poverty and welfare impact

As particular types of a general social-safety net, MIG schemes are expected to support a minority of deprived individuals excluded from the mainstream.[4] However, the configuration of social and economic deprivation in CEE countries reveals considerably impoverishment among the 'included', and the 'risk of poverty' is unevenly distributed between rural and urban areas, families with children and ethnic groups. The mismatch between the assumptions about poverty and its context-specific determinants undermines the effectiveness of MIG schemes.

Table 10.1 shows that the indicators of relative poverty and income inequality in CEE countries do not differ substantially from the EU-25 average; nonetheless, the rates of subjective economic strain are considerably higher, peaking at twice the EU-25 average in Bulgaria and Romania. The 'objective' indicator of the value of the poverty threshold also points at deeper scarcity in CEE countries among those situated below the 'at risk of poverty' line.

Unlike in Western Europe, in CEE countries the incidence of poverty has been considerably higher in rural areas throughout the transition period. Child poverty is not associated with immigrant status, but with a traditional family model, with three or more children (European Commission, 2008). Single-parent families are more exposed to poverty, but (as compared to the EU-15) they represent a smaller proportion of families with dependent

Table 10.1 Poverty and social inequality in CEE countries in 2006

	BG	CZ	HU	PL	RO	SK	EU-25 Average
Subjective economic strain (% of respondents)*	75.4	n.d.	45.7	35.3	61.9	42.3	27.8
Gini coefficient	24	25	33	33	33	28	30
Relative poverty rate	14	10	16	19	19	12	16
Poverty gap	17	17	24	25	23	20	22
Poverty threshold for a family of two adults with two dependent children in EURO**	153	444	362	266	98	257	–
Poverty threshold for a family of two adults with two dependent children in PPS**	356	816	591	503	226	546	–

Note: Own calculations for subjective economic strain, as indicated by answering the question, 'How do you feel about your household's income nowadays' with 'Difficult' or 'Very difficult living on present income'. The Czech Republic was not included in the ESS third round.

Source: ESPROSS, October 2008; *ESS 3rd Round (2006); **Joint Report on Social Inclusion (2008).

children. These differences in the configuration of problems are hardly reflected in the design of activation policies: farmers engaged in subsistence agriculture face difficulties in accessing micro-credits; courses of vocational qualification are organized almost exclusively in the cities and attendants ought to cover the costs of transportation; child benefits are modest and their means-tested components do not increase proportionally with the number of children (European Commission, 2008).

The favourable treatment of families with dependent children in the MIG programmes is either absent or inconsistent (see also Szikra and Tomka, this volume), exempting only means-tested child benefits from the imputed income of households. In Slovakia child allowance is exempted; in Romania, only its means-tested component, while scholarships are imputed; in Bulgaria, only the one-off payment at birth, and there is no universal child allowance. In the Czech Republic and Poland, all family benefits constitute imputed income. In Hungary, after the 2006 modifications, the amount of the benefit depends on household structure, but all sources of income are imputed.

Whereas total social expenditures slightly increased during the transition in all CEE countries (mainly due to increasing costs of sustaining the pension system), expenditures on social assistance benefits were kept low or even decreased. As shown in Table 10.2, Hungary, the Czech Republic and Slovakia report welfare efforts (measured as percentage of GDP spent on benefits for families, children, housing and social exclusion) close to the EU-25 average in 2005, whereas Poland, Bulgaria and Romania lag behind. The poverty reduction effectiveness of social assistance and family benefits[5] also presents a very uneven picture. Hungary performs better than the EU-25 on average. The Czech Republic slightly exceeds the EU-25 average in terms of absolute poverty reduction, but it is below in terms of relative reduction. The other four CEE countries score well below the EU-25 average in both respects. Again, Bulgaria and Romania register considerably below poverty reduction effectiveness.

For a general assessment on the impact of MIG schemes, three empirical dimensions were investigated: *welfare input* ('welfare effort'), *output* ('social

Table 10.2 Expenditures on income-support benefits and the poverty reduction effectiveness

	BG	CZ	HU	PL	RO	SK	EU-25 Average
Expenditures on income-support benefits (% of GDP)	1.5	2.0	3.2	1.3	1.7	2.4	3.0
Absolute poverty reduction	4.0	2.0	6.0	12.0	7.0	17.0	10.0
Relative poverty reduction	16.0	11.7	25.0	54.5	35.0	56.6	38.4

Source: ESPROSS, October 2008. Own calculations for absolute and relative poverty reduction.

citizenship') and *outcome* (the effects of welfare provisions on the extent and depth of social and economic deprivation) (Gough, 2005; Kvist, 2007).

On the input dimension, the main indicator is the national welfare effort to tackle the risks of poverty and social exclusion, computed using the ESSPROS methodology, which excludes administration costs.[6] The figures from Table 10.3 indicate that total social expenditures in 2005 were the lowest in Romania (14.2 per cent of GDP); however, cumulative expenditures on benefits for families and children, housing and social exclusion transfers were higher in Romania than in Bulgaria and Poland. Welfare effort was the highest, and the closest to the European average, in Hungary. The ranking of countries is similar in terms of relative allocations from their overall social spending. Hungary and Slovakia allocate more, whereas Bulgaria and Poland allocate significantly less. Paradoxically, the two countries that directed the highest share of GDP towards financing social assistance benefits were Hungary, which has no MIG scheme, and the Czech Republic, which has the lowest at-risk-of-poverty rate. Romania and Bulgaria, the countries with the highest poverty rates and relatively generous eligibility conditions, spent the smallest shares of GDP for poverty and social inclusion benefits.

On the output dimension, the net income of social assistance recipients as a proportion of the at-risk-of-poverty threshold serves as an indicator of the extent at which benefits secure the social right to subsistence or to a decent minimum (see Table 10.4). The relative values of social assistance benefits are the highest in Poland and Slovakia. For single adults, social assistance benefits provide an amount which is less than half of the poverty threshold in Hungary, and only slightly higher than that in Romania and Bulgaria. Similar figures were reported for Western Europe (Pena-Casas, 2005; Standing, 2003), asserting that MIG benefits provide rather a neo-liberal *minima moralia* than the social right to a decent minimum.

Table 10.3 Welfare effort for means-tested income support benefits in 2005

	BG	CZ	HU	PL	RO	SK	EU-25 Average
Total social expenditures	16.1	19.1	21.9	19.6	14.2	16.9	27.2
As % of GDP (2005)							
Family and children	1.1	1.4	2.5	0.8	1.4	1.9	2.1
Housing and social exclusion n.e.c.	0.4	0.6	0.7	0.5	0.3	0.5	0.9
As % of total state social expenditures (2005)							
Family and children	6.8	7.5	11.8	4.4	10.2	11.3	8
Housing and social exclusion n.e.c.	2.7	3.1	3.1	2.5	2.1	3.2	3.5

Source: ESPROSS, October 2008. Latest data available.

Table 10.4   Net income of social assistance recipients as % of the at-risk-of-poverty threshold for two jobless household types in 2005

	BG	CZ	HU	PL	RO	SK
Single adult	59	66.6	35	88.5	56.4	95
Married couple with two dependent children	79.1	85.9	29.1*	103.5	84	98

Note: *In the case of Hungary, the very small figure in the case of married couples with children is confusing because it ignores the universal financial support received by families with dependent children, which is around €104 for two children.

Source: ESPROSS, 2008. Own calculations for Bulgaria, Romania and Slovakia, based on data provided by National Statistical Institutes. Latest data available.

On the outcome dimension, indicators of benefit coverage, targeting and adequacy were used. According to World Bank estimations based on national household budget surveys, in none of the six CEE countries did the coverage of the benefit exceed 4 per cent in 2002–2004. In 2005, the coverage of the benefits (see Table 10.5) was slightly higher in Romania and Bulgaria, and the targeting was also better in these countries: 58 per cent of beneficiaries in Bulgaria and 62 per cent in Romania were from the lowest consumption quintile. In Bulgaria, the adequacy of the benefit was relatively higher (both overall and in the case of the bottom quintile) (Shopov, 2007). For Romania, there are no comparable data available.[7] However, for those situated below the national consumption poverty threshold[8] in 2002, benefit coverage was reported at 7.8 per cent and adequacy at 31.2 per cent, meaning that social assistance benefits were enough to cover less than one third of overall household expenditures (Teşliuc et al., 2003). In the same period, in Hungary the coverage and the adequacy were slightly lower, but families with dependent children could supplement their incomes with the more generous family allowances. In Poland, the targeting of benefits was precarious, as only 26 per cent of welfare recipients were from the poorest consumption quintile (World Bank, 2007).

To conclude, the effectiveness of social safety nets in CEE countries presents an uneven picture. The Czech Republic and Hungary are close to or even exceed the EU-25 average in terms of welfare input and output, whereas Bulgaria, Poland, Slovakia and Romania fell behind. In terms of policy outcomes, all countries have similarly low rates of coverage (from 2 per cent of the population in Hungary to 4 per cent in Romania) and poor benefit adequacy (from 15 per cent of total consumption in Hungary to 35 per cent in Bulgaria).

Proving deservingness: eligibility conditions and means-testing

The adoption of welfare-to-work policies might seem a neo-liberal path-departure, but the legacy of the socialist welfare state is a highly

Table 10.5 Coverage, targeting and adequacy of social assistance benefits in the lowest and the highest consumption quintiles in 2002–2004*

Country (year)	Coverage			Targeting		Adequacy		
	Total	Lowest quintile	Highest quintile	Lowest quintile	Highest quintile	Total	Lowest quintile	Highest quintile
Bulgaria (2003)	3%	8%	1%	58%	7%	35%	47%	12%
The Czech Rep. (2004)	3.6%	n.d.	n.d.	n.d.	n.d.	n.d.	n.d.	n.d.
Hungary (2004)	2%	6%	1%	42%	8%	15%	27%	10%
Poland (2004)	3%	5%	1%	26%	9%	24%	35%	18%
Romania (2002)	3.9%	11.7%	0.3%	62%	2%	Only for those below the poverty line: 31.2%		
Slovakia (2004)	3.3%	n.d.	n.d.	n.d.	n.d.	n.d.	n.d.	n.d.

Note: *More recent data on these indicators were not available at the time of writing.

Source: The World Bank country studies on social security: Ringold and Kasek (2007) for Hungary, Poland, Slovakia and the Czech Republic, Teşliuc (2007) for Romania and Shopov (2007) for Bulgaria. Quintiles based on household consumption per capita: the lowest quintile comprises those 20% of the population who live in the households with the lowest level of consumption per capita. Benefit adequacy computed only for recipient households, as the average share of the benefit from household consumption.

commodifying one (Deacon, 2000; Popescu, 2004a). The changes of social safety nets in CEE countries consisted not in the commodification of labour (which has already existed), but in the possibility to commodify needs. This bring on the distinction between 'deserving' and 'undeserving' poor, and the necessity to safeguard 'legitimate receipt'.

Social workers are supposed to act as 'gatekeepers' for the 'undeserving' poor, holding some discretionary power in establishing the right to benefits. Means-testing requires an estimation of informal income; but how much of that is really imputed depends on the unspoken 'negotiations' between social workers, beneficiaries and local authorities. As social interactions, these 'negotiations' are strongly marked by what the actors label as 'self-help' or 'idleness', promoting welfare-dependency or social justice.

The imputation of informal, irregular *potential* income as *actual* income and diminishing the amount of benefits accordingly constitutes not only a means of cost-containment, but also a way to discipline beneficiaries to commodify their workforce in the 'right way', on the formal labour market. Romania set national standards for imputing income from *potential* informal work during the agricultural season; therefore most of the households with up-to-work family members do not receive benefits for this period, although their entitlement is maintained. This is important for upholding their insurance in the public health-care system (Popescu and Rat, 2008).

The punitive nature of MIG schemes can be identified not only in the obligation to prove willingness to work, but also in overbureaucratization and the stigmatization of beneficiaries. Several documents needed for claiming benefits and maintaining entitlement cannot be obtained from local authorities, and applicants ought to acquire them from territorial-regional offices, which implies additional costs for applicants from rural areas. Following Offe (1982), one may remark that the bureaucracy of MIG has more to do with the disciplinary nature of the welfare state than with the quest to ensure fairness, while the ability to prove deservingness is negatively correlated with the extent of need (Offe, 1982; Standing, 2003). Social enquiries at claimants' homes and community work taking place in public places and consisting of 'dirty' tasks (such as cleaning parks or ditches, or repairing the buildings of public institutions) produce the stigmatization of recipients. Potential beneficiaries may renounce claiming benefits in order to avoid humiliation, while the public perception of community work is just useless foot-dragging. In August 2006, Romania adopted particularly stigmatizing rules: local authorities ought to post at a visible place the list of persons receiving social aid, the schedule of community work and the names of those supposed to perform the tasks.[9] The implementation of MIG became more transparent, allegedly in order to discard previous accusations of abusive granting of benefits. In rural areas, the new measures determined an increase in the non-claiming of benefits by impoverished but 'respectable' members of the local community, thus precisely those defined as the 'deserving' poor (Rat, 2007).

When the amount of benefits is too low, individuals fail to convert them into the necessary human and social resources in order to move out of poverty. The EAPN (2005) set 12 criteria for the quality of activation policies, the last one asserting that the amount of benefits should be enough 'to guarantee the security needed for activation' and 'a positive incentive to face the extra costs and risk when resuming a job after' (EAPN, 2005). Inadequately small benefits force recipients to supplement their incomes with various forms of informal work and appeal to other forms of assistance, which perpetuate their situation of 'dependency' (Paugam, 2003, p. 47), but also their stereotyping as 'abusers' of welfare.

The stigma of 'welfare dependency', commonly understood as abusive long-term reliance on welfare, not only reinforces already existing social divisions between the worse-off and the better-off strata, but also strengthens public expectations for the disciplinary role of social policies and diverts attention from the responsibility of the government to tackle persistent poverty. This effect is particularly evident in the case of 'Gypsies'. The use of the 'Gadje' label for the Roma minority is deliberate, and highlights reference to the stereotype of Gypsies, and not the Roma ethnics as such. Given that Gypsies are seen to be 'lazy' and 'thieves' (World Bank, 2005), the public blame for their poverty falls upon them, not on the government, whose responsibilities were seldom publicly accounted. In the case that the majority of beneficiaries are considered to be Gypsies, governments can avoid public sanction by shifting responsibility towards the 'undeserving' poor themselves.

Incentives for work and the disciplinary face of MIG

Providing assistance for the development of human and social 'capital' and incentives for engagement on the formal labour market constitutes on inherent part of MIG schemes. Standing (2003) argues that European welfare states are marked by a 'shift away from social protection to *human capital*' (Standing, 2003, p. 2) and behavioural conditions for welfare receipt: the obligation to accept any available job and undertake vocational requalification when necessary. Given that in CEE countries had educational systems weakly adjusted to the emergent market economies, highly regulated labour markets and a conspicuous lack of trained staff for programmes of vocational counselling, the implementation of activation measures was tardy and difficult. MIG schemes provided another pillar to strengthen the functioning of these programmes, by linking benefits to willingness to training and contractual work.

Means-tested cash transfers do not aim primarily at decommodifying needs and work (Esping-Andersen, 1990), but at permitting up-to-work individuals to 'commodify' their situation of social and economic depriv-ation in order to get (through training, counselling and financial support) 'marketable skills' (Ferrera et al., 2000) and gainfully 'sell' their workforce on the market. On the ideational dimension of the policy process, the depart-ure from the social-democratic quest for de-commodification towards the neo-liberal workfare and last resort social protection can be identified in the evolutions of CEE welfare states as well (Kovács, 2002; Popescu, 2004b), which are excepted to 'increase [their] productive function, to improve [their] social investment and empowerment capacities' (Cerami, 2008b).

The shift from *market-correcting* to *market-setting policies* (Lendvai, 2008) becomes apparent in the recommendation of the EU with respect to social policy design, and the goals of creating 'an inclusive society'. Lendvai (2008) argues that for CEE new member states there is an overlap between the pressures for market-setting stemming from two different sources: first, the EU-integration and its requirements to adjust social policies in order to make the European common market functional; second, the internal pres-sures of post-socialist liberalization and marketization (Lendvai, 2008). The envisaged harmonization of social protection in the EU following a model of 'social citizenship' (Marshall, 1950) ranks neither among the priorities of nation states, nor of the European Union (Carmel, 2005).

In the case of MIG schemes, eligibility regulations and conditions for maintaining entitlement provide the first tier of constraints to integration on the formal labour market. In all countries, applicants should prove that up-to-work persons in the household are either employed or actively seek-ing for work, enrolled in formal education or attending courses of voca-tional qualification. Some exceptions apply, such as in the case of persons caring for small children or functionally dependent adults (especially eld-erly) in the household. The obligation of unemployed beneficiaries to prove that they are registered jobseekers constitutes not only an indicator of dis-ciplinary state intervention, but also an overt measure of workforce control. This was acknowledged by the designers of the national MIG programme in Romania, who expected that unrecorded unemployed would register at the Labour Force Office in order to be eligible for MIG, and consequently the accuracy of official statistics on labour force would improve (Grecu et al., 2004).

In order to reduce work disincentives and inactivity traps, there is a favourable treatment of households with incomes from contractual employ-ment. In the Czech Republic only 70 per cent of earnings and 85 per cent of sickness and unemployment benefits are taken into account when estab-lishing benefit amounts; in Slovakia, 75 per cent of earnings, pensions and occasional income up to twice the amount of the subsistence minimum. In Romania, households with at least one gainfully employed person receive a 15 per cent bonus to the amount of the benefit, and they are not sup-posed to perform community work. However, given the very low eligibility threshold in Romania, households with a formally employed member are practically not eligible to receive the MIG benefit. In Bulgaria there are no explicit work incentives: the gap between the amount of social benefits and wages is large enough to constrain individuals to move out from welfare. The fact that in Bulgaria and Romania the amount of welfare benefits is too small to provide disincentives for work has already been pointed out by previous studies (Milcher and Zigova, 2005, p. 5).

Community work constitutes a means to control and limit unregistered work while being on welfare. In Bulgaria, unemployed recipients of social aid, who are not engaged in courses of vocational training, should perform at least five days of community work per month. In the Czech Republic, Slovakia and Poland they should perform community service organized by municipalities. In Romania, only one 'delegate' of the household has this obligation, and the required hours of labour depend on the value of the benefit. In Hungary, recipients of local social assistance benefits are allowed to present a certificate of occasional labour and they are exempted from community work (Lehoczky, 2007).

In the same vein of measures falls the control upon the territorial mobility of beneficiaries. In Bulgaria, households lose eligibility when anybody from the household travels abroad (except due to health problems or the death of a close relative). In Romania, the offices for work abroad report directly to the welfare offices the list of registered labour migrants; households with undocumented migrants lose eligibility when nobody performs the required community work or there is evidence of undeclared income sources.

Poverty and welfare receipt in the care of the Roma minority

Minority populations are considered more vulnerable to new social risks, especially those associated with irregular employment, and existing social divisions are 'crossed-over' (Taylor-Gooby, 2004) and further deepened by cleavages in terms of exposure to social contingencies. Survey data from CEE countries indicates that the risk of poverty and social exclusion is much higher in the case of the Roma (European Commission, 2004a; Ringold, 2000; Ringold et al., 2003; Szelényi, 2002), and disproportionately more Roma than non-Roma families receive means-tested income support transfers (Milcher and Zigova, 2005; UNDP, 2003).

National statistics on welfare receipt do not offer data split by ethnicity, given that claimants are not required to state their ethnic affiliation on the submitted forms. This regulation tries to combat the possibility of negative discrimination; nevertheless, it prohibits any objective account of welfare receipt among ethnic minorities (Cahn, 2004; Rat, 2005). Survey research leaves room to overestimating poverty and welfare receipt among the Roma, due to the fact that persons from segregated, poor communities, are easier to be identified as Roma and included in the sample than 'integrated' Roma persons living among the mainstream. The latter might also decline revealing their ethnic identity to the interviewers, in the context of strong negative prejudices against 'the Gypsies'. The result is a vicious circle of understating the proportion of the 'invisible' Roma with average living standards, and overstating those 'visible' because of their pauperism or (at the other extreme) conspicuous affluence.

Expert evaluations show concerns for 'welfare dependency' among the Roma, although they admit that the amount of benefits received is low (Fleck and Rughiniş, 2008; Ringold et al., 2003; UNDP, 2003). The World Bank argues for the need to 'break the cycle of poverty and social exclusion' (World Bank, 2003), the UNDP warns that the Roma should avoid the 'dependency trap' (UNDP, 2003), while the European Commission recommends an approach which 'promotes the social inclusion of the Roma within existing policies' (European Commission, 2004b). There are no European directives on specific measures to improve the situation of the Roma, and the first European Roma Summit taking place in September 2008 raised strong critiques on behalf of Roma organizations. All CEE countries agreed to participate in the international programme *The Decade of Roma Inclusion 2005–15* initiated and co-financed by the Open Society Institute Budapest, with the support of the World Bank, the UNDP and the European Commission.

The social stigma of 'welfare dependence', with the connotation of abusive reliance on welfare, adds new prejudices to those of the Roma being 'lazy', 'dirty' and 'dishonest' (World Bank, 2005). On the discursive level, one may feel the déjà vu of the 'underclass' debate, while in some academic papers Wilson's 'structural underclass' (Wilson, 1992) was embraced as a useful concept for analysing the plight of the Roma (Szelényi, 2002). Other scholars (most notably Stewart, 2002) contest the utility of this framework and draw attention to the processes of social segregation which perpetuate the vulnerability of the Roma despite their participation in local networks of kinship and informal economy (Fleck and Rughiniş, 2008; Stewart, 1997; Toma, 2005) and programmes of social protection (Milcher and Zigova, 2005; Rat, 2005).

The social safety net might provide a 'survival strategy' (Fleck and Rughiniş, 2008; UNDP, 2003), however, as shown in Table 10.6, the majority of Roma households do not receive any state support for unemployment or social assistance benefits: 66 per cent of the Roma households in Bulgaria, 71 per cent in Hungary and 60 per cent in Romania. As compared to the Czech Republic and Hungary, in Bulgaria and Romania Roma households receive much smaller amounts of state social transfers, both contributory and non-contributory benefits. In Romania, 87 per cent of the Roma and 94 per cent of the non-Roma households that were benefiting from state transfers for children received actually less than €25 per month in 2005. One

Table 10.6 Poverty and social transfers among the Roma in CEE countries

	Bulgaria		The Czech Rep.		Hungary		Romania	
	Majority living in the proximity of the Roma	Roma	Majority living in the proximity of the Roma	Roma	Majority living in the proximity of the Roma	Roma	Majority living in the proximity of the Roma	Roma
Income poverty – threshold set at $4.3 (PPP) per person per month; for the Czech. Rep.: $11 (PPP)								
Poverty rate	6	49	9	25	5	8	20	67
Poverty gap	1	15	2	3	2	3	6	25
% of households receiving unemployment, local social assistance benefits								
None	91	66	n.d.	n.d.	71	48	90	60
Up to €25	2	8	1.3	1.3	0	1	4	18
€25–50	2	12	2.3	3.0	2	1	3	14
€51 or more	1	11	8.7	48.3	24	47	2	4
% of households receiving state transfers for children								
None	79	49	n.d.	n.d.	55	22	64	41
Up to €10	8	11	1.3	0.3	0	0	19	17
€11–25	6	19	6.1	3.4	7	6	13	31
€25 or more	3	18	21.5	41.1	35	70	2	7

Note: Poverty rates computed after social transfers, all income sources included. Data not included in the survey, but its Roma population is considerably smaller than the other CEE countries.
Source: UNDP, 2005.

may hardly speak about abusive reliance on state support when the level of benefits is very low.

The Slovak social security reforms in 2004 determined serious unrest among the Roma population (European Roma Information Office, 2004). In Hungary, the recent changes concerning regular social assistance granted to needy households also fuel tensions between the Roma minority and the Hungarian majority, given that the former are overrepresented among welfare recipients (Pallagi, 2007; Lehoczky, 2007). In Romania, the regulations on including potential earnings from seasonal work in the imputed income of households constitutes a form of indirect discrimination against the Roma, who can neither gain a decent living from occasional labour, nor renounce that and rely on state protection. Bulgaria's regulation of refusing social benefits to those claimants who have travelled abroad during the past 12 months can be interpreted as a form of controlling Roma migration abroad, in the context of problems faced by the neighbouring Romania with respect to alleged Roma migrants in France and Italy.[10]

Majority populations contest the deservingness of the 'Gypsies', given than 'their' contributions to the national budget are far below 'their' revenues from social spending. Public discourse is marked by the 'othering' of the Roma and treating 'their' welfare rights and duties not in terms of social citizenship (which is by definition *individual*), but rather as the reliance of an un-integrated *community* on public charity. The boundaries of this community are largely hetero-defined and based on negative stereotypes, while the label of 'Gypsies' weights more than the social category of Roma ethnics. Coining the forms of direct and indirect discrimination of the Roma as straightforward racism ignores the specific historical context from Central and Eastern Europe and ethnographic evidence on the enactment of multi-layered social divisions in everyday interactions (Fleck and Rughiniş, 2008; Hann, 2000; Stewart, 1997, 2002; Szelényi, 2002; Toma, 2005). For social policies, such an approach might be 'misleadingly counterproductive, creating racism where it does not exist' (Hann, 2002, p. 94) and concealing the adverse forms of providing 'access' to resources and services. As discussed in the previous parts of this chapter, social safety nets contain such patterns of 'disempowering inclusion' (Anthias, 2001) by imputing income from informal work (Romania), prohibiting travel abroad (Bulgaria), treating families with many children unfavourably (Slovakia) or maintaining a decentralized, discretionary system of social assistance benefits (Hungary).

Conclusion

The evolutions of social safety nets in Central and Eastern Europe were marked by the imperatives of structural adjustment to the emergent market economies, which implied a tighter targeting of benefits in order to contain costs and the use of social assistance as a means of workforce management.

These opened a window for policy transfer (Haggard and Kaufman, 2008) and the 'soft' advice of the European Union gained increasing salience as European integration became a national quest that could further legitimize the social costs of transition. However, there was a contradiction between formal compliance with EU recommendations and poor implementation of social assistance programmes, which can be interpreted as a form of covert resistance to the pressures of EU-level policy coordination, invoking the lack of administrative and financial capacities.

On the other hand, the ineffectiveness of social safety nets, in particular the MIG scheme, is also rooted in the mismatch between the configuration of deprivation and social divisions in CEE countries, and the assumptions about poverty and the ways to tackle it which are embedded in the European approach on the risks of poverty and social exclusion. Policymakers embraced the new ideology of 'social inclusion', but only paid lip-service to it so far (Kovács, 2002). The context-specific adaptations of social safety nets through the particularities of entitlement conditions and means-testing suggest that these were primarily aiming at increasing the capacities of workforce control, limiting the informal sector and the territorial mobility of the economically deprived. Meanwhile, the allocation of provisions, social-assistance services and measures of workforce activation were hardly adequate to overcome social and economic disadvantage on the long run, especially in the case of the Roma minority.

The 'new social risk' of poverty and social exclusion in Central and Eastern Europe is manifold, rooted in multilayered social divisions which make certain categories particularly vulnerable to the new social and economic environment of emergent knowledge-based economies (Armingeon, 2004; Cerami, 2008b). At the ideational dimension, the new discourse on social exclusion conceals these inequalities beyond the banner of 'inclusion through workforce activation', restating the old distinction between the 'deserving' versus the 'undeserving' poor, and pushing the problem of persistent inequalities at the margins of the policy debate (Castel, 2003). The question is whether social safety nets 'empower through de-commodification' (Cerami, 2008b), or rather provide forms of 'unfavourable inclusion' (Sen, 2000) that discipline behaviour, 'commodifying' needs and workforce. In the search for an answer, this chapter explored the configuration of social safety nets in CEE countries, the repercussions of entitlement conditions, means-testing and the efficacy of work incentives. The comparative analysis indicates that the implementation of social assistance programmes in the second decade of post-socialist transition remains loaded with institutional pathways of 'disempowering inclusion' (Anthias, 2001) of the socioeconomically deprived.

11
Devolution of Social Protection Arrangements

Natascha Van Mechelen and Veerle De Maesschalck

Introduction

Decentralization reforms in CEE countries have been an essential component of the overall transformation process that took place after the collapse of the former communist regimes. It entered public thought as a panacea to the political, economical and social problems that emerged because of and during the transformation. It also featured prominently in social policy reforms, particularly in the case of social assistance. Local government involvement in the financing and administration of social assistance schemes has been widely promoted by various international organizations as holding the key to reducing the financial cost of such schemes through improved targeting. However, the theory of fiscal federalism provides us with sound theoretical arguments against decentralization of social assistance. According to this theoretical framework, fundamental constraints on redistribution by lower level governments would negatively affect the generosity of poverty relief systems and facilitate a 'race to the bottom'.

This chapter focuses on the relationship between the generosity of social assistance benefits and the involvement of sub-national governments in various dimensions of social policy-making (that is the administration, decision-making and funding of social assistance schemes) and discusses the potential implications of the current trend towards decentralization in CEE countries for the adequacy of social assistance benefit levels. The issue is here approached empirically by means of a cross-sectional study of the general (that is non-categorical) social assistance scheme in 21 OECD-countries. Our analysis shows that although extreme forms of decentralization are generally associated with inadequate minimum income provision, more restricted versions of decentralization do not necessarily result in low benefit levels. More particularly, we find that social assistance benefit packages are invariably below the poverty line (at least in the less generous municipalities) in countries where municipalities take autonomous decisions with regard to a substantial part of the benefit package (for example, where they are left free to set the level of basic rates or housing benefits). At the same time, benefit levels are usually above the poverty line in countries where central governments set the basic social assistance rates and housing benefits while sharing funding liabilities with the local government level. We conclude that the current trend towards more local involvement in minimum income provision in CEE countries will not necessarily lead to inadequate benefits provided that there is strong central steering, in the sense of both strict national guidelines regarding benefit standards and a normative system of fiscal equalization.

The first part of this chapter illustrates how decentralization of welfare provisions, and thus of social assistance systems, in transition countries fitted in an overall trend of transferring powers to lower government levels. Part two is an empirical assessment of the relationship between (de)centralization and benefit generosity of social assistance schemes in 21 OECD countries. This part empirically documents the cross-national variation in the involvement of local or regional government levels in the regulation, financing and implementation of social assistance schemes, and presents the results of our empirical analysis. The final part draws conclusions and contains prior conditions to decentralization from the perspective of adequate benefit levels.

Decentralization and means-testing in CEE countries after the transition

Decentralization reforms

Decentralization is an important, though often overlooked, element of the transition process of Central and Eastern European (CEE) countries. In fact, decentralization – or the transfer of powers and resources from higher to lower levels in the political system – can be considered as intrinsic to the transformation since changing the role of the state and the market fundamentally was one of its basic aims while the process itself meant moving away from a centrally controlled, command-driven economy towards more politically, economically and administratively decentralized and market-based structures (Czike et al., 2002; Ferge, 2001b; World Bank, 2001).

From a political and administrative point of view, decentralization reforms were regarded as a way to leave behind decades of central dominance and control (Ringold, 2005; Ringold and Kasek, 2007; World Bank, 2001). In this respect, decentralization has had a strong symbolic meaning. It can be seen as a way to legitimize the new power and demonstrate that things had moved away from the old, repressive and intrusive political apparatus. As a matter of fact, decentralization has often been considered to be an integral part of the democratization process in the former communist countries (Czike et al., 2002; Illner, 1998). From an economic perspective, decentralization had to bring solutions to the failures and limits of the state-run and planned economies. After the collapse of the old regimes, the extent of government involvement in society and the size of the public sector became increasingly incompatible with the introduction of a market-democracy and with the neo-liberal thinking that gained ground in post-communist societies. There was thought to be no alternative but to reduce the role of the state in the economy and to decentralize to markets and private provision of goods (Czike et al., 2002; World Bank, 2001).

Decentralization also played a significant role in the transformation of the social provisions of the former socialist countries of Central and Eastern Europe. Although, under the old system too, central governments used regional and local branches to deliver social services, the bulk of decisions were made at the centre (World Bank, 2001). Under the new regimes, local governments that previously lacked real decision-making power increasingly received more responsibility for the provision of key services in the area of social policy. As Ringold (2005) states, 'they became direct providers of cash benefits, managers of health facilities, operators of institutions for the elderly, employers of participants in public work programs and contractors of social assistance services'. Means-tested income schemes of the last resort were often the first scheme to be decentralized (Sipos and Ringold, 2005). Though to a different extent, many CEE-countries have transferred the power and responsibility for social assistance from the state administration to lower levels of government. Though today most CEE social assistance schemes are still regulated at the national level, local governments are increasingly involved in the administration and financing of the general safety net.

Means-testing in CEE countries

In Central and Eastern Europe, basic social assistance safety nets to supplement labour-centred social security were developed only recently. Until the late 1980s, the main instrument of minimum income protection in CEE countries was near-universal employment at low pay accompanied by work-based welfare systems (old-age pensions, health-related transfers and family benefits), together with regulated and subsidized prices (of food, clothing, housing, and so on) and services (for example (nearly) free health care and education). Since social services (even food) were in major part allocated through industrial enterprises, employment was a crucial condition to gain access to social support (Manning, 2004; Standing, 1997). For those incapable of taking an active part in working life social assistance systems provided a safety net (Cerami, 2006). However, as Milanovic (1995) states, neither in terms of its size nor with regard to its concentration on the poor did social assistance have the role that it typically has in the West. On the one hand, this was due to the fact that poverty was not (at least officially) widespread; on the other hand there was little sympathy for the poor as such. Policymakers saw poverty as a social pathology – experienced by individuals who did not conform to the idea of the good communist worker (Milanovic, 1995). Highly selective and stigmatized services were developed to cater for them (Cantillon et al., 2008).

With the transformation from centrally planned to market economies, the existing core pillars of social protection were augmented and expanded and new social provisions were developed to alleviate the anticipated welfare consequences. Prominent among the new social programmes was the enactment of an unemployment scheme to cope with an expected explosion of unemployment (Manning, 2004). For those not entitled to such replacement benefits, means-tested social assistance safety nets were introduced. One of the key features of these means-tested schemes was the establishment of a minimum income level (also called guaranteed income level) as a poverty threshold. All households and citizens that found themselves below the poverty line established by law had the right to social assistance benefits.

In the years immediately after the transition social benefits were typically generous and easy accessible. It has been noted that officials were rather reluctant to apply a strict means-test, mainly for feasibility reasons (Cerami, 2006). The fact that the existence of transfer systems often triggers unwanted behavioural responses and the sustainability of the new measures in the longer run were usually not taken into account (Góra and Schmidt, 1998). Yet another reason for this might be that, as various authors have pointed out, that the political legitimacy of the governments at the time largely depended on the effectiveness of these new welfare programmes as an anti-poverty device (Cerami, 2006; Kaufman, 2007; Manning, 2004; Vanhuysse, 2006a). As the profound economic and labour market changes resulted in massive job losses (and unemployment) and the old state-run forms of protection (such as consumer and enterprise subsidies) were disappearing, these new schemes became an important facilitating factor in the widespread acceptance of both the market economy and procedural democracy.

However, as the financial cost of these programmes rapidly rose far and above what had been foreseen, the idea soon gained ground that these early measures needed restructuring (Manning, 2004). Diminished financial capacity made it hard to continue providing the same level of social provision as in the pre- or early post-transition era and as a result the existing welfare institutions were dismantled. These social reforms took place against the background of political and economic forces arguing (under the influence of recommendations by international organizations like the IMF, the World Bank and the OECD) for neo-liberal restructuring (privatization, elimination of enterprise subsidies and so on). In order to become more 'market conforming' (Ferge, 1997), benefit generosity and duration were substantially cut back, especially for the unemployed but also for social assistance claimants.

This first round of restructuring, which mainly consisted in a restriction of eligibility requirements for unemployment insurance, resulted in an enormous expansion of means-tested support of the last resort (Góra and Schmidt, 1998). Indeed, according to Standing (1997), the drift to selectivity, and the related growth of the number of social assistance claimants, has been the most important trend in Central and Eastern European social protection systems during the 1990s (Boeri and Keese, 1992; Boeri and Edwards, 1998). The growing reliance on social assistance schemes, however, placed the systems under great fiscal pressure. National governments found themselves again urged to carry out fundamental reforms, now not only in the wider framework of social protection but also within social assistance schemes. The central issue in the reforms of social assistance schemes has become how to improve targeting (Milanovic, 1995; Ringold and Kasek, 2007; Sipos and Ringold, 2005; Standing, 1997). The current policy challenge in CEE countries exists in enhancing poverty relief efficiency by concentrating spending just to those in need and therefore at the same time also to all those in need (Standing, 1997).

It is important to stress that the increased stress on targeting as a tool for improving efficiency has not only been a process fuelled from within. It is as much the result of several exogenous factors of which the recommendations of international organizations (the World Bank, the IMF, the OECD and so on) are said to be the most important (Deacon, 2000; Sipos and Ringold, 2005). These organizations repeatedly stress the need to cut social expenditures and seriously promote a shift from universal to selective social assistance systems as the most efficient means to rationalize social spending. Note that these organizations have played an equally central role in the trend towards more decentralization already mentioned. As a matter of fact, the arguments in favour of decentralization and pro-targeting are not unrelated, given that decentralization is often conceived as the best way to enhance targeting of social assistance schemes (Dillinger and Fay, 1999; Ringold and Kasek, 2007). Such arguments find substance particularly in theoretical models claiming local governments to be better informed than central authorities of practical circumstances affecting the local implementation of policies. The assertion that decentralization facilitates targeting is also supported by the theory of 'laboratory federalism'. According to this view, federalism provides fertile conditions for policy innovation because it creates at the lower level multiple governments, any one of which might take the lead in experimenting with new solutions; it can thus unleash policy innovation on a local level that would not win sufficient support on a national level (Hueghlin and Fenna, 2006). Once given policies have been shown to work, one may see a demonstration effect whereby new policies (or policy models) are taken up by other decentralized units (sometimes resistant jurisdiction) or by the central government. However, this argument is not restricted to federal states: it may in fact hold for any country where both policy-making and implementation are transferred to lower levels of government.

It is noteworthy that there is still considerable disagreement regarding the exact impact of international organizations on social policy reforms in CEE countries. Particularly, studies on path-conforming elements in present CEE social policy have often qualified the importance of international organizations in shaping the post-communist welfare state. The discourse and guidelines of the European Union, World Bank, or the International Monetary Fund for that matter, are in these studies invariably portrayed as vehicles which CEE policymakers may use or not use for achieving the social policy objectives which they have inherited from the pre-transition period. Path-dependency somehow suggests that recommendations of such international agencies are a relevant force only to the extent that they fit within some pre-existing anti-poverty strategy. The legacy of communist institutions, the specificity of national conditions and situations (Sengoku, 2004), the confusing and inconsistent signals sent out by the international agencies (Deacon and Hulse, 1997), are all elements which are brought up to criticize the impact of international recommendations on the decentralization and regionalization processes in the countries of Central and Eastern Europe (Baun and Marek, 2006; Sipos and Ringold, 2005).

Hence, what we see is that the characteristics of the social assistance in CEE countries are often interpreted in terms of path-dependency, rather than being responses to international pressures. A widespread idea seems to exist that the welfare state as it has been developed since 1989 still carries many of the hallmarks of communist social policy. Note, however, that there is considerable disagreement on precisely which features of current provisions for the poor can be seen as reflective of the communist support system. Focusing on the inadequacy of social provisions, Ferge (2001b), for instance, argues that the CEE countries inherited from state socialism 'a deep-seated aversion to assistance based on rights (instead of discretion) together with strong prejudices against the "undeserving" poor'. Furthermore, Ferge identifies the legacy of many decades of communism as one of the main reasons (in conjunction with, among other things, financial hardship and the weakness of civil society) why the neo-liberal, residual welfare strategy, promoted by prominent international institutions (in particular the World Bank, OECD and IMF), was so easily adopted in CEE countries. Ferge clearly suggests that, in the CEE countries, the prospect of a non-categorical, generous and adequate safety net is not very favourable. A similar pessimistic view concerning the development of an equitable social policy can be found in Standing (1997). As Standing perceives it, there exists a tolerance of impoverishment in the CEE countries, caused by long-term experience of communism, where income security was only provided in conditions where liberty was denied. Cerami (2006), on the other hand, focuses on the increasingly important role that social assistance schemes have played in the anti-poverty strategy of CEE countries during the past decade and argues that these schemes can be linked to the principles of solidarity which already featured prominently in the social policy debate during the communist era. More particularly, Cerami points out that in many CEE countries minimum income guarantees – such as the minimum income level – had already been established 'well before the concept of "social minima" was introduced in France in 1988' (Cerami, 2006).

Decentralization and benefit generosity: an empirical comparative analysis

CEE social safety nets in comparative perspective

Since the late 1990s, in order to fight poverty most OECD states have a universal means-tested programme in place, that is a scheme that provides cash benefits to everyone who is defined as needy, irrespective of their working capacity. Hungary is the major exception: means-tested aid is here provided through several categorical programmes (Micklewright and Nagy, 1998). Within the OECD there are only few countries without universal – that is non-categorical – means-tested programmes. Turkey and Greece are the main exceptions apart from Hungary. However, in the strictest sense of the word, the prevailing social protection systems in the UK, Ireland, Australia, New Zealand and the US are not universal schemes that guarantee cash benefits to all the needy. In the UK, Ireland and New Zealand the safety net merely consists of various complementary categorical schemes. In the United Kingdom, for instance, non-able-bodied persons with insufficient resources can claim Income Support (if working fewer than 16 hours a week), able-bodied persons are entitled to an income-based Jobseekers Allowance (if working fewer than 16 hours a week), and low-income households working at least 16 hours a week are eligible for Working Tax Credit. However, because these programmes are closely aligned, they are often considered together as a universal guaranteed minimum income (Walker and Wiseman, 2003). Minimum income provision in Ireland, Australia and New Zealand is organized along similar lines. The US, for its part, deviates in another sense: the federal government does not provide cash benefits for all needy households, but only in-kind benefits such as food stamps and Medicaid. The Temporary Assistance for Needy Families programme (TANF) does encompass means-tested cash benefits, but only to households with children.

Although most CEE countries have universal means-tested schemes, there are some significant differences between minimum income provision in CEE countries on the one hand and the workings of safety nets in Western Europe on the other hand. For one thing, although in most CEE countries eligibility conditions and (minimum) benefit amounts are laid down by law, it is often argued that welfare payments are highly discretionary. Arbitrary decision-making on the part of local authorities is said to cause widespread non-payment and ad hoc selectivity, particularly in Poland (Cerami, 2006; Góra and Schmidt, 1998; Standing, 1997) and Hungary (Ferge and Juhász, 2004). In practice, financial support is often restricted to the so-called deserving poor, while many of those needing income support are excluded. Moreover, humiliating practices such as home visits and the stigma associated with social assistance seriously aggravate the problem of low take-up rates (Ferge, 1997). In addition, Heikkilä and Kuivalainen (2002) assert that CEE countries (that is the Czech Republic, Latvia and Bulgaria) use stricter means-tests and work requirements than the old EU member states in their cross-country study (Belgium, France, Finland and Ireland). In this chapter, however, we focus on two other characteristics of social assistance schemes: benefit levels and the degree of decentralization.

Cantillon et al. (2008) conclude on the basis of a comparison of social assistance benefits in 19 European countries (including six CEE countries) that the level of minimum income protection offered to the able-bodied poor in Latvia, Lithuania, Hungary, Poland, Slovakia and the Czech Republic is relatively low in purchasing power terms. At the same time, however, they argue that this holds less true in relative terms. For instance, in Poland and the Czech Republic, the gap between the social assistance benefit and equivalized median household income is less pronounced than in some West European countries. Although in both countries financial transfers for the poor are not entirely adequate (in the sense that benefit packages for social assistance claimants are below 50 per cent of the median standardized household income), they are no less generous than in, for instance, France and Norway. In fact, they induce less of a poverty gap than in the US, Canada, Portugal or Spain where the social assistance income amounts on average to 14 per cent to 35 per cent of median household income, compared to 44 per cent in the Czech Republic and 49 per cent in Poland[1] (see also Figure 11.1).

Despite the general trend towards decentralization, CEE countries differ quite substantially in the degree to which municipalities are involved in social assistance delivery. Table 11.1 arranges the OECD countries by the manner in which their general social assistance programmes are decentralized. Under the general social assistance schemes, households often receive different types of means-tested benefits: a basic rate to cover the general cost of living (food, clothes, and so on) and supplementary benefits that are linked to specific costs (housing, heating, and so on.) Households with children also receive family benefits or, as the case may be, specific allowances for lone parents, which may or may not be means-tested. These allowances are not always organized and provided at the same level of government. In Norway and Iceland, for example, social assistance claimants receive a centrally established housing allowance, while the level of the basic rate and other supplementary benefits is determined by every municipality separately. In order to ascertain in the empirical analysis which competency divisions provide for socially effective benefits and which do not, we measure the degree of decentralization for each of three income components: the basic rates, the housing allowances and the other supplementary benefits. In Table 11.1, we do not make this distinction, but we rather arrange the various countries by the level of government at which the total net income

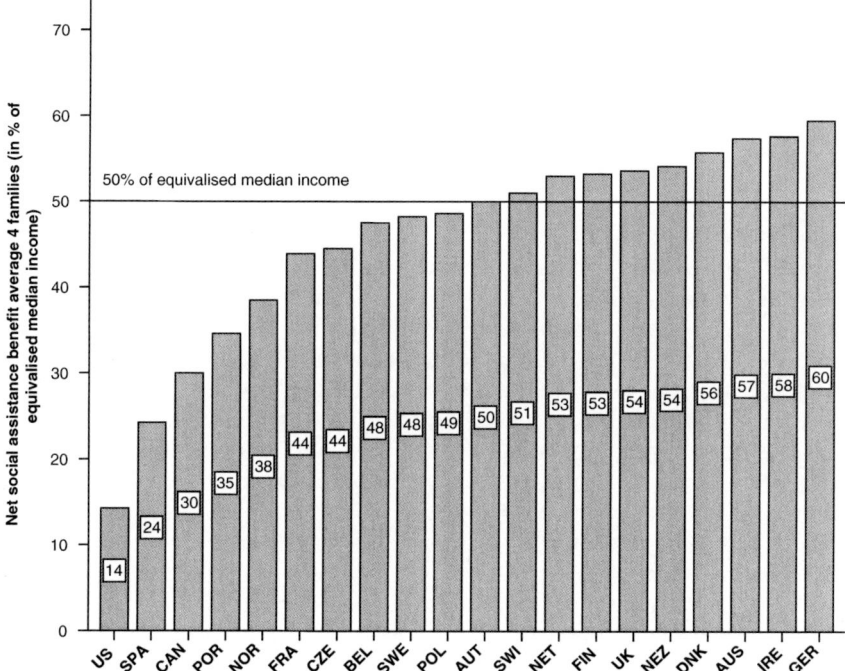

Figure 11.1 Net social assistance benefits as percentage of equivalized median household income, 20 OECD countries (2004)

Source: Own calculations based on OECD (2004).

Table 11.1 Decentralization of social assistance benefits in 25 OECD countries (2004)

No decentralization	Deconcentration	Decentralization
Luxembourg	Australia, Ireland, New Zealand, United Kingdom, Slovak Republic	*To meso level:* Austria, Canada, (Germany,) (France,) Italy, Spain, Switzerland, United States *To local level:* Czech Republic, Belgium, Denmark, Finland, (Germany,) (France,) Iceland, Japan, Netherlands, Norway, Portugal, Poland, Sweden

Sources: OECD, 2004: national reports; MISSOC, 2005; national data (particularly from websites of institutions involved in the regulation or implementation of the benefits analysed).

of the social assistance claimant is determined. This means that countries where the basic rates for social assistance claimants and housing allowances are the same across the nation, but where local government holds the explicit competency to decide on additional benefits, are subsumed under the group of regimes where the local authorities have decisive competency over the overall income package for social assistance recipients.

As shown in Table 11.1, there is just one OECD country, Luxembourg, where general social assistance has not been decentralized in any way. That is to say, the Luxembourg central government has not transferred fiscal, political or administrative responsibilities to lower levels of government. It is the central government that lays down the eligibility criteria and the benefit amounts (of basic rates as well as housing allowances and other supplementary benefits) and that carries the full financial burden of the system.

In the other OECD countries, competencies are to some extent transferred to a sub-central government agency. In Ireland, the United Kingdom, Australia, New Zealand and the Slovak Republic social assistance delivery is deconcentrated. This means that basic rates and supplementary benefits for social assistance recipients are regulated and financed by the central government and administered by regional (Ireland, Australia, New Zealand and the United Kingdom (standard rates)) or local (the Slovak Republic and the United Kingdom (housing benefits)) agencies which are under the direct supervision of the central government.

In Austria, Canada, Italy, Spain, Switzerland, France, Germany and the US, social assistance is decentralized to a meso-level government. In the first five of these countries, the provinces, regions or cantons have full competency in relation to both basic benefits and supplements for social assistance claimants. So each jurisdiction takes autonomous decisions with regard to the eligibility criteria, the benefit amounts and the funding of the system as a whole. In Switzerland, the variation in benefit amounts between cantons is however restricted through national guidelines which, though not binding, are more or less adhered to by all cantons. In Germany, social assistance is the responsibility of the Länder, but the extent of variation in the application of eligibility criteria and payment levels is limited as federal legislation defines basic rules on entitlement and benefit amounts. A similar system is in place in France. The French government is the main regulator and financer of the minimum income guarantee but leaves the implementation of the social assistance mostly to the departments, in cooperation with the municipalities. In the United States, the broad outlines of minimum income protection are provided in federal programmes (largely financed by the federal authorities), such as the Food Stamp Programme, Medicaid and TANF. However, individual states are free to develop and finance more broadly accessible and more generous social assistance programmes. In 1998, some 18 of the 52 states had their own cash assistance programmes (Walker and Wiseman, 2003). In most countries where social assistance is organized at the meso-level, local authorities are also involved in policy implementation, and sometimes also in its financing, but the degree to which this is the case may vary considerably from region to region. Germany and France are exceptions here, as local responsibilities are to some extent determined by national regulations. In CEE countries, such federalized social assistance schemes are non-existent.

In many CEE countries, as in many OECD countries, the general social assistance regime has been devolved directly from central government to the municipalities. Except for some cases, where local involvement is mostly administrative (like in Portugal and France until 2005), this implies first and foremost that the municipalities are made responsible for the financial side of social assistance benefits and/or supplementary benefits. However, in most countries the central government does meet part of the cost. In Poland, Belgium, Denmark and Japan, municipalities receive a transfer per social assistance recipient that covers part of the social assistance benefit. The proportion that the municipality contributes to the basic allowance (that is excluding housing allowances and supplementary benefits) varies from 25 per cent in Japan to more than 75 per cent in Poland. In the Czech Republic, the national government carries the entire burden of basic rates while the municipalities are financially responsible for the supplementary benefits. In Finland, Germany, Iceland, the Netherlands, Norway and Sweden, municipalities receive a general government grant which covers either some part of the totality of their social expenditures (Sweden) or the major part of their expenses on means-tested benefits (the Netherlands). The size of the block grant usually depends on local indicators, such as the unemployment rate, the urbanization rate, and so on.

In countries where social assistance programmes are funded with local resources, the local authorities generally have a say in determining benefit amounts. As Table 11.2 shows, however, the margin that municipalities have at their disposal varies strongly from country to country. In Japan and the Netherlands, benefit amounts, supplements and possible deviations thereof are laid down by law, so that little room is left for a municipal policy on social assistance benefits.[2] In the Czech Republic, Denmark, Finland, Germany and Sweden, the national legislator determines how basic benefits and housing allowances should be calculated. Yet the municipalities have room to adapt the eventual social assistance income to the local socio-economic context, as they can decide quasi-autonomously on the level of the supplementary benefits. Although little research has been conducted into this matter, it is generally assumed that, in these countries, minimum income protection of the poor varies strongly depending on where they live. Intercommunal differences in minimum protection are probably even greater in Belgium where only the basic amount is regulated nationally, while municipalities are left free to decide on eligibility criteria for and the benefit amounts of housing allowances and other supplements. In Iceland, Norway and Poland, the municipalities can, within nationally imposed

Table 11.2 Main local responsibilities in the delivery of social assistance benefit packages in 13 OECD countries (2004)

Mere administration	Administration + limited funding responsibilities and power of decision	Administration + substantial share of funding + regulation supplementary benefits (excluding housing benefits)	Administration + substantial share of funding + regulation supplementary benefits (including housing benefits)	Administration + substantial share of funding + regulation basic rate & supplementary benefits (excluding housing benefits)
France	Czech Rep.	Denmark	Belgium	Iceland
Portugal	Japan	Finland		Norway
	Netherlands	Germany		Poland
		Sweden		

Sources: OECD, 2004: national reports; MISSOC, 2005; national data (particularly from websites of institutions involved in the regulation or implementation of the benefits analysed).

limits, even determine the basic amounts. However, housing allowances are fixed at the national level in these countries.

Empirical findings: decentralization and adequate social assistance benefit levels

As we have seen, despite the general trend towards more decentralization, CEE countries still vary a lot in the degree to which local governments are involved in social assistance delivery. In the Slovak Republic, there has been no real decentralization: social assistance benefits are provided through local agencies that are under direct control of the central government rather than through local governments. At the other extreme, the Polish central government merely determines a maximum rate which leaves substantial freedom for local policymakers to develop their own approach to poverty relief. In between is the Czech Republic, where local autonomy is restricted to those supplementary benefits other than housing benefits.

In this section we empirically assess the relationship between decentralization and the adequacy of social assistance benefit levels. We use the level of the net social assistance benefit package (including child benefits and housing benefits) as percentage of 50 per cent of median standardized household income as a rough indicator of the adequacy of social assistance schemes. However, note that the adequacy of minimum income provisions does not only depend on benefit levels but also on other factors, such as the accessibility of the scheme and take-up rates for which, however, no cross-country comparable data are available.

As we have stated above, various international organizations put substantial pressure on CEE countries to transfer minimum income provision to local governments in order to improve the efficiency of poverty relief. However, there is a real danger that decentralization leads to better targeting at the cost of less adequate benefit levels. There are in fact several theoretical models claiming that decentralization exerts a downward pressure on social assistance benefit levels (for example, the veto player approach to the welfare state (Castles, 1999; Obinger, 1998). Without doubt the most prominent among these models is the theory of fiscal federalism. This theory provides us with sound theoretical reasons to believe that decentralization puts fundamental restraints on redistribution due to interjurisdictional fiscal competition. At the heart of fiscal federalism is the 'voting with their feet' hypothesis: if citizens are faced with an array of jurisdictions that offer different types or levels of public goods and services, then each citizen will choose the jurisdiction that best satisfies his or her own particular demands (Brown and Oates, 1987; Tiebout, 1956). Consequently, the socially weak will tend to move to regions where social benefits are high, while better-off households and enterprises shall be inclined to move out of such regions, because they are made to carry the burden of generous redistribution in the shape of high taxation and social contributions. Regions with generous protection schemes will consequently face rising costs and an increasingly narrow financial base. A decentralization of redistribution policy will thus compel jurisdictions to compete with one another in trying to become the least attractive to individuals who are highly dependent upon social protection. In the longer term, this dynamics will lead to a 'race to the bottom', whereby social protection is gradually eroded.

To what extent do our data support the view that decentralization is detrimental for the adequacy of social assistance benefit levels? Comparing the degree to which social assistance programmes in the countries have been decentralized (see Tables 11.1 and 11.2) and social assistance benefit levels (Figure 11.1), we notice that all countries with adequate benefits (those at the upper end of Figure 11.1) belong either to the group where social assistance programmes are run almost exclusively by the central government (Australia, New Zealand, UK and Ireland), or to the group where social assistance schemes have been devolved to the municipal level through co-financing schemes, but where the power of decision-making of those municipalities is quite limited, given that either the amounts involved are imposed nationally or strict guidelines are issued regarding both basic rates and housing allowances for social assistance recipients (the Netherlands, Finland, Denmark and Germany). Conversely, the countries where universal minimum income protection is found to be inadequate to prevent income poverty (those in the lower end of the distribution in Figure 11.1) are those where the regional or local authorities are granted ample room to devise local social assistance policy. In the United States, Spain and Canada, minimum income entitlements for the needy but capacitated are determined at the meso-level government. In Poland and Norway this decision-making competency lies primarily with the municipalities. In short, we find that countries with adequate welfare payments are generally characterized by a low or modest degree of decentralization whereas countries where the financial aid to those who are able-bodied but poor is the least adequate tend to have very decentralized welfare provisions. One conclusion that clearly emerges from the above comparison is that there is a significant negative impact of decentralization on social assistance benefit adequacy.

Indeed, our data suggest that extreme forms of decentralization, where the autonomy of municipalities in setting benefit packages is quite substantial, are associated with inadequate benefit levels. The negative impact of excessive local freedom is best illustrated by the cases of Norway, Belgium and Poland. All three countries have rather restricted national guidelines relating to benefit amounts for social assistance claimants as well as benefit levels below the poverty line. However, it is noteworthy that the inadequacy of social assistance benefits is often a geographically concentrated phenomenon. For instance, empirical studies of Norwegian and Belgian municipalities have demonstrated that local benefit rates are much more generous in large cities than in small municipalities (Ashworth et al., 2002; Lien and Pettersen, 2004). Figure 11.1 is based on the minimum rate for social assistance benefits in Belgium and on the average benefit amount in Norway. However, in both countries, there are, most probably, a number of municipalities that provide quite adequate benefits for social assistance claimants (for Norway see Bradshaw and Mayhew, 2006; for Belgium see Van Mechelen and Bogaerts, 2008). Therefore, it seems fair to say that the most problematic consequence of drastic decentralization is the large inter-regional variation in benefit levels, which often results in quite inadequate benefit levels in the least generous regions. This finding holds not only for local but also for federalized social assistance schemes (Van Mechelen, forthcoming).

However, it is important to stress that our data support the view that decentralization negatively affects benefit generosity only as far as extreme versions of decentralization are concerned. As the cases of Denmark, Finland, Germany and possibly Sweden show, decentralization per se is not by definition harmful for the adequacy of benefits. It appears that countries where the involvement of local authorities in the administration and funding of social assistance is substantial, yet restricted under central legislation or guidelines regarding benefit standards, the level of basic rates and housing allowances for social assistance recipients is often adequate, that is above 50 per cent of median household income (see Table 11.3). Although in Denmark, Finland and Germany municipalities are fiscally responsible for poverty relief, there is no race to the bottom because the national regulation with regard to rate-setting prevents the municipalities from providing the poor with 'poor' benefits.

Note that, although national benefit standards seem to play a crucial role in the provision of a nationwide and adequate minimum, they are by

Table 11.3 Local involvement in the delivery of social assistance and social assistance benefit levels in 13 OECD countries (2004)

	Mere administration	Administration + limited funding responsibilities and power of decision	Administration + substantial share of funding + regulation supplementary benefits (excluding housing benefits)	Administration + substantial share of funding + regulation basic rate or housing benefits + regulation other supplementary benefits
Adequate benefits		Netherlands	Denmark Finland Germany	
No adequate benefits	France Portugal	Czech Republic	Sweden[3]	Belgium Norway Poland

Sources: OECD, 2004 and related national reports; MISSOC, 2005; national data (particularly from websites of institutions involved in the regulation or implementation of the benefits analysed).

no means a sufficient condition. Take for example the French case or the Portuguese case. In both countries social assistance benefits are quite low, although there are strict national standards. One explanation for the difference between Portugal, France and possibly the Czech Republic on the one hand and Denmark, Finland and Germany on the other hand might be that in Portugal, France and the Czech Republic municipalities have scarcely any financial responsibility. It might be that central governments are only willing to set adequate benefit levels if municipalities are at least partially financially responsible for the scheme, so that national policymakers have reason to believe that benefits are efficiently administered. It seems that national benefit standards are particularly associated with adequate benefit levels if combined with both administrative and fiscal decentralization.

In short, our data suggest that the key to adequate minimum income provision is either a social assistance scheme that is run almost exclusively by the central government (cf. Australia, New Zealand, UK and Ireland) or to strike a happy medium between local and central responsibilities (cf. the Netherlands, Finland, Denmark and Germany). Given the alleged link between decentralization and targeting, the latter option (local administration and local (co-)financing under strict central guidelines) may be considered the most preferable way to organize a social assistance scheme. Analysing the efficiency of means-tested benefit systems, Holsch and Krause (2004) come to a very similar conclusion. Comparing poverty reduction efficiency of social assistance in five EU countries, they find that social assistance schemes with a medium degree of decentralization (France, Germany and Finland) perform much better than either extremely centralized (UK) or extremely decentralized systems (Italy).

Of course, one may ask whether the finding that this happy medium between local and central responsibilities is compatible with adequate minimum provision also holds within the context of CEE countries. More particularly, the question is whether the association between the mix of administrative, fiscal and political decentralization mentioned above and adequate benefit levels is related to specific circumstances or additional conditions. For one thing, the budgetary constraints of municipalities may be a crucial factor underlying the effectiveness of locally financed benefits. For example, the recent experience in Bosnia and Romania has shown that there is a danger in the context of strong local fiscal responsibility that local governments are unable to pay out social benefits that are otherwise well targeted because they lack adequate budgets or real opportunities to raise local taxes (Ringold and Kasek, 2007; Sipos and Ringold, 2005). Consequently, the World Bank strongly argues in favour of earmarked central government grants in order to ensure that each municipality has enough financial resources at its disposal to provide aid to the poor. Note that in Table 11.3 the majority of countries with adequate but locally co-financed social assistance schemes have fiscal equalizing mechanisms in place in order to redistribute funds from relatively wealthy municipalities to poorer ones (Germany, the Netherlands, Finland and Sweden). Indeed, as Davey (2003) has argued, one of the essential elements of decentralization is a normative system of fiscal equalization that ensures national standards to be realistically achieved despite differences in local revenue bases. However, he also notes that most post-communist countries inherited intergovernmental finance systems (funded partially, if not completely, by local revenues and bearing the costs of local public services) characterized by a certain degree of redistribution but lacking a normative basis. Instead, they were subjected to arbitrary variation in annual budgets and much political bias in its application which resulted in strong disincentives for revenue mobilization or cost discipline.

Another important factor in the effectiveness of locally financed social assistance schemes is probably the capacity of central governments to monitor and to ensure that national eligibility rules as well as the centrally determined means tests are correctly applied. After all, it is easy to see that high benefits will induce local policymakers to limit access to the benefit scheme by the vigour with which national guidelines are applied. As Schwager (1997) notes, high benefits may result in low proportions of poor persons who actually obtain it. In CEE countries the danger of decreasing administrative integrity is perhaps even greater than in Western Europe, given that, as we have already seen, various studies present a rather pessimistic picture regarding the rights attached to social assistance (Cerami, 2006; Ferge and Juhász, 2004; Góra and Schmidt, 1998; Standing, 1997).

All in all, it appears that further analyses are required to gauge how exactly the happy medium of central and local responsibilities is achieved.

More research is needed to determine how exactly the adequacy of social safety net can be improved through the framework of regulatory and fiscal decentralization. And what is especially important in the specific case of Central and Eastern European countries is to gain insight into how the relationship between political and fiscal decentralization on the one hand and social assistance benefit generosity inter-relates with context variables such as economic development and local bureaucratic capacities.

Conclusion

Probably the most important trend in CEE social protection systems during the 1990s has been the enormous expansion of means-tested support of the last resort. This trend is prompted, at least partially, by the recommendations of international organizations like the World Bank and the OECD who believe that the current policy challenge in CEE countries exists in enhancing poverty relief efficiency by better targeting. Such international recommendations on social policy tend to intensify the already ongoing process of decentralization, as more local government involvement in social assistance delivery is often conceived as the best way to improve targeting.

Comparing CEE social safety nets with other OECD countries, we see that the level of minimum income protection offered to the able-bodied poor is relatively low, at least if measured in purchasing power terms. However, in some CEE countries (for example the Czech Republic and Poland) the gap between the social assistance benefit and equivalized median household income is less pronounced than in some West European countries (for example France and Norway). Despite the general trend towards decentralization, CEE countries still differ quite substantially in the degree to which municipalities are involved in social assistance delivery. In Poland, local policymakers have a large degree of freedom to develop their own approach to poverty relief, while in the Slovak Republic local governments are formally excluded from the implementation of social assistance.

Part two of this chapter has empirically assessed to what degree decentralization represents a real threat to the adequacy of minimum income provision. The theory of fiscal federalism provides us with sound theoretical arguments to believe that decentralization exerts a downward pressure on social assistance adequacy. However, we find adequate social assistance benefits (that is above 50 per cent of median standardized household income) not only in countries where the central government is the main actor in social assistance delivery but also in countries with decentralized social assistance schemes, provided that the degree of decentralization is limited. More particularly, we usually find benefit levels above the poverty line in countries where the involvement of local authorities in the administration and funding of social assistance is substantial, yet restricted under central legislation or guidelines regarding benefit standards (for example, Germany, Denmark and Finland). Our data only support the view that decentralization has a downward impact on social assistance benefit levels in so far as unrestrained forms of decentralization are concerned. Countries where there are no strict national guidelines relating to benefit standards (such as Poland, Norway and Belgium) are generally associated with inadequate minimum income provision, at least in the less generous municipalities. In short, our data show that although extreme forms of decentralization are generally associated with inadequate minimum income provision, more restricted versions of decentralization do not necessarily result in low benefit levels. Therefore we have argued that the key to adequate minimum income provision is either the complete exclusion of local governments in social assistance delivery or to strike a happy medium between local and central responsibilities. Given the alleged link between decentralization and enhanced targeting, the latter option may be the most preferable way to organize a social assistance scheme. In addition, we have seen that the majority of countries with adequate but locally co-financed social assistance schemes have fiscal equalizing mechanisms in place in order to redistribute funds from relatively wealthy municipalities to poorer ones (for example, Germany, the Netherlands and Finland). This finding suggests that the happy medium associated with adequate benefit levels, and which in broad outline consists of local administration, central regulation and shared financial responsibilities, is especially facilitated by a normative system of fiscal equalization.

All this means that the current trend towards more local involvement in minimum income provision in CEE countries will not necessarily lead to inadequate benefits, provided that a number of conditions apply. First, it seems that adequate nationwide minimum standards require strong central steering, in the sense of both strict national guidelines regarding benefit standards and a normative system of fiscal equalization. In addition, we have argued that the compatibility of the above mix of central and local responsibilities with adequate benefit levels may be related to the bureaucratic capacities of both central and local governments.

12
The Impact of the EU Social Inclusion Strategy: the Czech Case*

Tomáš Sirovátka and Miroslava Rákoczyová

Introduction

The European Union launched a new strategy to fight against poverty and social exclusion at the Lisbon summit in March 2000. It was agreed that the objectives outlined might be best achieved by the Open Method of Coordination (OMC) which has been formerly used to implement the guidelines of the European Employment Strategy since 1997. The 'social inclusion' agenda emerged after the summit in Nice (December 2000) when all EU member states have been obliged to elaborate and to submit to the European Commission the National Action Plans on Social Inclusion – NAPSIs (Council of the European Union, 2000a, 2000b). This agenda (understood as *soft law*) is based on development of common discourses, key concepts and policy principles (Radaelli, 2003; Daly, 2008) rather than on directives of *hard law*. The new member states which joined the EU in 2004 have been invited to elaborate on the Joint Memorandum on Social Inclusion in 2003, and since 2004 to draft the NAPSI for 2004–2006. What is completely new in the European agenda of social inclusion now being implemented in post-communist countries through OMC – when compared to the already established 'emergency' policies – is an explicit requirement to adopt a complex strategy and to mobilize actors and resources to address most aspects of social exclusion understood as multidimensional phenomena. At the same time, new resources to be used for that purpose are available through European structural funds. The interesting question is to what extent this agenda would facilitate both discursive and policy-making change as a mechanism of 'path-departure'. The Czech case may serve as illustration of this since – as we will show below – the discursive and policy context there is less supportive of such a change than is the case in other CEE post-communist countries. Thus identification of any signs of 'path-departure' in the Czech case would support assumption about the impact of social inclusion agenda in these countries.

This chapter explores to what extent the European agenda of social inclusion has changed the discourse and process of policy-making in the Czech Republic in the specific field of social policy – protection against risks of poverty and social exclusion. In addition to a secondary analysis of various sets of national and international data and of the content of the NAPSI 2004–06 and 2006–08, we draw from information obtained through 75 focused semi-structured interviews conducted in 2005 in the Czech Republic at the national (18), regional (31) and local (26) levels, with actors who had been involved in the preparation of the NAPSI 2004–06 at the national level, and those who deal with the agenda directly contained in the NAPSI at the regional and local levels. In addition, eight semi-structured interviews were carried out with various actors in mid-2006. We also use information obtained through the international survey *Evaluation of Mainstreaming Social Inclusion* (2006), carried out by the Combat Poverty Agency and its national partners in nine European countries including 126 Czech respondents from public administration and NGOs.

The chapter is organized as follows. In the first section we discuss the potential of the social inclusion agenda and the Open Method of Coordination to influence the national strategy in this field. In the second section we assess development of public and policy discourse and previously existing approach of Czech social policy to poverty and social exclusion. The third section focuses on the implementation of the social inclusion agenda in the Czech Republic. The concluding section summarizes the findings and discusses the future prospects of social inclusion agenda in the Czech Republic. Alhough this is a national case study we are comparing the Czech case mainly with the other CEE post-communist countries in several crucial repects.

Social inclusion agenda

The 'old' EU members' experience with implementing the social inclusion agenda using the OMC dates from 2000. What is being emphasized when referring to the *social OMC* is that a new system of governance is being applied, grounded on cooperation, political bargaining, bottom-up policy-making, experimenting and institutional learning, establishing policy guidelines, setting benchmarks and qualitative indicators, concrete national targets and monitoring system via peer-group review and transfer of good practice (compare De la Porte et al., 2001; Begg and Berghman, 2002; Radaelli, 2003; O'Connor, 2005; Theobald and Kern, this volume). Yet assessments of its potential and effective contribution are not particularly clear-cut. On the one hand, the agenda is seen as beneficial in many respects. First, it brings the problem of social inclusion in the centre of public discourse and attention of public policy, raising general awareness of the issue (Abrahamson, 1997; O'Connor, 2005). At the same time, it provides language codes and understanding (Jepsen and Serrano Pascual, 2005) that may generate a considerable potential of *cognitive effect* and *institutional learning* (for example De la Porte and Pochet, 2004). Cerami (in this volume) distinguishes several forms of the institutional change and considers *ideational and discursive institutional change* to be one of the main mechanisms according to which transformation in institutional relations occur. Radaelli (2003, pp. 7–8) speaks of the legitimating function of the new agenda implemented through OMC and about initiating the process of *ideational convergence*: '[...] policymakers converge in their assessment of causal mechanisms at work in policy areas, definitions of desirable and unacceptable policies, and beliefs about how policies work'.

On the other hand criticism is directed mainly at the absence of enforcement mechanisms and the lack of formal EU-level competence (Goetschy, 1999), the structural asymmetry between economic or 'market-making' and social protection or 'market-correcting' interests at the European level (Ferrera et al., 2002; Scharpf, 2002): while the economic sphere of decision-making is strongly Europeanized and is based on binding regulations (Copenhagen EMU criteria in particular), the social sphere is governed by soft regulations, 'restricted by lack of intergovernmental agreement' (Scharpf, 2002, pp. 157–8) and cannot have a great influence over national decision-making. A number of authors argue that, after all, it is the level of political commitment of national actors that is crucial for implementation of social inclusion measures. Schaefer (2004, p. 2) even indicates a negative form of institutional learning when arguing that national governments 'learn to restrict the autonomy of supranational actors as a result of past experiences'. The employment strategy or the NAPSI may in some cases represent a mere *rhetoric exercise* – when the national strategic programme documents do not contain anything more than what would have been done anyway (Scharpf, 2002).

The assumption of the decisive role of political commitment of the actors involved in the agenda is also behind the recommendations by Commission for developing social inclusion plans at the regional and local level (compare Marlier et al., 2007) and for involvement of multiple actors in the formulation of the NAPSI (including members of excluded groups), since the strategy of social inclusion might be influenced by the pressure of social forces inside the member states (De la Porte et al., 2001; O'Connor, 2005, p. 358). Some other authors seek solution rather in a greater degree of bindingness of the OMC based on adoption of binding minimum thresholds related to national conditions across the European Union (Scharpf, 1999, 2002) or in a *hybrid strategy* based on combination of tools of hard law/directives with the OMC (Trubek and Trubek, 2005). We may conclude that legitimacy of the social inclusion agenda in the eyes of key actors is a crucial condition for *internalization* of the corresponding policy discourse by policymakers which facilitates the process of *institutional learning* (adopting and transforming ideas, norms, concepts and policy procedures) and also its usage as a specific instrument (*lever*) to advance some policy goals and measures. The result of such a process would be a specific kind of *domestification* of this agenda. Regarding post-communist countries, some studies emphasize that the assumption about the asymmetry between economic and social agendas is particularly relevant in view of dominance of the EU's economic convergence criteria before joining the European single currency (Potůček, 2004), and the delegitimation of the values of solidarity and social cohesion, leading to deviation from Europeanization of social policy (Ferge and Juhász, 2004).

On the other hand, the launching of the agenda for social inclusion in the new member states can be perceived as a 'policy window', 'window of opportunity' (Lendvai, 2004, p. 321; Cerami, this volume) if *enabling factors* such as socioeconomic and political situation would be favourable (as Cerami and Stanescu, this volume, suggest). As such, if considered as legitimate, it might eventually facilitate institutional learning, discursive change and modification of existing approaches to social problems. Besides, the European funds enlarge available resources and criteria, conditioning their allocation directly enforcing the process of institutional learning and facilitating the establishment of new policy communities at the local level.

Discursive climate for social inclusion in the Czech Republic

There is interdependence between policy discourse and public attitudes to the policies[1] on one side and the implemented policies on the other side. The argument was raised by Esping-Andersen (1990) and Baldwin (1990) that solidaristic policies of the welfare state are based on the formation of class interests and class coalitions interested in these policies while solidaristic policies contribute to the formation of class coalitions supporting such policies. Later Svallfors (1997) brought evidence on how different welfare regimes further certain attitudes at the expense of others. These impacts are due to several mechanisms: formation of class interests and coalitions, formation of short-term self-interests and formation of values and norms concerning justice and solidarity (compare Larsen, 2006, pp. 14–23). Sabbagh and Vanhuysse (2006, pp. 608–9) suggest that one way in which welfare regimes may affect public attitudes is through the political discourse of fairness, desert, need, necessity and worthiness that accompanies welfare policies. Liberal and radical regimes which stigmatize welfare 'dependency' and emphasize individual responsibility may lead citizens to support only programmes that either benefit them disproportionately or that reduce benefits to needs-tested minimum levels.

In the Czech Republic, two specific features of the policy discourse are highly relevant for public attitudes towards agenda of social inclusion. First, the *ideational domination* of the ruling political actors seems to be strong due to weak role of the social partners and civic society in general (compare for example Howard, 2003). Second, in the Czech Republic, the normative public discourse on policy and politics has for years been diverging from the actual policy-making process, while the policy coordinative discourse orienting policymakers in their decisions has not been much developed (Schmidt, 2008). Vanhuysse (2006b, pp. 1125–9) refers in this context to the Czech brand of economic and social 'exceptionalism' within the CEE pool: throughout the 1990s, Václav Klaus' governments were de facto proactively social-democratic in their social policies, and only merely apparently (that is, *rhetorically*) neo-liberal.

Following the neo-liberal rhetoric of the political elites – that rejected the ideas of social solidarity and the welfare state in general and was echoed in the mass media – the issue of poverty and social exclusion was 'individualized', with individual deficits being considered to be the main cause of the problem of poverty and social exclusion by both the public and policymakers. In mid-2003, we conducted an enquiry among 344 employees occupying decisive posts at all 77 local employment offices in the country. They defined as the most momentous cause of high unemployment 'an insufficient motivation to take up a job as a consequence of low wages, but high social benefits' (the average answer on the scale from 1 to 7 was 2.29). The most influential measure in terms of reducing unemployment was believed to be 'an adequate setting of the level and conditions of social benefits' (1.88). This corresponds with the prevailing public attitudes towards solidarity and social policy. In comparison with the citizens of the other post-communist countries, the Czech public most strongly supports the idea that the most important causes of poverty are the individual ones (56 per cent, while the average for new member states is 40 per cent), especially laziness (34 per cent compared to average of 26 per cent) and 'bad luck' (22 per cent compared to average of 14 per cent). See Table 12.1.

On the other hand the Czechs are citizens in post-communist countries among the the least supportive to the idea that poverty is due to '*injustice in society*' (21 per cent, while the average for new member states is 42 per cent: twice as high). Not only are Czechs rather sceptical about the deservingness of people considered to be socially excluded, they are also rather in favour of restricting redistribution to the poor and supportive to the principles of merit in the social security system. In September 2007, 37.5 per cent of Czechs agreed that social assistance benefits were being misused (while 36 per cent were undecided and 21 per cent were against the statement). At the same time 39 per cent considered the social security system as unjust.[2]

These preferences correspond with the earlier tradition of Bismarckian social security, only partially disrupted by the communist regime (see Cerami, 2006; Inglot, this volume) and with the findings by Sabbagh and Vanhuysse (2006, pp. 612–15) indicating that welfare state attitudes are clustered and that the 'market-based' cluster entails attribution of poverty

Table 12.1 The perceived causes of poverty (in %)

	Because they have been unlucky	Because of laziness and lack of willpower	Total personal causes	Because there is much injustice in our society	It's an inevitable part of progress	Total social causes	None of these	Do not know
EU-27	19	20	39	37	13	50	6	5
EU-15	21	18	39	36	13	49	6	5
NMS 12	14	26	40	42	10	52	6	5
Czech Rep.*	22 (15)	34 (42)	56 (57)	21 (21)	13 (18)	34 (39)	6	4 (4)
LT	15	39	54	31	11	42	3	1
LV	13	36	49	34	12	46	4	1
SK	19	30	49	35	10	45	3	3
EE	14	28	42	31	19	52	3	3
PL	12	29	41	41	10	51	3	5
RO	13	20	33	47	10	57	3	7
HU	13	18	31	56	10	66	5	2
BG	11	11	22	59	9	68	3	2

Sources: Special Eurobarometer 279 (2007, p. 34) 'Poverty and Social Exclusion' (adapted). European values study, 1999.

Note: * Numbers in parentheses refer to results in 1999.

to individual failures with individualism (mimimum delivery of welfare) and with work ethic support this explanation. In this context the hypothesis may be suggested that strong support of liberal policies would counteract influence of the EU's solidaristic policies and it will form a barrier for domestication of the social inclusion agenda in the Czech Republic.

Indeed, the initial shift of the communicative 'official' political discourse towards solidarity and fight against social exclusion associated with the process of Czech Republic's accession into the European Union has been rather temporary: 'The key for European social policy will be the fight against unemployment, poverty and social exclusion, healthy income policy and achievement of the European standards in legislative protection of labour' (government declaration, 2002, section 6.1 on Social Policy). Although similar wordings have appeared also in the government declarations of coalitions led by the Social Democrats from 2004 and 2005, the official communicative policy discourse was dominated more and more by individual attributions of blame for social exclusion and corresponding policy proposals. The new centre-right government which came into power in autumn 2006 stated that the 'social system has to work in benefit of those who are *truly needy* and lead to the well-understandable requirement that work should pay off' (emphasis added). The declaration only mentioned social exclusion briefly and in connotation with the *misuse* of social benefits and personal social services (Programové, 2007, p. 17, emphasis added). Similarly, the measures implemented within the package of the 'social reforms' aimed to stabilize the public finance and consisting mostly of cuts of benefits and/or restricting entitlements have been in most of cases explained (beside necessity of savings) by objectives to improve work incentives and to avoid misuse of benefits.[3]

In sum, the attitudes and discourse of the public and policymakers in the Czech Republic are not very supportive of the agenda of social inclusion understood as a balanced and multidimensional approach (recently European Commission, 2008). Vanhuysse (2006b, and in this volume) considers the strategy of 'protest avoidance' to be a key motive of policy-making in post-communist countries. Such a strategy is socially divisive since it leads to provision of specific welfare entitlements to different groups. In this case the policy discourse on individualizing the causes of poverty enables – as we see – in the latter stage of policy-making, the key actors reasoning about cuts in social security and making them more legitimate to the public. This all makes implementation of the social inclusion agenda more difficult. The legitimacy gap is larger in the Czech Republic than in any other post-communist CEE country.

Czech social policy, poverty and social exclusion

In contrast to the strong neo-liberal discourse, 'social acceptability' was from the very start a core concern of political representations who paid great attention to protecting the population against the negative impacts of transformation (Tomeš, 1991; Vanhuysse, 2006a, 2006b; Haggard and Kaufman, this volume; Cerami and Stanescu, this volume). They managed to do so in the long term, with a strong emphasis on prevention of poverty (Sirovátka, 2000). Post-1989, a social safety net was created consisting of social assistance and unemployment benefits. In addition, social insurance schemes and family-related benefits were redesigned as highly redistributive in favour of low-income groups, providing good guarantees of minimum income and almost universal coverage.

The effectiveness of the Czech system of benefits in eliminating poverty was assessed as among the very highest in Europe (Sainsbury and Morissens, 2002; Guio, 2005). This is a remarkable achievement considering that overall social expenditure amounted to only 19 per cent of GDP in 2004, while the European average was about 26 per cent and in Sweden it was close to 32 per cent (European Commission, 2007, Annex, p. 158). The at-risk-of poverty rate as defined by Eurostat (share of population below 60 per cent of median equivalized income) stand by 2005 at 10 per cent (CZSO, 2007; European Commission, 2007) compared with the European average of 16 per cent and CEE countries like Poland (21 per cent), Hungary or Slovakia (both 13 per cent). On the other hand poverty and exclusion from the labour market is concentrated to specific vulnerable groups. The Czech Republic, like other post-communist CEE countries, does not provide unemployed or inactive persons in 'productive' age groups with too generous replacement ratios. In recent years, in line with 'individalization discourse', their revaluation lagged behind salary increases. For example, Van Mechelen and De Maesschalck (in this volume), using a poverty threshold of 50 per cent of median equivalized income in 2004, rank Czech among those OECD countries which provide rather 'inadequate' benefits, below 25 per cent of poverty threshold.

The Czech Republic traditionally preferred to avoid high unemployment by means of deliberate anti-bankruptcy policy known as 'bank socialism' (Vanhuysse, 2006b, pp. 1128–9). Unemployment, unlike in Hungary, Poland and Slovakia, never increased above the 10 per cent threshold. But less attention was paid to the access of really marginalized groups to the labour market and the long-term unemployed represented about half of unemployment stock (CZSO, 2007). Active labour market policy expenditure during 2004–2006 achieved only 0.12–0.14 per cent of GDP and the number of ALMP participants ranged between only 0.96 and 1.16 per cent of labour force. In countries with similar unemployment rate in these years (between 7 and 8 per cent) such as Finland, Hungary, Portugal and Sweden, we see their expenditure to be considerably higher in 2006: 0.89 per cent, 0. 28 per cent, 0.61 per cent and 1.36 per cent respectively (Employment Outlook, 2008).

In sum, Czech social policy appears at least partially successful, given that it has managed to establish a system of compensating those on low incomes who are most at risk of poverty and preventing mass unemployment (see also Inglot, this volume; Vanhuysse, this volume). On the other hand, there remains room for improvement as regards active inclusion of labour market outsiders and poverty reduction of marginalized groups. However, all the circumstances described above slowed down domestication of the social inclusion agenda: namely the coincidence of the strong individualizing discourse on social exclusion with effective social safety and absence of excessive unemployment leads to lower legitimacy of the social inclusion agenda.

Agenda for social inclusion in the Czech Republic at the national level: approach, targets and programme documents

The 'obligatory' EU agenda for social inclusion brought a fresh general perspective on existing social problems into public and political discourse. However, weak real political support for the agenda (legitimacy gap) made itself felt in the content of the first NAPSI for 2004–2006, which focused primarily on the analysis of social problems while using the concept of social exclusion and gave an overview of existing measures aimed at combating poverty and social exclusion. On the other hand, it showed that commitment to translate the general principles of the social inclusion strategy into measures in various areas of national policy-making was low. The formulation of the first NAPSI in 2004–2006 resembled rather a 'technological process' (Lendvai, 2004) of applying administrative procedures, means of expression, and coordinating measures in this area than real policy turnover (point of departure). Legitimacy gap was manifested also in the very status granted to the social inclusion agenda within other governmental agendas. The NAPSI has emerged through standard procedure as any other proposal by Ministry of Labour and Social Affairs, not as a national strategy. It was drawn by the Department of Social Services of the Ministry of Labour and Social Affairs although with assistance of an appointed Interdepartmental Committee for Preparation of NAPSI and involvement of other partners including non-governmental organizations. Before it was submitted to the government, the plan had been open to comments and revision by other governmental departments the Ministry of Finances including.[4] Such circumstances of course play a significant role in both external and internal censorship.

The goals contained in Czech NAPSI 2004–06 were almost exclusively articulated in general terms and their achievement was therefore difficult to monitor. Neither were these goals ambitious. For example, the plan did not set elimination of poverty and social exclusion as the main goal – instead, its stated goal was 'to secure appropriate attention to issues of poverty and social exclusion and contribute to tackling these issues' (NAPSI, 2004, p. 5). Direct goals (even if formulated in general terms) appeared rarely in the NAPSI of the CR and those that had often been adapted from other programme documents.[5] Moreover, the general goals were not translated into suitable indicators in the Czech Action Plan that would allow for the monitoring of goals. Yet the Czech NAPSI did not even contain specific indirect or input targets or outcome targets (European Commission, 2005, p. 37; Marlier et al., 2007, p. 211). It contained only a single quantified goal that could qualify as an input target – the goal to raise the proportion of long-term unemployed people in active employment policy programmes to 20 per cent adapted from the National Action Plan on Employment. NAPSI was specific neither on financial resources, nor on responsibilities for accomplishing the goals or for meeting key measures.

The Czech formulation of the first NAPSI differed significantly from the other CEE countries. Both Hungarian and Polish NAPSI 2004–06 contained sets of quantified targets (including direct ones[6]) as well as sets of relevant indicators aimed to monitor the progress in the fight against social exclusion. In the case of Poland these targets were set for a longer period until 2010. Compared to the Czech NAPSI, these action plans were also much more ambitious. For example, Poland set a target to reduce extreme poverty (i.e. the share of people living below subsistence minimum) from almost 12 per cent in 2003 to 5 per cent by 2010. The Slovak government formulated the goals of NAPSI 2004–06 in rather general terms; however, these were accompanied by quantifiable indicators (and, furthermore, the following NAPSI of the Slovak Republic included also quantified direct and outcome targets). The different approach of CEE countries to their first NAPSIs, including different levels of setting quantified targets, when the Czech Republic was a laggard, was also identified by the European Commission (2005a, pp. 38–9).

According to many key actors in the Czech Republic whom we interviewed the NAPSI 2004–06 lacked the ambition to identify new strategies or solutions. It is precisely these traits that made the plan politically acceptable for key political actors. At the same time the declarative nature of the action plan undermines the legitimacy of the national strategy of social inclusion, as the actors at the regional and local levels do not believe that that there is political commitment in place to make the necessary capacities and resources available to tackle pressing problems.

Had the institutional learning process facilitated by the launching of the social inclusion agenda later met with an adequate level of legitimacy and political commitment as *enabling factor* (Cerami and Stanescu, this volume) it would have been possible to expect a shift in the general role and status of the NAPSI 2006–08. This, however, was not the case and, instead, we witnessed further reduction in the content of the plan, although the European Commission has repeatedly recommended that the member states set about to formulate specific, quantified and ambitious goals (European Commission, 2004b, 2005b). In line with the Commission's direction, the

Czech Republic set itself so-called priority targets, which were, however, very general and broad (for example the target to promote lifelong learning of elderly people and their possibility to live in their home environment for as long as possible, or the target to promote field work and assistance programmes targeted especially at excluded Roma communities). There were only two quantified targets in the Czech NAPSI 2006–08, and these, moreover, had an input character: (a) drawing and implementing 14 development plans for regional social services and (b) involving a minimum of 200 local municipalities in the planning of social services at the local level by 2008. No surprise that the criticism of vagueness of the NRSPSI 2006–08 by the Commission was again much stronger in the Czech case than in the case of Hungary, Poland or Slovakia (European Commission, 2007).

The main shift in focus at this stage was the *individualization* of the social inclusion agenda in the sense that the already existing approach and policy discourse strongly influenced the domestic social inclusion agenda. For example, in chapter 2 of the NRSPSI 2006–08 we can repeatedly find great emphasis on incentives and promotion of individual competences of the excluded (MPSV, 2006, p. 9).

Lastly, an obvious aspiration to maximize flows from the EU funds in this area is not accompanied by an effort in coordination of the agenda, which would secure consistency between funded projects and objectives of social inclusion (which appear rather vague). Such a discrepancy is not specific for the administration of agenda of social inclusion: recently Vobecká (2009) documented a similar approach within the Czech rural development policies.

What was new in the Czech NAPSI 2006–08 was the emphasis on on the as yet insufficient mainstreaming and especially on lacking mechanism for involving people with direct experience of poverty in the drafting of policies. This innovation can be interpreted as *institutional learning* – this is a reflection of the *implementation deficit* concerning the social inclusion strategy at lower levels of public administration. Similarly, although the plan challenged a broader spectrum of public policies to take into account the principle of social inclusion (particularly by increasing awareness and knowledge), it had largely abandoned the multidimensional approach adopted in the previous NAPSI 2004–06, as it focused itself predominantly on social services. Even this is further proof of institutional learning: our interviews with members of the Interdepartmental Committee for Preparation of NAPSI indicated that the authors of the proposal who came from Department of Social Services (Ministry of Labour and Social Affairs) regarded those areas that fall within the competence of other departments – or those that are largely dependent on other departments – as hardly receptive to a substantial change of policy due to lacking political commitment while feeling opportunities to use social inclusion agenda for achieving faster progress in 'their field' of social services. This is an illustration of how some domestic actors involved used the 'European agenda of social OMC' as a resource to push through their objectives – the leverage effect (Erhel et al., 2005) leading to domestication of European social policy (Zeitlin, 2005).

Implementation of the agenda of social inclusion in practice: the learning process and barriers to learning

When it comes to assessing the causes of social exclusion and possible solutions by the interviewed key actors at the national, regional and local level, there is a dominant tendency towards 'individualization' of the problem of social exclusion and, subsequently, propensity for moralizing discourse in approaching social inclusion (see Lister, 2004) while far less emphasis is placed on participation in the life of society with respect to access to civil rights. Besides, there is a marked difference between experts and political representatives. Professionals who work in this sector partially internalize the concept of social inclusion by learning its general meaning and the usage of it in connection with their professional orientation and projects carried. This is transparent in their critical reflections on implementation deficits – see Table 12.3 below. In contrast the representatives of regional and local political authorities have so far more or less neglected the concept – which can be explained by their not very high level of political commitment to this agenda. Tackling the problems of social exclusion gains neither legitimacy nor support of the general public, which tends to individualize the problem of social exclusion and sometimes calls for complete exclusion – for example, for moving the Roma out of their community (see also Gabal, 2006, p. 92). Gabal (2006, p. 16) finds that about 60 per cent of the socially excluded Roma communities have emerged in the past ten years, in part due to the deliberate strategy of municipalities aimed to remove them from, and/or concentrate them in, some localities. If the degree of political commitment concerning the agenda of social inclusion varies even in other European countries (see Table 12.2), then in the Czech Republic it is generally lower than elsewhere.

   The survey of mainstreaming social inclusion confirms that relevant actors in the field of social inclusion in the Czech Republic perceive the agenda mainly as an administrative task of the central government. Furthermore, the agenda's real significance and implementation are inhibited by low political priority attached to it across all levels of public administration and, especially, at the lower administrative levels. We oberve that social inclusion is considered to be key political priority at the central level by only 35 per cent of the 'experts' involved in it in the Czech Republic (compared with the average for nine EU countries of 46 per cent). On top of that the prioritizing of the social inclusion agenda is considered to be the lowest in the Czech Republic among nine EU countries at the regional and local level (11 per cent against 30 and 35 per cent, respectively). In general, the

Table 12.2 'Are the policies against poverty and social exclusion a key political priority? Answer: 'to a (very) great extent', selected countries with more than 60 respondents-experts from all levels of public administration as well as representatives of NGOs and social partners, N in parentheses, (in per cent)

	At the central level	At the regional level	At the local level
United Kingdom	65.6 (116)	46.5 (114)	39.4 (114)
Ireland	48.4 (91)	27.8 (90)	17.7 (90)
France	18.6 (70)	31.4 (68)	26.5 (68)
Portugal	40.9 (88)	–	43.0 (86)
Bulgaria	62.8 (121)	41.5 (121)	56.6 (122)
Average for 9 countries	46.3 (702)	29.5 (573)	35.1 (700)
Czech Republic	35.4 (121)	11.1 (125)	11.0 (125)

Source: Based on dataset from the Mainstreaming Social Inclusion survey (O'Kelly, 2007), countries: IRELAND, NORWAY, SCOTLAND, ENGLAND, WALES, FRANCE, NETHERLANDS, CZECH REPUBLIC, SLOVAKIA, PORTUGAL, BULGARIA, own computations.

commitment at the local level in other European countries involved in the study was perceived as close to the one at the national level. A gap similar to the Czech situation was identified only in Ireland, where O'Kelly (2007, p. 48) sees as a reason the fragmentation of political support to individual issues rather than overall policy of social inclusion at the local level. In the Czech Republic, this may be accompanied also by the novelty of the social inclusion/exclusion agenda and its top-down implementation into public policy.

The *implementation gaps* were identified in the area of coordination, allocation of resources and involvement of NGOs and excluded people. In such a situation, it is not surprising that the overall impact of central policy formulated in NAPSI is seen as very low. As Table 12.3 shows, an implementation of the agenda is also perceived as problematic in other European countries. However, the problems with coordination especially are much more obvious in the Czech Republic than elsewhere. Specifically, in the Czech Republic only 11–15 per cent of experts consider social inclusion policies to be 'to a (very) great extent' coordinated at the central, regional and local level, compared to the average for nine EU countries of 20 and 29 per cent respectively. Also the influence of the excluded persons and the NGOs, as well as the overall impact of the NAPSIs, is considered as somewhat lower in the Czech Republic than elsewhere (see Table 12.3).

When interviewed, the professionals were often able to formulate appropriate and desirable approaches and measures addressing the problems. This may be a signal that a new discourse and a new agenda – in combination

Table 12.3 Various items characterizing implementation of the social inclusion agenda

	Coordination of policies against poverty and social exclusion			Resources in governmental policies	Influence of excluded persons	Influence of NGOs	Impact of the NAPSI
	Central government	Regional level	Local level				
United Kingdom	19.0 (110)	18.4 (98)	15.6 (96)	21.4 (113)	8.8 (114)	13.3 (106)	13.6 (81)
Ireland	23.1 (91)	6.4 (78)	23.6 (85)	16.3 (86)	17.5 (86)	32.6 (84)	30.6 (85)
France	16.9 (70)	28.6 (70)	23.5 (68)	7.4 (68)	8.8 (68)	18.8 (69)	7.8 (66)
Portugal	33.7 (86)	28.6 (108)	15.4 (104)	11.4 (87)	25.8 (81)	35.9 (78)	20.1 (80)
Bulgaria	68.5 (118)	41.4 (104)	60.0 (108)	38.6 (122)	33.0 (115)	35.9(105)	75.2 (109)
Average for 9 countries	28.8 (663)	20.1 (494)	25.8 (614)	19.8 (681)	16.0 (656)	27.6(634)	28.3 (605)
Czech Republic	12.8 (102)	11.2 (108)	15.4 (104)	18.0 (117)	10.3 (107)	21.3(108)	22.2 (108)

Answer: 'to a (very) great extent', selected countries with more than 60 respondents-experts, N in parentheses, in per cent
Source: Based on dataset from the Mainstreaming Social Inclusion survey (O'Kelly, 2007), own computations.

with professional knowledge of a problem – initiate the process of the institutional learning and improvement of abilities of both individuals and institutions, leading to the advancement of policies in the area of social inclusion since its legitimacy is rising among some actors involved. For example, the notions of social exclusion and inclusion appeared, for the first time, in the new Act on Social Services (no 108/2006, par. 3). This Act introduced a broader definition of social services (including also labour market-related services aiming at labour market inclusion, etc.) and an increased emphasis on the standard of social services' quality. Besides, under this Act, regional authorities have been obliged to elaborate mid-term plans on the development of social services.

However, what seems to have facilitated internalization and domestication of the concept and principles of social inclusion at lower levels of public administration even more markedly than the programme documents of the NRSPSI, is the availability of financial support from the European structural funds – and the European Social Fund (ESF) in particular. ESF in the projects of which key actors to a greater or lesser extent (wish to) participate is not perceived merely as a financial resource but also as a powerful instrument of establishing social exclusion/inclusion concerns in the agenda at all levels of public administration.

Conclusion

While social policy-making in the Czech Republic has been mainly concerned with and successful in eliminating poverty, until now it has been to large extent influenced by a discourse of individual failure, blaming the individuals or groups exposed to social exclusion. The corresponding policy orientation gained in influence during the period of 2004–2007 after the initial absorption of the EU communicative discourse associated with introduction of the 'social OMC'. This agenda is 'blocked' by a legitimacy gap larger than in any post-communist CEE country. This is an important reason why the agenda for social inclusion has not brought about a noticeable shift in the practical orientation of Czech social policy. To begin with, there seem to be inconsistencies in the programme document's contents. While aspirations concerning general objectives are rather low, a discrepancy is apparent between the general objectives and goals laid down in the National Action Plans on Social Inclusion (NAPSI 2004–06 and NRSPSI 2006–08) and the lack of specification and breakdown into operational goals and financial and institutional capacities to secure the meeting of these goals.

Second, key actors interviewed in our research highlight implementation deficits in the social inclusion agenda in the Czech Republic. Lendvai (2004, pp. 324–5) argues that the performance gap is a major barrier to implementing the European Union agendas in the post-communist countries which is attributable to insufficient resources, coordination of the different levels and areas of public governance, and weakness of key actors the state including and lack of cooperation among them. Despite the above stumbling blocks, our findings also indicate that there is a strong potential for institutional learning, particularly on the part of professionals in the field, including non-governmental, non-profit organizations. Although there is not much evidence about the direct (real) impact of this learning process on the agenda of social inclusion at this stage in the Czech Republic, at least the process of changing the discourse has been initiated. This is most visible in the area of social services, where both programme documents and financial resources of the ESF played a visible role (leverage effect).[7]

Two conclusions can be drawn as regards further advancement of the agenda of social inclusion. The impact of bottom-up learning in connection with projects of the European Social Fund has probably been underestimated so far and deserves further intensive research although they imply a rather instrumental approach. Second, the low legitimacy of the social inclusion agenda could possibly improve as a result of bottom-up benchmarking, thanks to professionals with participation of the non-governmental sector and people with direct experience of social exclusion in the formulation of the agenda. The shift in the policy discourse is in place, generated by professionals and NGOs under support of academic research. Lastly, this case study illustrates that discursive change does impact policy to some extent, although in the Czech case this impact is rather embryonic. The key blocking factor is the competing discourse on individualization of poverty and social exclusion prevailing in mainstream policy and supported by the public, with bottom-up actors such as NGOs and professionals only slowly gaining influence. Both the legitimacy gap and the performance gap concerning the social inclusion agenda may be explained by the exceptionally strong individualizing attitudes and discourse on social exclusion on the one hand and seemingly successful anti-poverty measures, which have enabled to narrow the scope of poverty and long-term unemployment while leading to their concentration to the specific groups of population, on the other hand. There are some indications that awareness is rising, and discursive change and the institutional learning process is somewhat faster in other CEE post-communist countries, where NAPSIs convincingly display more commitment and professionalism in specifying the objectives to be achieved and the instruments/resources to be used in various policy fields.

Concluding Remarks

13
The Eastern European Welfare State in Comparative Perspective*
Stephan Haggard and Robert R. Kaufman

Introduction

Until recently, the study of the welfare state was confined largely to the advanced industrial countries. However, the recent transitions in Eastern Europe substantially widen the canvas on which comparisons might be drawn. In addition, new literature has emerged on the evolution of social policy in the middle-income countries of Latin America and East Asia as well (Huber, 2002; Kapstein and Milanovic, 2002; Brooks, 2007; Segura-Ubiergo, 2007; Haggard and Kaufman, 2008; Rudra, 2008).

Yet this wider canvas also raises important questions of both theory and method. The literature on the advanced welfare state has generated a plethora of competing hypotheses about the determinants of social policy, drawn mainly from the Western European experience. Do we expect these hypotheses to be portable to other settings, even though they were developed with reference to a limited range of cases? Or do we believe that generalizations will inevitably have to be more localized, reflecting for example legacies of state socialism, late development or colonialism that fundamentally differentiate these countries from the advanced industrial states?

This question about theoretical priors is intimately related to how we choose cases to compare in the first place. Should our ambition be global: to develop theories of social policy that cover a wide array of cases? Are there gains to be had from more limited cross-regional comparisons, for example, between Western and Eastern Europe or across middle-income countries? Or are we on safer ground to focus on differences within a well-defined region that shares – and thus controls for – a number of historical commonalities? The latter strategy undergirds many of the chapters in this book, which explore some of the commonalities and differences in social policy that have emerged since the great transformation of the socialist countries of Eastern Europe in the 1990s.

In our view, however, the proper answer to these questions is 'all of the above'; there is much to be gained from theorizing and comparing across a number of different levels. But there are always trade-offs as well; broad comparisons may miss nuance, but more focused ones risk overemphasizing differences that may narrow or fall away altogether with somewhat greater distance. Since our comparative advantage lies largely in the developing world, we focus on the gains that might be had from comparing the Eastern European experience with the middle-income countries of East Asia and Latin America.

We begin in the first section with a comparison of the modalities of welfare provision across the three regions at the onset of their democratic transitions and with a brief analysis of the reasons for their divergent trajectories. Against this backdrop, we engage a number of the chapters in this volume that address the nature and determinants of social policy under communist rule. In the second section, we discuss how post-communist systems were affected by democratization and economic shocks of the 1980s and 1990s, again with reference to the contributions in this volume. To what extent does social policy show continuity with the socialist era (suggesting path-dependence) as opposed to taking altogether new forms (in the language of this book, 'path-departing')? To what extent have the countries of the region converged or diverged in the models that they have adopted, and why?

Contrasting welfare systems in Eastern Europe, Latin America and East Asia: origins and evolution

Our point of departure is the sharp contrast we have found between the welfare systems that had evolved in Eastern Europe by the late communist period and concurrent developments in the middle-income countries of Latin America and East Asia throughout the 1980s (Haggard and Kaufman, 2008).[1] As is also true of other regions, there are important differences among the Eastern European countries. Nevertheless, all shared a number of important characteristics that proved highly consequential to developments following the collapse of communist rule; Table 13.1 provides a stylized summary of these inter-regional differences.

In Eastern Europe, social policy was anchored by an overarching employment guarantee, but also by a strong commitment to education and training, universal coverage with respect to health care and pensions, and widespread use of family allowances. These commitments began as occupational ones following the communist seizure of power in the late 1940s, but were gradually extended and transformed over the post-war period into universal citizenship rights.

In Latin America, most countries established occupationally based social insurance and health systems in the mid-twentieth century that favoured formal sector workers but typically excluded informal urban workers and the rural sector. In contrast to Eastern Europe, social insurance coverage rarely reached more than 50 per cent of the population except in relatively

Table 13.1 Regional welfare models *c.*1980

	Latin America	East Asia	Eastern Europe
Social insurance (primarily health insurance and pensions)	Extensive protection through public systems or contributory systems with some public financing. Coverage is partial and unequal in most countries.	Limited public provision of social insurance outside of state sector workers. Purely contributory and compulsory savings systems in some countries for limited segments of the workforce.	Coverage initially based on employment in state enterprises, gradually universalized.
Basic health services	Unequal and incomplete public coverage; de facto reliance on private provision and financing.	Emphasis on public health and basic health services in some countries, but limited public provision and reliance on private provision and financing.	Universal government provision provided free at point of delivery.
Education	Access to primary education expands in 1960s and 1970s, but high drop-out and repetition rates and low quality. Significant regional inequalities. Biases toward tertiary education.	Early emphasis on expansion of access to primary education, followed by expansion of secondary education. Relative high rates of completion and low drop-out rate.	Universal primary and secondary education, but with strong emphasis on vocational training and manpower planning.

Continued

Table 13.1   Continued

	Latin America	East Asia	Eastern Europe
Labour markets	Labour codes include extensive protections for formal sector workers, contributing to labour market rigidities and dualism.	Relatively flexible labour markets.	Centralized manpower planning and wage setting. Guaranteed employment, supplemented over time by unemployment insurance following 'market socialist' experiments.

Source: Haggard and Kaufman (2008, p. 5).

large welfare states such as Costa Rica, Chile and Uruguay, and in those cases coverage was by no means universal. The provision of basic social services also showed a marked iniquity in distribution, re-enforcing rather than mitigating long-standing patterns of inequality.

In Asia, social insurance was even more limited and, where it did exist, was provided through mandated individual savings programmes that had little or no redistributive component. Nonetheless, governments attached a high priority to the provision of primary and secondary education, and, somewhat more unevenly, to public health and basic health services.

Origins and evolution of welfare systems in Latin America and East Asia

The origins of these contrasting policy regimes can be traced to political realignments that occurred in the early to mid-twentieth century, and to development strategies that accompanied or followed these realignments. The realignments can be identified by changes in the composition of ruling elites and in the extent to which these new elites co-opted, controlled or repressed urban labour unions and political movements representing the working class and the peasantry.[2] Although we see intra-regional variation with respect to these realignments, a combination of longer-run historical factors and international circumstances resulted in important similarities within regions. Development strategies also showed important regional commonalities. Latin American countries tended to opt for sustained import-substitution approaches, a number of East Asian countries pursued export-oriented growth models beginning in the 1960s, and communist rule ensured the pursuit of state socialist economic models in Eastern Europe. We begin with brief sketches of the Latin American and East Asian experiences before turning to a more extended discussion of the Eastern European cases.

In Latin America, critical realignments occurred as a result of reformist challenges to the oligarchic rule of the late nineteenth and early twentieth century (Collier and Collier, 1991). An important contrast with both Eastern Europe and East Asia is that these challenges pre-dated the great power rivalry of the Cold War era; new contenders for power could not count on sustained support from powerful external patrons. Instead, they formed cross-class coalitions that included segments of organized labour and in some instances popularly based parties. As a consequence, blue-collar and middle-sector unions gained legal status, political influence and new social protections.

However, anti-oligarchic coalitions generally included some segments of the land-owning class, which continued to control large segments of the rural population through land ownership, patron–client relations and localized resort to force. Urban-based political challengers were thus unable to penetrate the countryside to the same extent as in Eastern Europe and East Asia; and as a result, peasants remained politically marginalized and the countryside relatively disadvantaged in the provision of social insurance and services.

The cross-class coalitions formed during these realignments were conducive to import-substitution industrialization, first as a response to the economic shocks of the 1920s and 1930s and then as a more self-conscious development strategy after the Second World War. ISI allowed both state enterprises and private firms in the import-substituting sectors to accommodate relatively generous welfare entitlements for the organized urban working class. Such policies contributed to labour market dualism among urban workers and to well-known biases against agriculture and the rural sector; the social insurance systems that developed in the region both reflected and re-enforced these biases. Moreover, the structural characteristics of import-substituting economies also had adverse effects on the overall distribution of income and reduced incentives for governments, firms and workers to invest in human capital and in education in particular.

In the developing countries of East and Southeast Asia (South Korea, Taiwan, Malaysia, the Philippines and Singapore), critical realignments came later than in Latin America. In the aftermath of the Pacific war, a number of countries gained independence but were quickly swept up into Cold War dynamics. Unlike in Latin America, alliances with the United States (and Britain in Singapore and Malaysia) provided crucial support for new conservative elites to pursue political projects that dramatically weakened labour, social-democratic left and rural political movements. Across the region conservative, anti-communist governments came to power following independence; similar patterns are visible in Thailand, which had not been colonized. With external support, these governments beat back the challenge from the left in the cities, forestalled or defeated armed insurgencies in the country-side, and in varying degrees reached into the rural areas for support.

The turn toward export-oriented growth occurred well after the conservative political realignments of the Cold War period. Nonetheless, outward-oriented strategies exhibited an elective affinity with conservative political rule and subsequently influenced the incentives of governments, firms and workers with respect to social policy. On the one hand, strategies dependent on the export of labour-intensive manufactures put a premium on labour market flexibility and made governments and firms highly resistant to payroll taxes and social insurance benefits that would increase the cost of labour. The authoritarian regimes in the region, whether established early in the post-war period or after brief periods of semi-democratic rule, maintained far more limited systems of public protection than was the case in either Eastern Europe or Latin America. On the other hand, export-oriented growth strengthened incentives to expand access to primary, secondary and vocational education to enhance the productivity of the workforce and, to a lesser extent, motivated the expansion of basic public health services as well.

The Eastern European experience in comparative perspective

In Eastern Europe, as in East Asia, political realignments reflected Cold War politics. In these countries, however, Soviet influence prevailed. As in East Asia, the post-war liberation initially unleashed a wide spectrum of new social forces. Early social initiatives – prior to the communist seizure of power – reflected these pressures from below as well as a range of distinctive social policy legacies that are given particular weight in the contribution of Tomasz Inglot. As Inglot argues (this volume) intra-regional differences in these earlier legacies impacted welfare initiatives undertaken by communist regimes in the post-Stalinist period as well as the 'emergency' measures undertaken during the transition. With the consolidation of power by Communist parties, however, came the destruction of social democratic and peasant parties, as well as independent unions, and a significant convergence in the approach to the role of the state. The distinctive features of socialist social policy were therefore not given by accommodation of labour and the left, as was the case in the European social democracies, but by the political, economic and organizational logic of the command economy.

Prior to the communist realignment, the trajectory of Eastern European welfare development bore a striking resemblance to concurrent patterns in Latin America. The chapters in this volume by Szikra and Tomka, Inglot, Aidukaite, and particularly Cerami and Stanescu on Bulgaria and Romania, underline not only the Bismarckian nature of pre-Second World War social insurance systems but the highly stratified nature of the benefits extended under them. However, new communist governments quickly centralized power and initiated state-led industrialization drives that fundamentally transformed the economic and social order. The strategy rested on high levels of investment in basic industry, financed by primitive accumulation through the mobilization of labour and a squeeze on the countryside.

The commitment to full employment and government provision of social insurance and services emerged as side-effects of the nationalization and socialization of the economy (in the Baltics, a somewhat similar trajectory occurred through the incorporation of Estonia, Latvia and Lithuania directly into the Soviet Union). Unlike either Latin America or Asia, the state provided protection to workers not only through the conduct of social policy, but more directly through its role as employer. Labour was 'decommodified' but in a socialist rather than social democratic fashion: administrative decisions determined job placements and wages, and while employment was guaranteed workers were viewed as instruments of the socialist planning process. The mobilization of rural labour into the industrial sector transformed large segments of the peasantry, provided upward mobility and was accompanied by a dramatic narrowing of intersectoral wage differences. However, pay was initially low, in line with the overall objective of squeezing wages and consumption in order to maximize capital investment.

A distinctive feature of the socialist employment system is the difficulty in disentangling the wage and non-wage components of total compensation. The state took on the obligation not only for employment but for the provision of basic foodstuffs, typically at subsidized prices. Housing was also the responsibility of the state – although it was continually in short supply – and enterprises provided other social amenities as well, from childcare to group vacations. The precise nature of the social contract thus depended heavily on the enterprise and the priority it enjoyed within the overall planning process.

If we focus on public commitments to social insurance, however, the communist regimes in Eastern Europe fall at the opposite end of the spectrum from the limited state involvement of their Asian counterparts. In addition to the state's commitment to full employment and provision of basic consumer goods and housing, the absence of private markets for social insurance and services meant that the financing and provision of pensions, health care and other social services of necessity fell to the state.

At the outset of the socialist era, some occupationally based differentiation existed in the industrial sector and agriculture was excluded from the system. As Szikra and Tomka note, 'industrial workers, members of the armed forces, the party and state bureaucracy were privileged. Parallel to this process was the politically motivated elimination of social rights obtained earlier and the discrimination of certain social groups, most of all, farmers, occurred in the early communist period'. But as Szikra and Tomka also argue – and we concur – the seeds of a kind of socialist universalism were sewn by the economic strategy itself. Benefits extended to urban workers necessarily covered a larger and larger share of the population as the industrial sector grew. Just as important, the collectivization of agriculture effectively brought the peasantry into the socialist welfare state, a marked contrast with the marginalization of the countryside that persisted in Latin America.

Needless to say, the socialist social contract was by no means the result of democratic politics, or even bargaining with affected interests; on these grounds, Szikra and Tomka question whether the Eastern European countries under communism can even be called 'welfare states' at all. Nevertheless, social policy provided a tool for post-Stalinist elites to secure political acquiescence if not support, and in turn generated relatively stable expectations about the benefits the state would provide.

The interests, expectations and institutions formed through these social policy interventions posed some constraints on governments even during the socialist era, as the Polish government's run-ins with Solidarity showed. However, they affected even more strongly the political battles over social policy that unfolded in the new democracies that emerged in the1980s and 1990s, as we will argue in the next section.

Implications of the socialist legacy

This abbreviated account – which emphasizes the central role of the Communist seizures of power and the subsequent convergence on very similar welfare models – raises several important analytic and empirical issues addressed in this volume. A core issue is whether the historical legacies of the pre-Second World War period had more enduring consequences than we suggest, either for the socialist welfare state or even for the post-transition period. In a series of important contributions, Inglot (2003, 2008, this volume) argues they did; as a result, he emphasizes differences across the Eastern European countries even during the socialist era.

Inglot's theoretical starting point is a variant of historical institutionalism in which previous institutions and policies are never completely eradicated but rather experience a continual 'layering'. The contrasts he draws between Czechoslovakia and Hungary provide an example. The Czech socialist welfare state originated both in the interwar period and in policy and institutional innovations prior to the Stalinist seizure of power in the late 1940s. The institutional cornerstone of the Czech welfare state was the establishment of a powerful welfare ministry, the direct involvement of unions, and a strong 'social democratic' orientation in social policy. This orientation persisted during the post-communist period.

Hungary, by contrast, failed to develop a coherent welfare model prior to the transition to state socialism in the late 1940s. As a result, Inglot argues, the expansion of entitlements in Hungary was much slower than in Czechoslovakia and 'had neither the breadth, consistency nor the transformative character of the Czechoslovak National Insurance Act'. Although coverage and benefits expanded during the 1970s, the system reflected a very particular political compromise 'between ambitious welfare reformers who sought a modernized, and wide-ranging "societal policy" and the economic planners of the New Economic Mechanism (NEM) who preferred the existing, more limited social insurance system under tight fiscal controls'. Partly as a result, post-1989 social policies fell under the sway of interior or finance ministries that treated welfare issues through a fiscal lens, while trade union bureaucracies lacked the organizational muscle or political clout to influence the path of entitlements.

We take up the evolution of policy during the post-transition period in the next section. Regarding the earlier period, however, we are more inclined toward the view of Szikra and Tomka which also emphasizes the transformative impact of Communist rule. They note some of the idiosyncratic factors that produced differences across the Eastern European countries, for example, in Poland as a result of the fact that collectivization was not pushed as aggressively and in that country's somewhat different approach to the granting of family benefits. Moreover, they also suggest that the structuring of welfare bureaucracies in the interwar period had lasting effects. On the other hand they also show how the privileges accorded under the Bismarckian systems were fundamentally upended and the entitlements that they oversaw were transformed by state socialism. Differences persisted initially but subsequently narrowed over time, even in the face of somewhat different political histories and different degrees of experimentation with market socialism.

The causal factors producing such convergence included fundamental features of the state socialist model. Most central in our view were the effective employment guarantee and the monopolization of provision of all social services – including most notably pensions, health and family policy – by the state. Even countries that began the post-war period at quite different levels of development and correspondingly divergent social structures – say, Czechoslovakia and Bulgaria – converged not only on quite common social policy models but even on comparable levels of social spending. Although we place primary emphasis on economic features of state socialism, this convergence was undoubtedly re-enforced by some common *political* features of post-Stalinism, including the effort by Communist political elites to elicit a modicum of support and maintain labour productivity.

Inglot certainly has identified an important research project that pushes against many conventional views of the communist era. And the significance of institutional layering may gain weight in the consideration of particular policy areas, such as family policy. However, as Inglot himself notes path-departing moves are more likely following crises and regime changes that bring new authoritarian elites to power and the instauration of communist rule was a crisis-driven authoritarian regime change par excellence. Moreover, the distinctive characteristics of the Eastern European trajectory under state socialism become particularly apparent when placed against the patterns we have sketched in Latin America, which showed a number of intriguing commonalities with interwar Eastern Europe with respect to both social structure and even social policy.

Democracy, economic performance, welfare legacies and the reform of social contracts in Latin America, East Asia and Eastern Europe

The 1980s and 1990s witnessed profound political and economic changes across the developing and socialist world. Transitions to democratic rule were defining elements of this period, and constitute a key background factor in understanding the course of social policy in Eastern Europe as well. But welfare legacies and changed economic circumstances were equally if not more important in setting the agenda and subsequent course of social policy.

In the Eastern European countries, welfare legacies and economic circumstances pushed governments in very different directions. On the one hand, with the transition to market-oriented economies, it was difficult or impossible to sustain certain features of the old system such as employment guarantees, price subsidies and in-kind benefits. As in Latin America, moreover, deep recessions and very tight fiscal constraints threatened the sustainability of the social insurance and comprehensive services of the communist era. These economic pressures were already visible in during the 1980s; the chapters by Inglot and Szikra and Tomka both note the strains on the late socialist model. However, these constraints were particularly evident with the onset of the transitional recessions of the early 1990s.

During the early years of the transition, such circumstances led several prominent observers (Ferge, 1991, 1997; Deacon, 1992) to fear that Eastern European countries would undertake a decisive 'liberal' transformation of their welfare systems. Economic crises – and particularly those accompanied by fiscal constraints and high inflation – as well as the transition to the market had both direct and indirect effects on social policy commitments. Sheer fiscal constraints limited the capacity of governments to sustain existing commitments or to make credible commitments to new benefits, while the rollback of the state sector reduced the capacity to use state-owned enterprises as a vehicle for the delivery of entitlements.

Crises also had important political effects. They increased the influence of technocrats, the international financial institutions and domestic policy networks that favoured economic reform. These reform coalitions had wide-ranging policy agendas that included macroeconomic stabilization and a variety of market-oriented policies, but typically included reforms of the social sector, as Orenstein argues most vigorously.

But crises and the concomitant influence of the international financial institutions were not the only causal factor at work. The course of social policy also depended heavily on prior social policy choices. Despite the severe fiscal constraints under which the new Eastern European democracies operated, the socialist welfare legacy had offsetting political consequences. Most citizens had been incorporated into a dense network of social entitlements. Even where the value of these protections and the quality of services had deteriorated, scaling them back posed serious political risks, even, as Vanhuysse (2006a; Cerami and Vanhuysse, this volume) has argued, to democracy itself. In general, the wider the coverage and the more effective the services provided, the more difficult for reformers to strip away existing entitlements or to 'sell' alternative, market-oriented means of financing and delivery.

As the chapters in this volume show, there is substantial and significant debate on precisely how to characterize the new Eastern European model. Some contributions stress neo-liberal elements in the new Eastern European welfare states. In his discussion of the policy influence of the World Bank and other international financial institutions, Orenstein emphasizes the shift toward multipillar pension systems that accorded a significant role for personal accounts and private management. Rat notes the disciplinary nature of Minimum Income Guarantee (MIG) schemes in their obligation to seek employment, in the over-bureaucratization and stigmatization of beneficiaries, and in their overlay with earlier patterns of social exclusion, for example vis-à-vis the Roma populations.

But with the benefit of hindsight, early fears that crisis and economic reform would strip away basic social entitlements have clearly been moderated and nuanced. Rat's analysis, for example, sees the failures of the MIG programmes not so much as a triumph of neo-liberalism, but as a more complex policy failure that is rooted in fundamental features of European MIG schemes themselves and difficulties of implementation when they are extended to very different economic and social contexts. As Szikra and Tomka argue, the 'modal pattern' of social policy in Eastern Europe after the transition is by no means an Anglo-Saxon or liberal one; rather it is a hybrid that includes not only liberal principles, but also social democratic, conservative and even some communist elements.

Characterizing policy developments

The hybrid nature of Eastern Europe's evolving welfare systems poses at least two analytical challenges for arguments focusing on path-dependence between the communist and post-communist eras. First, there are questions of measurement and categorization: identifying the nature and extent of ongoing adaptations of social policy systems and deciding whether they represent path-dependent or path-departing developments and against what standards. As we see from the chapters by Orenstein and Inglot, there is no unambiguous way to establish these benchmarks; the significance of similar pension reforms can be interpreted in quite different ways. The second and ultimately more important challenge is to identify the causal factors behind whatever changes have occurred, a challenge we take up more explicitly in the next section.

Once again, some cross-regional comparisons may help shed light on these issues. First, economic performance since 1980 has shown wide variation across the three regions of interest to us. As implied above, these differences have had important implications for social policy. Until 1997, most of the East Asian countries managed to escape the debilitating financial and transitional crises of the 1980s and 1990s. Good macroeconomic performance both improved the fiscal position of governments and strengthened the hand of political actors arguing for an expansion of social commitments and weakened the force of technocratic arguments for reform or retrenchment. A little-remarked feature of the global social policy landscape is the quite dramatic expansion of entitlements in the high-growth Asian countries – Thailand and particularly Korea and Taiwan – following their transitions to democratic rule.

The region-wide crisis of 1997–98 posed similar constraints to those seen in Latin America and Eastern Europe and triggered policy reforms as well. But fiscal pressures were more widely viewed as cyclical, rather than long-term and structural. As a result governments had greater latitude to respond to demands for social protection and the new entitlements put in place following the transition to democratic rule generally survived it intact.

Latin America and Eastern Europe faced far more severe economic constraints, but in the context of very different welfare legacies that appeared to influence the way governments responded. With the exception of Costa Rica and the countries of the southern cone, most Latin American welfare states were deep but not wide. They involved heavy public expenditures on social insurance, but benefits were not universal and in some cases were limited to a quite narrow set of beneficiaries. Moreover, the distribution of social services was also highly uneven. Where coverage was wider, as in Uruguay, Argentina and Costa Rica, efforts to reform the system of social insurance and services faced greater political resistance from constituents, even in the face of strong fiscal constraints.

Where coverage had been narrow and unequal, it proved somewhat more difficult for beneficiaries to defend the status quo. Market-oriented reformers gained traction over the social policy agenda, for example, in the privatization of pensions. Politicians also faced stronger political incentives to expand entitlements in cases where they had been distributed in a highly unequal fashion, even if it implied a reallocation of resources away from existing beneficiaries: Colombia, Brazil and Venezuela provide examples of this second pattern.

Two particular differences between the Eastern European and Latin American response to economic crisis are noteworthy. First, new democratic governments in Eastern Europe attached a much higher priority to the establishment of social safety nets aimed at compensating formal sector workers displaced by economic reform, what Inglot calls the 'emergency' welfare state. These safety net programmes were by no means uniform in their design or generosity, and initial commitments were not necessarily sustained over time (see Rat's contribution to this volume in particular). Nonetheless, the contrast with Latin American is striking. Although Latin American governments did move toward targeted assistance and the improvement of access to health and education, compensation for unemployed formal sector workers was much less of a priority and was more likely to take a targeted and residualist form. Moreover, as Rat shows, initial emergency measures in Eastern Europe – which generated substantial criticism in the region – were gradually supplemented with the institution of MIG schemes, an integrated rights-based approach to social assistance that reflects a fundamentally different, and ultimately European, approach to poverty reduction than anything visible in Latin America.

Second, the socialist inheritance resulted in a very different approach to the reform of existing social insurance and services. In Latin America, the combination of fiscal constraints and narrow coverage made social insurance entitlements particularly vulnerable to financial rationalization and limited the scope for expansion. In Eastern Europe, by contrast, publics expected that the government would maintain these social insurance functions on a universal basis at low – or even no – cost. As a result, even where de jure changes appeared to reflect fundamental departures – for example, in a shift toward social insurance principles – governments maintained entitlements de facto. Even the framing of policy changes differed. Initial 'reforms' were cast in terms of *increasing* public expenditures rather than the standard elements of neo-liberal welfare reforms, such as reallocating resources, shifting the financing burden toward households, or increasing the efficiency of provision through greater reliance on private actors.

When structural reforms were undertaken, such as moving toward social insurance means of health-care financing or introducing multipillar pension systems, public responsibilities remained much more extensive than in Latin American countries. Unlike Latin America, the public pillar in Eastern Europe remained the largest component of the new pension systems, and as Orenstein observes, none moved toward a fully substitutive approach pioneered by Chile and later adopted by Mexico (Haggard and Kaufman, 2008, p. 209). Similarly, despite some movement toward privatization in health care, public spending in 2005 averaged almost three-quarters of all health-care spending in Eastern Europe, while private insurance covered only 2 per cent of private-sector expenditures. In Latin America, in contrast, the share of public spending was only 55 per cent; and private insurance had made considerable inroads by 2005, constituting almost 28 per cent of all private spending (Haggard and Kaufman, 2008, p. 213).

In these and other areas, principles of universalism were typically maintained de facto if not de jure. Governments found it extremely difficult to rationalize the finances of these systems, and programmes operated on soft budget constraints surprisingly similar to those seen during the socialist era.

It is important to emphasize that social policy in Eastern Europe by no means eliminated the human costs associated with the transition; the rise in unemployment, inequality and poverty is well documented. Cerami and Stanescu show high levels of those at risk for poverty even after taking transfers into account, and Rat's comparative analysis in this volume shows variations in, and shortcomings of, minimum income guarantee schemes. Nonetheless, the contrast with Latin America is striking. Only in the larger welfare states such as Costa Rica and Uruguay were pre-existing entitlements maintained to the same extent or new ones created. Rat's careful analysis of the data shows that the effect of transfers on poverty fall short of European standards; however, the magnitude and effects of these transfers far exceeds the various targeted programmes pioneered in Latin America (Haggard and Kaufman, 2008, pp. 216–18).

In sum, viewed from our particular comparative perspective, we are more inclined to interpret the Eastern European cases as exhibiting strong path-dependencies in the post-transition period. Path-dependence does not necessarily mean that existing policies and institutions are retained intact; this is a misleading benchmark. Rather it means that pre-existing policies exert influence on what is politically feasible in identifiable ways. We argue that politicians and technocrats were inclined to retain core principles, such as effective universalism, as well as broadly similar levels of coverage even in the face of quite compelling economic constraints and international pressures to adjust policies in a more liberal direction.

Explaining continuities and changes

What are the precise mechanisms for such persistence in the course of social policy and how might we explain cases that deviate from this predicted pattern? In his theoretical overview of institutional change, Cerami emphasizes the micro-institutional sources of persistence and change. In drawing our contrast between Eastern Europe and Latin America, our argument has been more straightforwardly political. In the first instance, existing entitlements influence public opinion and through public opinion the electoral calculus of politicians. The electoral constraint helps explain one puzzle that pops up in a number of chapters and in our view does not receive adequate attention: the fact that the parties that dominate the post-communist political landscape in most countries often do not differ substantially in their approaches to social policy; we return to departures from this observation in more detail below.

However, we agree with Cerami that these constraints on government operated not only through the electoral connection alone, but through the constellation of social policy interests and at the micro-institutional level. Past welfare policies created complex interest group and institutional constraints on welfare reform, from civil servants and public service providers, unions with an institutional stake in the welfare system, to civil society organizations carrying the banner for pensioners and other affected groups.

Before turning to these domestic arguments in more detail, it is worth beginning with a discussion of international factors since they provide an important context, interact in complex ways with domestic influences and constitute an important argument in a number of the contributions. In the most radical statement of international effects, Cerami and Stanescu explore the 'misfit' model, under which the greater the initial divergence between domestic politics and institutions, the more likely countries are to have to adjust to the external political environment.

However, a close reading of the full array of the chapters in this volume leaves a very different impression about the effects of international pressures, which in some cases push toward liberalizing change and in others serve to widen and deepen social policy commitments. It is clear that in the economically constrained countries of Latin America and Eastern Europe, the international financial institutions have played a crucial role in framing the discourse about social policy choices. Orenstein (2008, and this volume) makes a compelling empirical case for the role of the World Bank in promoting and shaping pension reform in a liberal direction. And Cerami (this volume) conceptualizes the role of the IFIs as purveyors of new ideas that can reframe debates and interact with past beliefs in ways that produce significant policy changes. However, as we have noted, these ideas appear to have gained less traction in Eastern Europe than elsewhere. Moreover, it is important to note that other chapters in the volume discuss the direct and indirect effects of the EU (Theobold and Kern, Sirovátka and Rákoczyová, Cerami and Stanescu, and Rat) which by no means represents a political force for the adoption of neo-liberal social policies. In sum, countries vary both in the extent to which they are 'vulnerable' to IFI policy discourse and financial influence, and also in the nature of the international organizational pressures to which they are even subject in the first place.

We are sceptical, therefore, about putting too much weight on international factors as a source of liberalizing change. First, as our discussion of cross-regional differences indicates, we are dubious about the starting premise of these arguments: that social policy is converging in a neo-liberal direction. To the extent that neo-liberal international forces are operating – as they certainly are – the extent of their influence appears highly conditional on domestic political circumstance.

In addition, other international influences in Eastern Europe, particularly the pull of social democratic and conservative Western European models, work in the *opposite* direction of restraining liberal reform. It is clear that membership in the European Community, European aid and technology transfer, and intellectual influences have all operated in providing a menu of social policy models from which to choose (Jacoby, 2004). To the extent that international influences are operating, they do so not only through the 'hard' influence of conditionality, but also through 'softer' processes of diffusion that are heavily mediated by domestic political influences (Weyland, 2004; Brooks, 2005).

Our reading of the contributions to the volume is that they typically begin with an acknowledgement of the political effects of the socialist legacy, even if their analytic purpose is subsequently to explore variation. The overview by Szikra and Tomka provides the most explicit discussion of those, such as Deacon (1993), who anticipated a possible turn toward neo-liberal social models. Their conclusion is worth citing at some length.

> All in all, the welfare system retained its mixed character in East Central Europe, even though, with a different composition. The communist features disappeared quickly and the mix of social democratic and conservative principles has prevailed. These patterns were deeply rooted not only in institutions but also in public attitudes. According to polls, the majority of the electorate has favoured a combination of universalistic social welfare arrangements (especially in health care) and work-related benefits (cash benefits).

Similar observations echo through the other country chapters as well. In the conclusion to his chapter on the Visegrad countries, Inglot notes that with the possible exception of Slovakia in the early 2000s – to which we return below – 'we could observe clear continuity in terms of the welfare discourse, institutional consolidation, and also in maintaining a rather destabilizing pattern or alternating expansion and retrenchment of social expenditures'. However, he also notes that 'the first two elements to a large extent augmented the negative effects of the third one' and that 'generally, all four countries fared quite well in terms of upholding the accumulated social insurance rights and providing immediate assistance to the jobless under extremely difficult conditions of economic collapse and rising unemployment'.

The discussion of Bulgaria and Romania by Cerami and Stanescu presents a variant of the political argument for path-dependence that emphasizes the socio-political structure of those two countries and the resulting political deadlock. 'Political parties in both countries were... confronted, once again in their history, by the dilemma of simultaneously ensuring convergence of rural areas to urban standards, while promoting, at the same time, further modernization of urban areas so as to ensure a faster alignment towards the standards present in other CEE and Western countries.' Parties resisted the tax increases that would be required to achieve this objective, but none were willing to curtail the existing distribution of benefits either.

Even in the Baltics, home of some of the more wide-ranging economic reforms, important components of path-dependence remain. Aidukaite emphasizes that despite the weakness of left parties and labour and some distinctive national cleavages – to which we return in a moment – the future of the Baltic welfare state is unlikely to be neo-liberal. She references 'cognitive Europeanization' as a factor, but also the same political constraints that we have emphasized: 'citizens in the Baltic states reject the idea of a strong paternalistic state, but they still want to have a universal and comprehensive social protection system'.

In sum, it is important in any comparative exercise to be clear about benchmarks. As members of the European Union, it is understandable that the countries of Eastern Europe would look toward their Western neighbours as important points of reference. Yet their lower levels of wealth and the wrenching challenges of transition continue to set them apart. Our point of reference is one that reaches beyond the Eastern European region, but towards middle-income developing countries rather than Europe. From this perspective, we note commonalities with other countries in profound economic crises that have challenged the viability of existing commitments and pressed governments and citizens to make difficult adjustments. Yet we also see a process of change in social policy commitments that is surprisingly incremental, particularly when placed against the enormity of the economic and social transformation associated with the collapse of state socialism. Politics appears to play a central role in this incrementalism, or path-dependence. Fiscal constraints and international influences do give rise to neo-liberal reform efforts, but the political reaction to them is negative and either forces incumbent governments to resist liberalizing pressures in the first place, retreat from reforms, or leads to the election of new governments that undertake at least partial reversals.

Path-dependent and path-departing developments: intra-regional variations

In the preceding analysis, we have been inclined to see evidence of a 'modal' social policy transition path in Eastern Europe that includes strong 'emergency' responses to the dislocations of the transition, convergence on social insurance models, and the maintenance of wide coverage. However, differences across countries exist, to be sure, reflecting for example variation in the socialist status quo ante and in features of the post-transition political and economic landscape, such as the timing and depth of crises and the strength of left parties.

It is beyond the scope of this chapter to explore variation at the level of particular policies, although this is in our view probably the most effective strategy for getting at the precise institutional mechanisms of persistence and change. This approach is adopted with good effect in the chapter by Rat on minimum income guarantee schemes in particular. But we can make a modest contribution to the debate by focusing at the country level on several outliers that appear to exhibit more 'path-departing' patterns of social policy and reviewing some of the causal factors that might influence observed variation; indeed, we think that much more still needs to be done to sharpen up the intra-regional comparisons by being more explicit about the political and institutional differences that appear to drive them.

There can be little doubt that the debate over the course of Eastern European social policy has been heavily influenced by the more extensively studied Visegrad cases: Poland, Hungary and the Czech Republic. Yet some interesting opportunities for comparison can arise by pitting these 'core' cases against Slovakia and the Baltic countries. The Slovak reforms of the early 2000s rank among the most decisive in the region. With respect to pensions, the reform established a relatively large second pillar. The reform of the health-care system increased the scope for private insurers and providers, rationalized public provision and introduced limits on the scope of public responsibilities. The government also managed to tighten eligibility requirements and reduce the size and duration of welfare payments.

It is important to put these liberalizing reforms in comparative perspective. The pension privatization retained the effective universalism of the system, and was sold in part by arguing that replacement rates would rise. Health-care reforms were similarly coupled with a restatement of the commitment to universalism, promises to improve the quality of care, and important concessions to low-income households. And as Inglot points out, 'the government proved unable to withstand social pressure in favor of the return to a much universal, Czechoslovak-style system of family support'. In these crucial respects, the system maintained important links to the commitments of the socialist era.

Nonetheless, it is worth asking why Slovakia went as far as it did. A number of factors of contributed, including external ones. Slovakia experienced a strong wave of public support for integration with Europe following the isolation of the Mečiar years. Given its past history – and arguably its relative weakness – the external constraints on fiscal policy associated with accession were particularly strong. However, these external factors need to be understood in the context of the ideological cohesion of the ruling coalition after 2002 and the fragmentation and isolation of the opposition as well, a point made implicitly in the treatment of Bulgaria and Romania by Cerami and Stanescu as well. Foreign models were appealing to the extent that they were congruent with domestic political realignments that occurred following the 'second round' crises of the mid-1990s in both countries, but particularly in Bulgaria. In sum, these cases suggest that an important line of future comparative work lies in teasing out the extent to which partisan differences did in fact influence social policy choices.

The Baltics certainly raise this issue as well, given that socialist parties fared more badly here than they did elsewhere in the region. The account by Aidukaite notes the dominance of right-liberal coalitions from the onset of the transition in Estonia and Latvia and the fact that the Social Democratic Party in Lithuania had become a centrist party by the early 2000s and in any case ruled in coalition with other parties. However, Aidukaite also notes a second theoretically interesting explanation for the path of social policy in the Baltics: the national question raised by the presence of significant Russian populations in Latvia and Estonia. These Russian populations are formally disenfranchised in both countries, and their numbers will almost certainly decline looking forward. Nonetheless, ethnic and linguistic heterogeneity might have been a block to the pursuit of more robust social policies, as a number of economic theories of public goods have noted. Vanhuysse (this volume) makes a similar point about the role of heterogeneity. She notes that the weakness of the unions in the Baltics is due in part to the way in which broad coalitions of at-risk workers could not form because of ethnic appeals that divided indigenous from Russian-speaking economic losers. Although their populations are much smaller, the social exclusion of the Roma populations might also affect how broader social policy is crafted, introducing elements of targeting, means-testing and work requirements that might not be as stringent were those at the bottom ethnically homogenous with the rest of the population.

Partisanship and social heterogeneity are certainly not the only candidates for explaining the variance in the path of social policy among the Eastern European cases. Elsewhere, we have also explored the possible effects of the timing and extent of the economic shocks of the 1990s and the speed with which governments adopted market-oriented reforms. However, the main point we seek to emphasize is that the effects of these (and other) causal factors are conditional: they operate in some range that is set by the social policy inheritance. To the extent that this social policy inheritance was broadly shared across the countries in the region – which we believe it was – its influence can only be seen clearly through comparative analysis with reference cases outside the region.

Conclusion

The study of the post-socialist welfare state is not only of significance in its own right; engagement with these cases, and the excellent work contained in this volume, promises to deepen our understanding of the more general political processes of redistribution, insurance and service provision. We close with a few suggestions – including to ourselves! – about how that process might best be advanced.

First, it is important that scholars working on the welfare state in post-socialist and developing countries devise metrics and push hard to collect the data – both qualitative and quantitative – that will permit more focused comparisons. Debates about path-dependent and path-departing change hinge ultimately on devising measures of social policy and welfare outcomes and comparing them across cases – both within and outside Eastern Europe – and over time. The early stages of research on the region are naturally devoted to simply figuring out what happened, in part through the construction of narratives. But as with the evolution of the literature on the advanced welfare state, further progress will come by establishing clear metrics that allow for more focused and systematic analysis.

Second, as we have emphasized throughout this essay, such metrics are always instruments of comparison. In this regard, we were particularly struck by the emphasis many chapters placed on the Western European experience, and the powerful typology of the advanced welfare states offered by Esping-Andersen (1990) in particular. Yet it is important to recall that Esping-Andersen's typology gains its force in part from his very close reading of the distinctive history of the Western European cases, for example, in the particular nature of their party systems and, in his later work, in the changing nature of the economic and employment structure (Esping-Andersen, 1999). It is not clear that such a typology necessarily travels to other settings, nor, do we believe, would Esping-Andersen expect it too; one of his most important injunctions is that social policy arises in complex bundles of complementary policies and is not well understood in simple terms of 'more and less'.

A common finding in many of the chapters in this volume is that the Eastern European cases represent 'hybrid' forms of social policy that draw on each of the main Western European models. Yet in the end, the utility of this observation is limited. It implicitly privileges an explanation of social policy that focuses on external factors and emulation, and distracts us from figuring out the political and social drivers of the particular complexes of policy that have arisen in the Eastern European setting.

We have suggested that middle-income developing countries provide a different lens through which to view the Eastern European cases, in part because these countries remain much poorer than Western Europe. But even if the Western European referrant is maintained it may be useful to move beyond the logic of hybrid forms to focus on the distinctive features of Eastern European social policy.

A final point is the importance of pushing the research on the Eastern European welfare state down the causal chain towards it social consequences. Most of the chapters in this volume – and our own work we should add – has been focused primarily on policy. But any meaningful strategy of comparison of the welfare state must ultimately engage its consequences for a variety of outcomes, from poverty and inequality, to physical quality of life measures, to economic outcomes such as the efficiency of labour markets, competitiveness and even economic growth. In the first instance, we are interested in the welfare state because we are interested in human welfare. But the distributional outcomes of social policy are also critically important for understanding the political economy of continuity and change: they shape both the identity of key social and political actors and how they respond to the ongoing pressures on the welfare state.

14
Epilogue: Lessons Learnt and Open Questions

Claus Offe

The remarkable collection of country studies as well as studies of issue areas in social policy that Cerami and Vanhuysse have assembled in this volume marks a step forward in charting the *terra incognita* of welfare states in the new member states which joined the EU in 2004 and 2007. Apart from the one and a half small Mediterranean islands of Malta and the southern part of Cyprus, all new member states share the quality of having emerged, after 1989, from the economic, social and political regime of state socialism. One of the recurrent themes throughout the chapters of this volume is the following question: To what extent can the evolution of CEE welfare states be accounted for in terms of path-dependency and the continuity of state socialism as well as those institutional patterns that were adopted in the region during the interwar period – and to what extent do we encounter path-departures that were conditioned by the two dominant novelties of (a) the breakdown of state socialism with the subsequent deep transformation crisis and (b) the accession of the new members to the European Union and its patterns of capitalist democracy, as well as the conditionalities governing Eastern Enlargement. In dealing with these questions, the authors share an analytical frame that dominates much of the academic literature on current affairs in CEE. Stated at the most general level, this frame suggests that what we see happening in the region must be accounted for in terms of a joint outcome of 'the past' and 'the West'.

As far as the past is concerned, the vanished state socialist institutional system had nurtured, during its rule of roughly 40 years, expectations and notions of social justice that persisted after its demise, most importantly the expectation that government must take responsibility for high levels of employment. 'Well after the transition, expectations about an expansive role for the state remained extremely high' (Haggard and Kaufman, 2008, p. 308). Moreover, institutional legacies, most importantly a strongly 'Bismarckian' pattern of providing for social security, were inherited by countries of the region from the interwar period. Concerning 'Western' determinants of the shape of welfare state transformations in the region,

there are also two factors of influence. One is the role of international financial institutions, such as the World Bank, in making strong and 'conditionalist' suggestions as to how post-socialist states must adjust their pension
and health systems when they were facing huge revenue deficits under the
impact of the transformation crises of the first half of the 1990s. The other
Western factor is the European Union and the eastward diffusion of the
various welfare state models of its member states. This role has been interpreted as following a 'push' and a 'pull' mechanism. The push mechanism,
originating with the EU Commission and the treaties of Maastricht (1992)
and Amsterdam (1997), became effective when the prospects for Eastern
Enlargement began to necessitate the 'rationalization of social expenditure'
(Haggard and Kaufman, 2008, p. 344) in what were becoming candidate
countries. But at least equally strong was a pull factor, which consisted in
CEE political elites looking for templates in West European welfare states
and drawing upon proposals coming from international organizations (the
World Bank, ILO, Council of Europe, OECD) in order to adjust their own
systems accordingly (Schimmelfennig and Sedelmeier, 2005).

To these two complex bundles of variables, we might be well advised to
add two more, namely the power position, political resources and strategic
opportunities that political elites enjoy and that (various categories of) non-
elites are to a greater or lesser extent deprived of – such as strong trade
unions. In contrast to the external parameters of 'the past' and 'the West',
these are internal variables which unfold their causal impact within the
new political institutions and socioeconomic conditions of the new member states; as such, these variables are promising candidates for explaining
variation among – rather than common features and trajectories of – states in
the region. The author who most clearly and consistently adopts the analytical perspective of power resources and strategic action is Pieter Vanhuysse,
both in his chapter in this volume as well as in his earlier book (Vanhuysse,
2006a). Needless to say, the two analytical perspectives are in no way mutually exclusive, as external actors (both representing the EU and the 'past' of
post-socialist societies) do wield power, too, and as domestic power holders are, on their part, empowered by the conditions and opportunities that
emerged in the sequence of breakdown, transformation and eventually EU
integration. For the features of this sequence allow us to understand which
power resources enjoyed by elites of the old regime could be preserved and
converted into the context of the new one, and which could not (Stark and
Bruszt, 1998).

Instead of dwelling on these issues of building and combining causal variables and models, I want to use the limited space of these concluding reflections to focus upon two sets of factors that are, as it were, to be located at
the very beginning of welfare state transformation in the region, on the
one part, and at the very end of it. Less cryptically put, I want to address
the prevailing values, ideas, social norms, attitudes and expectations, i.e. the

ideas that inform both elites and non-elites. I also want to focus upon the performance, achievements, or final *outcomes* of social policies in the new member states, the ways in and the extent to which they actually provide security and life chances to their constituencies/clients and are thus effective in fighting exclusion.

The underlying value system of CEE welfare states

Any system of social security and the provision of services draws an implicit demarcation line. This line divides categories of risks and contingencies that belong to a sphere that the respective individuals affected by such conditions can be expected to *cope with by their own means*, on the one hand, from those categories of conditions that *call for collective provisions*, on the other. If I suffer from a common cold, I am, according to the logic of most welfares states and health systems, on this side of the line, as I am supposed to know what to do (and actually act upon that knowledge) in order to achieve a speedy recovery and to pay for whatever it costs to get there. In contrast, if I suffer from pneumonia, the remedial measures to be taken are typically specified by, provided for, and financed through public and other collective arrangements (insurance, licensed medical institutions, tax-subsidized occupational health plans, etc.). In this way, welfare states can be looked at as sorting machines which assign deserts, rights or legitimate needs-to-be-taken-care-of to categories of people in specified conditions, while leaving other conditions to the sphere of what is considered 'normal': you have to cope with them by your own means, relying on markets and family support, or, failing that, simply accept them as unfortunate facts of life. Within welfare states and longitudinally, this demarcation line is never fixed and essentially contested. But cross-sectionally and between welfare states, the location of this divide differs greatly between individual states as well as types of welfare states.

As becomes evident from various chapters in this volume, the state socialist culture of social policy has located this moral demarcation line very far away from the extreme of market-mediated private provision and very close to the opposite extreme of the comprehensive caring state. The basic fact that there was, at least officially, no labour 'market', but a pervasive system of administrative allocation of labour to jobs and status rights of jobholders was (rightly, for the duration of the system) seen as a blanket protection of the entire population from the risk of unemployment. Expectations of non-elites converged with the strategic orientation of the monopolistic ruling party in that benevolent state paternalism should govern most spheres of need (including, for instance, basic food, housing, education, vacation trips) of most categories of persons (Offe, 1993). Strategically, the institutions that were designed to embody and implement this set of social policy norms operated in the service of the objectives of keeping workers dependent, disciplined and acquiescent, of rewarding loyalty towards the regime (as well as threatening sanctions for disloyalty), preventing 'petit bourgeois individualism' and social differentiation among the worker-citizens, and to motivate work effort and productivity through the comprehensive guarantee of (job, income, housing, health, civic, etc.) security. Services and benefits were allocated to a large extent at the point of production and through managerial discretion, rather than on the basis of individual rights that could be enforced in court. The system that provided security was distinctively 'productivist' in that social rights of citizenship (as opposed to status rights of workers) played at best a marginal role.[1] Collectivist and paternalist care privileged those preparing themselves for playing productive roles in schools and universities, those presently involved in the process of production and the reproductive function women (as well as in the process of the state's administering, policing and protecting society from its 'enemies'), while people outside of (re)productive roles, mostly pensioners, were significantly worse off in terms of social protection. (The latter fact provides reason to caution against mistaking state socialist social policy for being based on 'citizenship'; rather, effective citizenship was based upon the performance of the various 'productive' roles just mentioned.)

I have focused upon this highly consistent set of norms, institutions and strategies (which presumably were mutually reinforcing) in order to address the question: What happens to the *norms* in case the *institutions* are no longer in place (be it due to the fact that they are no longer affordable as a consequence of the privatization of enterprises and ensuing transformation crises, be it due to liberalization and democratization as a consequence of which state paternalism is exposed to challenges and hard budget constraints)? My tentative answer is that norms and expectations that belong to the 'comprehensive paternalist care' syndrome just reviewed *do not vanish* with the corresponding institutions, but survive them for a substantial period of time and may even gain in strength (as it were, due to effects of nostalgia) when their supporters have to face the consequences of such institutional patterns' disappearance under the impact of incipient democratic capitalism.

If I am not mistaken, there is a pervasive though implicit hierarchy in the interest scholars take in welfare states after state socialism. Much of the comparative literature focuses upon the Visegrad states and the Baltic states, while much less data and analysis seems to be available on the two South-East European member states of Bulgaria and Romania. Even less widely covered are conditions and developments in the Western Balkans, with the rest (Ukraine, Moldova, Belarus, Russia) remaining almost entirely a matter for country specialists. There is very little, also in this volume, about the GDR, the most prosperous of the CMEA states. An obvious (if under-utilized in the scholarly literature) place to test the hypothesis (or 'cultural lag theory' of transitions from state socialism) is the part of Germany that used to be, until the formal end of that state through unification in 1990, the demographic and territorial basis of the GDR (Alesina and Fuchs-Schündeln, 2007). Even after a time of almost 20 years since the end of the German case of state socialism, the normative demarcation line between public and individual responsibilities continues to clearly show up in opinion surveys comparing East German and West German samples. Like in a natural experiment, the ex-GDR (the only example of transition through state *merger*, or the death of one state, as contrasting to the six CEE cases of transition through the *separation* of states, or state births) allows us to study the robust afterlife of the normative underpinnings and guiding ideas of state socialism. To summarize just a few findings from recent German surveys, East Germans favour a significantly more substantive definition of 'democracy' compared to the formal and procedural definition that West Germans apply. Of Eastern respondents, 55 per cent (vs. 39 per cent in the West) believe that 'democracy' implies that the state provides jobs and is responsible for reducing unemployment, and 40 per cent of them (vs. 26 per cent in the West) think that a truly democratic state must take control over the banks. Similarly, in 2006 74 per cent believed that 'socialism is a good idea badly implemented', a statement that only 49 per cent in the West agreed to. The surviving semantic of 'democracy' is strongly associated in the region with distributive justice and high levels of state-sponsored protection. Hence the perceived deficiencies of 'democratic' outcomes, thus understood, explains the significantly greater dissatisfaction with 'how democracy works' in the East as compared with the West.

As the transition from state socialism to democratic capitalism that took place in the region after 1989 is without any historical precedent, and as it also was not guided by some revolutionary project or programme (but rather 'happened' unexpectedly), there was no coherent model or template according to which the transformation was to be conducted. Hence the distinctive pattern of (social) policy-making that is richly and convergently described in the chapters of the present volume. The making of post-socialist welfare states occurred in a mode of emergency policy-making, the recalibration of existing institutions under many economic and political constraints, according to a pattern of ad hoc measures and bricolage, with many turns, a high degree of volatility, and the result of 'faceless' hybrids being adopted in the various countries that differed both from each other and from the existing, ideologically somewhat consistent welfare states in Western Europe, be they of the 'social democratic', 'conservative' or '(neo-)liberal' variety. Conditions in some of the countries under study here were shaped, moreover, by their specific ethnic composition and ethnic tensions and religious cultures (which do not show up in these chapters as possible independent variables for explaining welfare state structures and trajectories).

Outcomes: Security, inclusion and the distribution of life chances

As we know, new member states are generally poorer that the old ones, and they are going to remain so for a generation or more. They are also relatively poor performers in terms of a 'just' distribution of life chances. Merkel and Giebler (2009) have undertaken a heroic though instructive attempt to build an 'Index of Social Justice' (ISJ) and apply it to 30 OECD countries, among them the four members of the Visegrad group. The Index has values from 1 (worst) to 10 (best) and consists of seven dimensions of social justice (poverty prevention, education, labour market performance, social expenditure on health and cohesion, income distribution, intergenerational justice, anti-discrimination policies), each of them operationalized by one or more pertinent empirical indicators. The resulting index is weighted, with poverty weighted by the factor 4, education by 3, and labour market performance 2. In spite of these somewhat arbitrary quantitative operations, the results are remarkably plausible. All five Scandinavian countries are at the top of the list of 30 countries, most of the Continental old member states are in the second quarter of the ranking, followed by Slovakia (rank 14), Czech Republic (15), Hungary (16) and Poland (with a distant rank 26, just above South Korea). As these four countries are, together with Slovenia, the economic and political 'success stories' among the new member states, the remaining five (on which comparable data are not available) are likely to fare considerably worse. At the same time, the 'social justice' performance of the four countries is mostly better, according to these measures, than that of the Anglo-Saxon welfare states, following on ranks 18 (Australia), 21 (UK) and 24 (USA).

Another way to measure welfare state outcomes is to look at degrees of subjective satisfaction with conditions in post-transition and post-accession. The European Bank of Reconstruction and Development (2007) has generated an extensive data base by which these questions can be answered. One question concerned the priorities for 'extra (government) investment'. Without exception, 'health care' was named as the number one priority in all ten countries, with 'pensions' being a close-running number two. This pattern seems to reflect the widely held view that social protection remains deficient in these two core areas of any welfare state. Another set of questions concerned the preferability of 'democracy' and 'market economy' as compared to other political/economic systems. An interesting finding is not so much the level of positive answers (which were roughly between one-half and three-quarters in the case of 'democracy' and between two-fifths and three-fifths in the case of 'market economy'), but the distribution of favourable opinions across age and income categories. Again, an amazing uniformity emerges. With two exceptions (Slovenia, Hungary) the strongest supporters of democracy are to be found in the 18–34 age bracket and the 'upper' income category, while the agreement of older and poorer persons was consistently lower and dropped in many cases below the 50 per cent line. This pattern shows up even more distinctively in the case of support for the market economy, where virtually only the young and the better-off are above the 50 per cent line (again, with the exception of Slovenia). A final

item to be considered here are responses to the statement: 'All things considered, I am satisfied with my life now.' Again, the peak values of positive
answers are to be found among the young and the wealthy (i.e., those least
dependent upon social security, poor relief and welfare state services) while
the majority of the non-young and the non-wealthy almost consistently
drop below the 50 per cent line (again, with the exception of Slovenia and,
here, Estonia). These findings leave us with the question: Are post-transition
welfare states, as well as the institutional structure of the economy and
the polity, preferred just by the minorities of those who have succeeded
under them (or at any rate hope to do so)? If so, there is little reason to
believe that the performance of these institutions has so far earned them
the widely shared trust and credibility that they may depend upon for the
sake of their stability. From findings like these it seems safe to conclude that
CEE welfare states have a substantial distance to travel before they reach
the standards set by western Continental cases, to say nothing about the
Scandinavian ones. The consolidation of their democracies and their firm
integration into the EU institutional framework will only be safe if they
actually manage to bridge that gap.

Welfare state development and the ongoing dynamics within the enlarged European Union

Nicholas Barr (2005, p. 16) has nicely summarized the strategic dilemma
that underlies the European politics of accession/enlargement. This
dilemma, according to him, is captured by two questions: (1) 'Were the
accession arrangements [as they were negotiated by EU-15 elites with candidate countries] sufficiently *parsimonious* for EU politicians to sell them to
their electorates?' In this perspective, arrangements may not be '*too* generous'. Conversely, the other question had to be asked: (2) 'Were the proposed
arrangements *sufficiently* generous that politicians in the accession countries could sell them to *their* electorates?' (my emphasis). Between these two
limiting conditions, a 'meeting ground' had to be found. Yet it was (and
remains under the post-accession turbulences) uncertain whether such a
meeting ground does at all exist or whether the maximum defined by the
answer to the first question remains *below* the minimum defined by the
answer to the second question. In other words, there is the possibility that
the two local equilibria do not add up to an encompassing equilibrium.

There was also a clear asymmetry as to the dominant motivations on
either side. As seen from the vantage point of the new member states, joining the EU involves the *political* sacrifice (in terms of the sovereignty of,
after 1989, newly independent nation states with their strong memories of
being forcibly integrated into the Soviet supranational systems of CMEA
and the Warsaw Pact) to comply with the rule of European 'external governance' (Schimmelfennig and Sesselmeier, 2004) It implies, inter alia, the

adoption of the *acquis communautaire* with its 85,000 pages of legal norms, in the making of most of which new member states had no say, as well as compliance with the Maastricht convergence criteria. This sacrifice remains politically tolerable at the level of domestic politics of new member states only to the extent it is seen to be offset by tangible *economic* gains that EU integration is seen to yield in terms of growth and prosperity. The perspective of the old member states of EU-15 is a perfect mirror image of this trade-off of political and economic considerations. Here, *economic* sacrifices that most of West European economies make, at least in the short run, in terms of the outflow of investment and EU funds as well as the inflow of migrant labour, are to be compensated for in terms of enhanced prospects for *political stability* within the new capitalist democracies of the CEE region (Fuchs and Offe, 2009). Either of these two balances show symptoms of stress and precariousness at the end of the first decade of the twenty-first century.

As to the CEE balance, gains of prosperity and security that the new capitalist political economies enjoy, together with their new welfare states and their supranational integration into the EU, are widely seen to be too moderate and too unequally distributed to compensate for the loss of national autonomy. Rather unsurprisingly, and given the weakness of liberal traditions of political culture in the region, this imbalance provides vast political opportunities for ethno-nationalist, populist and anti-European mobilization within virtually all of the new member states. (Mungiu-Pippidi, 2007) Such responses will also be fuelled by the experience that the financial market crisis is affecting EU member states in highly unequal ways, with the new member states being in a vastly inferior position, compared to at least some of the old member states and given the unwillingness and incapacity of the latter[2] to engage into an EU-wide effective crisis management, as it comes to defending new member states' economies against the impact of the crisis. These economies are to a large extent dependent economies, concerning both their financial as well as their manufacturing sectors. As an illustration of the latter, the Hungarian government has claimed just before the accession of that country in 2004 that a full 40 per cent of the Hungarian GDP was generated by German subsidiaries in Hungary, a figure that highlights an extreme degree of vulnerability in case the German economy should contract (Sinn, 2003, pp. 65–6). The pattern is clearly confirmed by financial market developments in early 2009: Dependency means that if 'we' catch a cold, 'they' will begin to suffer from pneumonia. Hence the widely asked question in the CEE region, among elites and non-elites alike: Was accession really worth the sacrifices in terms of *political autonomy* that it involved?

As to the Western version of the equation, there are growing doubts as to whether the logic of Eastern Enlargement, namely the logic of investing, through opening capital and labour markets to the region and offering assistance out of EU funds, will actually yield the hoped-for returns in terms of political stability in CEE and Europe-wide cooperation. If anything, these doubts are being heightened (or at least justified) by the perception of symptoms of an anti-liberal, ethnocentric and also anti-European backlash to be observed on the scene of politics in many of the new member states. Mungiu-Pippidi (2007, p. 9) lists the following indicators of this backlash: advance of populist groups, political radicalization, weak majorities, factional behaviour within unstable parties and governing coalitions, occasional violations of democratic standards (such as the rigging of elections). Apart from tiny Slovenia, even the best economic growth performers of the region – Czech Republic, Poland, Hungary – have all been backsliding in assessments of their democratic evolution between 2000 and 2007. Internally unstable and externally (concerning the European integration agendas) uncooperative political elites are clearly giving rise to doubts in the old member states: Was enlargement really worth the effort in terms of the *economic burdens* it involved? Unsurprisingly, these doubts intensify at a time when not just global financial and economic crises emerge but, more specifically, when accession itself is a done deal and conditionality has lost most of its pre-2007 leverage. For on 'the day after accession ... , the influence of the EU vanishes like a short term anesthetic' (Mungiu-Pippidi, 2007, p. 16).

The speculation may not be far off the mark that the conditions that 'Brussels', for example, the old member states, had imposed upon candidate countries were as severe as they were exactly because the closing of the conditionalist window of opportunity could be anticipated. As old member states 'did what they could', prospective new members had to do what they could, and arguably more than that. Nicholas Barr (2005) has raised a question that is clearly up to future historians to provide a conclusive answer to. The question is this: Have the terms of accession (for example, the *acquis* plus the convergence criteria of the Stability and Growth Pact) as they were defined by the old member states actually *helped* the economic and political transition in the post-socialist region of Central and Eastern Europe? Barr cautiously suggests that 'considerable worker protection', as mandated by the *acquis*, in combination with macroeconomic conditionality (for example, tough budget constraints resulting from convergence criteria) 'unnecessarily aggravated the costs of transition' (20) and prevented the new member states from sustaining the 'high welfare spending directly connected with transition, for example unemployment benefits and poverty relief' (17). Under the constraints imposed by accession, even robust growth may be prevented from translating into equally robust social protection. It remains to be seen how remaining deficiencies in social protection and poverty relief affect political stability in the region once elite strategies of 'divide and pacify' (Vanhuysse, 2006a) may be no longer viable.

I have been considering here, in an admittedly speculative manner, causal relationships between four macro variables: (1) the conditions of accession; (2) their impact upon economic performance in old as well as new member states; (3) the consequences for welfare state performance; and (4) political stability (rule of law and democratic consolidation). First, whether accession conditionality promotes or weakens economic performance in the region is a question the answer to which is unlikely to be equally valid in the short term vs. the long run, for immediate geographic neighbours of the old member states vs. the more remote countries. Yet economic performance of the new member states remains inferior to that in the old member states, and very likely to remain so for the foreseeable future. In 2010, it is only the Czech Republic and Slovenia which are forecast to surpass the 50 per cent mark of GDP per capita, with the yardstick of 100 per cent being the EU-15 average. Even if highly optimistic assumption should turn out to be true, for example a 3.5 per cent annual growth rate for the EU-10 and 1.5 per cent for the EU-15, the forecast for 2030 is that only the two top regional performers, the Czech Republic and Slovenia, will perform slightly better than the EU-15 average (data quoted from Fuchs and Offe, 2009, Table 2). Growth performance may be affected by EU membership in various ways. Access of manufactured and agricultural products to Western markets is clearly critical, as is foreign direct investment, itself partly a dependent variable of political stability. Yet the regulatory regime of the *acquis*, the brain drain of skilled manpower, the economic dependency upon Western economies, as well as the budgetary convergence constraints may all play a role in reducing growth rates.

Second, welfare state development and the proportion of social expenditure is related to GDP per capita by the rule of thumb that the *percentage* of welfare spending increases with the *absolute size* of GDP. This equation, however, is likely to be significantly modified by the fact that the economies of the new member states must compete for investment through maintaining comparative advantages in terms of labour costs, including non-wage costs of labour such as contributions to social security systems. The other major parameter of competition is the rate of direct (corporate) and indirect taxation. Several of the new member states have adopted very low flat rates for these taxes (in Bulgaria, as low as 10 per cent), which implies significant revenue constraints and severe limitations on social spending. Third, there must be some kind of causal link between growth performance and welfare spending/social security, on the one hand, and political stability/democratic consolidation, on the other. The nature and direction of these causal links remains a matter of great scholarly as well as political interest, with the players within the political party system, the patterns of political culture, and the structure of interest representation playing mediating roles.

Concerning the third of the above causal links – the impact of social policy generosity upon political stability – is clearly of key interest to the authors and readers of the present volume. Much of current research suggests that the stability of the democratic regime form depends on good welfare state performance. For instance, Carles Boix (2004) has suggested the straightforward argument that conflicts of interest can be processed within the framework democratic procedures only as long the losers of an election (or other forms of collectively binding decision-making) have reasons to hope for a better outcome of the next election or negotiation. Such hope, in turn, is supported if 'the political and organizational resources of both the majority and the minority become more balanced'. 'The distribution of income may affect the chances of introducing and sustaining a democratic regime'...because 'as the less well-off grow richer and their income comes closer to that of high-income voters, economic tensions decline', and both the rich and the less rich are increasingly inclined to accept an existing democratic regime or supranational authority. This reasoning is confirmed by the fact that the probability of democratic breakdown is up to 6.6 per cent per year in societies with a Gini Index of above .50, while it has been zero between 1950 and 1990 in societies with a Gini Index of below .35 (Boix, 2004, p. 2). Similarly, the stability of institutions of regional inte-gration (such as the EU and its logic of supranational authority-pooling) depends on the relative socioeconomic homogeneity of its constituent member states. Yet with the second round of Eastern Enlargement in 2007, the EU-27 shows a Gini of .399, worse than the US (.394), and exactly a third of the total population of EU-27 live below half the median of the original EU-6 core countries. Such findings allow the conclusion: Unless income and social security can be enhanced and brought to some convergence, both within individual member countries and between them, liberal democra-cies within the new member states as well as their stable institutional inte-gration into the EU will be jeopardized.

All these empirical patterns, analytical categories, theoretical explan-ations and predictions may, however, already have begun to undergo a process which renders them obsolete. As we enter the new era of global economic and financial crisis to which the new member states of the EU are significantly more vulnerable than most of the old ones, neither eco-nomic nor political developments can be grasped by pre-crisis concepts and assumptions, let alone predicted or shaped.

Notes

1 Introduction: Social Policy Pathways, Twenty years after the Fall of the Berlin Wall

* Equal authors, listed alphabetically.

1. Czech Republic, Estonia, Hungary, Latvia, Lithuania, Poland, Slovakia and Slovenia.
2. Bulgaria and Romania.
3. The EU-15 group of countries includes Austria, Belgium, Denmark, Finland, France, Germany, Greece, Ireland, Italy, Luxembourg, Netherlands, Portugal, Spain, Sweden and United Kingdom.
4. See, furthermore, Milanovic (1998), World Bank (2005), Milanovic and Ersado (2008), OECD (2008), and Aidukaite (2009). On the role of EU accession in CEE welfare development, see Barr (2005), Cerami (2008a), Fuchs and Offe (2009).
5. On the role of legacies in CEE institutional and welfare state development, see furthermore Ekiert and Hanson (2003), Kornai et al. (2001), Inglot (2003, 2008), Szikra (2004), Tomka (2004), Cerami (2006, 2009), Haggard and Kaufman (2008), *Social Policy and Administration* (2009), Szelényi (2009a).
6. This is exemplified in the work by Immergut (1992), Pierson (2000, 2004), Bonoli and Palier (2001), Hinrichs (2001), Thelen (2004), Streeck and Thelen (2005), Palier and Martin (2007), Seeleib-Kaiser (2008) or Palier (2009).
7. Ibid.
8. On the role of ideas and discourse, see for instance Schmidt (2000, 2002, 2008) and Béland (2005, 2007). On the role of international institutions driving this process within CEE, see Deacon (2007), Deacon and Stubbs (2008) and Orenstein et al. (2008).
9. See, for instance, Sabatier and Jenkins-Smith (1993) and Boussaguet et al. (2006). A powerful example is the shift from 'embedded liberalism' (Ruggie, 1983) in the first three decades of the post-war period, to 'monetarism' (McNamara, 1998) since the 1980s.
10. On gender issues in Western welfare states, see, especially, Lewis (1992), Sainsbury (1996), O'Connor et al. (1999), Orloff (2006). On familism and defamilialization, see furthermore Esping-Andersen (1996b, 1999); on CEE see Fodor and Glass et al. (2002), Pascall and Kwak (2007), Fodor (2006), Szelewa and Polakowski (2008). On new social risks, see Taylor-Gooby (2004), Armingeon and Bonoli (2006), Kitschelt and Rehm (2006), Cerami (2008b) and Vanhuysse (2008a).
11. As Haggard and Kaufman (2008, p. 46, italics in original) put it, the outcomes of these critical realignments 'reflect not only the initial strength of these groups but also the strategies of political elites and the resources available to either incorporate subaltern groups into the political system or exclude them from it. [...] What matters is the *subsequent* political and organizational capacity of the working class, the peasantry, and the parties that govern them'.
12. The CIS region includes Armenia, Azerbaijan, Belarus, Georgia, Kazakhstan, Kyrgyzstan, Moldova, Russia, Tajikistan, Turkmenistan, Ukraine and Uzbekistan.
13. Bulgaria, Czech Republic, Estonia, Hungary, Latvia, Lithuania, Poland, Romania, Slovakia and Slovenia.

14. A third, one-member, political economy model is represented by Slovenia, which is not studied in this volume. Slovenia occupies an exceptional place within post-communist Central Europe as it is the only case characterized by a neo-corporatist type of political economy with a strong institutional position for organized labour, high spending on social protection and high levels of complex exports (Bohle and Greskovits, 2006, 2007; also Feldmann, 2007; Vanhuysse, 2007).

15. See, for instance, Deacon (1992), Barr (2005), Elster et al. (1998), Ferge (1992, 2001), Nelson (1997, 2001), Manning (2004), Potůček (2004, 2008), Szalai (2005a) and Cook (2007a).

16. For instance, the temporally progressive reduction of weak ties among once-similar labour market outsiders who were newly divided into either unemployed or abnormally retired status, combined with the struggle for resources between unemployment and pensions programmes, would have further increased their need to rely on informal work as the most effective way to cope with economic welfare reductions (see Vanhuysse 2006a, 2006b).

2 Social Policy in East Central Europe: Major Trends in the Twentieth Century

1. We use the term 'communist' here because that is most commonly used in the English-speaking world for the totalitarian, state-socialist dictatorships in this region, although 'state-socialism' would be more precise. We also use the terms 'Western' and 'Eastern' Europe, although we know that it is a constructed concept that crystallized during the Cold War. To mark that this sharp division cannot be upheld any more we put the terms in quotation marks when first using them.

2. Remarkably enough, the successors of earlier communist parties became the most eager political players to push for neo-liberal reforms of pension systems all over East Central Europe.

3 Mechanisms of Institutional Change in Central and Eastern European Welfare State Restructuring

* Acknowledgements: The author would like to thank Karl Hinrichs, Tomasz Inglot, Mitchell A. Orenstein, Dorottya Szikra, Béla Tomka, Pieter Vanhuysse and Jonathan Zeitlin for their valuable comments and critiques on an early draft of this chapter. It goes without saying that whatever faults remain are entirely my own responsibility.

1. For recent exceptions, see Inglot (2008) and Haggard and Kaufman (2008).

2. For this section I have greatly benefited from discussions with Frank Ettrich, to whom I am grateful.

3. The term 'recalibration' seems, however, to have been suggested by Jonathan Zeitlin.

4. The *self-fulfilling prophecy* occurs when an initial belief (whether false or true) results in a behaviour that sooner or later makes the initial belief a reality. Robert K. Merton's famous example was based on the insolvency of a bank caused by false rumours about its bankruptcy. These rumours led the depositors to withdraw their money and to close their bank accounts, ultimately letting the bank really go bankrupt.

5. For an early sceptical review of private schemes, see ILO (2000).
6. Please note that during communism, the main trade union was responsible for the management of social insurance funds. This autonomy, however, was only virtual, since the trade union was under direct control of the Communist Party.

4   Power, Order and the Politics of Social Policy in Central and Eastern Europe

* Acknowledgements: I am grateful to the European Centre for Social Welfare Policy and Research in Vienna for providing me with an excellent research environment during the writing of this chapter, and to Alfio Cerami, Sean Hanley and Jana Vobecka for helpful comments and suggestions.

1. For a critique of hardnosed coordinating and efficiency-enhancing accounts in politics, see Vanhuysse (2002); on Moe's views of power, see Vanhuysse and Sulitzeanu-Kenan (2009).
2. See, for instance, Dowding (1992), Korpi (1983, 2001), Levi (2003), Offe (1984), Offe and Wiesenthal (1986) and Olson (2000). While Moe's arguments hold water as a general critique of mainstream rational choice theories, his specific theory of power in education politics is theoretically overstated and empirically doubtful on a number of counts (Vanhuysse and Sulitzeanu-Kenan, 2009).
3. Recent applications of blame avoidance theory to social policy retrenchment include Haggard and Kaufman (2008), and Pierson (2001). On loss aversion and status quo bias, see Kahneman and Tversky (2000), Fernandez and Rodrik (1991). On the reform benefit/costs distribution, see Vis and Van Kersbergen (2007), Haggard and Kaufman (2008).
4. For instance, in 1995, 1998 and 2003, unemployment in Poland ranged between 1.5 and 4.4 per cent among university graduates and between 35.5 and 39 per cent among those with basic vocational education (Paczynska, 2005, p. 594).
5. Marek Gora, personal communication (December 2008). To cushion the impact of this change, a new temporary system of 'bridging pensions' was introduced, available for a limited group of workers. The bridging pensions are outside the universal (basic/mandatory) system, unlike the previous early retirement schemes.
6. See e.g. Aidukaite (2006, and this volume), Bite and Zagosarkis (2003), Cerami (2006), Leppik and Kruuda (2003), Müller (2002), Paas et al. (2004), Trumm (2006), Ringold and Kasek (2007); World Bank (2006). On welfare politics in the former Soviet Union and contemporary Russia, see, respectively, Cook (1993) and Cook (2007a).
7. Yet, while citizenship laws were later liberalized, still 22 per cent of registered Latvian residents were non-citizens as late as 2003, while in Estonia by 2002 still 13 per cent of residents did not have any citizenship at all and 6 per cent still held Russian citizenship (Smith-Sivertsen, respectively Lagerspetz and Vogt, 2004, cited in Bohle and Greskovits, 2007, p. 451).
8. David Laitin (1998, p. 97) notes that 'Russian leaders in Estonia were not deaf to these themes and understood the "game" the nationalizing elites were playing. They felt that the Estonian government was trying to squeeze the Russians out of the republic that Estonians considered their own.' Yet, 'only a limited percentage [of Estonian and Latvian Russians] seriously considered leaving' (Laitin, 1998, p. 354). See also Bloom (2007).
9. *Net* emigration was small in the Baltic states between 1996 and 2001, as immigration by exiles living abroad (accounting for between 1.54 and 1.73 per cent of

the Latvian population) almost compensated for an emigration rate of between 1.62 and 2.12 per cent. In 1995, Latvian immigration even exceeded emigration. Emigration to the former USSR was more characteristic for elderly cohorts, with younger cohorts mainly emigrating to the West (Bite and Zagorskis, 2003, pp. 8–9). Similarly, immigration represented between 0.10 and 0.11 per cent of the Estonian population in 1995–2000, while emigration ranged from 0.14 to 0.66 per cent (Leppik and Kruuda, 2003, p. 16).

10. As I pointed out elsewhere (Vanhuysse, 2007), Margaret Thatcher's politically convenient *regional* targeting of unemployment ensured that Tory economic reform costs disproportionately affected the north and north-west of England and the Midlands, which had the highest concentration of manufacturing industry and, crucially, were safe Labour Party seats anyway.

11. See Bite and Zagorski (2003, pp. 66, 97; World Bank, 2006). These were higher poverty rates than for other groups. For comparison, poverty rates were between 17 and 23 per cent among households with two children in this period. As in Hungary and Poland, Latvian pensioners were comparatively well off. Among households with two pensioners, poverty ranged from 9 to 17 per cent.

12. See endnote vii. Other research on Latvia, particularly Laitin's (1998, 2007) and Bloom's (2007) studies of Russians' reaction to forced assimilation and Bloom's (2008) analysis of fiscal appeasement, is largely consistent with such a power politics interpretation.

13. See Offe (this volume), Vanhuysse (2008b). The *Journal of Democracy* (2007) devoted a special section to the question: 'Is East-Central Europe Backsliding?' This backsliding appears to validate Greskovits's (1998) lucid early prediction of a low-equilibrium brand of democracy.

14. See Burke (2009), Barry (2009).

15. Own computations from Institute for Democracy and Electoral Assistance, see: www.idea.int (retrieved 11 July 2008). Equivalent turnout rates in the same period for Western countries such as Sweden Germany and the UK were 84, 79 and 69 per cent respectively.

5 Czech Republic, Hungary, Poland and Slovakia: Adaptation and Reform of the Post-Communist 'Emergency Welfare States'

1. For more detailed analysis of the developmental paths of the welfare state in East Central Europe see Inglot (2008).

2. Even the allegedly radical mandatory, private pension plans in Poland, Hungary and Slovakia are dwarfed by the size of the main, public pillar. All these new plans are also carefully regulated and managed by the state and, as the most recent economic turmoil in Slovakia demonstrates, are in fact reversible (Palata, 2008).

3. See for example 'Polityka Społeczna w Czechosłowacji', *Praca i Opieka Społeczna*, nos. 1 and 2. Warsaw, 1949.

4. All statistical references included in this chapter are based on original data collected by the author from various government and independent sources in East Central Europe. GDP figures are probably about 2 per cent lower then corresponding official figures in relation to the Net Material Product (NMP). For more specific and complete data please see Inglot (2008).

5. In this respect, one major departure from the national tradition has been the emphasis on 'individual savings' rather than on 'occupational plans' that existed in the interwar and immediate post-war periods.
6. See 'Social reform: Less money as of January' 2007.
7. See Ministerstwo Pracy i Polityki Społecznej (Ministry of Labour and Social Policy), Projekt ustawy z dn. 21 kwietnia, 2007 o emeryturach kapitałowych z zakładow ubezpieczeń emerytalnych. www.mps.gov.pl/bip/download/USTAWA%20ZUE%2026_04_07v.pdf- (accessed 20 April 2008).
8. Actually, the Hungarians were the first foreign delegation to visit Warsaw after the declaration of the martial law to 'offer advice and comfort to the Polish comrades and share the similar experiences of the Hungarian Communist Party' (Tischler, 2007).
9. This includes the almost intractable crisis of early retirement privileges for numerous professions that continues unabated to this day. According to the ZUS statistics in 2004 pensions for miners, teachers and rail workers alone represented a little over 20 per cent of old age benefits paid, but in 2006 it was already 35 per cent (Fandrejewska, 2008).
10. In Poland opportunities for foreign investment of the private pension funds remain heavily restricted by the government (Ostrowska, 2008).
11. In 1993 the IMF agreed to offer an assistance package to Slovakia under strict conditions that included immediate change in the social insurance institutions (Macha and Woleková, 1998).
12. Interviews by author – Renata Balintová, 5 June 2002, Michal Szábo, 4 June 2002 and Marek Jakoby, 6 June 2002.
13. A similar process of migration of labour away from the public sector employment and its networks of benefits has been under way in Hungary already since the early 1980s (Seleny, 2006).
14. For a rare example of a study of the public sector lobbies see Sznajder (2006).

6   The Transformation of Welfare Systems in the Baltic States: Estonia, Latvia and Lithuania

* Acknowledgements: I would like to thank the editors for their useful comments. For advice provided on political parties in Estonia, Latvia and Lithuania, I would like to thank Mare Ainsaar, Feliciana Rajevska and Arvydas Guogis.

1. GDP has, however, started to decline since 2008. This might be negatively influenced by the current financial crisis affecting the US financial market with consequences for the rest of Europe and the world due to increasing global trade and competition.
2. For more details about the social security systems of the Baltic states, see Aidukaite (2006).

7   Welfare State Transformations in Bulgaria and Romania

1. For the concept of *policy window*, see Kingdon (1995).
2. For an interesting discussion on how the interaction of structural economic developments and the micro-institutional welfare state arrangements can influence institutional change, see Haüsermann (2009)'s considerations on the transformation of the Swiss welfare state.
3. On modernization theory, see Zapf (1994). However, opponents of *modernization theory* have criticized its simplicity in explaining extremely complex and

problematic processes of social and institutional change. Modernity has, in fact, too often become synonymous of the West, while the existence of other, different forms of modernity has systematically been neglected or underestimated (Ettrich, 2005). In addition, while emphasizing processes of differentiation and rationalization, modernization theory has not paid serious attention to the self-destructive mechanisms that may exist in capitalist societies (Offe, 1986).

4. For an analysis of welfare reform trajectories in Continental Europe, see Esping-Andersen (1996a) and Palier (2009).

9 Elder Care Systems: Policy Transfer and Europeanization

* Acknowledgements: The authors would like to thank Alfio Cerami, Pieter Vanhuysse, the other authors of the book and Frank Bönker for valuable comments on an earlier draft. It goes without saying that whatever faults remain are entirely our own responsibility.

1. www.provinz.bz.it/index_d.asp; www.provinz.bz.it/sozialwesen/pflegesicherung. htm. We would like to thank Prof. Costanzo Ranci, Politecnico di Milano, Italy for this valuable information.

10 The Impact of Minimum Income Guarantee Schemes in Central and Eastern Europe

* Acknowledgements: I am grateful to Alfio Cerami, Irina Culic, Livia Popescu and Pieter Vanhuysse for their valuable comments on earlier drafts of this chapter.

1. 'A guaranteed minimum income is the expression of a universal non-contributory subjective and non-discretionary right to social assistance, granted generally under the form of a means-tested differential income. As main pillar of a dedicated scheme, it acts as (part of) the ultimate safety net of social protection in order to prevent individual or households, which are not covered by other social protection schemes and with insufficient resources to support themselves, to fall into (severe) poverty or under decent living standards as perceived in national societies' (Pena-Casas, 2005, p. 18).

2. Bradshaw et al. (1996) use the following criteria in order to cluster OECD welfare states based on their social assistance component: total extent, cost and coverage of social assistance cash transfers; the relative level of benefits provided; the central/ local dimension in regulation and administration; the operation of means-test (whether the unit of benefit allocation is the nuclear family or extended besides that, the tightness of means-tests, and the extent to which some categories of income are disregarded); the degree of discretion in determining the benefit receipt (Eardly et al., 1996, p. 165).

3. OECD countries were clustered into seven groups: *selective welfare systems* (Australia and New Zealand), *public assistance states* (USA), welfare states with integrated safety nets (Britain, Canada, Ireland and Germany), *dual social assistance* (France and Benelux countries), *rudimentary assistance* (Southern Europe and Turkey), *residual social assistance* (Nordic countries), *highly decentralized systems with strong local discretion* (Austria and Switzerland) (Eardly et al., 1996).

4. Minimum Income Guarantee Schemes were inspired by the French *Revenue Minimum d'Insertion* designed in 1988 as a means to provide state social protection for those outside of the insurance system (Paugam, 2003). It was replaced by *Revenu Minimum d'Activité* in 2004, which set stricter conditions on proving active employment-seeking.

5. The reason for merging the four categories of expenditures (reported in ESSPROS as two distinct categories of expenditures) consists of the fact that in each case universal family benefits and insurance-based maternity or childcare indemnities are combined with means-tested income support benefits.

6. Means-tested social benefits presume regular social enquiries and frequent re-evaluations of eligibility. In Romania, the country with the lowest level of total social expenditures, administration costs accounted for 0.02 per cent of the GDP, social expenditures net of administration costs being 14.7 per cent in 2004 (source: Romanian National Statistical Institute, 2004).

7. The World Bank report computed benefit adequacy as the percentage of social security benefits in the *overall income of the whole quintile*, not only in the case of recipient households. This led to misleading data, which indicates that only 4.1 per cent of household budget comes from social assistance.

8. The national poverty threshold was set at 60 per cent of median consumption per equivalent household member, including the value of goods produced within the household for domestic consumption (relevant mostly in rural areas). Equivalence scale: (no. of adults + 0.5*no. of children)$^{0.9}$ (Teşliuc et al., 2003).

9. See Methodological Guidelines of the amendment of the Law on the Minimum Income Guarantee, H.G. 1010/09.08.2006, Art. 29.

10. After the removal of visa requirements for Romania in 2002, the deviant behaviour (begging, theft, prostitution, illegal trade, etc.) of Romanian citizens of allegedly Roma ethnicity was often in the headlines of Romanian as well as international mass media. Following Romania's integration within the EU, France enacted regulations for paying financial compensation (€200) to those Romanian citizens of Roma ethnicity who lack contractual work and accept to leave to country. In Italy, in November 2007, tensions between Italian citizens and Romanian citizens working in Italy escalated after the violent crime of a Romanian citizen of Roma ethnicity against an Italian lady, who died shortly afterwards.

11   Devolution of Social Protection Arrangements

1. Note here, however, that the OECD estimate of the net social assistance package in Poland is based on the maximum social assistance rate that can be granted by local governments. In practice, however, many municipalities presumably provide benefits substantially below the maximum rate.

2. Note that activation allowances are not included here. Supplementary benefits refer here only to allowances for specific expenses such as heating, clothing, furniture, etc.

3. Note here that in Figure 11.1 the data possibly somewhat underestimate the level of the social assistance packages in Sweden, since several other studies on benefit levels come to substantially higher (and adequate) outcomes for Sweden (Cantillon et al., 2004; Bradshaw and Mayhew, 2006).

12   The Impact of the EU Social Inclusion Strategy: the Czech Case

* The study was undertaken with the support of the research plan by the Research Institute of Labour and Social Affairs (MPS 4577300901) and research grant of the Ministry of Labour and Social Affairs, Czech Republic no. 1 J 028/04 – DP2 (Social Cohesion in a Differentiated Society). The authors are grateful to the editors – Pieter Vanhuysse and Alfio Cerami – for helpful comments and suggestions.

1. The policy discourse (and policy-making) is reflecting the attitudes and preferences of the public (classical theory of democracy) while the policymakers are shaping and manipulating the preferences of the public by offering ideas, selective information (public choice theory); this is by changing discourse and attitudes/preferences.
2. 39 per cent were undecided, 22 per cent considered it as being just. Answers missing to 100 per cent – those who did not respond. The survey 'Social inclusion and social policy' conducted by Sirovátka and Mareš (agency FOCUS, random sampling, N= 1,300).
3. See webpages of the Ministry of Labour and Social Affairs: www.mpsv.cz, 'sociální reformy' update 7 November 2007, date accessed 20 December 2008.
4. Interview with a member of the Committee for preparation the NAPSI. This is a standard procedure for handling with all the documents prepared within Ministry of Labour and Social Affairs which illustrates well the low status and competences of the Committee for NAPSI when the NAPSI is considered to be a standard product of this ministry, not a national strategy.
5. These are for example the goals to eliminate all forms of discrimination and to remove obstacles to education and qualification of the Roma (by 2020) or the goal to reduce unemployment among the Roma, which were adapted from the Conception of Roma Integration.
6. Following the rhetoric of European Commission, direct outcome targets are those targets that directly indicate a reduction in poverty and social exclusion in a key policy domain (unemployment, low income, poor housing/homelessness, educational disadvantage, poor health) (European Commission, 2004a).
7. For example, the agenda of social inclusion of the Roma minority has been recognized in the strategic documents and the programme of field social work carried out by the leading NGO in the country ('People in Need') has been supported from the ESF for several years (and presented in the EC Peer Review Programme on social inclusion in 2005).

13   The Eastern European Welfare State in Comparative Perspective

* We are grateful for thoughtful comments on this chapter by Alfio Cerami, Tomasz Inglot, Mitchell Orenstein and Pieter Vanhuysse.
1. The countries included in our study are Korea, Malaysia, the Philippines, Singapore, Taiwan and Thailand in Asia; Argentina, Bolivia, Brazil, Chile, Colombia, Costa Rica, Mexico, Peru, Uruguay and Venezuela in Latin America; and Bulgaria, the Czech Republic, Hungary, Poland, Romania and Slovakia in Eastern Europe.
2. In this regard, we share some of the theoretical priors of the power resource approach, which traces the nature of social policy to the strength of labour and the left.

14   Epilogue: Lessons Learnt and Open Questions

1. Even today, social policy ideas such as basic income guarantees are virtually unknown in the region.
2. 'There is no joint fiscal policy, no joint tax policy, no joint policy on which industries to subsidize or not', writes the *New York Times* (2 March 2009) in an article titled 'Growing Economic Crisis Threatens the Idea of One Europe'.

Bibliography

Aasland, A. (1998) Ethnicity and Unemployment in the Baltic States. *International Politics*, 35, 353–70.

Aasland, A. and Fløtten, T. (2001) Ethnicity and Social Exclusion in Estonia and Latvia. *Europe-Asia Studies*, 53, 1023–49.

Åberg, Y. and Hedström, P. (2005) Quantitative Research, Agent-Based Modelling and Theories of the Social. IN Hedström, P. (ed.) *Dissecting the Social: On the Principles of Analytical Sociology*. Cambridge, Cambridge University Press.

Abrahamson, P. (1997) Combating Poverty and Social Exclusion in Europe. In W. Beck, L., Van Der Maesen, L. and Walker, A. (eds) *The Social Quality of Europe*. The Hague, Kluwer Law International.

Aidukaite, J. (2004) The Emergence of the Post-Socialist Welfare State. The Case of the Baltic States: Estonia, Latvia and Lithuania. *Södertörns Doctoral Dissertations No. 1*. Södertörns, Södertörns University College.

—— (2005) Who are the Winners and Losers of the Transition in the Baltic States? Citizens' Satisfaction with the Material Well-Being. Paper presented at the ESPANET annual conference, Fribourg, 22–24 September.

—— (2006) The Formation of Social Insurance Institutions of the Baltic States in the Post-socialist Era. *Journal of European Social Policy*, 16, 259–70.

—— (2009) *Poverty, Urbanity and Social Policy: Central and Eastern Europe Compared*. New York, Nova Sciences Publishers.

Alber, J. (1995) A Framework for the Comparative Study of Social Services. *Journal of European Social Policy*, 5, 131–50.

Alber, J. and Köhler, U. (2004) *Health and Care in an enlarged Europe. European Foundation for the Improving of Working Conditions*. Luxembourg, Official Publications of the European Communities.

Alesina, A. and Fuchs-Schündeln, N. (2007) Good-Bye Lenin (or not?): The Effect of Communism on People's Preferences. *American Economic Review*, 97, 1507–28.

Alesina, A. and La Ferrara, E. (2005) Ethnic Diversity and Economic Performance. *Journal of Economic Literature*, 43, 762–800.

Amenta, E. (2003) What We Know about the Development of Social Policy: Comparative and Historical Research in Comparative and Historical Perspective. In Mahoney, J. and Rueschemeyer, D. (eds) *Comparative Historical Analysis in Social Sciences*. New York, Cambridge University Press.

Anderson, C. (2001) Desperate Times Call for Desperate Measures? Unemployment and Citizen Behavior in Comparative Perspective. In Bermeo, N. (ed.) *Unemployment in the New Europe*. Cambridge, Cambridge University Press.

Andorka, R., Kondratas, A. and Tóth, I. G. (1994) *A jóléti rendszer átalakulása Magyarországon: felépítése, kezdeti reformjai és javaslatok [The Transformation of the Welfare System: Structure and Reform Proposals]*. Budapest, A Magyar-Nemzetközi Kék Szalag Bizottság 3. sz. Gazdaságpolitikai tanulmánya.

Andorka, R. and Tóth, I. G. (1992) A szociális kiadások és a szociálpolitika Magyarországon [Social Expenditures and Social Policy in Hungary]. In Andorka, R., Kolosi, T. and Vukovich, G. (eds) *Társadalmi riport 1992. [Social report, 1992]*. Budapest, Tárki.

Anthias, F. (2001) The Concept of 'Social Divisions' and Theorizing Social Stratification: Looking at Ethnicity and Class. *Sociology*, 35, 835–54.

Antonnen, A., Baldock, J. and Sipilä, J. (2003) *The Young, the Old and the State. Social Care Systems in Five Industrial Nations*. Cheltenham, UK, Edward Elgar.

Armingeon, K. (2004) The Politics of Old and New Social Risk Coverage: Class, Age, and Gender. *The Annual Meeting of the American Political Science Association*. Hilton Chicago and the Palmer House Hilton, 2 September 2004.

Armingeon, K. and Bonoli, G. (eds) (2006) *The Politics of Postindustrial Welfare States. Adapting Post-War Social Policies to New Social Risks*. London/New York, Routledge.

Arrowsmith, J., Sisson, K. and Marginson, P. (2004) What Can 'Benchmarking' Offer the Open Method of Co-ordination? *Journal of European Public Policy*, 11, 311–28.

Ashworth, J., Heyndels, B. and Smolders, C. (2002) Redistribution as a Local Good: An empirical Test for Flemish Municipalities. *Kyklos*, 55, 27–56.

Atkinson , A. B., Cantillon, B., Marlier, E. and Nolan, B. (2005) *Taking Forward the EU Social Inclusion Process*. Luxembourg, European Commission.

Atkinson, T. C., Marlier, E. and Nolan, B. (2002) *Social Indicators: The EU and Social Inclusion*. Oxford, Oxford University Press.

Bachrach, P. and Baratz, M. S. (1962) Two Faces of Power. *American Political Science Review*, 56, 947–52.

Baldwin, P. (1990) *The Politics of Social Solidarity. Class Bases of the European Welfare State 1875–1975*. Cambridge, Cambridge University Press.

Balintová, R. (2002) Deputy Director for Strategy, Social Insurance Agency, Socialna Poistovna, Bratislava. Slovakia, interview 5 June.

Barbier, J.-C. (2004) Research on 'Open Methods of Coordination' and National Social Policies: What Sociological Theories and Methods? Paper presented at ISA RC 19 Conference, Paris, September.

Barr, N. (ed.) (2005) *Labor Markets and Social Policy in Central and Eastern Europe: The Accession and Beyond*, Washington, DC, World Bank.

Barr, N. (2007) London School of Economics and former World Bank official, 5 February.

Barry, B. (1974) Review Article: Exit, Voice and Loyalty. *British Journal of Political Science*, 14, 79–107.

Barry, E. (2009) More Riots in the Baltics. *International Herald Tribune*. Saturday 17 January.

Barysch, K. (2009) New Europe and the Economic Crisis. Briefing Note, February 2009. London, Centre for European Reform.

Bates, R., De Figueredo, R. J. P. and Weingast, B. R. (1998) The Politics of Interpretation: Rationality, Culture, and Transition. *Politics and Society*, 26, 603–38.

Batty, I. (1997) Mandatory Pension Funds in Hungary and Poland. *Benefits and Compensation International*, 4, 2–7.

Baun, M. and Marek, D. (2006) Regional Policy and Decentralization in the Czech Republic. *Regional & Federal Studies*, 16, 409–28.

Bautzová, L. (2006) Waiting for a Pension. *New Presence: The Prague Journal of Central European Affairs*, 7, 14–15.

Beattie, R. and McGillivray, W. (1995) A Risky Strategy: Reflections on the World Bank Report Averting the Old Age Crisis. *International Social Security Review*, 48, 5–22.

Becker, C. (2005) Professor of Economics, Duke University, May.

Becker, C. M., Seitenova, A. S. and Urzhumova, D. S. (2005) Pension Reform in Central Asia: An Overview. *PIE Discussion Paper Series 260*. Hitotsubashi University.

Begg, I. and Berghman, J. (2002) Introduction: EU Social (Exclusion) Policy Revisited? *Journal of European Social Policy*, 12, 179–94.

Beichelt, T. (2008) Dimensions of Europeanisation. In Bafoil, F. and Beichelt, T. (eds) *Européanisation. D'Ouest en Est. Coll. Logiques Politiques*. Paris, L'Harmattan.

Béland, D. (2005) Ideas and Social Policy: An Institutionalist Perspective. *Social Policy & Administration*, 39, 1–18.

—— (2007) Ideas and Institutional Change in Social Security: Conversion, Layering, and Policy Drift. *Social Science Quarterly*, 88, 20–38.

—— (2009) Ideas, Institutions and Policy Change. *Journal of European Public Policy*, 16(5), 701–18.

Béland, D. and Marier, P. (2006) The Politics of Protest Avoidance: Labor Mobilization and Social Policy Reform in France. *Mobilization*, 11, 377–91.

Bernotas, D. and Guogis, A. (2006) *Globalizacija, socialinė apsauga ir Baltijos šalys [Globalization, Social Policy and the Baltic States]*. Vilnius, Mykolo Romerio Universitetas.

Bettio, F. and Plantenga, J. (2004) Comparing Care regimes in Europe. *Feminist Economics*, 10, 85–113.

Bite, I. and Zagorskis, V. (2003) Study on the Social Protection Systems in the 13 Applicant Countries: Latvia Country Study, European Commission – Employment and Social Affairs DG.

Bloom, S. (2007) Competitive Assimilation or Strategic Nonassimilation? The Political Economy of School Choice in Latvia. *Comparative Political Studies*, 41, 947–70.

—— (2008) Which Minority is Appeased? Coalition Potential and Redistribution in Latvia and Ukraine. *Europe-Asia Studies*, 60, 1575–600.

BMFSFJ (Bundesministerium Für Familie, S., Frauen Und Jugend) (1994) *Politik für ältere Menschen – Stand, Stellenwert und Entwicklungsmöglichkeiten der Aging Policy in den Mitgliedsstaaten der Europäischen Gemeinschaft und den EFTA-Staaten*, Stuttgart, Kohlhammer.

Boeri, T., Burda, M. and Köllö, J. (1998) *Mediating the Transition: Labor Markets in Central and Eastern Europe*. New York, CEPR.

Boeri, T. and Edwards, S. (1998) Long-Term Unemployment and Short-Term Unemployment Benefits: The Changing Nature of Non-Employment Subsidies in Central and Eastern Europe. *Empirical Economics*, 23, 31–54.

Boeri, T. and Keese, M. (1992) Labour Markets and the Transition in Central and Eastern Europe. *OECD Economic Studies*. Paris, OECD.

Boeri, T. and Terrell, K. (2002) Institutional Determinants of Labor Reallocation in Transition. *Journal of Economic Perspectives*, 16, 51–76.

Bohle, D. (2007) The New Great Transformation: Liberalization and Social Protection in Central Eastern Europe. Paper prepared for presentation at the second ESRC seminar: '(Re)distribution of Uncertainty', Warwick Business School, University of Warwick, 2 November.

Bohle, D. and Greskovits, B. (2006) Capitalism Without Compromise: Strong Business and Weak Labor in Eastern Europe's New Transnational Industries. *Studies in Comparative International Development*, 41, 3–25.

—— (2007) Neoliberalism, Embeddded Neoliberalism, and Neocorporatism: Paths towards Transnational Capitalism in Central-Eastern Europe. *West European Politics*, 30, 443–66.

Boix, C. (2004) The Institutional Accomodation of an Enlarged Europe. *Europäische Politik (04)*. Bonn, Friedrich Ebert Stiftung.

Bonoli, G. (2007) Time Matters. Postindustrialization, New Social Risks, and Welfare State Adaptations in Advanced Industrial Democracies. *Comparative Political Studies*, 40, 495–520.

Bonoli, G. and Palier, B. (2001) How Do Welfare States Change? Institutions and their Impact on the Politics of Welfare State Reform in Western Europe. In Leibfried, S. (ed.) *Welfare State Futures*. Cambridge, Cambridge University Press.

—— (2007) When Past Reforms Open New Opportunities: Comparing Old-age Insurance Reforms in Bismarckian Welfare Systems. *Social Policy & Administration*, 41, 555–73.

Borrás, S. and Jacobsson, K. (2004) The Open Method of Co-ordination and New Governance Patterns in the EU. *Journal of European Public Policy*, 11, 185–208.

Börzel, T. A. and Risse, T. (2003) Conceptualising the Domestic Impact of Europe. In Featherstone, K. and Radaelli, C. M. (eds) *The Politics of Europeanization*. Oxford, Oxford University Press.

Boussaguet, L., Jacquot, S. and Ravinet, P. (eds) (2006) *Dictionnaire des Politiques Publiques*. Paris, Sciences Po Les Presses.

Bradshaw, J. and Mayhew, E. (2006) Family Benefit Packages. In Bradshaw, J. and Hatland, A. (eds) *Social Policy, Employment and Family Change in Comparative Perspective*. Cheltenham (UK)/Northampton (USA), Edward Elgar.

Braithwaite, J., Grootaert, C. and Milanovic, B. (2000) *Poverty and Social Assistance in Transition Countries*. London, Macmillan.

Bridgman, B. (2008) Why Are Ethnically Divided Countries Poor? *Journal of Macroeconomics*, 30, 1–18.

Brinton, M. and Nee, V. (eds) (1998) *The New Institutionalism in Sociology*. New York, Russel Sage Foundation.

Brodin, H. (2005) *Does Anybody Care? Public and Private Responsibilities in Swedish Eldercare 1940–2000*. University of Umeå.

Brooks, S. M. (2004) International Financial Institutions and the Diffusion of Foreign Models for Social Security Reform in Latin America. In Weyland, K. (ed.) *Learning from Foreign Models in Latin American Policy Reform*. Washington, DC and Baltimore, MD, Woodrow Wilson Center and Johns Hopkins University Press.

—— (2005) Interdependent and Domestic Foundations of Policy Change: The Diffusion of Pension Privatization around the World. *International Studies Quarterly*, 49, 273–94.

—— (2007) *Social Protection and the Market: The Transformation of Social Security Institutions in Latin America*. Cambridge, Cambridge University Press.

Brown, C. C. and Oates, W. E. (1987) Assistance to the Poor in a Federal System. *Journal of Public Economics*, 32, 307–30.

Bulmer, S., Dolowitz, D., Humphreys, P. and Padgett, S. A. (2007) *Policy Transfer in European Union Governance. Regulating the Utilities*. London and New York, Routledge.

Burau, V., Theobald, H. and Blank, R. H. (2007) *Governing Home Care: A Cross-National Comparison*. Cheltenham, UK, Edward Elgar.

Burke, J. (2009) Eastern Europe Braced for a Violent 'Spring of Discontent'. *The Observer*, Sunday 18 January 2009.

Butorá, M. and Butorová, Z. (1993) Slovakia: The Identity Challenges of the Newly Born State. *Social Research*, 4, 705–36.

Cahn, C. (2004) Void at the Centre: (The Lack of) European Union Guidance on Ethnic Data. *Roma Rights Quarterly*, 2, www.errc.org/cikk.php?cikk=1995.

Cain, M. and Surdej, A. (1999) Transnational Politics of Public Choice? Explaining Stalled Pension Reforms in Poland. In Cook, L. J., Orenstein, M. A. and Rueschemeyer, M. (eds) *Left Parties and Social Policy in Postcommunist Europe*. Boulder, CO, Westview Press.

Cameron, D. (1978) The Expansion of the Public Economy: A Comparative Analysis. *American Political Science Review*, 72, 1243–61.

Campbell, J. L. (2004) *Institutional Change and Globalization.* Princeton NJ, Princeton University Press.

Campell, A. and Morgan, K. (2005) Federalism and the Politics of Old-age Care in Germany and the United-States. *Comparative Political Studies*, 38, 1–28.

Campbell, J. L. and Pedersen, O. K. (2001) Introduction. In Campbell, J. L. and Pedersen, O. K. (eds) *The Rise of NeoLiberalism and Institutional Analysis.* Princeton, Princeton University Press.

Cantillon, B., Van Mechelen, N. and Schulte, B. (2008) Minimum Income Policies in Old and New EU Member States. In Alber, J., Fahey, T. and Saraceno, C. (eds) *Handbook of Quality of Life in the Enlarged European Union.* London/New York, Routledge.

Carmel, E. (2005) Governance and the Constitution of a European Social. In Newman, J. (ed.) *Remaking Governance. Peoples, Politics, and the Public Sphere.* Bristol, Policy Press.

Casey, B. H. (2004) Pension Reform in the Baltic States: Convergence with 'Europe' or with 'the World'? *International Social Security Review*, 57, 19–45.

Cashu, I. (2005) *The World Bank and Pension Reform in Romania.* Syracuse, NY, Syracuse University.

Castel, R. (2003) *From Manual Workers to Wage Laborers. Transformation of the Social Question.* New Brunswick and London, Transaction Publishers.

Castles, F. G. (1986) Whatever Happened to the Communist Welfare State? *Studies in Comparative Communism*, 19, 213–26.

—— (1999) Decentralization and the post-war political economy. *European Journal of Political Research*, 36, 27–53.

Castles, F. G. and Obinger, H. (2008) Worlds, Families, Regimes: Country Clusters in European and OECD Area Public Policy. *West European Politics*, 31.

Cerami, A. (2006) *Social Policy in Central and Eastern Europe. The Emergence of a New European Welfare Regime.* Berlin, LIT Verlag.

—— (2008a) Europeanization and Social Policy in Central and Eastern Europe. In Bafoil, F. and Beichelt, T. (eds) *Européanisation. D'Ouest en Est. Coll. Logiques Politiques.* Paris, L'Harmattan.

—— (2008b) New Social Risks in Central and Eastern Europe: The Need for a New Empowering Politics of the Welfare State. *Czech Sociological Review*, 44, 1089–110.

—— (2009a) The Politics of Social Security Reforms in Czech Republic, Hungary, Poland and Slovakia. In Palier, B. (ed.) *A Long-Good Bye to Bismarck? The Politics of Reforms in Continental Europe.* Amsterdam, Amsterdam University Press.

—— (2009b) Welfare State Developments in the Russian Federation: Oil-Led Social Policy and the 'Russian Miracle'. *Social Policy & Administration*, 43(2), 105–20.

Chandler, M. (2002) Tax Collection and the Shadow Economy in the Baltics. Paper presented at the conference 'Unofficial Activities in Transition Countries: Ten Years of Experience', Zagreb, 18–19 October.

Chłon-Dominczak, A. and Móra, M. (2003) Commitment and Consensus in Pension Reform. In Holzmann, R., Orenstein, M. A. and Rutkowski, M. (eds) *Pension Reform in Europe: Process and Progress.* Washington, DC, World Bank.

Citi, M. and Rhodes, M. (2006) New Modes of Governance in the European Union: A Critical Survey and Analysis. In Jørgensen, K. E., Pollack, M. and Rosamond, B. (eds) *Handbook of European Union Politics.*

Coleman, J. S. (1986) Social Theory, Social Research, and a Theory of Action. *American Journal of Sociology*, 91, 1309–35.

Collier, R. and Collier, D. (1991) *Shaping the Political Arena: Critical Junctures, the Labor Movement, and Regime Dynamics in Latin America*. Princeton, NJ, Princeton University Press.

Consensus Phare (1999a) *Bulgaria Survey. Project number ZZ-9710–0016*. Brussels, Phare Consensus.

—— (1999b) *Romania Survey. Project number ZZ-9710–0016*. Brussels, Phare Consensus.

Consensus Programme (1998) *Recent Reforms in Organisation, Financing and Delivery of Health Care*. Brussels, European Commission.

Cook, L. (1993) *The Soviet Social Contract and Why it Failed*. Cambridge, MA, Harvard University Press.

—— (2007a) *Postcommunist Welfare States: Reform Politics in Russia and Eastern Europe*. Ithaca, NY, Cornell University Press.

—— (2007b) Negotiating Welfare in Postcommunist States. *Comparative Politics*, 40, 41–62.

Corneo, G. and Gruner, H. P. (2002) Individual Preferences for Political Redistribution. *Journal of Public Economics*, 83, 83–107.

Council of Europe (2001) Promoting the Policy Debate on Social Exclusion from a Comparative Perspective. Strasbourg, Council of Europe.

Council of the European Union (2000a) Presidency Conclusions. Lisbon, European Council, 23 and 24 March, www.europarl.europa.eu/summits/lis1_en.htm.

—— (2000b) Presidency Conclusions. Nice, European Council, 7, 8 and 9 December. http://ec.europa.eu/employment_social/gender_equality/docs/2000/euro_council_nice_en.pdf.

Crouch, C. (2005) *Capitalist Diversity and Change. Recombinant Governance and Institutional Entrepreneurs*. Oxford, Oxford University Press.

Crowley, S. and Ost, D. (eds) (2001) *Workers after Workers' State: Labor and Politics in Postcommunist Eastern Europe*. Latham, CT, Rowman and Littlefield Publishers, Inc.

Čsú (CZSO) (2007) *Survey on Incomes and Living Conditions 2005*. Prague Czech Statistical Office.

Culic, I. (2008) Eluding Exit and Entry Controls: Romanian and Moldovan Immigrants in the European Union. *East European Politics & Societies*, 22, 145–70.

Czech Social Security Administration (2004) *80 Years of Social Insurance*, Prague, CSSZ.

Czike, K., Krémer, B. and Tausz, K. (2002) The Impact of Decentralization on Social Policy in Hungary, Latvia and Ukraine. In Tausz, K. (ed.) *The Impact of Decentralization on Social Policy*. Budapest, Open Society Institute/Local Government and Public Service Reform Initiative.

Daly, M. (2008) Wither EU Social Policy? An Account and Assessment of Developments in the Lisbon Social Inclusion Process. *Journal of Social Policy*, 37, 1–19.

Darvas, Á. (2000) *Utak és tévutak. Családtámogatási rendszerek Közép-Kelet-Európában a rendszerváltás óta. (Doktori disszertáció.) [Roads and Dead Ends. Family Policies in Central and Eastern Europe after the Transition. PhD Thesis.]* Budapest, ELTE University.

Davey, K. (2003) Fiscal Decentralization. In Unpan (ed.) http://unpan1.un.org/intradoc/groups/public/documents/UNTC/UNPAN017650.pdf.

Davis, N. Y. (1997) *Gender and Nation*. London, Sage Publications.

De Deken, J. J. (1994) Social Policy in Postwar Czechoslovakia. The Development of Old-Age Pensions and Housing Policies during the Period 1945–1989. *EUI Working Paper SPS no. 94/13*. Florence, European University Institute.

De la Porte, C. and Deacon, B. (2002) Contracting Companies and Consultants: The EU and Social Policy of Accession Countries. *GASPP Occasional Paper No. 9/2002*. Helsinki, STAKES.
—— (2004) The EU and Social Policy of Accession Countries: The Case of Lithuania. *Policy Studies*, 25, 121–37.
De la Porte, C. and Pochet, P. (2004) The European Employment Strategy: Existing Research and Remaining Questions. *Journal of European Social Policy*, 14(1), 71–9.
De la Porte, C., Pochet, P. and Room, G. (2001) Social Benchmarking, Policy Making and New Governance in the EU. *Journal of European Social Policy*, 11, 291–307.
De Oliveira, F. (ed.) (1994) *Social Security Systems in Latin America*. Washington, DC, Inter-American Development Bank.
Deacon, B. (1983) *Social Policy and Socialism*. London, Pluto Press.
—— (1992) *The New Eastern Europe: Social Policy, Past, Present and Future*. London, SAGE.
—— (1993) Developments in East European Social Policy. In Jones, C. (ed.) *New Perspectives on the Welfare State in Europe*. London and New York, Routledge.
—— (1997) International Organizations and the Making of Post-Communist Social Policy. In Deacon, B., Hulse, M. and Stubbs, P. (eds) *Global Social Policy International Organizations and the Future of Welfare*. London, Sage Publications.
——(2000) Eastern European Welfare States: The Impact of the Politics of Globalization. *Journal of European Social Policy*, 10, 146–61.
—— (2007) *Global Social Policy & Governance*. London, SAGE Publications.
Deacon, B. and Hulse, M. (1997) The Making of Post-communist Social Policy: The Role of International Agencies. *Journal of Social Policy*, 26, 43–62.
Deacon, B. and Stubbs, P. (eds) (2007) *Social Policy and International Interventions in South East Europe*. Cheltenham UK, Edward Elgar.
Deacon, B. and Szalai, J. (1992) *Social Policy in the New Eastern Europe*. Aldershot, Avebury.
Deficit (Nadwyżka) (2004) budżetu w wybranych krajach UE w 2004 r. (w proc. PKB)."[Budget deficit (surplus) in the selected countries of the EU in 2004 (in % GDP)]. *Rzeczpospolita Online*. 21 March 2005, www.rzeczpospolita.pl/teksty/ wydanie_050321/ekonomia_a_1–1.F.jpg.
Dillinger, W. and Fay, M. (1999) From Centralized to Decentralized Government. *Finance & Development*, 36(4), 19–21.
Dimaggio, P. J. and Powell, W. W. (1991) Introduction. In Powell, W. W. and Dimaggio, P. J. (eds) *The New Institutionalism in Organizational Analysis*. Chicago, University of Chicago Press.
Dowding, K. (1996) *Power*. Minneapolis, University of Minnesota Press.
—— (2006) Three-Dimensional Power: A Discussion of Steven Lukes' Power: A Radical View. *Political Studies Review*, 4, 136–45.
Drahokoupil, J. (2008) *Globalization and the State in Central and Eastern Europe: The Politics of Foreign Direct Investment*. London, Routledge.
Dreifelds, J. (1996) *Latvia in Transition*. Cambridge, Cambridge University Press.
EAPN (2005) Can Activation Schemes Work for Social Inclusion? EAPN Criteria for 'Good' Activation. Brussels, European Anti-Poverty Network.
Eardly, T., Bradshaw, J., Ditch, J., Gough, J. and Whiteford, P. (1996) Social Assistance in OECD Countries. Synthesis Report, Vol. I. London, UK Department of Social Security.
Ebbinghaus, B. (2005) Can Path Dependence Explain Institutional Change? Two Approaches Applied to Welfare State Reform. *MPIfG Discussion Paper 05/2*. Cologne, Max-Planck-Institut für Gesellschaftsforschung.

Ebbinghaus, B. (2006) *Reforming Early Retirement in Europe, Japan and the USA*. Oxford, Oxford University Press.

Edwards, S. (1998) The Chilean Pension Reform: A Pioneering Program. In Feldstein, M. (ed.) *Privatizing Social Security*. Chicago, IL and London, University of Chicago Press.

Eisen, R. and Mager, H. C. (eds) (1999) *Pflegebedürftigkeit und Pflegesicherung in ausgewählten Ländern Europas*. Opladen, Leske/Budrich.

Ekiert, G. and Hanson, S. E. (eds) (2003) *Capitalism and Democracy in Central and Eastern Europe. Assessing the Legacy of Communist Rule*. Cambridge, Cambridge University Press.

Ellerman, D. (2001) *Sounding the Alarm on Neo-Chilean 'Pension Reforms': The Case of Kazakhstan*. Washington, DC, The World Bank.

Elster, J. (1998) A Plea for Mechanisms. In Hedström, P. and Swedberg, R. (eds) *Social Mechanisms: An Analytical Approach to Social Theory*. Cambridge, Cambridge University Press.

Elster, J. and Hylland, A. (eds) (1986) *Foundations of Social Choice Theory*. Cambridge, Cambridge University Press.

Elster, J., Offe, C. and Preuss, U. K. (1998) *Institutional Design in Post-Communist Societies: Rebuilding the Ship at Sea*. Cambridge, Cambridge University Press.

Epstein, R. A. (2006) Cultivating Consensus and Creating Conflict: International Institutions and the Depoliticization of Postcommunist Economic Policy. *Comparative Political Studies*, 39, 1019–42.

—— (2008) Transnational Actors and Bank Privatization. In Orenstein, M. A., Bloom, S. and Lindstrom, N. (eds) *Transnational Actors in Central and Eastern European Transitions*. Pittsburgh, CA, University of Pittsburgh Press.

Erhel, C., Mandin, L. and Palier, B. (2005) *The Leverage Effect. The Open Method of Coordination in France*. Brussels, P.I.E. – Peter Lang.

Esping-Andersen, G. (1990) *The Three Worlds of Welfare Capitalism*. Cambridge, Polity Press.

—— (1996a) After the Golden Age? Welfare State Dilemmas in a Global Economy. In Esping-Andersen, G. (ed.) *Welfare States in Transition. National Adaptations in Global Economies*. London, Sage.

—— (1996b) Welfare States without Work: the Impasse of Labor Shedding and Familialism in Continental European Social Policy. *Welfare States in Transition: National Adaptations in Global Economies*. London, Sage Publications.

—— (1999) *The Social Foundations of Postindustrial Economies*. Oxford, Oxford University Press.

—— (2002) A New Gender Contract. In Esping-Andersen, G., Gallie, D., Hemerijck, A. and Myles, J. (eds) *Why We Need a New Welfare State*. Oxford, Oxford University Press.

Esping-Andersen, G., Gallie, D., Hemerijck, A. and Myles, J. (2002) *Why We Need a New Welfare State*. Oxford, Oxford University Press.

Estonica (2008) The Estonian Political Landscape. Society. Online Article. *Estonica*. Encyclopedia about Estonia, www.estonica.org/eng/lugu.html?kateg=38&menyy_id=1222&alam=47&leht=2.

Eto, M. (2001) Public Involvement in Social Policy Reform: Seen from the Perspective of Japan's Elderly Care Insurance Scheme. *Journal of Social Policy*, 30, 17–36.

Ettrich, F. (2005) *Die andere Moderne. Soziologische Nachrufe auf den Staatssozialismus*. Berlin, Berliner Debatte.

—— (2008) Personal communication: Institutional Mechanisms as Social Mechanisms. Erfurt, University of Erfurt, 30 May.

European Bank for Reconstruction and Development (EBRD) (2007) *Life in Transition. A Survey of People's Experiences and Attitudes.* London, EBRD.

European Commission (2004a) The Situation of the Roma in an Enlarged European Union. Brussels, The European Commission, Directorate General for Employment and Social Affairs.

—— (2004b) Joint Report on Social Inclusion. *Document drawn up on the basis of COM (2003) 773 final.* Luxembourg, DG Employment and Social Affairs. http://ec.europa. eu/employment_social/publications/2005/keaq04001_en.pdf.

—— (2005a) Report on Social Inclusion 2004. An Analysis of the National Action Plans on Social Inclusion (2004–2006) submitted by the 10 new Member States. *Document drawn up on the basis of SEC (2004) 256 final.* Luxembourg, DG Employment and Social Affairs. http://ec.europa.eu/employment_social/spsi/docs/ social_inclusion/sec256printed_en.pdf.

—— European Commission (2005b) *Working Together, Working Better: A New Framework for the Open Coordination of Social Protection and Inclusion Policies in the European Union,* Brussels, European Commission. http://ec.europa.eu/social/main. jsp?catId=547.

—— (2007a) Mutural Information System on Social Protection. In European Commission (ed.) *Directorate-General from Employment, Social Affairs and Equal Opportunities.* Brussels.

—— (2007b) Joint Report on Social Protection and Social Inclusion. In European Commission (ed.) *Directorate-General from Employment, Social Affairs and Equal Opportunities.* Brussels.

—— (2008) Renewed Social Agenda. Opportunities, Access and Solidarity in 21st Century. *COM (2008) 412 final.* Brussels, European Commission. http://ec.europa. eu/social/main.jsp?catId=547.

European Foundation for the Improvement of Living and Working Conditions (EFILWC) (2004) *Health and Care in an Enlarged Europe.* Luxembourg, Office for Official Publications of the European Communities.

European Roma Information Office (2004) *On-line Newsletter March,* www.erionet.org.

Eurostat (2008) *Statistics in Focus. Populations and Social Condititions.* Luxembourg, Eurostat. http://epp.eurostat.cec.eu.int/portal/.

Eyal, G., Szelényi, I. and Townsley, E. (1998) *Making Capitalism without Capitalists: The New Ruling Elites in Eastern Europe.* London, Verso Books.

Falkner, G. and Treib, O. (2007) Three Worlds of Compliance or Four? The EU15 Compared to New Member States. Vienna, Institute for Advanced Studies.

Falkner, G., Treib, O., Hartlapp, M. and Leiber, S. (eds) (2005) *Complying with Europe? The Impact of EU Minimum Harmonisation and Soft Low in the Member States.* Cambridge, Cambridge University Press.

Fandrejewska, A. (2008) Emerytalne zaniepokojenie [Pension anxiety]. *Rzeczpospolita Online.* 10 March. www.rp.pl/artykul/5,104828.html.

Featherstone, K. and Radaelli, C. M. (eds) (2003) *The Politics of Europeanization.* Oxford, Oxford University Press.

Feldmann, M. (2007) The Origins of Varieties of Capitalism: Lessons from Post-Socialist Transition in Estonia and Slovenia. In Hancké, B., Rhodes, M. and Thatcher, M. (eds) *Beyond Varieties of Capitalism.* Oxford, Oxford University Press.

Ferge, Z. (1979) *A Society in the Making: Hungarian Social and Societal Policy, 1945–1975.* London, Penguin.

—— (1991) Social Security Systems in the New Democracies of Central and Eastern Europe: Past Legacies and Possible Futures. In Cornia, G. A. and Sipos, S. (eds)

Children and the Transition to the Market Economy. Safety Nets and Social Policies in Central and Eastern Europe. Aldershot, Avebury.

—— (1992) Social Policy Regimes and Social Structure. In Ferge, Z. and Kolber, J. E. (eds) *Social Policy in a Changing Europe*. Frankfurt/M. and Boulder, CO, Campus.

—— (1997) The Changed Welfare Paradigm: The Individualization of the Social. *Social Policy and Administration*, 31, 20–44.

—— (2001a) Welfare and 'Ill-fare' Systems in Central-Eastern Europe. In Sykes, R., Palier, B. and Prior, P. M. (eds) *Globalization and European welfare States. Challenges and Change*. New York, Palgrave.

—— (2001b) European Integration and the Reform of Social Security in the Accession Countries. *European Journal of Social Quality*, 3, 9–25.

—— (2008) Is There a Specific East Central European Welfare Culture? In Van Oorschot, W., Opielka, M. and Pfau-Effinger, B. (eds) *Culture and Welfare State,Values of Social Policy from a Comparative Perspective*. Cheltenham, Edward Elgar.

Ferge, Z. and Juhász, G. (2004) Accession and Social Policy: The Case of Hungary. *Journal of European Social Policy*, 14, 233–51.

Ferge, Z. and Tausz, K. (2002) Social Security in Hungary: A Balance Sheet after Twelve Years. *Social Policy and Administration*, 36, 176–99.

Ferge, Z., Tausz, K. and Darvas, A. (2002) *Combating Poverty and Social Exclusion*. Budapest, International Labour Office.

Fernandez, R. and Rodrik, D. (1991) Resistance to Reform: Status Quo Bias in the Presence of Individual-Specific Uncertainty. *American Economic Review*, 81, 1146–55.

Ferrera, M., Hemerijck, A. C. and Rhodes, M. (eds) (2000) *The Future of Social Europe: Recasting Work and Welfare in the New Economy*. Oeiras, Celta Editora.

Ferrera, M., Matsaganis, M. and Sacchi, S. (2002) Open Coordination against Poverty: the New EU Social Inclusion Process. *Journal of European Social Policy*, 12, 227–39.

Fiorina, M. P. (1995) Rational Choice and the New(?)Institutionalism. *Polity*, XXXVIII, 107–15.

Fleck, G. and Rughiniş, C. (eds) (2008) *Vino mai aproape [Come Closer]*. Bucharest, Human Dynamics, PHARE RO 2004/016–722.01.01.01.

Flora, P. and Alber, J. (1981) Modernization, Democratization, and the Development of Welfare States in Western Europe. In Flora, P. and Heidenheimer, A. J. (eds) *The Development of Welfare States in Europe and America*. New Brunswick, Transaction Books.

Flora, P., Kuhnle, S. and Urwin, D. (1999) *State Formation, Nation-Building, and Mass Politics in Europe. The Theory of Stein Rokkan*. Oxford, Oxford University Press.

Fodor, É. (2006) A Different Type of Gender Gap: How Women and Men Experience Poverty. *East European Politics and Societies*, 20, 14–39.

Fodor, É., Glass, C. and Al., E. (2002) Family Policies and Gender in Hungary, Poland and Romania. *Communist and Post-Communism Studies*, 35, 475–90.

Förster, M. F. and Tóth, I. G. (1999) *Családi támogatások és gyermekszegénység a kilencvenes években Csehországban, Magyarországon és Lengyelországban [Family Support and Child Poverty in the Czech Republic, Hungary and Poland in the 1990s]*. Budapest, TÁRKI.

Fuchs, S. and Offe, C. (2009) Welfare State Formation in the Enlarged European Union. Patterns of Reform in the Post-Communist New Member States. In Rumford, C. (ed.) *The SAGE Handbook of European Studies*. London, Sage.

Fultz, E. (2004) Pension Reform in EU Accession Countries: Challenges, Achievements, and Pitfalls. *International Social Security Review*, 57, 3–24.

—— (2005) ILO Central and Eastern Europe Team, May.

Gabal, I. (2006) Analýza sociálně vyloučených romských lokalit a absorpční kapac-
ity subjektů působících v této oblasti [The Analysis of the Socially Excluded Roma
Localities and Absorption Capacity of the Subjects Involved in this Field]. Prague,
Gabal Analysis and Consulting, research report for MLSA.

Gábos, A. (2000) Családok helyzete és családtámogatások a kilencvenes években
[Families and Family Support in the 1990s]. In Kolosi, T., Tóth, I. G. and Vukovich,
G. (eds) *Társadalmi Riport 2000 [Social report, 2000]*. Budapest, TÁRKI.

Gans-Morse, J. and Orenstein, M. A. (2006) Postcommunist Welfare States: The
Emergence of a Continental-Liberal World. Paper presented at the 38th National
Convention of the American Association for the Advancement of Slavic Studies,
November. Washington, DC.

Garrett, G. (1998) *Partisan Politics in the Global Economy*. Cambridge, Cambridge
University Press.

Garud, R. and Karnøe, P. (2001) Path Creation as a Process of Mindful Deviation. In
Garud, R. and Karnøe, P. (eds) *Path Dependence and Creation*. Mahwah, Lawrence
Erlbaum.

Gedeon, P. (1995) Hungary: Social Policy in Transition. *East European Politics and
Societies*, 3, 433–58.

Gehlbach, S. (2006) A Formal Model of Exit and Voice. *Rationality and Society*, 18,
395–418.

Gillion, C., Turner, J., Bailey, C. and Latulippe, D. (2000) *Social Security Pensions:
Development and Reform*. Geneva, International Labour Office.

Glootz, T. (2003) Der Weg des europäischen Wohlfahrtsstaates. Angleichung der
Alterssicherungssysteme im 20. Jahrhundert. Berlin, Humboldt-Universität zu Berlin.

Goetschy, J. (1999) The European Employment Strategy: Genesis and Development.
Journal of Industrial Relations, 5, 117–37.

Goodin, R. E. (1996) Institutions and Their Design. In Goodin, R. E. (ed.) *The Theory
of Institutional Design*. Cambridge, Cambridge University Press.

Góra, M. and Schmidt, C. M. (1998) Long-Term Unemployment, Unemployment
Benefits and Social Assistance: The Polish Experience. *Empirical Economics*, 23,
55–85.

Góralska, H. and Wiktorow, A. (1988) System ubezpieczeń społecznych i świadczeń
socjalnych w krajach RWPG [The System of Social Insurance and Welfare Benefits
in the Countries of the COMECON]. In Winiewski, M. (ed.) *Ubezpieczenia społeczne
i świadczenia socjalne (no.2 vol. 1) [Social Insurance and Welfare Benefits (no.2 vol.
1)]*. Warsaw, Instytut Pracy i Spraw Socjalnych/Towarzystwo Wolnej Wszechnicy
Polskiej [Institute of Labor and Social Affairs/Polish Society for the Cultivation of
Education].

Götting, U. (1998) *Transformation der Wohlfahrtsstaaten in Mittel- und Osteuropa. Eine
Zwischenbilanz*. Opladen, Leske und Budrich.

Gough, I. (2001) Social Assistance Regimes: a Cluster Analysis. *Journal of European
Social Policy*, 11, 165–170.

—— (2005) European Welfare States. Explanations and Lessons for Developing
Countries. *New Frontiers of Sociology*. Arusha.

Grabbe, H. (2006) *The EU's Transformative Power: Europeanization through Conditionality
in Central and Eastern Europe*. Basingstoke, Palgrave Macmillan.

Granovetter, M. (1992) Economic Action and Social Structure: The Problem of
Embeddedness. In Granovetter, M. and Swedberg, R. (eds) *The Sociology of Economic
Life*. Boulder, Westview Press.

Graziano, P. and Vink, M. P. (eds) (2007) *Europeanization: New Research Agendas*.
Basingstoke, Palgrave Macmillan.

Grecu, M., Şerbănescu, A. and Hang, D. (2004) *Evaluation of the Implementation of the Minimum Income Guarantee.* Durham, UK Department for International Development and the World Bank, Birks Sinclair & Associates Ltd, Mountjoy Research Centre.

Greskovits, B. (1998) *The Political Economy of Protest and Patience.* Budapest, CEU Press.

Guillén, A. M. and Palier, B. (2004) Introduction: Does Europe Matter? Accession to EU and Social Policy Developments in Recent and New Member States. *Journal of European Social Policy,* 14, 203–9.

Guio, A. C. (2005) *Poverty and Social Exclusion in the EU-25. Statistics in Focus.* Luxembourg, Eurostat.

Guodis, A., Bernotas, D. and Uselis, D. (2000) *Lietuvos politinių partijų samprata apie socialinę apsaugą [Political Parties in Lithuania and their Understandings of Social Policy].* Vilnius, Phare.

Guogis, A. and Koht, H. (2009) Why not the Nordic Model of Welfare State in Lithuania? Trends in Lithuanian and Norwegian Social Policies. In Aidukaite, J. (ed.) *Poverty, Urbanity and Social Policy: Central and Eastern Europe Compared.* New York, Nova Sciences Publishers.

Haggard, S. and Kaufman, R. (1995) *The Political Economy of Democratic Transitions.* Princeton, NJ, Princeton University Press.

—— (2008) *Development, Democracy, and Welfare States.* Princeton, NJ, Princeton University Press.

Hall, P. A. (1986) *Governing the Economy.* New York, Oxford University Press.

—— (1993) Policy Paradigm, Social Learning and the State: the Case of Economic Policy-Making in Britain. *Comparative Politics,* 25 April, 275–96.

—— (1997) Institutions, Interests and Ideas in the Comparative Political Economy of the Industrialized Nations. In Lichbach, M. and Zuckerman, A. (eds) *Comparative Politics: Rationality, Culture and Structure.* New York, Cambridge University Press.

Hall, P. A. and Taylor, R. C. R. (1996) Political Science and the Three New Institutionalisms. *Political Studies,* 44, 936–57.

Hall, P. A. and Thelen, K. (2009) Institutional Change in Varieties of Capitalism *Socio-Economic Review,* 7, 7–34.

Haney, L. (2000) Familial Welfare: Building the Hungarian Welfare Society, 1948–1968. *Social Politics,* 7, 101–22.

—— (2002) *Inventing the Needy: Gender and Politics of Welfare in Hungary.* Berkeley and Los Angeles, University of California Press.

Haney, L. and Pollard, L. (2003) In a Familial Way: Theorizing State and Familial Relations. In Haney, L. and Pollard, L. (eds) *Families of a New World: Gender, Politics, and State Development in a Global Context.* New York, Routledge.

Hanley, S. (2008) Special Review Section, Advances in the Study of Post-Communist States and Public Administrations: Re-Stating Party Development in Central and Eastern Europe? *Czech Sociological Review,* 44, 1155–76.

Hann, C. (ed.) (2000) *Postsocialismus.* London, Routledge.

Hantrais, L. (2004) *Family Policy Matters: Responding to Family Change in Europe.* Bristol, Policy Press.

Hardin, R. (1982) *Collective Action.* Baltimore, MD, Johns Hopkins.

Hartl, J. and Večernik, J. (1992) Economy, Policy and Welfare in Transition. In Ferge, Z. and Kolberg, J. E. (eds) *Social Policy in a Changing Europe.* Frankfurt am Main, Kampus Verlag.

Haskova, H. (2007) Public and Privat Childcare and Pre-School Education in the pre-1989 and post-1989 Czech Society. Paper presented at Conference 'The German

Half-Day Model: A European Sondernweg? The "Time Politics" of Childcare, Pre-School Education and Elementary School Education in Post-War Europe'. Cologne, 1–3 March.

Hasselmann, C. (2006) *Policy Reform and the Development of Democracy in Eastern Europe.* Aldershot, UK and Burlington, VT, Ashgate Publishing Company.

Haüsermann, S. (2009) Reform Opportunities in a Bismarckian Latecomer: Restructuring the Swiss Welfare State. In Palier, B. (ed.) *A Long-Good Bye to Bismarck? The Politics of Reforms in Continental Europe.* Amsterdam, Amsterdam University Press.

Hay, C. (2001) The 'Crisis' of Keynesianism and the Rise of NeoLiberalism in Britain: An Ideational Institutionalist Approach. In Campbell, J. L. and Pedersen, O. K. (eds) *The Rise of NeoLiberalism and Institutional Analysis.* Princeton, NJ, Princeton University Press.

Hay, C. (2006) Constructivist Institutionalism. In Rhodes, R. A. W., Binder, S. A. and Rockman, B. A. (eds) *The Oxford Handbook of Political Institutions.* Oxford, Oxford University Press.

Heclo, H. (1994) Ideas, Interests and Institutions. In Dodd, L. and Jillson, C. (eds) *The Dynamics of American Politics. Approaches and Interpretations.* Boulder, CO, Westview Press.

Hedström, P. (2008) Studying Mechanisms to Strengthen Causal Inferences in Quantitative Research. In Box-Steffensmeier, J. M., Brady, H. E. and Collier, D. (eds) *The Oxford Handbook of Political Methodology.* Oxford, Oxford University Press.

Hedström, P. and Swedberg, R. (1998) Social Mechanisms: An Introductory Essay. In Hedström, P. and Swedberg, R. (eds) *Social Mechanisms: An Analytical Approach to Social Theory.* Cambridge, Cambridge University Press.

Heidenreich, M. and Bischoff, G. (2008) The Open Method of Co-ordination: A Way to the Europeanization of Social and Employment Policies? *Journal of Common Market Studies*, 46, 497–532.

Heidmets, M. (ed.) (2008) *Estonian Human Development Report 2007.* Eesti Ekspressi Kirjastuse AS, Tallinn.

Heikkilä, M. and Kuivalainen, S. (2002) Using Social Benefits to Combat Poverty and Social Exclusion: Opportunities and Problems from a Comparative Perspective European Synthesis Report. *Trends in Social Cohesion.* Strasbourg, Council of Europe.

Hemerijck, A. C. (2007) Towards Developmental Welfare Recalibration in Europe. ISA RC 19 Conference 'Social Policy in a Globalizing World' Florence, 6–8 September.

—— (2010) *In Search of a New Welfare State.* Oxford, Oxford University Press.

Hervey, T. (2008) The European Union's Governance of Health Care and the Welfare Organizations' Agenda. *Regulation & Governance*, 2, 102–20.

Hinrichs, K. (2001) Elephants on the Move: Patterns of Public Pension Reform in OECD Countries. In Leibfried, S. (ed.) *Welfare State Futures.* Cambridge, Cambridge University Press.

Hirschman, A. O. (1970) *Exit, Voice and Loyalty: Responses to Decline in Firms, Organizations and States.* Cambridge, MA, Harvard University Press.

—— (1978) Exit, Voice, and the State. *World Politics*, 31, 90–107.

Hivatal, K. S. (1982) *Magyar Statisztikai Évkönyv, 1981 [Hungarian Statistical Yearbook, 1981].* Budapest, KSH.

Hölsch, K. and Kraus, M. (2004) Poverty Alleviation and the Degree of Decentralization in European Schemes of Social Assistance. *Journal of European Social Policy*, 14(2), 143–64.

Holzinger, K., Knill, C. and Arts, B. (2008) *Environmental Policy Convergence in Europe. The Impact of International Institutions and Trade.* Cambridge and New York, Cambridge University Press.
Holzmann, R. and Hinz, R. (2005) *Old Age Income Support in the 21st Century: An International Perspective on Pension Systems and Reform.* Washington, DC, World Bank.
Hooghe, L. and Marks, G. (2001) *Multi-Level Governance and European Integration.* Lanham, Md., Rowman and Littlefield.
Hooghe, M. (2007) Social Capital and Diversity. *Canadian Journal of Political Science,* 40, 709–32.
Howard, M. M. (2003) *The Weakness of Civil Society in Post-Communist Europe.* Cambridge, Cambridge University Press.
Hristov, T. (2008) Bulgaria. Deliverable 2. Desk Research. *EUREQUAL. Social Inequality and Why it Matters for the Economic and Democratic Development and Its Citizens: Post-Communist Central and Eastern Europe in Comparative Perspective.* Oxford, University of Oxford.
Huber, E. (ed.) (2002) *Models of Capitalism: Lessons for Latin America.* College Station, Pennsylvania State University Press.
Hueghlin, T. O. and Fenna, A. (2006) *Comparative Federalism. A Systematic Inquiry.* Ontario, Broadview Press Ltd.
Ikegami, N., Yamauchi, K. and Yamada, Y. (2003) The Long-term Care Insurance Law in Japan: Impact on Institutional Care Facilities. *International Journal of Geriatric Psychiatry,* 18, 217–21.
Illner, M. (1998) Territorial Decentralisation: An Obstacle to Democratic Reform in Central and Eastern Europe. In Kimball, J. D. (ed.) *The Transfer of Power: Decentralization in Cental and Eastern Europe.* Budapest, The Local Government and Public Service Reform Initiative.
ILO (2000) *World Labour Report 2000, Income Security and Social Protection in a Changing World.* Geneva, ILO.
Immergut, E. M. (1992) *Health Politics: Interests and Institutions in Western Europe.* Cambridge, Cambridge University Press.
Indokolás (1890) *Indoklás 'az ipari és gyári alkalmazottaknak betegség esetében való segélyezéséről' szóló törvényjavaslathoz [Justification to the Bill of 'Benefits for Industrial and Factory Workers in Case of Sickness'].* Budapest, Pesti Könyvnyomda Rt.
Inglot, T. (1995) The Politics of Social Policy Reform in Post-communist Poland: Government Responses to the Social Insurance Crisis During 1989–1991. *Communist and Postcommunist Studies,* 3, 361–73.
——. (2003) Historical Legacies, Institutions, and the Politics of Social Policy in Hungary and Poland, 1989–1999. In Ekiert, G. and Hanson, S. E. (eds) *Capitalism and Democracy in Central and Eastern Europe. Assessing the Legacy of Communist Rule.* Cambridge, Cambridge University Press.
——. (2008) *Welfare States in East Central Europe, 1919–2004.* Cambridge, Cambridge University Press.
International Bank for Reconstruction and Development (1992) *Hungary: Reform of Social Policy and Expenditures.* Washington, DC, International Bank for Reconstruction and Development.
International Social Security Association (ISSA) (2006) *Social Security Programs Throughout the World: Bulgaria and Romania.* Geneva, International Social Security Association.

Iversen, T. (2005) *Capitalism, Democracy and Welfare.* Cambridge, Cambridge University Press.

Izuhara, M. (2003) Social Inequality under a New Social Contract: Long-term Care in Japan. *Social Policy and Administration*, 37, 395–410.

Jackowiak, C. (ed.) (1991) *Rozwój Ubezpieczeń Społecznych w Polsce [The Development of Social Insurance in Poland].* Wrocław, Zaklad Narodowy im. Ossolińskich.

Jacoby, W. (2004) *The Enlargement of the European Union and NATO: Ordering from the Menu in Central Europe.* Cambridge, Cambridge University Press.

—— (2008) Minority Traditions and Postcommunist Politics. How Do IGOs Matter? In Orenstein, M. A., Bloom, S. and Lindstrom, N. (eds) *Transnational Actors in Central and Eastern European Transitions.* Pittsburgh, University of Pittsburgh Press.

Jakoby, M. (2002) M.E.S.A. 10, Center for Economic and Social Analyses. Bratislava, Slovakia, interview 6 June.

James, E. (1996) Providing Better Protection and Promoting Growth: A Defence of Averting the Old Age Crisis. *International Social Security Review*, 49, 3–20.

Javeline, D. (2003) The Role of Blame in Collective Action: Evidence from Russia. *American Political Science Review*, 97, 107–21.

Jepsen, M. and Serrano Pascual, A. (2005) The European Social Model: An Exercise in Deconstruction. *Journal of European Social Policy*, 15, 231–45.

Jesse, M., Habicht, J., Aaviksoo, A., Koppe, A., Irs, A. and Thomson, S. (2004) *Health Care Systems in Transition: Estonia.* Copenhagen, WHO Regional Office for Europe, on behalf of the European Observatory on Health Systems and Policies.

Journal of European Public Policy (JEPP) (2008) Special Issue: Beyond Conditionality: International Institutions in Postcommunist Europe after Enlargement. *Journal of European Public Policy*, 15.

Kabaj, M. (1995) Polityka pełnego zatrudnienia w Republice Czeskiej [Policy of Full Employment in the Czech Republic]. *Polityka Społeczna [Social Policy]*, 4, 20–3.

Kaelble, H. (2005) Der europäische Wohlfahrtsstaat: Geschichte und transnationale Seite. In Linzbach, C., Lübking, U., Scholz, S. and Schulte, B. (eds) *Die Zukunft der sozialen Dienste vor der europäischen Herausforderung.* Baden-Baden, Nomos.

Kahneman, D. and Tversky, A. (eds) (2000) *Choices, Values and Frames.* Cambridge, Cambridge University Press.

Kalnins, V. (2003) Party System. Latvian Institute of International Affairs LIIA. October 2001. Updated by Mikko Palonkorpi in August 2003. Online Article. www.balticdata.info/latvia/politics/latvia_politics_legislative_power_parliament_political_scene_party_system_basic_information.htm.

Kamerman, S. B. and Kahn, A. J. (eds) (1978) *Family Policy. Government and Families in Fourteen Countries,* New York, Columbia University Press.

Kapstein, E. and Milanovic, B. (eds) (2002) *When Markets Fail: Social Policy and Economic Reform.* New York, Russell Sage Foundation.

Katzenstein, P. (1985) *Small States in World Markets.* Ithaca, NY, Cornell University Press.

Katznelson, I. (2003) Periodization and Preferences: Reflections on Purposive Action in Comparative Historical Social Science. In Mahoney, J. and Rueschemeyer, D. (eds) *Comparative Historical Analysis in the Social Sciences.* Cambridge, Cambridge University Press.

Kaufman, R. R. (2007) Market Reform and Social Protection : Lessons from the Czech Republic, Hungary, and Poland. *East European Politics & Societies*, 21, 111–25.

Kazepov, Y. and Sabatinelli, S. (2005) Minimum Income and Social Integration – Institutional Arrangements. Ground Paper for the European Commission Peer-Review in the Field of Social Inclusion. Brussels, European Commission.

Keck, M. E. and Sikkink, K. (1998) *Activists beyond Borders: Advocacy Networks in International Politics*. Ithaca, NY, Cornell University Press.

Kern, K. (2000) *Die Diffusion von Politikinnovationen. Umweltpolitische Innovationen im Mehrebenensystem der USA*. Opladen, Leske+Budrich.

Keune, M. (2008) *EU Enlargement and Social Standards: Exporting the European Social Model*. Brussels, ETUI-REHS.

King, L. (2002) Postcommunist Divergence: A Comparative Analysis of the Transition to Capitalism in Poland and Russia. *Studies in Comparative International Development*, 37, 3–34.

—— (2007) Central European Capitalism in Comparative Perspective. In Hancké, B., Rhodes, M. and Thatcher, M. (eds) *Beyond Varieties of Capitalism*. Oxford, Oxford University Press.

Kingdon, J. (1995) *Agendas, Alternatives, and Public Policies*, 2nd edn. New York, HarperCollins.

Kitschelt, H. and Rehm, P. (2006) New Social Risk and Political Preferences. In Armingeon, K. and Bonoli, G. (eds) *The Politics of Postindustrial Welfare States. Adapting Post-War Social Policies to New Social Risks*. London and New York, Routledge.

Kivisaar, S. and Scots, A. (2006) The Development of Formal and Informal Care in Estonia. Unpublished report. Tartu, Estonia.

Kohl, H. (2008) Where Do Trade Unions Stand in Eastern Europe Today? Stock-Taking after EU Enlargement. *Int. Politics and Society*, 3, 107–30.

Korbel, J. (1977) *Czechoslovakia in the Twentieth Century: The Meanings of Its History*. New York, Columbia University Press.

Kore, J. (2005) Social Policy Development in Estonia in Liberal Political and economical Circumstances. Paper presented at the FAFO, seminar 9–10 June, Oslo, Fafo Institute for Labour and Social Research. www.fafo.no/Oestforum/Estland/juri_kore.pdf.

Kornai, J. (1992) *The Socialist System: The Political Economy of Communism*. Oxford, Oxford University Press.

—— (1996) Paying the Bill for Goulash Communism: Hungarian Development and Macro Stabilization in a Political-Economy Perspective. *Social Research*, 63, 943–1040.

Kornai, J., Haggard, S. and Kaufman, R. (eds) (2001) *Reforming the State: Fiscal and Welfare Reform in Post-Socialist Countries*. Cambridge, Cambridge University Press.

Korpi, W. (1983) *The Democratic Class Struggle*. London, Routledge & Kegan Paul.

—— (2000) Faces of Inequality: Gender, Class and Patterns of Inequalities in Different Types of Welfare States. *Social Politics*, 7, 127–91.

—— (2001) Contentious Institutions: An Augmented Rational-Action Analysis of the Origins and Path Dependency of Welfare State Institutions in Western Countries. *Rationality and Society*, 13, 235–83.

—— (2006) Power Resources and Employer-Centered Approaches in Explanations of Welfare States and Varieties of Capitalism. *World Politics*, 58, 167–206.

Korpi, W. and Palme, J. (2003) New Politics and Class Politics in the Context of Austerity and Globalization: Welfare State Regress in 18 Countries, 1975–95. *American Political Sciences Review*, 97, 425–46.

Köstler, U. (1999) Pflegesicherung in Luxemburg. In Eisen, R. and Mager, H.-C. (eds) *Pflegebedürftigkeit und Pflegesicherung in ausgewählten Ländern*. Opladen, Leske+Buderich.

Kovács, J. M. (2002) Approaching the EU ans Reaching the US? Rival Narratives on Transforming Welfare Regimes in East-Central Europe. *West European Politics*, 25, 175–204.

Koven, S. and Michel, S. (1993) *Mothers of a New World: Maternalist Politics and the Origins of Welfare States*. New York, Routledge.

Král, J. (2003) Deputy Director for Social Insurance, Ministry of Labor and Social Affairs, Prague, Czech Republic, interview 2 April.

Kramer, M. (1997) Social Protection Policies and Safety Nets in East-Central Europe: Dilemmas of the Postcommunist Transformation. In Kapstein, E. and Mandelbaum, M. (eds) *Sustaining the Transition: The Social Safety Net in Postcommunist Europe*. New York, Council of Foreign Relations Books, Brooking Institution Press.

Kuhn, T. S. (1970) *The Structure of Scientific Revolutions* (2nd edn). Chicago, IL, University of Chicago Press.

Kurtz, M. (1999) Chile's Neo-Liberal Revolution: Incremental Decisions and Structural Transformation, 1973–1989. *Journal of Latin American Studies*, 31, 399–427.

Kvist, J. (2007) State Generosity, Social Rights and Obligations. In Clasen, J., Siegel, N. (ed.) *Investigating Welfare State Change*. Cheltelham, Edward Elgar.

Kvist, J. and Saari, J. (2007) *The Europeanization of Social Protection*. Bristol, Policy Press.

Laitin, D. (1998) *Identity in Formation: The Russian-Speaking Populations in the Near Abroad*. Ithaca, NY, Cornell University Press.

—— (2007) *Nations, States, and Violence*, Oxford, Oxford University Press.

Lamaute, D. (1998–2005) Pension Specialist, USAID, multiple interviews.

Lamping, W. and Rüb, F. W. (2004) From the Conservative Welfare State to an 'Uncertain Else': German Pension Politics in Comparative Perspective. *Policy & Politics*, 32, 169–92.

Lamura, G. (2007) Italy's Familistic Approach to Elderly Care and the New Role of Migrant Home Care Workers. In Burau, V., Theobald, H. and Blank, R. H. (eds) *Governing Home Care: A Cross-National Comparison*. Cheltenham, Edward Elgar.

Larsen, A. C. (2006) *The Institutional Logic of Welfare Attitudes*. Aldershot, Ashgate.

Lauristin, M. (2003) Social Contradictions Shadowing Estonia's 'Success Story'. *Demokratizatsiya*. Autumn 2003. Online Article, http://findarticles.com/p/articles/mi_qa3996/is_200310/ai_n9310188.

Lebihan, B. and Martin, C. (2008) Cross-Border Diffusion of Ideas towards a Convergence of the LTC Policies: a Comporative Analysis of the French Compromise. ESPAnet (Network for European Social Policy Analysis) Annual Conference. Helsinki.

Lehoczky, Z. (2007) Sok bába közt elvész a gyermek!" [Inadequacies of the law on regular social assistance]. *Work instead of welfare!* Budapest, Hungarian Office for Labour and Social Protection.

Leibfried, S. (1992) Towards a European Welfare State? On Integrating Poverty Regimes into the European Community. In Ferge, Z. and Kolberg, J. E. (eds) *Social Policy in a Changing Europe*. Frankfurt am Main, Kampus Verlag.

Leinsalu, M., Vågerö, D. and Kunst, A. (2004) Increasing Ethnic Differences in Mortality in Estonia after the Collapse of the Soviet Union. *J Epidemiology and Community Health*, 58, 583–9.

Leitner, S. (2003) Varieties of Familialism. The Caring Function of the Family in Comparative Perspective. *European Societies*, 5, 353–75.

Lelkes, O. (2000) A Great Leap Towards Liberalism? The Hungarian Welfare State. *International Journal of Social Welfare*, 9, 92–102.

Lendvai, N. (2004) Review Essay: The Weakest Link? EU Accession and Enlargement: Dialoguing EU and Post-Communist Social Policy. *Journal of European Social Policy*, 14, 319–33.

Lendvai, N. (2005) Remaking European Governance: Transition, Accession and Integration. In Newman, J. (ed.) *Remaking Governance. Peoples, Politics and the Public Sphere.* Bristol, Policy Press.

—— (2008) Incongruities, Paradoxes, and Varieties: Europeanization of Welfare in the New Member States. Paper presented at the ESPAnet conference, Helsinki, 18–20 September.

Leppik, L. (2005) Impact of the EU Social Policy in a New Member State – Reflections on the Estonian Case. In Palola, E. and Savio, A. (eds) *Refining the Social Dimension in an Enlarged EU.* Helsinki, STAKES.

Leppik, L. and Kruuda, R. (2003) Study on the Social Protection Systems in the 13 Applicant Countries: Estonia Country Study, European Commission – Employment and Social Affairs DG.

Lepsius, R. M. (1990 [1977]) *Interessen, Ideen Institutionen.* Opladen, Westdeutscher Verlag.

Lessenich, S. (2003) Frozen Landscapes Revisited: the Dynamics of Inertia in the European Social Model. ESPAnet (Network for European Social Policy Analysis). Annual Conference – Changing European Societies: the Role of Social Policy. Copenhagen.

Levi, M. (2003) Organizing Power: The Prospects for an American Labor Movement. *Perspectives on Politics,* 1, 45–68.

Levy, J. (2005) Redeploying the State: Liberalization and Social Policy in France. In Streeck, W. and Thelen, K. (eds) *Beyond Continuity.* Oxford, Oxford University Press.

Lewis, J. (1992) Gender and the Development of Welfare Regimes. *Journal of European Social Policy,* 2, 159–73.

—— (2000) Gender and Welfare Regimes. In Lewis, G., Gerwitz, S. and Clarke, J. (eds) *Rethinking Social Policy.* London, Sage.

Lien, S. and Pettersen, P. A. (2004) Local Government and Welfare Generosity: Municipality Spending on Social Welfare. *Scandinavian Political Studies,* 27, 343–65.

Lijphart, A. (1997) APSA Presidential Address: Unequal Participation: Democracy's Unresolved Dilemma. *American Political Science Review,* 91, 1–14.

Linz, J. J. and Stepan, A. (1996) *Problems of Democratic Transition and Consolidation. Southern Europe, South-America, and Post-Communist Europe.* Baltimore and London, Johns Hopkins University Press.

Lister, R. (2004) *Poverty.* Cambridge, Polity Press.

Lukes, S. (1974) *Power: A Radical View.* London, Macmillan.

Macadam, D., Tarrow, S. and Tilly, C. (2001) *Dynamics of Contention.* Cambridge, Cambridge University Press.

Macha, M. (2002) The Political Economy of Pension Reform in the Czech Republic. In Fultz, E. (ed.) *Pension Reform in Eastern and Central Europe. Vol 2. Restructuring of Public Pension Schemes: Case Studies of the Czech Republic and Slovenia.* Budapest, ILO.

Macha, M. and Woleková, H. (1998) Komparace vývoje statni sociální podpory v ČR a SR [Comparison of the Development of Government Social Assistance in Czech Republic and the Slovak Republic]. In Potůček, M. and Radičová, I. (eds) *Sociální politika v Čechách a na Slovensku po roce 1989 [Social Policy in the Czech Republic and Slovakia after 1989].* Prague, Karolinum.

Macinskas, C. (1971) *Socialinis draudimas Lietuvoje ir kova dėl jo 1919–1940 metais [Social insurance in Lithuania between 1919–1940].* Vilnius, Mintis.

Madrid, R. L. (2003) *Retiring the State: The Politics of Pension Privatization in Latin America and Beyond,* Stanford, CA, Stanford University Press.

Mager, H.-C. and Manegold, N. (1999) Pflegesicherung in Österreich. In Eisen, R. and Mager, H.-C. (eds) *Pflegebedürftigkeit und Pflegesicherung in ausgewählten Ländern.* Opladen, Leske+Buderich.

Manning, N. (2004) Diversity and Change in Pre-Accession Central and Eastern Europe since 1989. *Journal of European Social Policy,* 14, 211–32.

March, J. G. and Olsen, J. P. (1989) *Rediscovering Institutions: The Organizational Basis of Politics.* New York, Free Press.

Marchenko, G. (1998) Head, Pension Reform Working Group, Republic of Kazakhstan, 1 July.

Marlier, E., Atkinson, A. B., Cantillon, B. and Nolan, B. (2007) *The EU and Social Inclusion. Facing the Challenges.* Bristol, The Policy Press.

Marshall, T. H. (1950) *Citizenship and Social Class and Other Essays.* Cambridge, Cambridge University Press.

Matsumoto, K. (2003) Erfahrungen mit der japanischen Pflegeversicherung. *Vortrag der der Gesellschaft für Versicherungswissenschaft und -gestaltung e.V.* Cologne.

Mayntz, R. (2002) Zur Theoriefähigkeit makro-sozialer Analysen. In Mayntz, R. (ed.) *Akteure – Mechanismen – Modelle. Zur Theoriefähigkeit makro-sozialer Analysen.* Frankfurt am Main, Kampus Verlag.

—— (2003) Mechanisms in the Analysis of Macro-Social Phenomena. Cologne, Max Planck Institute for the Study of Societies.

Mcnamara, K. R. (1998) *The Currency of Ideas. Monetary Politics in the European Union.* Ithaca and London, Cornell University Press.

Mečiar, V. (1993) Nie ma groźby nacjonalizmu [There is no threat of nationalism], an interview with Xavier Gautier. *Rzeczpospolita (Warsaw),* 25, 5 (reprinted from *Le Figaro*).

Merkel, W. and Giebler, H. (2009) Measuring Social Justice and Sustainable Governance in the OECD. In Stiftung, B. (ed.) *Sustainable Governance Indicators 2009.* Gütersloh, Bertelsmann.

Merton, R. K. (1968) The Self-Fulfilling Prophecy. In Merton, R. K. (ed.) *Social Theory and Social Structure.* New York, The Free Press.

Meyer, J. (1996) *Der Weg zur Pflegeversicherung,* Frankfurt/Main, Mabuse.

Michel, S. (2006) Introduction: Perspectives on Child Care, East and West. *Social Politics,* 13, 145–50.

Micklewright, J. and Nagy, G. (1998) Unemployment Assistance in Hungary. *Empirical Economics,* 23, 155–75.

Milanovic, B. (1995) Poverty, Inequality, and Social Policy in Transition Economies. *World Bank Policy Research Working Paper.* Washington, DC, World Bank.

—— (1998) *Income, Inequality and Poverty during the Transition from Planned to Market Economy.* Washington, DC, World Bank.

Milanovic, B. and Ersado, L. (2008) Reform and Inequality during the Transition. An Analysis Using Panel Household Survey Data, 1990–2005. *Policy Research Workiing Paper 4780.* Washington, DC, World Bank.

Milcher, S. and Zigova, K. (2005) The Impact of Social Policies on Self-Relaince Incentives for Roma in Central and Eastern Europe. *Ekonomika,* 69, 1–19.

Ministerstwo Pracy I Polityki Społecznej [Ministry of Labour and Social Policy] (2007) *Projekt ustawy z dn. 21 kwietnia, 2007 o emeryturach kapitałowych z zakładow ubezpieczeń emerytalnych [Ministry proposal of the law on the private pensions paid from the pension insurance institutions, 21 April 2007].* Warsaw, Ministry of Labour and Social Policy. www.mps.gov.pl/bip/download/USTAWA%20ZUE%2026_04_07v.pdf.

Ministry of Labour and Social Affairs (MPSV) (2004) *Národní akční plán sociálního začleňování 2004–2006 [National Action Plan for Social Inclusion 2004–2006].* Prague, Ministry of Labour and Social Affairs of the Czech Republic.

—— (2006) *Národní strategická zpráva o sociální ochraně a sociálním začleňování 2006–2008 [National strategic report on social protection and social inclusion].* Prague, Ministry of Labour and Social Affairs of the Czech Republic.

—— (2007) Analýza vývoje zaměstnanosti a nezaměstnanosti v ČR v roce 2006 [The analysis of development of employment and unemployment in the Czech republic in 2006]. Prague, Ministry of Labour and Social Affairs of the Czech Republic. http://portal.mpsv.cz/sz/stat.

Ministry of Labour, Social Affairs and the Family (2001) *Social Policy: Slovak Republic.* Bratislava, Ministry of Labour, Social Affairs and the Family.

Minkoff, J. and Turgeon, L. (1977) Income Maintanence in the Soviet Union in Eastern and Western Perspective. In Horowitz, I. L. (ed.) *Equity, Income and Policy.* New York and London, Praeger.Mitchell, B. R. (1980) *European Historical Statistics, 1750–1975.* London, Macmillan.

Moe, T. M. (2006) Political Control and the Power of the Agent. *Journal of Law, Economics, and Organization,* 22, 1–29.

Müller, K. (1999) *The Political Economy of Pension Reform in Central-Eastern Europe.* Cheltenham, UK/Northhampton, MA, Edward Elgar.

—— (2000) Pension Privatization in Latin America. *Journal of International Development,* 12, 507–18.

—— (2002a) Old-Age Security in the Baltics: Legacy, Early Reform, and Recent Trends. *Europe-Asia Studies,* 54, 725–48.

—— (2002b) From the State to the Market? Pension Reform Paths in Central-Eastern Europe and the Former Soviet Union. *Social Policy and Administration,* 36, 156–75.

—— (2003) *Privatising Old-Age Security: Latin America and Eastern Europe Compared.* Aldershot, Edward Elgar.

Müller, K., Ryll, A. and Wagener, H.-J. (eds) (1999) *Transformation of Social Security: Pensions in Central and Eastern Europe.* Heidelberg, Physica-Verlag.

Mungiu-Pippidi, A. (2007) Is East Central Europe Backsliding? EU Accession is no End of History. *Journal of Democracy,* 18, 8–16.

Myles, J. and Pierson, P. (2001) The Comparative Political Economy of Pension Reform. In Pierson, P. (ed.) *The New Politics of the Welfare State.* Oxford, Oxford University Press.

Nelson, J. M. (2004) External Models, International Influence, and the Politics of Social Sector Reforms. In Weyland, K. (ed.) *Learning from Foreign Models in Latin American Policy Reform.* Washington, DC and Baltimore, MD, Woodrow Wilson Center and Johns Hopkins University Press.

Noelke, C. (2008) Social Protection, Inequality and Labour Market Risks in Central and Eastern Europe. In Kogan, I., Cebel, M. and Noelke, C. (eds) *Europe Enlarged: A Handbook of Education, Labour and Welfare Regimes in Central and Eastern Europe.* Bristol, The Policy Press, pp. 63–97.

North, D. C. (1990) *Institutions, Institutional Change, and Economic Performance.* Cambridge, Cambridge University Press.

Nospickel, C. (2005) EU-Erweiterung: Die Entwicklung der Sozialen Dienste in den neuen und künftigen Mitgliedsstaaten Mittel- und Osteuropas. In Linzbach, C., Lübking, U., Scholz, S. and Schulte, B. (eds) *Die Zukunft der sozialen Dienste vor der Europäischen Herausforderung.* Baden-Baden, Nomos.

Obinger, H. (1998) Federalism, Direct Democracy and Welfare State Development in Switzerland. *Journal of Public Policy*, 18, 241–63.

O'Connor, J. S., Orloff, A. S. and Shaver, S. (1999) *States, Markets, Families: Gender, Liberalism and Social Policy in Australia, Canada, Great Britain and the United States*. Cambridge, Cambridge University Press.

O'Connor, J. (2007) Convergence in European Welfare State Analysis: Convergence of What? In Kvist, J. (ed.) *Investigating Welfare State Change. The Problem of the Dependent Variable*. London, Edward Elgar.

O'Connor, J. S. (2005) Policy Coordination, Social Indicators and the Social Policy Agenda in the European Union. *Journal of European Social Policy*, 15, 345–61.

OECD (2006) *Long-term Care for Older People*. Paris, OECD.

—— (2007) *Social Expenditures Database 1980–2003*. Paris, OECD.

—— (2008a) *Employment Outlook*. Paris, OECD.

—— (2008b) *Growing Unequal? Income Distribution and Poverty in OECD Countries*. Paris, OECD.

Offe, C. (1982) Some Contradictions of the Modern Welfare State. *Critical Social Policy*, 2, 7–14.

—— (1984) *Contradictions of the Welfare State*. Boston, MA, MIT Press.

—— (1986) Die Utopie der Null-Option. Modernität und Modernisierung als politische Gütekriterien. *Soziale Welt*, 7, 94–11.

—— (1993) The Politics of Social Policy in Eastern European Transitions: Antecedents, Agents, and Agenda of Reform. *Social Research*, 60, 649–85.

—— (2006) *Strukturprobleme des kapitalistischen Staates. Veränderte Neuausgabe*. Frankfurt/New York, Campus.

Offe, C. and Wiesenthal, H. (1986) Two Logics of Collective Action: Theoretical Notes on Social Class and Political Form. In Offe, C. (ed.) *Disorganized Capitalism*. Cambridge, MA, MIT Press.

O'Kelly, K. (2007) *The Evaluation of Mainstreaming Social Inclusion in Europe*. Brussels, European Commission.

Okrasa, W. (1987) Social Welfare in Poland. In Le Grand, J. and Okrasa, W. (eds) *Social Welfare in Britain and Poland*. London, STICERD.

Olson, M. (2000) *Power and Prosperity: Outgrowing Communist and Capitalist Dictatorships*. New York, Basic Books.

Olsson, S. E. O. (1990) *Social Policy and Welfare State in Sweden*. Lund, Arkiv.

Opinie Do Senackiego Projektu Inicjatywy Ustawodawczej O Ubezpieczeniach Spolecznych (Mpips, M., Zus) [Ministry of Labor and Social Policy, Ministry of Finance, Social Insurance Institution], (1992 (October)) *Comments on the Senate Legislative Proposal on the Reform of Social Insurance (manuscript for internal use)*. Warsaw, Biuro Studiow i Analiz Kancelarii Senatu.

Orenstein, M. (1998) A Genealogy of Communist Successor Parties in East-Central Europe and the Determinants of Their Success. *East European Politics and Societies*, 12, 472–99.

—— (2008a) *Privatizing Pensions: The Transnational Campaign for Social Security Reform*. Princeton, NJ, Princeton University Press.

—— (2008b) Out-Liberalizing the EU: Pension Privatization in Central and Eastern Europe. *Journal of European Public Policy*, 15, 899–917.

Orenstein, M. A., Bloom, S. and Lindstrom, N. (eds) (2008) *Transnational Actors in Central and Eastern European Transitions*. Pittsburgh, University of Pittsburgh Press.

Orenstein, M. A. and Haas, M. R. (2005) Globalization and the Development of Welfare States in Central and Eastern Europe. In Glatzer, M. and Rueschemeyer,

D. (eds) *Globalization and the Future of the Welfare State*. Pittsburgh, Pittsburgh University Press.

Orloff, A. S. (2006) Farewell to Maternalism. In Levy, J. D. (ed.) *The State After Statism*. Cambridge, MA, Harvard University Press.

Ost, D. (2005) *The Defeat of Solidarity: Anger and Politics in Postcommunist Europe*. Ithaca/London, Cornell University Press.

Ostrowska, K. (2008) OFE musza miec wiecej mozliwosci [Private Pension Funds must have more opportunities]. *Rzeczpospolita Online*. 12 March. www.rp.pl/artykul/105476.html.

Paas, T., Hinnosaar, M., Masso, J. and Szirko, O. (2004) *Social Protection in the Baltic States*. Tartu, Tartu University Press.

Paczynska, A. (2005) Inequality, Political Participation, and Democratic Deepening in Poland. *East European Politics and Societies*, 19, 573–613.

Pacolet, J., Bouten, R., Lanoye, H. and Versieck, K. (2000) *Social Protection for Dependency in Old Age*. Aldershot, Ashgate.

Palacios, R. (2003) Pension Reform in the Dominican Republic. *Social Protection Discussion Paper 0326*, Washington, DC, World Bank, December.

Palacios, R. J. and Pallares-Miralles, M. (2000) *International Patterns of Pension Provision*. Washington, DC, World Bank.

Palata, L. (2008) "Nacjonalizacja po słowacku [Nationalization Slovak-style]. *Gazeta Wyborcza (Gazeta.pl)*, 4. http://wiadomosci.gazeta.pl/Wiadomosci/2029020,80353,5883835.html.

Palier, B. (ed.) (2009) *A Long-Good Bye to Bismarck? The Politics of Reforms in Continental Europe*. Amsterdam, Amsterdam University Press.

Palier, B. and Guillén, A. M. (2004) Introduction: Does Europe Matter? Accession to EU and Social Policy Developments in Recent and New Member States. *Journal of European Social Policy*, 14, 203–11.

Palier, B. and Martin, C. (2007) Editorial Introduction. From 'a Frozen Landscape' to Structural Reforms: The Sequential Transformation of Bismarckian Welfare Systems. *Social Policy and Administration*, 41, 535–54.

Palier, B. and Surel, Y. (2005) Les « Trois I » et l'Analyse de l'Etat en Action. *Revue Française de Science Politique*, 55, 7–32.

Pallagi, I. (2007) önkormányzati feladatok, a közmunka szerepe és lehetőségei a segélyezettek életében [The Roles of Local Councils, Opportunities for Community Work and its Importance in the Lives of Welfare Recepients]. *Work Instead of Welfare!*, Budapest, The Hungarian Office for Labour and Social Protection.

Paluckiene, J. (2000) Post-Socialist Welfare State and Gender: A Comparative Study in the Baltic States. In Taljunaite, M. (ed.) *Streaming Towards Social Stability, Social Studies Vol. 4*. Vilnius, Lithuanian Institute of Philosophy and Sociology.

Parties and Elections in EU (2008) *Parties and Elections in EU. The Database about Parliamentary Elections and Political Parties in Europe, 1997–2009 by Wolfram Nordsieck*. www.parties-and-elections.de/.

Pascall, G. and Kwak, A. (2005) *Gender Regimes in Transition in Central and Eastern Europe*. Bristol, Policy Press.

Paugam, S. (2003) The Revenu Minimum d'Insertion (RMI) in France: The Limits of a Progressive Social Policy. In Standing, G. (ed.) *Minimum Income Schemes in Europe*. Geneva, International Labour Office, pp. 29–53.

Pena-Casas, R. (2005) *Minimum income standards in enlarged EU: Guaranteed Minimum Income Schemes*. Brussels, Observatoire Social Europeén.

Pettai, V. and Kreuzer, M. (1999) Party Politics in the Baltic States: Social Bases and Institutional Context. *East European Politics and Societies*, 13, 148–89.

Pfau-Effinger, B. (2004) Culture and Welfare State Policies: Reflections on a Complex Interrelation. *Journal of Social Policy*, 34, 1–18.
—— (2005) Culture and Welfare State Policies: Reflections on a Complex Relation. *Journal of Social Policy*, 34, 3–20.
Pierson, C. (2006) *Beyond the Welfare State. The New Political Economy of Welfare*. Cambridge, Polity Press.
Pierson, P. (1994) *Dismantling the Welfare State? Reagan, Thatcher, and the Politics of Retrenchment*. Cambridge, Cambridge University Press.
—— (1996) The Path to European Integration: A Historical Institutionalist Analysis. *Comparative Political Studies*, 29, 123–63.
—— (1998) Irresistible Forces, Immovable Objects: Post-industrial Welfare States Confront Permanent Austerity. *Journal of European Public Policy*, 5, 539–60.
—— (2000) Increasing Returns, Path Dependence, and the Study of Politics. *American Political Science Review*, 94, 251–68.
—— (ed.) (2001) *The New Politics of the Welfare State*. Oxford, Oxford University Press.
—— (2004) *Politics in Time. History, Institutions and Social Analysis*. Princeton, NJ, Princeton University Press.
Piñera, J. (2006) Secretary of Labor and Social Security, Republic of Chile, January, interview via email.
Piven, F. F. (2008) ASA Presidential Address: Can Power from Below Change the World? *American Sociological Review*, 73, 1–14.
Piven, F. F. and Cloward, R. A. (1977) *Poor People's Movements*. New York, Vintage Books.
—— (1993) *Regulating the Poor*. New York, Vintage Books.
Pochet, P. (2003) Pensions: The European Debate. In Clark, G. L. and Whiteside, N. (eds) *Pension Security in the 21st Century*. Oxford, Oxford University Press.
Political Studies Review (2006) Review Symposium on Steven Lukes' Power: A Radical View. *Political Studies Review*, 4, 115–75.
Polityka Społeczna W Czechoslowacji [Social Policy in Czechoslovakia] (1949) Praca i Opieka Społeczna [Labor and Social Care] *Polityka społeczna w Czechoslowacji [Social Policy in Czechoslovakia]*.
Popescu, L. (2004a) *Politici sociale Est-Europene intre paternalism de stat si responsabilitate individuala*, Cluj-Napoca, Presa Universitara Clujeana.
Popescu, L. (2004b) Romanian Post-Communist Social Policy. Towards the Third Way. In Seelisch, W. (ed.) *Soziale Verantwortung in Europa. Analysen und professionelles Handeln in verschiedenen Hilfesystemen*. Darmstadt, Bogen Verlag.
Popescu, L. and Rat, C. (2008) Quasi-Marketization and Security in Health Care Systems: The Case Study of the North-Western Region of Romania. *Studia Universitatis Babes-Bolyai, Seria Sociologia*, 53, 79–99.
Potůček, M. (1999) Havel versus Klaus: Public Policy Making in the Czech Republic. *Journal of Comparative Public Policy Analysis: Research and Practice*, 1, 163–76.
—— (2004) Accession and Social Policy: The Case of the Czech Republic. *Journal of European Social Policy*, 14, 253–66.
—— (2008) Metamorphoses of Welfare States in Central and Eastern Europe. In Seeleib-Kaiser, M. (ed.) *Welfare State Transformations. Comparative Perspectives*. Basingstoke, Palgrave Macmillan.
Potůček, M. and Radičová, I. (eds) (1998) *Sociální politika v Čechách a na Slovensku po roce 1989 [Social Policy in the Czech Republic and Slovakia after 1989]*. Prague, Karolinum.

Programové Prohlášení Vlády (Government Declaration) (17 January 2007). www. vlada.cz/scripts/detail.php?id=20780.

Putnam, R. D. (2007) E Pluribus Unum: Diversity and Community in the Twenty-First Century. *Scandinavian Political Studies*, 30, 137–74.

Queisser, M. (2000) Pension Reform and International Organizations: From Conflict to Convergence. *International Social Security Review*, 53, 31–45.

Radaelli, C. M. (2003) *The Open Method of Coordination: A New Governance Architecture for the European Union?* Stockholm, SIEPS, available from www.sieps.su.se.

Radičová, I. and Potůček, M. (1998) Porovnanie vývoja českej a slovenskej social-nej politiky po roku 1989. In Potůček, M. and Radičová, I. (eds) *Sociální politika v Čechách a na Slovensku po roce 1989*. Prague, Karolinum.

Rajevska, F. (2005) Social Policy in Latvia. Welfare State under Double Pressure. *Project 'Poverty, Social Assistance and Social Inclusion – Development in Estonia and Latvia in a Comparative Perspective'. FAFO-report 498.*

Ranci, C. (2007) Crisis and Transformation of the Italian Care Model: Beyond Familism, the Role of the Market, and Public Policy. ESPAnet (Network for European Social Policy Analysis), Annual Conference. Vienna.

Rashid, M., Rutkowski, J. and Fretwell, D. (2005) Labor Markets. In Barr, N. (ed.) *Labor Markets and Social Policy in Central and Eastern Europe*. Washington, DC, World Bank.

Rat, C. (2005) Romanian Roma, State Transfers, and Poverty. *International Journal of Sociology*, 35, 85–93.

—— (2007) *Implementarea masurilor de protectie sociala bazate pe testarea mijloacelor in judetul Cluj [The Implementation of Means-Tested Social Protection in Cluj County].* Cluj-Napoca, Presa Universitara Clujeana.

Rauch, D. (2005) Institutional Fragmentation and Social Service Variation: a Scandinavian Comparison. University of Umeå.

Regnard, P. (2007) *Minimum Wages 2007. Variations from 92 to 1570 euro Fross per Month', Statistics in Focus. Population and Social Conditions,* Luxembourg, European Communities and Eurostat.

Ringold, D. (2000) Roma and the Transition in Central Eastern Europe: Trends and Challenges. Washington, DC, World Bank

—— (2005) The Course of the Transition. Growth, Inequality and Poverty. In Barr, N. (ed.) *Labor Markets and Social Policy in Central and Eastern Europe. The Accession and Beyond.* Washington, DC, World Bank.

Ringold, D. and Kasek, L. (2007) Social Assistance in the New EU Member States: Strengthening Performance and Labor Market Incentives. *World Bank Working Paper* Washinton, DC, World Bank.

Ringold, D., Orenstein, M. A. and Wilkens, E. (2005) *Roma in an Expanding Europe: Breaking the Poverty Cycle,* Washington, DC, World Bank.

Risse, T., Cowles, M. G. and Caporaso, J. (2001) Europeanization and Domestic Change: Introduction. In Cowles, M. G., Caporaso, J. and Risse, T. (eds) *Transforming Europe. Europeanization and Domestic Change.* Ithaca/London, Cornell University Press.

Roberts, K. M. (2008) The Mobilization of Opposition to Economic Liberalization. *Annual Review of Political Science*, 327–49.

Rogers, E. (2003) *Diffusion of Innovations*, 5th edn. New York, Free Press.

Rose, R. (2005) *Learning from Comparative Public Policy.* London and New York, Routledge.

Rudra, N. (2008) *Globalization and the Race to the Bottom in Developing Countries: Who Really Gets Hurt?* New York, Cambridge University Press.

Ruggie, J. G. (1983) International Regimes, Transactions and Change: Embedded Liberalism in the Post-War Economic Order. In Krasner, S. (ed.) *International Regimes.* Ithaca and London, Cornell University Press.

Sabatier, P. A. (1999) *Theories of the Policy Process.* Boulder, CO, Westview Press.

Sabatier, P. A. and Jenkins-Smith, H. (eds) (1993) *Polica Change and Learning: An Advocacy Coalition Approach.* Boulder, CO, Westview Press.

Sabbagh, C. and Vanhuysse, P. (2006) Exploring Attitudes Towards the Welfare State: Students' Views in Eight Democracies. *Journal of Social Policy,* 35, 607–28.

Sainsbury, D. (1996) *Gender, Equality and Welfare States.* Cambridge, Cambridge University Press.

Sainsbury, D. and Morissens, A. (2002) Poverty in Europe in the Mid-1990s: The Effectiveness of Means-Tested Benefits. *Journal of European Social Policy.* 12, 307–27.

Saxonberg, S. and Sirovátka, T. (2006) Failing Family Policies in Eastern Europe. *Journal of Comparative Policy Analysis,* 8, 185–202.

Saxonberg, S. and Szelewa, D. (2007) The Continuing Legacy of the Communist Legacy? The Development of Family Policies in Poland and the Czech Republic. *Social Politics,* 14, 351–79.

Scarpetta, S. and Wörgötter, A. (eds) (1995) *The Regional Dimension of Unemployment in Transition Economies.* Paris, OECD.

Schaefer, A. (2004) Beyond the Community Method: Why the Open Method of Coordination Was Introduced to EU Policy-Making. *European Integration online Papers (EIoP),* 8, http://eiop.or.at/texte/2004–013a.htm.

Scharpf, F. W. (1997) *Games Real Actors Play. Actor-Centered Institutionalism in Policy Research.* Boulder, CO, Westview Press.

—— (1999) *Governing in Europe Effective and Democratic.* Oxford, Oxford University Press.

—— (2002) The European Social Model: Coping with the Challenges of Diversity. *Journal of Common Market Studies,* 40, 645–70.

Schimmelfennig, F. and Sedelmeier, U. (2004) Governance by Conditionality: EU rule transfer to the candidate countries of Central and Eastern Europe. *Journal of European Public Policy,* 11, 661–79.

Schimmelfennig, F. and Sedelmeier, U. (eds) (2005) *The Europeanization of Central and Eastern Europe.* Ithaca, NY, Cornell University Press.

Schludi, M. (2005) *The Reform of Bismarckian Pension Systems. A Comparison of Pension Politics in Austria, France, Germany, Italy and Sweden.* Amsterdam, Amsterdam University Press.

Schmidt, V. A. (2000) Values and Discourse in the Politics of Adjustment. In Scharpf, F. W. and Schmidt, V. A. (eds) *Welfare and Work in the Open Economy, Volume I: From Vulnerability to Competitiveness.* Oxford, Oxford University Press.

—— Schmidt, V. A. (2002) *The Futures of European Capitalism.* Oxford, Oxford University Press.

—— (2006) *Democracy in Europe. The EU and National Polities.* Oxford, Oxford University Press.

—— (2008) Discursive Institutionalism: The Explanatory Power of Ideas and Discourse. *Annual Review of Political Science,* 11, 303–26.

Schneider, F. (2007) Shadow Economies and Corruption All Over the World: New Estimates for 145 Countries. *Economics,* 1, 1–41.

Schulte, B. (2001) Altenhilfe in Europa. In Schriftenreihe Des Bundesministeriums Für Familie, S., Frauen Und Jugend Ed. Stuttgart.

Schwager, R. (1997) Matching Grants for Welfare Expenditures with a Decentralised Administration. *Finanzarchiv*, 53, 434–60.

Seeleib-Kaiser, M. (ed.) (2008) *Welfare State Transformations. Comparative Perspectives.* Basingstoke, Palgrave Macmillan.

Segura-Ubiergo, A. (2007) *The Political Economy of the Welfare State in Latin America: Globalization, Democracy, and Development.* New York, Cambridge University Press.

Seleny, A. (2006) *The Political Economy of State-Society Relations in Hungary and Poland.* New York, Cambridge University Press.

Sen, A. (2000) Social Exclusion: Concept, Application and Scrutiny *Social Development Papers No. 1.* Manila, Asian Development Bank.

Sengoku, M. (2004) Emerging eastern European welfare States: A Variant of the 'European' Welfare Model? In Tabata, S. and Iwashita, A. (eds) *Slavic Eurasia's Integration into the World Economy and Community.* Sapporo, Hokkaido University/ Slavic Research Center.

Shepsle, K. A. (1986) Institutional Equilibrium and Equilibrium Institutions. In Weisberg, H. F. (ed.) *Political Science: The Science of Politics.* New York, Agathon.

Shopov, G. (2007) Case Study Summary: Bulgaria Guaranteed Minimum Income. *Program Implementation Matters for Targeting Performance: Evidence and Lessons from the ECA Region.* Washington, DC, World Bank.

Sik, E. and Svetlik, I. (1990) Similarities and Differences. In Evens, A. and Wintersberger, H. (eds) *Shifts in the Welfare-Mix.* Frankfurt am Main, Kampus Verlag.

Simonazzi, A. (2008) Care Regimes and National Employment Models. Dipartimento di Economia Pubblica, University La Sapienza, Roma.

Sinn, H. W. (2003) *Ist Deutschland noch zu retten?* München, Econ.

Sipos, S. and Ringold, D. (2005) Evolution from inclusion and control to inclusion and participation. In Barr, N. (ed.) *Labor Markets and Social Policy in Central and Eastern Europe: The Accession and Beyond.* Washington, DC, World Bank.

Sippola, M. (2006) Nordic Manufacturing Companies in the Baltic States – Are They Diffusing or Evading the Nordic Industrial Relations Practices? *Baltic Rim Economies, Bimonthly Review 5.* Turku School of Economics, Pan-European Institute, www.tse.fi/FI/yksikot/erillislaitokset/pei/Documents/bre/Expert_article66_52006.pdf, (accessed on 29 June 2009).

Sirovátka, T. (2000) *Česká sociální politika na prahu 21. století. Efektivnost, selhávání, legitimita [The Czech Social Policy on the Eve on 21st Century. Effectiveness, Failures, Legitimacy].* Brno, Masarykova univerzita.

Sirovátka, T. E. A. (2003) *Problémy trhu práce a politiky zaměstnanosti [The Problems of Labour Market and Employment Policy, Research Report].* Brno, Masarykova univerzita.

Sissenich, B. (2005) The Transfer of EU Social Policy to Poland and Hungary. In Schimmelfennig, F. and Sedelmeier, U. (eds) *The Europeanization of Central and Eastern Europe.* Ithaca, NY, Cornell University Press.

—— (2007) *Building States without Society. European Union Enlargement and the Transfer of EU Social Policy to Poland and Hungary.* Lanham, Lexington Books.

Skocpol, T. (1995) Why I am an Historical-Institutionalist. *Polity*, 28, 103–6.

Snelbecker, D. (2005) Pension Reform in Eastern Europe and Eurasia: Experiences and Lessons Learned. In USAID (ed.) *Workshop for Practitioners on Tax and Pension Reform.* Washington, DC, USAID.

Social Policy and Administration (2009) Special Regional Issue: Eastern Europe. *Social Policy & Administration*, 432, 101–207.

Social Reform (2007) Social reform: Less money as of January. December 13, www.czech.cz/en/news/economy/social-reform-less-money-as-of-january/ (accessed on 29 June 2009).

Sotiropoulos, D. A., Neamtu, I. and Stoyanove, M. (2003) The Trajectory of Post-Communist Welfare State Development: The Cases of Bulgaria and Romania. *Social Policy & Administration*, 37, 656–73.

Stanculescu, M. and Zaman, C. (2006) Country Report: Romania. Annex. In *Balkandide. The Social Dimension in the Candidate Countries – Bulgaria, R., Croatia, and Turkey* (ed.). Brussels, European Commission.

Standing, G. (1996) Social Protection in Central and Eastern Europe: A Tale of Slipping Anchors and Torn Safety Nets. In Esping-Andersen, G. (ed.) *Welfare States in Transition: National Adaptations in Global Economies*. London, Sage.

—— (1997) The Folly of Social Safety Nets : Why Basic Income is Needed. *Eastern Europe Social Research*, 64, 1339–79.

—— (ed.) (2003) *Minimum Income Schemes in Europe*. Geneva, International Labour Office.

Stanek, V., Husáková, M. and Ošková, S. (2007) Transformation of Social Policy in the Slovak Republic. Paper presented at the annual ESPAnet (European Social Policy network) conference, Vienna, 22 September.

Stanovnik, T. and Fultz, E. (2004) The Collection of Pension Contributions: A Comparative Review. In Fultz, E. and Stanovnik, T. (eds) *The Collection of Pension Contributions: Trends, Issues, and Problems in Central and Eastern Europe*. Budapest, ILO.

Stark, D. (1996) Recombinant Property in East European Capitalism. *American Journal of Sociology*, 101, 993–1027.

Stark, D. and Bruszt, L. (1998) *Postsocialist Pathways. Transforming Politics and Property in East Central Europe*. Cambridge, Cambridge University Press.

Steinmo, S., Thelen, K. and Longstreth, F. (eds) (1992) *Structuring Politics: Historical Institutionalism in Comparative Analysis*. Cambridge, Cambridge University Press.

Stevens, J. N. (1985) *Czechoslovakia at the Crossroads: The Economic Dilemmas of Communism in Postwar Czechoslovakia*. Boulder, CO, East European Monographs/distributed by Columbia University Press.

Stewart, M. (1997) *The Time of the Gypsies*. Boulder, CO, Westview Press.

—— (2002) Deprivation, The Roma and 'The Underclass'. In Hann, C. (ed.) *Postsocialismus*. London, Routledge.

Streeck, W. and Thelen, K. (eds) (2005a) *Beyond Continuity. Institutional Change in Advanced Political Economies*. Oxford, Oxford University Press.

—— (2005b) Introduction: Institutional Change in Advanced Political Economies. In Streeck, W. and Thelen, K. (eds) *Beyond Continuity. Institutional Change in Advanced Political Economies*. Oxford, Oxford University Press.

Svallfors, S. (1997) Words of Welfare and Attitudes to Redistribution: A Comparison of Eight Western Nations. *European Sociological Review*, 13, 283–304.

Swank, D. (2002) *Global Capital, Political Institutions and Policy Change in Developed Welfare States*. Cambridge, Cambridge University Press.

Szabo, M. (2002) Deputy Minister of Labor and Social Affairs, Bratislava, Slovakia, interview 4 June.

Szalai, J. (2005a) *Socialism. An Analysis of its Past and Future*. Budapest/New York, CEU Press.

—— (2005b) Poverty and the Traps of Post-communist Welfare Reforms in Hungary: A Fourth World of Welfare Capitalism on the Rise. Annual Conference of RC19, ISA on 'Retheorizing Welfare States: Restructuring States, Restructuring Analysis'. Chicago, IL, Northwestern University.

—— (2005c) A joleti fogda [The Welfare Trap]. *Esely*, 1, 3–32.

Szalai, J. (2006) Poverty and the Traps of Postcommunist Welfare Reforms in Hungary: The New Challenges of EU-Accession. *Revija za Socijalnu Politiku,* 13, 309–333.
—— (2008) The Hungarian Bifurcated Welfare State. European Social Policy Analysis Network Annual Conference, Helsinki.
Szelényi, I. (2002) *Poverty, Ethnicity and Gender in Transition Countries.* Budapest, Akadémiai Kiadó.
—— (2009a) From Socialist Workfare to Capitalist Welfare State. In Morgan, G., Campbell, J., Crouch, C., Pedersen, O., Christensen, P. H. and Whitley, R. (eds) *Oxford Handbook of Comparative Institutional Analysis.* Oxford, Oxford University Press.
—— (2009b) Review of Janos Kornai, From Socialism to Capitalism. *Czech Sociological Review,* 45.
Szelewa, D. and Polakowski, M. (2008) Who Cares? Patterns of Care in Central and Eastern Europe. *Journal of European Social Policy,* 18, 115–31.
Szikra, D. (2000) The Beginnings of the Hungarian Welfare State in a Comparative Perspective. *Periodica Politecnica,* 10, 143–9.
—— (2004) The Thorny Path to Implementation: Bismarckian Social Insurance in Hungary in the Late 19th Century. *European Journal of Social Securit,* 6, 255–72.
—— (2005) Family and Child Support in a Postcommunist Society: Origins of the Mixed Hungarian Welfare Capitalism. In Cain, M., Gelazis, N. and Inglot, T. (eds) *Fighting Poverty and Reforming Social Security: What Can Post-Soviet States Learn from the New Democracies of Central Europe?* Washington, DC, Woodrow Wilson International Center.
—— (2008) Social Policy and Anti-Semitic Exclusion before and During World War II in Hungary. The Case of the Productive Social Policy. In Hauss, G. and Schulte, D. (eds) *The Dual Mandate. Social Work between Serving the State and Serving the Client.* Oplade, Barbara Budrich Publishers.
Szikra, D. (2009). From Bismarck to the New Pension Orthodoxy: The Historical Development of the Pension System in Hungary. In Petersen J.H. and Petersen, K. (eds.) The Politics of Age. Basic Pension Systems in a Comparative and Historical Perspective. Peter Lang, Frankfurt am Main, pp. 41–65.
Sznajder, A. (2006) *From Behemoths to Subsidiaries: The Politics of Steel Sector Restructuring and Privatization in Central and Eastern Europe.* PhD dissertation, Yale University.
Tanaka, Y. (2004) Between Self-responsibility and Social Security. In Kaelble, H. and Schmid, G. (eds) *Auf dem Weg zum transnationalen Sozialstaat.* Berlin, Edition Sigma.
Taylor-Gooby, P. (ed.) (2004) *New Risks, New Welfare. The Transformations of the European Welfare State.* Oxford, Oxford University Press.
Tepe, M. and Vanhuysse, P. (2009) Are Aging Welfare States on the Path to the Politics of Gerontocracy? Evidence from 18 OECD Democracies, 1980–2002. *Journal of Public Policy,* 29, 1–28.
Teşliuc, E., Pop, L. and Florescu, R. (2003) Protecting the Poor and Vulnerable. Background paper for the Poverty Assessment Report of the World Bank. Washington, DC, World Bank.
The Economist (2007a) Political Forces. Country Views Wire Latvia. From the Economist Intelligence Unit, Online article. 7 August 2007, www.economist.com/ Countries/Latvia/profile.cfm?folder=Profile-Political%20Forces.
The Economist (2007b) Political Forces. Country briefings Lithuania. From the Economist Intelligence Unit. Online article. 7 August 2007. www.economist.com/ Countries/Lithuania/profile.cfm?folder=Profile-Political%20Forces.
Thelen, K. (1999) Historical Institutionalism in Comparative Politics. *Annual Reveiw of Political Science,* 2, 369–404.

Thelen, K. (2004) *How Institutions Evolve. The Political Economy of Skills in Germany, Britain, the United States, and Japan*. Cambridge/New York, Cambridge University Press.

Therborn, G. (1995) *European Modernity and Beyond*. London, Sage.

Tiebout, C. M. (1956) A Pure Theory of Local Expenditures. *Journal of Political Economy*, 64, 416–24.

Tilly, C. (2001) Mechanisms in Political Processes. *Annual Review of Political Science*, 4, 21–41.

Tischler, J. (2007) Spokój nad Wisłą to łatwiejsze życie na Węgrzech [Peace on the Vistula means easier life in Hungary]. *Rzeczpospolita Online*. 8 December. www.rp.pl/artykul/75231.html.

Titma, M., Brandon Tuma, N. and Silver, B. (1998) Winners and Losers in the Postcommunist Transition: New Evidence from Estonia. *Post-Soviet Affairs*, 12(2), 114–35.

Titmuss, R. (1958) *Essays on the Welfare State*. London, Allen and Unwin.

Tjadens, F. (2007) Die offene Methode der Koordinierung im Bereich der Langzeitpflege – drei Jahre bedeutsamer Schritte. In Bundesministerium Für Familie, S., Frauen Und Jugend Ed. *Observatorium für die Entwicklung sozialer Dienste in Europa, Newsletter 1*.

Toma, S. (2005) Az en ciganyom. Informalis gazdasagi kapcsolatok ciganyok es magyarok kozt [My Gypsy. Informal economic relations between Gypsies and Hungarians]. *Erdélyi Társadalom*, 1, 25–50.

Tomeš, I. (1991) Social Reform: A Cornerstone in Czechoslovakia's New Economic Structure. *International Labour Review*, 130, 191–8.

—— (2002) Department of Social Insurance, Ministry of Labor and Social Affairs (MLSA), 1989–1991 and in the late 1960s, World Bank expert, ILO expert, Professor of social policy at Charles University in Prague. Interview Prague 12 June.

Tomka, B. (2004) *Welfare in East and West. Hungarian Social Security in an International Comparison 1918–1990*. Berlin, Akademie Verlag.

—— (2005) The Politics of Institutionalized Volatility: Lessons from East Central European Welfare Reforms. In Cain, M., Gelazis, N. and Inglot, T. (eds) *Fighting Poverty and Reforming Social Security: What Can Post-Soviet States Learn from the New Democracies of Central Europe?* Washington, DC, Woodrow Wilson International Center.

—— (2006) East Central Europe and the European Social Policy Model: A Long-Term View. *East European Quarterly*, 40, 135–59.

Toshkov, D. (2007) Transposition of EU Social Policy in the New Member States. *Journal of European Social Policy*, 17, 335–48.

Trubek, D. M. and Trubek, L. G. (2005) The Open Method of Coordination and the Debate over 'Hard' and 'Soft' Law. In Zeitlin, J., Pochet, P. and Magnusson, L. (eds) *The Open Metod of Coordination in Action. The European Employment and Social Inclusion Strategy*. Brussels, P.I.E. – Peter Lang.

Trumm, A. (2006) *EU-8 Social Policy Review: National Report of Estonia. Background paper*. Washington, DC, World Bank.

Tsolova, S., Noncheva, T., Tomev, L., Chobanov, D. and Stanchev, K. (2006) Country Report: Bulgaria. Annex. In *Balkandide. The Social Dimension in the Candidate Countries – Bulgaria, R., Croatia, and Turkey* (ed.). Brussels, European Commission.

Tymorek, K. (2008) Zasiłek macierzyński dla przedsiębiorczej kobiety [Maternity Benefit for Women Entrepreneurs]. *Rzeczpospolita Online*, 28 March, www.rp.pl/artykul/112949.html.

UNDP (2003) *The Roma in Central and Eastern Europe. Avoiding the Dependency Trap.* New York, UNDP.

—— (2008) *2007/2008 Human Development Index Rankings,* New York, UNDP. http://hdr.undp.org/en/statistics/.

Unicef (2006) *TransMonee Database.* Florence, Unicef Innocenti Research Centre.

—— (2008) *TransMonee Database.* Florence, Unicef Innocenti Research Centre.

Vachudova, M. (2005) *Europe Undivided,* Oxford, Oxford University Press.

Vachudova, M. A. (2008) The European Union. The Causal Behemoth of Transnationa Influence on Postcommunist Politics. In Orenstein, M. A., Bloom, S. and Lindstrom, N. (eds) *Transnational Actors in Central and Eastern European Transitions.* Pittsburgh, University of Pittsburgh Press.

Vanhuysse, P. (2001) The Political Economy of Pensions: Western Theories, Eastern Facts. *Journal of European Public Policy,* 8, 853–61.

—— (2002) Efficiency in Politics: Competing Economic Approaches. *Political Studies,* 50, 136–49.

—— (2004) The Pensioner Booms in Post-Communist Hungary and Poland: Political Sociology Perspectives. *International Journal of Sociology and Social Policy,* 24, 86–102.

—— (2006a) *Divide and Pacify. Strategic Social Policies and Political Protests in Post-Communist Democracies.* Budapest, CEU Press.

—— (2006b) Czech Exceptionalism? A Comparative Political Economy Interpretation of Post-Communist Policy Pathways. *Czech Sociological Review,* 42, 1115–36.

—— (2007) Workers without Power: Agency, Legacies, and Labour Decline in East European Varieties of Capitalism. *Czech Sociological Review,* 43, 495–522.

—— (2008a) Kneeling at the Altar of (Il-)liberalism: The Politics of Ideas, Job Loss and Union Weakness in East Central Europe. *International Labor and Working-Class History,* 73, 137–51.

—— (2008b) The New Political Economy of Skill Formation. *Public Administration Review,* 68, 954–8.

Vanhuysse, P. and Sulitzeanu-Kenan, R. (2009) Teacher's PAT? Multiple-Role Principal-agent Theory, Education Politics, and the Power of Bureaucrats. *Critical Studies in Education,* 50(2), 129–44.

Van Kersbergen, K. and Manow, P. (eds) (2009) *Religion, Class Coalitions, and Welfare States.* Cambridge, Cambridge University Press.

Van Mechelen, N. (forthcoming) *Barriers to Adequate Social Safety Nets.* Antwerp, University of Antwerp.

Van Mechelen, N. and Bogaerts, K. (2008) Aanvullende financiële steun in Vlaamse OCMW's. *Berichten/UA, Centrum voor Sociaal beleid Herman Deleeck.* Antwerpen, Universiteit Antwerpen.

Verhoeven, W.-J., Jansen, W. and Dessens, J. (2009) Losers in Market Transition: The Unemployed, the Retired, and the Disabled. *European Sociological Review,* 25, 103–22.

Vis, B. and Van Kersbergen, K. (2007) Why and How Do Political Actors Pursue Risky Reforms? *Journal of Theoretical Politics,* 19, 153–72.

Vobecká, J. (2009) Czech Rural Development Policies for Human Resources, Post-2004: A Tale of Muddeled Definitions Preventing Strategic Visions? *Central European Journal of Public Policy,* 3(1), 44–64.

Vodopivec, M., Worgotter, A. and Raju, D. (2003) Unemployment Benefit Systems in Central and Eastern Europe: A Review of the 1990s. *Social Policy Discussion Paper No. 0310.* Washington, DC, World Bank.

Walker, R. and Wiseman, M. (2003) *The Welfare State We Want? The British Challenge for American Reform,* Bristol, Policy Press.

Weaver, K. R. (1986) The Politics of Blame Avoidance. *Journal of Public Policy,* 6, 371–98.

—— (2008) Negative Feedback Effects and the Dynamics of Pension Policy Regime Change in Advanced Industrial Countries. Presentation held at Sciences Po, Paris (France), 13 May.

Weingast, B. R. (1998) Political Institutions: Rational Choice Perspectives. In Goodin, R. E. and Klingemann, H.-D. (eds) *A New Handbook of Political Science.* Oxford, Oxford University Press.

Weyland, K. (2005) Theories of Policy Diffusion. Lessons from Latin America Pensions Reform. *World Politics,* 57, 262–95.

Weyland, K. G. (2004) *Learning from Foreign Models in Latin American Policy Reform,* Washington, DC and Baltimore, Johns Hopkins University Press and Woodrow Wilson Center Press.

Wilensky, H. (2002) The Welfare State Convergence and Divergence. In Wilensky, H. L. (ed.) *Rich Democracies: Political Economy, Public Policy and Performance.* Berkeley, CA, University of California Press.

Wilson, D. (2002) *Minority Rights in Education. Lessons for the European Union from Estonia, Latvia, Romania and the Former Yugoslav Republic of Macedonia,* Right to Education Project. Unedited draft for the United Nations Sub-Commission on the Promotion and Protection of Human Rights. Lund, Sweden, Raoul Wallenberg Institute.

Wilson, W. J. (1992) *The Truly Disadvantaged.* Chicago, IL, Chicago University Press.

Woolfson, C. (2007) Labour Standards and Migration in the New Europe: Post-Communist Legacies and Perspectives. *European Journal of Industrial Relations,* 13, 199–218.

—— (2008) Social Dialogue and Lifelong Learning in the New EU Member States: 'Reform Fit' in Latvia. *Journal of European Social Policy,* 18, 79–87.

World Bank (1994) *Averting the Old-Age Crisis: Policies to Protect the Old and Promote Growth.* Oxford, Oxford University Press.

—— (2001) *Decentralization in the Transition Economies: Challenges and the road ahead,* Washington, DC, World Bank.

—— (2003) The Roma in an Expanding Europe. Breaking the Poverty Cycle. Washington, DC, World Bank.

—— (2005) *Growth, Poverty, and Inequality: Eastern Europe and the Former Soviet Union.* Washington, DC, World Bank.

—— (2006) *Latvia: Sharing the High Growth Dividend, A Living Standards Assessment.* Washington, DC, World Bank.

—— (2007) *Social Assistance in Central Europe and the Baltic States.* Washington, DC, World Bank.

Zapf, W. (1994) *Modernisierung, Wohlfahrtsentwicklung und Transformation. Soziologische Aufsätze 1987 bis 1994.* Berlin, Sigma.

Zeitlin, J. (2005) The Open Method of Coordination in Action. Theoretical Promise, Empirical Realities, Reform Strategy. In Zeitlin, J., Pochet, P. and Magnusson, L. (eds) *The Open Metod of Coordination in Action. The European Employment and Social Inclusion Strategy.* Brussels, P.I.E. – Peter Lang.

Żukowski, M. (2009) Social Policy Regimes in the European Countries. In Golinowska, S., Hengstenberg, P. and Żukowski, M. (eds) *Diversity and Commonality in European Social Policies: The Forging of a European Social Model.* Warsaw, Friedrich-Ebert-Stiftung and Wydawnictwo Naukowe Scholar.

Index